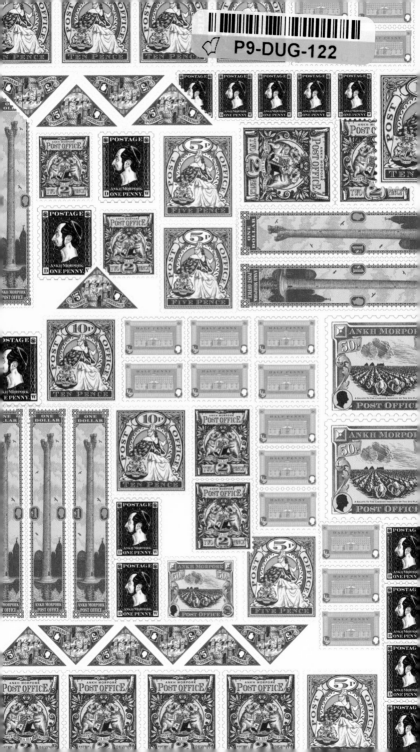

GOING POSTAL

A Discworld® Novel

BOOKS BY TERRY PRATCHETT

For Younger Readers

THE BROMELIAD TRILOGY
(containing *Truckers*, *Diggers*
and *Wings*)

TRUCKERS ✤

DIGGERS ✤

WINGS ✤

THE CARPET PEOPLE ✤

ONLY YOU CAN
SAVE MANKIND ✤

JOHNNY AND THE DEAD ✤

JOHNNY AND THE BOMB ✤

THE JOHNNY MAXWELL
TRILOGY
(containing *Only You Can Save Mankind*,
Johnny and the Dead and *Johnny and
the Bomb*)

JOHNNY AND THE DEAD
playscript (adapted by Stephen Briggs) ★

Discworld for Younger Readers

THE AMAZING MAURICE AND HIS
EDUCATED RODENTS ✤

THE AMAZING MAURICE AND HIS
EDUCATED RODENTS playscript
(adapted by Stephen Briggs) ★

THE WEE FREE MEN ✤

A HAT FULL OF SKY

For Adults of All Ages

The Discworld® series

THE COLOUR OF MAGIC ✤

THE LIGHT FANTASTIC ✤

EQUAL RITES ✤

MORT ✤

SOURCERY ✤

WYRD SISTERS ✤

PYRAMIDS ✤

GUARDS! GUARDS! ✤

ERIC ✤ ●

MOVING PICTURES ✤

REAPER MAN ✤

WITCHES ABROAD ✤

SMALL GODS ✤

LORDS AND LADIES ✤

MEN AT ARMS ✤

SOUL MUSIC ✤

INTERESTING TIMES ✤

MASKERADE ✤

FEET OF CLAY ✤

HOGFATHER ✤

JINGO ✤

THE LAST CONTINENT ✤

CARPE JUGULUM ✤

THE FIFTH ELEPHANT ✤

THE TRUTH ✤

THIEF OF TIME ✤

NIGHT WATCH ✤

MONSTROUS REGIMENT ✤

GOING POSTAL ✤

THE COLOUR OF MAGIC –
GRAPHIC NOVEL

THE LIGHT FANTASTIC –
GRAPHIC NOVEL

MORT: A DISCWORLD BIG COMIC
(illustrated by Graham Higgins) ●

GUARDS! GUARDS!: A DISCWORLD
BIG COMIC
(adapted by Stephen Briggs,
illustrated by Graham Higgins) ●

SOUL MUSIC: THE ILLUSTRATED SCREENPLAY
WYRD SISTERS: THE ILLUSTRATED SCREENPLAY
MORT – THE PLAY (adapted by Stephen Briggs)
WYRD SISTERS – THE PLAY (adapted by Stephen Briggs)
GUARDS! GUARDS! – THE PLAY (adapted by Stephen Briggs)
MEN AT ARMS – THE PLAY (adapted by Stephen Briggs)
MASKERADE (adapted for the stage by Stephen Briggs) ■
CARPE JUGULUM (adapted for the stage by Stephen Briggs) ■
LORDS AND LADIES (adapted for the stage by Irana Brown) ■
INTERESTING TIMES (adapted for the stage by Stephen Briggs) ◆
THE FIFTH ELEPHANT (adapted for the stage by Stephen Briggs) ◆
THE TRUTH (adapted for the stage by Stephen Briggs) ◆
THE SCIENCE OF DISCWORLD (with Ian Stewart and Jack Cohen) ✺
THE SCIENCE OF DISCWORLD II: THE GLOBE
(with Ian Stewart and Jack Cohen) ✺
THE DISCWORLD COMPANION (with Stephen Briggs) ●
THE STREETS OF ANKH-MORPORK (with Stephen Briggs)
THE DISCWORLD MAPP (with Stephen Briggs)
A TOURIST GUIDE TO LANCRE – A DISCWORLD MAPP
(with Stephen Briggs and Paul Kidby)
DEATH'S DOMAIN (with Paul Kidby)
NANNY OGG'S COOKBOOK
(with Stephen Briggs, Tina Hannan and Paul Kidby)
THE PRATCHETT PORTFOLIO (with Paul Kidby) ●
THE LAST HERO (with Paul Kidby) ●
THE CELEBRATED DISCWORLD ALMANAK (with Bernard Pearson)

GOOD OMENS (with Neil Gaiman)
STRATA
THE DARK SIDE OF THE SUN
THE UNADULTERATED CAT (cartoons by Gray Jolliffe) ●

✦ also available in audio/CD   ● published by Victor Gollancz
■ published by Samuel French   ◆ published by Methuen Drama
✺ published by Ebury Press   ★ published by Oxford University Press

GOING POSTAL

Terry Pratchett

BCA

This edition published 2004
by BCA
by arrangement with TRANSWORLD PUBLISHERS
The Random House Group Ltd

CN 133710

Typeset in Minion by
Falcon Oast Graphic Art Ltd

Printed and bound in Germany by
GGP Media GmbH, Pössneck

The 9,000 Year Prologue

THE FLOTILLAS OF THE DEAD sailed around the world on underwater rivers.

Very nearly nobody knew about them. But the theory is easy to understand.

It runs: the sea is, after all, in many respects only a wetter form of air. And it is known that air is denser the lower you go and lighter the higher you fly. As a storm-tossed ship founders and sinks, therefore, it must reach a depth where the water below it is just viscous enough to stop its fall.

In short, it stops sinking and ends up floating on an underwater surface, beyond the reach of the storms but far above the ocean floor.

It's calm there. Dead calm.

Some stricken ships have rigging; some even have sails. Many still have crew, tangled in the rigging or lashed to the wheel.

But the voyages still continue, aimlessly, with no harbour in sight, because there are currents under the ocean and so the dead ships with their skeleton crews sail on around the world, over sunken cities and between drowned mountains, until rot and shipworms eat them away and they disintegrate.

Sometimes an anchor drops, all the way to the dark, cold calmness of the abyssal plain, and disturbs the stillness of centuries by throwing up a cloud of silt.

One nearly hit Anghammarad, where he sat watching the ships drift by, far overhead.

He remembered it, because it was the only really interesting thing to happen for nine thousand years.

The One Month Prologue

THERE WAS THIS . . . DISEASE that the clacksmen got.

It was like the illness known as 'calenture' that sailors experienced when, having been becalmed for weeks under a pitiless sun, they suddenly believed that the ship was surrounded by green fields and stepped overboard.

Sometimes, the clacksmen thought they could fly.

There was about eight miles between the big semaphore towers and when you were at the top you were maybe a hundred and fifty feet above the plains. Work up there too long without a hat on, they said, and the tower you were on got taller and the nearest tower got closer and maybe you thought you could jump from one to the other, or ride on the invisible messages sleeting between them, or perhaps you thought that *you* were a message. Perhaps, as some said, all this was nothing more than a disturbance in the brain caused by the wind in the rigging. No one knew for sure. People who step on to the air one hundred and fifty feet above the ground seldom have much to discuss afterwards.

The tower shifted gently in the wind, but that was okay. There were lots of new designs in *this* tower. It stored the wind to power its mechanisms, it bent rather than broke, it acted more like a tree than a fortress. You could build most of it on the ground and raise it into place in an hour. It was a thing of grace and beauty. And it could send messages up to four times faster than the old towers, thanks to the new shutter system and the coloured lights.

At least, it would once they had sorted out a few lingering problems . . .

The young man climbed swiftly to the very top of the tower. For most of the way he was in clinging, grey morning mist, and then he was rising through glorious sunlight, the mist spreading below him, all the way to the horizon, like a sea.

He paid the view no attention. He'd never dreamed of flying. He dreamed of mechanisms, of making things work better than they'd ever done before.

Right now, he wanted to find out what was making the new shutter array stick *again*. He oiled the sliders, checked the tension on the wires, and then swung himself out over fresh air to check the shutters themselves. It wasn't what you were supposed to do, but every lines-man knew it was the only way to get things done. Anyway, it was perfectly safe if you—

There was a clink. He looked back and saw the snaphook of his safety rope lying on the walkway, saw the shadow, felt the terrible pain in his fingers, heard the scream and dropped . . .

. . . like an anchor.

CHAPTER ONE

The Angel

In which our Hero experiences Hope, the Greatest Gift – The Bacon Sandwich of Regret – Sombre Reflections on Capital Punishment from the Hangman – Famous Last Words – Our Hero Dies – Angels, conversations about – Inadvisability of Misplaced Offers regarding Broomsticks – An Unexpected Ride – A World Free of Honest Men – A Man on the Hop – There is Always a Choice

THEY SAY THAT THE PROSPECT of being hanged in the morning concentrates a man's mind wonderfully; unfortunately, what the mind inevitably concentrates on is that it is in a body that, in the morning, is going to be hanged.

The man going to be hanged had been named Moist von Lipwig by doting if unwise parents, but he was not going to embarrass the name, in so far as that was still possible, by being hung under it. To the world in general, and particularly on that bit of it known as the death warrant, he was Albert Spangler.

And he took a more positive approach to the situation and had concentrated his mind on the prospect of *not* being hanged in the morning, and most particularly on the prospect of removing all the crumbling mortar from around a stone in his cell wall with a spoon. So far the work had taken him five weeks, and reduced the spoon to something like a nail file. Fortunately, no one ever came to change the bedding here, or else they would have discovered the world's heaviest mattress.

It was the large and heavy stone that was currently the object of his attentions, and at some point a huge staple had been hammered into it as an anchor for manacles.

Moist sat down facing the wall, gripped the iron ring in both hands, braced his legs against the stones on either side, and heaved.

His shoulders caught fire and a red mist filled his vision but the block slid out, with a faint and inappropriate tinkling noise. Moist managed to ease it away from the hole and peered inside.

At the far end was another block, and the mortar around it looked suspiciously strong and fresh.

Just in front of it was a new spoon. It was shiny.

As he studied it, he heard the clapping behind him. He turned his head, tendons twanging a little riff of agony, and saw several of the warders watching him through the bars.

'Well *done*, Mr Spangler!' said one of them. 'Ron here owes me five dollars! I *told* him you were a sticker! He's a sticker, I said!'

'You set this up, did you, Mr Wilkinson?' said Moist weakly, watching the glint of light on the spoon.

'Oh, not us, sir. Lord Vetinari's orders. He insists that all condemned prisoners should be offered the prospect of freedom.'

'Freedom? But there's a damn great stone through there!'

'Yes, there is that, sir, yes, there is that,' said the warder. 'It's only the *prospect*, you see. Not actual free freedom as such. Hah, that'd be a bit daft, eh?'

'I suppose so, yes,' said Moist. He didn't say 'you bastards.' The warders had treated him quite civilly this past six weeks, and he made a point of getting on with people. He was very, very good at it. People skills were part of his stock-in-trade; they were nearly the whole of it.

Besides, these people had big sticks. So, speaking carefully, he added: 'Some people might consider this cruel, Mr Wilkinson.'

'Yes, sir, we asked him about that, sir, but he said no, it wasn't. He said it provided—' his forehead wrinkled '—occ-you-pay-shun-all ther-rap-py, healthy exercise, prevented moping and offered that greatest of all treasures which is Hope, sir.'

'Hope,' muttered Moist glumly.

'Not upset, are you, sir?'

'Upset? Why should I be upset, Mr Wilkinson?'

'Only the last bloke we had in this cell, he managed to get down that drain, sir. Very small man. Very agile.'

Moist looked at the little grid in the floor. He'd dismissed it out of hand.

'Does it lead to the river?' he said.

The warder grinned. 'You'd *think* so, wouldn't you? He was really *upset* when we fished him out. Nice to see you've entered into the spirit of the thing, sir. You've been an example to all of us, sir, the way you kept going. Stuffing all the dust in your mattress? Very clever, very tidy. Very *neat*. It's really cheered us up, having you in here. By the way, Mrs Wilkinson says ta very much for the fruit basket. Very posh, it is. It's got kumquats, even!'

'Don't mention it, Mr Wilkinson.'

'The Warden was a bit green about the kumquats 'cos he only got dates in his, but I told him, sir, that fruit baskets is like life: until you've got the pineapple off'f the top you never know what's underneath. He says thank you, too.'

'Glad he liked it, Mr Wilkinson,' said Moist absent-mindedly. Several of his former landladies had brought in presents for 'the poor confused boy', and Moist always invested in generosity. A career like his was all about style, after all.

'On that general subject, sir,' said Mr Wilkinson, 'me and the lads were wondering if you might like to unburden yourself, at this point in time, on the subject of the whereabouts of the place where the location of the spot is where, not to beat about the bush, you hid all that money you stole . . . ?'

The jail went silent. Even the cockroaches were listening.

'No, I couldn't do that, Mr Wilkinson,' said Moist loudly, after a decent pause for dramatic effect. He tapped his jacket pocket, held up a finger and winked.

The warders grinned back.

'We understand totally, sir. Now I'd get some rest if I was you, sir, 'cos we're hanging you in half an hour,' said Mr Wilkinson.

'Hey, don't I get breakfast?'

'Breakfast isn't until seven o'clock, sir,' said the warder reproachfully. 'But, tell you what, I'll do you a bacon sandwich. 'cos it's *you*, Mr Spangler.'

*   *   *

And now it was a few minutes before dawn and it was *him* being led down the short corridor and out into the little room under the scaffold. Moist realized he was looking at himself from a distance, as if part of himself was floating outside his body like a child's balloon ready, as it were, for him to let go of the string.

The room was lit by light coming through cracks in the scaffold floor above, and significantly from around the edges of the large trapdoor. The hinges of said door were being carefully oiled by a man in a hood.

He stopped when he saw the party arrive and said, 'Good morning, Mr Spangler.' He raised the hood helpfully. 'It's me, sir, Daniel "One Drop" Trooper. I am your executioner for today, sir. Don't you worry, sir. I've hanged dozens of people. We'll soon have you out of here.'

'Is it true that if a man isn't hanged after three attempts he's reprieved, Dan?' said Moist, as the executioner carefully wiped his hands on a rag.

'So I've heard, sir, so I've heard. But they don't call me One Drop for nothing, sir. And will sir be having the black bag today?'

'Will it help?'

'Some people think it makes them look more dashing, sir. And it stops that pop-eyed look. It's more a crowd thing, really. Quite a big one out there this morning. Nice piece about you in the *Times* yesterday, I thought. All them people saying what a nice young man you were, and everything. Er . . . would you mind signing the rope beforehand, sir? I mean, I won't have a chance to ask you afterwards, eh?'

'*Signing* the *rope*?' said Moist.

'Yessir,' said the hangman. 'It's sort of traditional. There's a lot of people out there who buy old rope. Specialist collectors, you could say. A bit strange, but it takes all sorts, eh? Worth more signed, of course.' He flourished a length of stout rope. 'I've got a special pen that signs on rope. One signature every couple of inches? Straightforward signature, no dedication needed. Worth money to me, sir. I'd be very grateful.'

'So grateful that you won't hang me, then?' said Moist, taking the pen.

This got an appreciative laugh. Mr Trooper watched him sign along the length, nodding happily.

'Well done, sir, that's my pension plan you're signing there. Now . . . are we ready, everyone?'

'Not me!' said Moist quickly, to another round of general amusement.

'You're a card, Mr Spangler,' said Mr Wilkinson. 'It won't be the same without you around, and that's the truth.'

'Not for me, at any rate,' said Moist. This was, once again, treated like rapier wit. Moist sighed. 'Do you really think all this deters crime, Mr Trooper?' he said.

'Well, in the generality of things I'd say it's hard to tell, given that it's hard to find evidence of crimes not committed,' said the hangman, giving the trapdoor a final rattle. 'But in the *specificality*, sir, I'd say it's very efficacious.'

'Meaning what?' said Moist.

'Meaning I've never seen someone up here more'n once, sir. Shall we go?'

There was a stir when they climbed up into the chilly morning air, followed by a few boos and even some applause. People were strange like that. Steal five dollars and you were a petty thief. Steal thousands of dollars and you were either a government or a hero.

Moist stared ahead while the roll call of his crimes was read out. He couldn't help feeling that it was so *unfair*. He'd never so much as tapped someone on the head. He'd never even broken down a door. He *had* picked locks on occasion, but he'd always locked them again behind him. Apart from all those repossessions, bankruptcies and sudden insolvencies, what had he actually done that was *bad*, as such? He'd only been moving numbers around.

'Nice crowd turned out today,' said Mr Trooper, tossing the end of the rope over the beam and busying himself with knots. 'Lot of press, too. *What Gallows?* covers 'em all, o' course, and there's the *Times* and the *Pseudopolis Herald*, prob'ly because of that bank what collapsed there, and I heard there's a man from the *Sto Plains Dealer*, too. Very good financial section – I always keep an eye on the used rope prices. Looks like a lot of people want to see you dead, sir.'

Moist was aware that a black coach had drawn up at the rear of the crowd. There was no coat of arms on the door, unless you were in on the secret, which was that Lord Vetinari's coat of arms featured a sable shield. Black on black. You had to admit that the bastard had style—

'Huh? What?' he said, in response to a nudge.

'I asked if you have any last words, Mr Spangler?' said the hangman. 'It's customary. I wonder if you might have thought of any?'

'I wasn't actually expecting to die,' said Moist. And that was it. He really hadn't, until now. He'd been certain that *something* would turn up.

'Good one, sir,' said Mr Wilkinson. 'We'll go with that, shall we?'

Moist narrowed his eyes. The curtain on a coach window had twitched. The coach door had opened. Hope, that greatest of all treasures, ventured a little glitter.

'No, they're not my *actual* last words,' he said. 'Er . . . let me think . . .'

A slight, clerk-like figure was descending from the coach.

'Er . . . it's not as bad a thing I do now . . . er . . .' *Aha, it all made some kind of sense now. Vetinari was out to scare him, that was it. That would be just like the man, from what Moist had heard. There* was *going to be a reprieve!*

'I . . . er . . . I . . .'

Down below, the clerk was having difficulty getting through the press of people.

'Do you mind speeding up a bit, Mr Spangler?' said the hangman. 'Fair's fair, eh?'

'I want to get it right,' said Moist haughtily, watching the clerk negotiate his way around a large troll.

'Yes, but there's a limit, sir,' said the hangman, annoyed at this breach of etiquette. 'Otherwise you could go ah, er, um for *days*! Short and sweet, sir, that's the style.'

'Right, right,' said Spangler. 'Er . . . oh, *look*, see that man there? Waving at you?'

The hangman glanced down at the clerk, who'd struggled to the front of the crowd.

'I bring a message from Lord Vetinari!' the man shouted.

'Right!' said Moist.

'He says to get on with it, it's long past dawn!' said the clerk.

'Oh,' said Moist, staring at the black coach. That damn Vetinari had a warder's sense of humour, too.

'Come *on*, Mr Spangler, you don't want me to get into trouble, do you?' said the hangman, patting him on the shoulder. 'Just a few words, and then we can all get on with our lives. Present company excepted, obviously.'

So this *was* it. It was, in some strange way, rather liberating. You didn't have to fear the worst that could happen any more, because this was it, and it was nearly over. The warder had been right. What you had to do in this life was get past the pineapple, Moist told himself. It was big and sharp and knobbly, but there might be peaches underneath. It was a myth to live by and so, right now, totally useless.

'In that case,' said Moist von Lipwig, 'I commend my soul to any god that can find it.'

'Nice,' said the hangman, and pulled the lever.

Albert Spangler died.

It was generally agreed that they had been good last words.

'Ah, Mr Lipwig,' said a distant voice, getting closer. 'I see you are awake. And still alive, at the present time.'

There was a slight inflection to that last phrase which told Moist that the length of the present time was entirely in the gift of the speaker.

He opened his eyes. He was sitting in a comfortable chair. At a desk opposite him, sitting with his hands steepled reflectively in front of his pursed lips, was Havelock, Lord Vetinari, under whose idiosyncratically despotic rule Ankh-Morpork had become the city where, for some reason, everyone wanted to live.

An ancient animal sense also told Moist that other people were standing behind the comfortable chair, and that it could be extremely uncomfortable should he make any sudden movements. But they couldn't be as terrible as the thin, black-robed man with the fussy little beard and the pianist's hands who was watching him.

'Shall I tell you about angels, Mr Lipwig?' said the Patrician pleasantly. 'I know two interesting facts about them.'

Moist grunted. There were no obvious escape routes in front of him, and turning round was out of the question. His neck ached horribly.

'Oh, yes. You were hanged,' said Vetinari. 'A very precise science, hanging. Mr Trooper is a master. The slippage and thickness of the rope, whether the knot is placed *here* rather than *there*, the relationship between weight and distance . . . oh, I'm sure the man could write a book. You were hanged to within half an inch of your life, I understand. Only an expert standing right next to you would have spotted that, and in this case the expert was our friend Mr Trooper. No, Albert Spangler is dead, Mr Lipwig. Three hundred people would swear they saw him die.' He leaned forward. 'And so, appropriately, it is of angels I wish to talk to you now.'

Moist managed a grunt.

'The first interesting thing about angels, Mr Lipwig, is that some-times, very rarely, at a point in a man's career where he has made such a foul and tangled mess of his life that death appears to be the only sensible option, an angel appears to him, or, I should say, *unto* him, and offers him a chance to go back to the moment when it all went wrong, and this time do it *right*. Mr Lipwig, I should like you to think of me as . . . an angel.'

Moist stared. He'd felt the snap of the rope, the choke of the noose! He'd seen the blackness welling up! He'd *died*!

'I'm offering you a job, Mr Lipwig. Albert Spangler is buried, but Mr Lipwig has a *future*. It may, of course, be a very short one, if he is stupid. I am offering you a job, Mr Lipwig. Work, for wages. I realize the concept may not be familiar.'

Only as a form of hell, Moist thought.

'The job is that of Postmaster General of the Ankh-Morpork Post Office.'

Moist continued to stare.

'May I just add, Mr Lipwig, that behind you there is a door. If at any time in this interview you feel you wish to leave, you have only to step through it and you will never hear from me again.'

Moist filed that under 'deeply suspicious'.

'To continue: the job, Mr Lipwig, involves the refurbishment and running of the city's postal service, preparation of the international packets, maintenance of Post Office property, et cetera, et cetera—'

'If you stick a broom up my arse I could probably sweep the floor, too,' said a voice. Moist realized it was his. His brain was a mess. It had come as a shock to find that the afterlife is this one.

Lord Vetinari gave him a long, long look.

'Well, if you wish,' he said, and turned to a hovering clerk. 'Drumknott, does the housekeeper have a store cupboard on this floor, do you know?'

'Oh, yes, my lord,' said the clerk. 'Shall I—'

'It was a joke!' Moist burst out.

'Oh, I'm sorry, I hadn't realized,' said Lord Vetinari, turning back to Moist. 'Do tell me if you feel obliged to make another one, will you?'

'Look,' said Moist, 'I don't know what's happening here, but I don't know *anything* about delivering post!'

'Mr Moist, this morning you had no experience at all of being dead, and yet but for my intervention you would nevertheless have turned out to be extremely *good* at it,' said Lord Vetinari sharply. 'It just goes to show: you never know until you try.'

'But when you sentenced me—'

Vetinari raised a pale hand. 'Ah?' he said.

Moist's brain, at last aware that it needed to do some work here, stepped in and replied: 'Er . . . when you . . . sentenced . . . Albert Spangler—'

'Well done. Do carry on.'

'—you said he was a natural born criminal, a fraudster by vocation, an habitual liar, a perverted genius and totally untrustworthy!'

'Are you accepting my offer, Mr Lipwig?' said Vetinari sharply.

Moist looked at him. 'Excuse me,' he said, standing up, 'I'd just like to check something.'

There were two men dressed in black standing behind his chair. It wasn't a particularly neat black, more the black worn by people who just don't want little marks to show. They looked like clerks, until you met their eyes.

They stood aside as Moist walked towards the door which, as promised, was indeed there. He opened it very carefully. There was nothing beyond, and that included a floor. In the manner of one who is going to try all possibilities, he took the remnant of spoon out of his pocket and let it drop. It was quite a long time before he heard the jingle.

Then he went back and sat in the chair.

'The prospect of freedom?' he said.

'Exactly,' said Lord Vetinari. 'There is always a choice.'

'You mean . . . I could choose certain death?'

'A choice, nevertheless,' said Vetinari. 'Or, perhaps, an alternative. You see, I *believe* in freedom, Mr Lipwig. Not many people do, although they will of course protest otherwise. And no practical definition of freedom would be complete without the freedom to take the consequences. Indeed, it is the freedom upon which all the others are based. Now . . . will you take the job? No one will recognize you, I am sure. No one ever recognizes you, it would appear.'

Moist shrugged. 'Oh, all right. Of course, I accept as natural born criminal, habitual liar, fraudster and totally untrustworthy perverted genius.'

'Capital! Welcome to government service!' said Lord Vetinari, extending his hand. 'I pride myself on being able to pick the right man. The wage is twenty dollars a week and, I believe, the Postmaster General has the use of a small apartment in the main building. I think there's a hat, too. I shall require regular reports. Good day.'

He looked down at his paperwork. He looked up.

'You appear to be still here, Postmaster General?'

'And that's *it*?' said Moist, aghast. 'One minute I'm being hanged, next minute you're employing me?'

'Let me see . . . yes, I think so. Oh, no. Of course. Drumknott, do give Mr Lipwig his keys.'

The clerk stepped forward and handed Moist a huge, rusted keyring full of keys, and proffered a clipboard. 'Sign here, please, Postmaster General,' he said.

Hold on a minute, Moist thought, this is only one city. It's got gates. It's completely surrounded by different directions to run. Does it matter what I sign?

'Certainly,' he said, and scribbled his name.

'Your *correct* name, if you please,' said Lord Vetinari, not looking up from his desk. 'What name did he sign, Drumknott?'

The clerk craned his head. 'Er . . . Ethel Snake, my lord, as far as I can make out.'

'*Do* try to concentrate, Mr Lipwig,' said Vetinari wearily, still apparently reading the paperwork.

Moist signed again. After all, what would it matter in the long run? And it would certainly be a long run, if he couldn't find a horse.

'And that leaves only the matter of your parole officer,' said Lord Vetinari, still engrossed in the paper before him.

'Parole officer?'

'Yes. I'm not completely stupid, Mr Lipwig. He will meet you outside the Post Office building in ten minutes. Good day.'

When Moist had left, Drumknott coughed politely and said, 'Do you think he'll turn up there, my lord?'

'One must always consider the psychology of the individual,' said Vetinari, correcting the spelling on an official report. 'That is what I do all the time and lamentably, Drumknott, you do not always do. That is why he has walked off with your pencil.'

Always move fast. You never know what's catching you up.

Ten minutes later Moist von Lipwig was well outside the city. He'd *bought* a horse, which was a bit embarrassing, but speed had been of the essence and he'd only had time to grab one of his emergency stashes from its secret hiding place and pick up a skinny old screw from the Bargain Box in Hobson's Livery Stable. At least it'd mean no irate citizen going to the Watch.

No one had bothered him. No one had looked at him twice; no one ever did. The city gates had indeed been wide open. The plains lay ahead of him, full of opportunity. And he was good at parlaying nothing into something. For example, at the first little town he came to he'd go to work on this old nag with a few simple techniques and ingredients that'd make it worth twice the price he'd paid for it, at least for about twenty minutes or until it rained. Twenty minutes would be enough time to sell it and, with any luck, pick up a better horse worth slightly more than the asking price. He'd do it again at the next town and in three days, maybe four, he'd have a horse worth owning.

But that would be just a sideshow, something to keep his hand in. He'd got three very nearly diamond rings sewn into the lining of his coat, a real one in a secret pocket in the sleeve, and a very nearly gold dollar stitched cunningly into the collar. These were, to him, what his saw and hammer are to a carpenter. They were primitive tools, but they'd put him back in the game.

There is a saying 'You can't fool an honest man' which is much quoted by people who make a profitable living by fooling honest men. Moist never knowingly tried it, anyway. If you did fool an honest man, he tended to complain to the local Watch, and these days they were harder to buy off. Fooling dishonest men was a lot safer and, somehow, more sporting. And, of course, there were so many more of them. You hardly had to aim.

Half an hour after arriving in the town of Hapley, where the big city was a tower of smoke on the horizon, he was sitting outside an inn, downcast, with nothing in the world but a genuine diamond ring worth a hundred dollars and a pressing need to get home to Genua, where his poor aged mother was dying of Gnats. Eleven minutes later he was standing patiently outside a jeweller's shop, inside which the jeweller was telling a sympathetic citizen that the ring the stranger was prepared to sell for twenty dollars was worth seventy-five (even jewellers have to make a living). And thirty-five minutes after that he was riding out on a better horse, with five dollars in his pocket, leaving behind a gloating sympathetic citizen who, despite having been bright enough to watch Moist's hands carefully, was about to go back to the jeweller to try to sell for seventy-five dollars a shiny brass ring with a glass stone that was worth fifty pence of anybody's money.

The world was blessedly free of honest men, and wonderfully full of people who believed they could tell the difference between an honest man and a crook.

He tapped his jacket pocket. The jailers had taken the map off him, of course, probably while he was busy being a dead man. It was a good map, and in studying it Mr Wilkinson and his chums would learn a lot about decryption, geography and devious cartography. They wouldn't find in it the whereabouts of AM$150,000 in mixed currencies, though, because the map was a complete and complex fiction. However, Moist entertained a wonderful warm feeling inside to think that they would, for some time, possess that greatest of all treasures, which is Hope.

Anyone who couldn't simply *remember* where he'd stashed a great big fortune deserved to lose it, in Moist's opinion. But, for now, he'd have to keep away from it, while having it to look forward to . . .

Moist didn't even bother to note the name of the next town. It had an inn, and that was enough. He took a room with a view over a disused alley, checked that the window opened easily, ate an adequate meal, and had an early night.

Not bad at all, he thought. This morning he'd been on the scaffold with the actual noose round his actual neck, tonight he was back in business. All he need do now was grow a beard again, and keep away from Ankh-Morpork for six months. Or perhaps only three.

Moist had a talent. He'd also acquired a lot of skills so completely that they were second nature. He'd *learned* to be personable, but something in his genetics made him unmemorable. He had the talent of not being noticed, for being a face in the crowd. People had difficulty describing him. He was . . . he was 'about'. He was about twenty, or about thirty. On Watch reports across the continent he was anywhere between, oh, about six feet two inches and five feet nine inches tall, hair all shades from mid-brown to blond, and his lack of distinguishing features included his entire face. He was about . . . average. What people *remembered* was the furniture, things like spectacles and moustaches, so he always carried a selection of both. They remembered names and mannerisms, too. He had hundreds of those.

Oh, and they remembered that they'd been richer before they met him.

At three in the morning, the door burst open. It was a real burst; bits of wood clattered off the wall. But Moist was already out of bed and diving for the window before the first of them hit the floor. It was an automatic reaction that owed nothing to thought. Besides, he'd checked before lying down, and there was a large water butt outside that would break his fall.

It wasn't there now.

Whoever had stolen it had not stolen the ground it stood on, however, and it broke Moist's fall by twisting his ankle.

He pulled himself up, keening softly in agony, and hopped along the alley, using the wall for support. The inn's stables were round the back; all he had to do was pull himself up on to a horse, any horse—

'Mr Lipwig?' a *big* voice bellowed.

Oh, gods, it was a troll, it *sounded* like a troll, a big one too, he didn't know you got any down here outside the cities—

'You Can't Run And You Can't Hide, Mr Lipwig!'

Hold on, hold on, he hadn't given his real name to *anyone* in this place, had he? But all this was background thinking. Someone was after him, therefore he would run. Or hop.

He risked a look behind him when he reached the back gate to the stables. There was a red glow in his room. Surely they weren't torching the place over a matter of a few dollars? How stupid! Everyone *knew* that if you got lumbered with a good fake you palmed it off on to some other sucker as soon as possible, didn't they? There was no helping some people.

His horse was alone in the stable, and seemed unimpressed to see him. He got the bridle on, while hopping on one foot. There was no point in bothering with a saddle. He knew how to ride without a saddle. Hell, once he'd ridden without pants, too, but luckily all the tar and feathers helped him stick to the horse. He was the world champion at leaving town in a hurry.

He went to lead the horse out of the stall, and heard the clink.

He looked down, and kicked some straw away.

There was a bright yellow bar, joining two short lengths of chain with a yellow shackle attached, one for each foreleg. The only way this horse would go anywhere was by hopping, just like him.

They'd clamped it. They'd bloody *clamped* it . . .

'Oh, Mr Lipppppwig!' The voice boomed out across the stable yard. 'Do You Want To Know The *Rules*, Mr Lipwig?'

He looked around in desperation. There was nothing in here to use as a weapon and in any case weapons made him nervous, which was why he'd never carried one. Weapons raised the ante far too high. It was much better to rely on a gift for talking his way out of things, confusing the issue and, if that failed, some well-soled shoes and a cry of 'Look, what's that over there?'

But he had a definite feeling that while he could talk as much as he liked, out here no one was going to listen. As for speeding away, he'd just have to rely on hop.

There *was* a yard broom and a wooden feed bucket in the corner. He stuck the head of the broom under his armpit to make a crutch and grabbed the bucket handle as heavy footsteps thudded towards the stable door. When the door was pushed open he swung the bucket as hard as he could, and felt it shatter. Splinters filled the air. A moment later there was the thump of a heavy body hitting the ground.

Moist hopped over it and plunged unsteadily into the dark.

Something as tough and hard as a shackle snapped round his good ankle. He hung from the broom handle for a second, and then collapsed.

'I Have Nothing But Good Feelings Towards You, Mr Lipwig!' boomed the voice cheerfully.

Moist groaned. The broom must have been kept as an ornament, because it certainly hadn't been used much on the accumulations in the stable yard. On the positive side, this meant he had fallen into something soft. On the negative side, it meant that he had fallen into something soft.

Someone grabbed a handful of his coat and lifted him bodily out of the muck.

'Up We Get, Mr Lipwig!'

'It's pronounced Lipvig, you moron,' he moaned. 'A v, not a w!'

'Up Ve Get, Mr Lipvig!' said the booming voice, as his broom/crutch was pushed under his arm.

'What the hell *are* you?' Lipwig managed.

'I Am Your Parole Officer, Mr Lipvig!'

Moist managed to turn round, and looked up, and then up again, into a gingerbread man's face with two glowing red eyes in it. When it spoke, its mouth was a glimpse into an inferno.

'A golem? You're a damn *golem*?'

The thing picked him up in one hand and slung him over its shoulder. It ducked into the stables and Moist, upside down with his nose pressed against the terracotta of the creature's body, realized that it was picking up his horse in its other hand. There was a brief whinny.

'Ve Must Make Haste, Mr Lipvig! You Are Due In Front Of Lord Vetinari At Eight O'Clock! And At Vork By Nine!'

Moist groaned.

'Ah, *Mr Lipwig*. Regrettably, we meet again,' said Lord Vetinari.

It was eight o'clock in the morning. Moist was swaying. His ankle felt better, but it was the only part of him that did.

'It walked all night!' he said. 'All damn night! Carrying a horse as well!'

'Do sit *down*, Mr Lipwig,' said Vetinari, looking up from the table and gesturing wearily to the chair. 'By the way, "it" is a "he". An honorific in this case, clearly, but I have great hopes of Mr Pump.'

Moist saw the glow on the walls as, behind him, the golem smiled.

Vetinari looked down at the table again, and seemed to lose interest in Moist for a moment. A slab of stone occupied most of the table. Little carved figurines of dwarfs and trolls covered it. It looked like some kind of game.

'*Mr* Pump?' said Moist.

'Hmm?' said Vetinari, moving his head to look at the board from a slightly different viewpoint.

Moist leaned towards the Patrician, and jerked a thumb in the direction of the golem.

'*That*,' he said, 'is *Mr* Pump?'

'No,' said Lord Vetinari, leaning forward likewise and suddenly, completely and disconcertingly focusing on Moist. '*He* . . . is Mr Pump. Mr Pump is a government official. Mr Pump does not sleep. Mr Pump does not eat. And Mr Pump, Postmaster General, *does not stop*.'

'And that means what, exactly?'

'It means that if you are thinking of, say, finding a ship headed for Fourecks, on the basis that Mr Pump is big and heavy and travels only at walking pace, Mr Pump will follow you. You have to sleep. Mr Pump does not. Mr Pump does not breathe. The deep abyssal plains of the oceans present no barrier to Mr Pump. Four miles an hour is six hundred and seventy-two miles in a week. It all adds up. And when Mr Pump catches you—'

'Ah, now,' said Moist, holding up a finger. 'Let me stop you there. I *know* golems are not allowed to hurt people!'

Lord Vetinari raised his eyebrows. 'Good heavens, wherever did you hear that?'

'It's written on . . . something inside their heads! A scroll, or something. Isn't it?' said Moist, uncertainty rising.

'Oh, dear.' The Patrician sighed. 'Mr Pump, just break one of Mr Lipwig's fingers, will you? Neatly, if you please.'

'Yes, Your Lordship.' The golem lumbered forward.

'Hey! No! What?' Moist waved his hands wildly and knocked game pieces tumbling. 'Wait! Wait! There's a *rule*! A golem mustn't harm a human being or allow a human being to come to harm!'

Lord Vetinari raised a finger. 'Just wait *one* moment, please, Mr Pump. Very well, Mr Lipwig, can you remember the next bit?'

'The next bit? What next bit?' said Moist. 'There isn't a next bit!'

Lord Vetinari raised an eyebrow. 'Mr Pump?' he said.

' "... Unless Ordered To Do So By Duly Constituted Authority",' said the golem.

'I've never heard *that* bit before!' said Moist.

'Haven't you?' said Lord Vetinari, in apparent surprise. 'I can't imagine who would fail to include it. A hammer can hardly be allowed to refuse to hit the nail on the head, nor a saw to make moral judgements about the nature of the timber. In any case, I employ Mr Trooper the hangman, whom of course you have met, and the City Watch, the regiments and, from time to time . . . other specialists, who are fully entitled to kill in their own defence or in protection of the city and its interests.' Vetinari started to pick up the fallen pieces and replace them delicately on the slab. 'Why should Mr Pump be any different just because he is made of clay? Ultimately, so are we all. Mr Pump will accompany you to your place of work. The fiction will be that he is your bodyguard, as befits a senior government official. We alone will know that he has . . . additional instructions. Golems are highly moral creatures by nature, Mr Lipwig, but you may find their morality a shade . . . old-fashioned?'

'Additional instructions?' said Moist. 'And would you mind telling me exactly what his additional instructions are?'

'Yes.' The Patrician blew a speck of dust off a little stone troll and put it on its square.

'And?' said Moist, after a pause.

Vetinari sighed. 'Yes, I *would* mind telling you exactly what they are. You have no rights in this matter. We have impounded your horse, by the way, since it was used in the committing of a crime.'

'This is cruel and unusual punishment!' said Moist.

'Indeed?' said Vetinari. 'I offer you a light desk job, comparative freedom of movement, working in the fresh air . . . no, I feel that my offer might well be unusual, but cruel? I think not. However, I believe we do have down in the cellars some ancient punishments which are *extremely* cruel and in many cases quite unusual, if you would like to try them for the purposes of comparison. And, of course, there is always the option of dancing the sisal two-step.'

'The what?' said Moist.

Drumknott leaned down and whispered something in his master's ear.

'Oh, I apologize,' said Vetinari. 'I meant of course the hemp fandango. It is your choice, Mr Lipwig. There is *always* a choice, Mr Lipwig. Oh, and by the way . . . do you know the *second* interesting thing about angels?'

'What angels?' said Moist, angry and bewildered.

'Oh, dear, people just don't pay attention,' said Vetinari. 'Remember? The first interesting thing about angels? I told you yesterday? I expect you were thinking about something else. The *second* interesting thing about angels, Mr Lipwig, is that *you only ever get one.*'

CHAPTER TWO

The Post Office

In which we meet the Staff – Glom of Nit – Dissertation on Rhyming
Slang – 'You should have been there!' – The Dead Letters – A Golem's
Life – Book of Regulations

THERE WAS ALWAYS AN ANGLE. There was always a price. There was always a *way*. And look at it like this, Moist thought: certain death had been replaced with uncertain death, and that was an improvement, wasn't it? He was free to walk around . . . well, hobble, at the moment. And it was just possible that somewhere in all this was a profit. Well, it *could* happen. He was good at seeing opportunities where other people saw barren ground. So there was no harm in playing it straight for a few days, yes? It'd give his foot a chance to get better, he could spy out the situation, he could make plans. He might even find out how indestructible golems were. After all, they were made of pottery, weren't they? Things could get broken, maybe.

Moist von Lipwig raised his eyes and examined his future.

The Ankh-Morpork Central Post Office had a gaunt frontage. It was a building designed for a purpose. It was, therefore, more or less, a big box to employ people in, with two wings at the rear which enclosed the big stable yard. Some cheap pillars had been sliced in half and stuck on the outside, some niches had been carved for some miscellaneous stone nymphs, some stone urns had been ranged along the parapet and thus Architecture had been created.

In appreciation of the thought that had gone into this, the good citizens, or more probably their kids, had covered the walls to a height of six feet with graffiti in many exciting colours.

In a band all along the top of the frontage, staining the stone in greens and browns, some words had been set in letters of bronze.

'"NEITHER RAIN NOR SNOW NOR GLO M OF NI T CAN STAY THESE MES ENGERS ABO T THEIR DUTY,"' Moist read aloud. 'What the hell does that mean?'

'The Post Office Was Once A Proud Institution,' said Mr Pump.

'And *that* stuff?' Moist pointed. On a board much further down the building, in peeling paint, were the less heroic words:

DONT ARSK US ABOUT:
rocks
troll's with sticks
All sorts of dragons
Mrs Cake
Huje green things with teeth
Any kinds of black dogs with orange eyebrows
Rains of spaniel's
fog
   Mrs Cake

'I Said It *Was* A Proud Institution,' the golem rumbled.

'Who's Mrs Cake?'

'I Regret I Cannot Assist You There, Mr Lipvig.'

'They seem pretty frightened of her.'

'So It Appears, Mr Lipvig.'

Moist looked around at this busy junction in this busy city. People weren't paying him any attention, although the golem was getting casual glances that didn't appear very friendly.

This was all too strange. He'd been – what, fourteen? – when he'd last used his real name. And heavens knew how long it had been since he'd gone out without some easily removable distinguishing marks. He felt naked. Naked and unnoticed.

To the interest of no one whatsoever, he walked up the stained steps and turned the key in the lock. To his surprise it moved easily, and the paint-spattered doors swung open without a creak.

There was a rhythmic, hollow noise behind Moist. Mr Pump was clapping his hands.

'Vell Done, Mr Lipvig. Your First Step In A Career Of Benefit Both To Yourself And The Vell-being Of The City!'

'Yeah, right,' muttered Lipwig.

He stepped into the huge, dark lobby, which was lit only dimly by a big but grimy dome in the ceiling; it could never be more than twilight in here, even at noon. The graffiti artists had been at work in here, too.

In the gloom he could see a long, broken counter, with doors and pigeon-holes behind it.

Real pigeon-holes. Pigeons were *nesting* in the pigeon-holes. The sour, salty smell of old guano filled the air, and, as marble tiles rang under Moist's feet, several hundred pigeons took off frantically and spiralled up towards a broken pane in the roof.

'Oh, shit,' he said.

'Bad Language Is Discouraged, Mr Lipvig,' said Mr Pump, behind him.

'Why? It's written on the walls! Anyway, it was a *description*, Mr Pump! Guano! There must be tons of the stuff!' Moist heard his own voice echo back from the distant walls. 'When was this place last open?'

'Twenty years ago, Postmaster!'

Moist looked around. 'Who said that?' he said. The voice seemed to have come from everywhere.

There was the sound of shuffling and the click-click of a walking stick and a bent, elderly figure appeared in the grey, dead, dusty air.

'Groat, sir,' it wheezed. 'Junior Postman Groat, sir. At your service, sir. One word from you, sir, and I will *leap*, sir, *leap* into action, sir.' The figure stopped to cough long and hard, making a noise like a wall being hit repeatedly with a bag of rocks. Moist saw that it had a beard of the short bristled type that suggested that its owner had been inter-rupted halfway through eating a hedgehog.

'*Junior* Postman Groat?' he said.

'Indeedy, sir. The reason being, no one's ever bin here long enough to promote me, sir. Should be Senior Postman Groat, sir,' the old man added meaningfully, and once again coughed volcanically.

Ex-Postman Groat sounds more like it, Moist thought. Aloud he said, 'And you work here, do you?'

'Aye, sir, that we do, sir. It's just me and the boy now, sir. He's keen, sir. We keeps the place clean, sir. All according to Regulations.'

Moist could not stop staring. Mr Groat wore a toupee. There may actually be a man somewhere on whom a toupee works, but whoever that man might be, Mr Groat was not he. It was chestnut brown, the wrong size, the wrong shape, the wrong style and, all in all, wrong.

'Ah, I see you're admirin' my hair, sir,' said Groat proudly, as the toupee spun gently. 'It's all mine, you know, not a prunes.'

'Er . . . prunes?' said Moist.

'Sorry, sir, shouldn't have used slang. Prunes as in "syrup of prunes", sir. Dimwell slang.* Syrup of prunes: wig. Not many men o' my age got all their own hair, I expect that's what you're thinking. It's clean living that does it, inside and out.'

Moist looked around at the fetid air and the receding mounds of guano. 'Well done,' he muttered. 'Well, Mr Groat, do I have an office? Or something?'

For a moment, the visible face above the ragged beard was that of a rabbit in a headlight.

'Oh, yes, sir, *techn'c'ly*,' said the old man quickly. 'But we don't go in there any more sir, oh no, 'cos of the floor. Very unsafe, sir. 'cos of the floor. Could give way any minute, sir. We uses the staff locker room, sir. If you'd care to follow me, sir?'

Moist nearly burst out laughing. 'Fine,' he said. He turned to the golem. 'Er . . . Mr Pump?'

'Yes, Mr Lipvig?' said the golem.

'Are you allowed to assist me in any way, or do you just wait around until it's time to hit me on the head?'

'There Is No Need For Hurtful Remarks, Sir. I Am Allowed To Render Appropriate Assistance.'

---

* Dimwell Arrhythmic Rhyming Slang: Various rhyming slangs are known, and have given the universe such terms as 'apples and pears' (stairs), 'rubbity-dub' (pub) and 'busy bee' (General Theory of Relativity). The Dimwell Street rhyming slang is probably unique in that it does not, in fact, rhyme. No one knows why, but theories so far advanced are 1) that it is quite complex and in fact follows hidden rules or 2) Dimwell is well named or 3) it's made up to annoy strangers, which is the case with most such slangs.

'So could you clean out the pigeon shit and let a bit of light in?'

'Certainly, Mr Lipvig.'

'You *can*?'

'A Golem Does Not Shy Away From Vork, Mr Lipvig. I Vill Locate A Shovel.' Mr Pump set off towards the distant counter, and the bearded Junior Postman panicked.

'No!' he squeaked, lurching after the golem. 'It's really not a good idea to touch them heaps!'

'Floors liable to collapse, Mr Groat?' said Moist cheerfully.

Groat looked from Moist to the golem, and back again. His mouth opened and shut as his brain sought for words. Then he sighed.

'You'd better come down to the locker room, then. Step this way, gentlemen.'

Moist became aware of the smell of Mr Groat as he followed the old man. It wasn't a bad smell, as such, just … odd. It was vaguely chemical, coupled with the eye-stinging aroma of every type of throat medicine you've ever swallowed, and with just a hint of old potatoes.

The locker room turned out to be down some steps into the basement where, presumably, the floors couldn't collapse because there was nothing to collapse into. It was long and narrow. At one end was a monstrous oven which, Moist learned later, had once been part of some kind of heating system, the Post Office having been a very advanced building for its time. Now a small round stove, glowing almost cherry-red at the base, had been installed alongside it. There was a huge black kettle on it.

The air indicated the presence of socks, cheap coal and no ventilation; some battered wooden lockers were ranged along one wall, the painted names flaking off. Light got in, eventually, via grimy windows up near the ceiling.

Whatever the original purpose of the room, though, it was now the place where two people lived; two people who got along but, nevertheless, had a clear sense of mine and thine. The space was divided into two, with a narrow bed against one wall on each side. The dividing line was painted on the floor, up the walls and across the ceiling. My half, your half. So long as we remember that, the line indicated, there won't be any more . . . trouble.

In the middle, so that it bestrode the boundary line, was a table. A couple of mugs and two tin plates were carefully arranged at either end. There was a salt pot in the middle of the table. The line, at the salt pot, turned into a little circle to encompass it in its own demilitarized zone.

One half of the narrow room contained an over-large and untidy bench, piled with jars, bottles and old papers; it looked like the work space of a chemist who made it up as he went along or until it exploded. The other had an old card table on which small boxes and rolls of black felt had been stacked with slightly worrying precision. There was also the largest magnifying glass Moist had ever seen, on a stand.

That side of the room had been swept clean. The other was a mess that threatened to encroach over the Line. Unless one of the scraps of paper from the grubbier side was a funny shape, it seemed that somebody, with care and precision and presumably a razor blade, had cut off that corner of it which had gone too far.

A young man stood in the middle of the clean half of the floor. He'd obviously been waiting for Moist, just like Groat, but he hadn't mastered the art of standing to attention or, rather, had only partly understood it. His right side stood considerably more to attention than his left side and, as a result, he was standing like a banana. Nevertheless, with his huge nervous grin and big gleaming eyes he radiated keenness, quite possibly beyond the boundaries of sanity. There was a definite sense that at any moment he would bite. And he wore a blue cotton shirt on which someone had printed 'Ask Me About Pins!'

'Er . . .' said Moist.

'Apprentice Postman Stanley,' mumbled Groat. 'Orphan, sir. Very sad. Came to us from the Siblings of Offler charity home, sir. Both parents passed away of the Gnats on their farm out in the wilds, sir, and he was raised by peas.'

'Surely you mean *on* peas, Mr Groat?'

'*By* peas, sir. Very unusual case. A good lad if he doesn't get upset but he tends to twist towards the sun, sir, if you get my meaning.'

'Er . . . perhaps,' said Moist. He turned hurriedly to Stanley. 'So you know something about pins, do you?' he said, in what he hoped was a jovial voice.

'Nosir!' said Stanley. He all but saluted.

'But your shirt says—'

'I know *everything* about pins, sir,' said Stanley. 'Everything there is to know!'

'Well, that's, er—' Moist began.

'Every single fact about pins, sir,' Stanley went on. 'There's not a thing I don't know about pins. Ask me anything about pins, sir. Anything you like at all. Go on, sir!'

'Well . . .' Moist floundered, but years of practice came to his aid. 'I wonder how many pins were made in this city last ye—'

He stopped. A change had come across Stanley's face: it smoothed out, lost the vague hint that its owner was about to attempt to gnaw your ear off.

'Last year the combined workshops (or "pinneries") of Ankh-Morpork turned out twenty-seven million, eight hundred and eighty thousand, nine hundred and seventy-eight pins,' said Stanley, staring into a pin-filled private universe. 'That includes wax-headed, steels, brassers, silver-headed (and full silver), extra large, machine- and hand-made, reflexed and novelty, but not lapel pins which should not be grouped with the true pins at all since they are technically known as "sports" or "blazons", sir—'

'Ah, yes, I think I once saw a magazine, or something,' said Moist desperately. 'It was called, er . . . *Pins Monthly*?'

'Oh dear,' said Groat, behind him. Stanley's face contorted into something that looked like a cat's bottom with a nose.

'That's for *hobbyists*,' he hissed. 'They're not true "pinheads"! They don't *care* about pins! Oh, they *say* so, but they have a whole page of needles every month now. Needles? Anyone could collect needles! They're only pins with holes in! Anyway, what about *Popular Needles*? But they just don't want to know!'

'Stanley is editor of *Total Pins*,' Groat whispered, behind Moist.

'I don't think I saw that one—' Moist began.

'Stanley, go and help Mr Lipwig's assistant find a shovel, will you?' said Groat, raising his voice. 'Then go and sort your pins again until you feel better. Mr Lipwig doesn't want to see one of your Little Moments.' He gave Moist a blank look.

'. . . they had an article last month about *pincushions*,' muttered Stanley, stamping out of the room. The golem followed him.

'He's a good lad,' said Groat, when they'd gone. 'Just a bit cup-and-plate in the head. Leave him alone with his pins and he's no trouble at all. Gets a bit . . . intense at times, that's all. Oh, and on that subject there's the third member of our jolly little team, sir—'

A large black and white cat had walked into the room. It paid no attention to Moist, or Groat, but progressed slowly across the floor towards a battered and unravelling basket. Moist was in the way. The cat continued until its head butted gently against Moist's leg, and stopped.

'That's Mr Tiddles, sir,' said Groat.

'*Tiddles?*' said Moist. 'You mean that really is a cat's name? I thought it was just a joke.'

'Not so much a name, sir, more of a description,' said Groat. 'You'd better move, sir, otherwise he'll just stand there all day. Twenty years old, he is, and a bit set in his ways.'

Moist stepped aside. Unperturbed, the cat continued to the basket, where it curled up.

'Is he blind?' said Moist.

'No, sir. He has his routine and he sticks to it, sir, sticks to it to the very second. Very patient, for a cat. Doesn't like the furniture being moved. You'll get used to him.'

Not knowing what to say, but feeling that he should say something, Moist nodded towards the array of bottles on Groat's bench.

'You dabble in alchemy, Mr Groat?' he said.

'Nosir! I practise nat'ral medicine!' said Groat proudly. 'Don't believe in doctors, sir! Never a day's illness in my life, sir!' He thumped his chest, making a *thlap* noise not normally associated with living tissue. 'Flannelette, goose grease and hot bread puddin', sir! Nothing like it for protecting your tubes against the noxious effluviences! I puts a fresh layer on every week, sir, and you won't find a sneeze passing my nose, sir. Very healthful, very natural!'

'Er . . . good,' said Moist.

'Worst of 'em all is soap, sir,' said Groat, lowering his voice. 'Terrible stuff, sir, washes away the beneficent humours. Leave things be, I say! Keep the tubes running, put sulphur in your socks and pay attention to your chest protector and you can laugh at anything! Now, sir, I'm sure a young man like yourself will be worrying about the state of his—'

'What's this do?' said Moist hurriedly, picking up a pot of greenish goo.

'That, sir? Wart cure. Wonderful stuff. Very natural, not like the stuff a doctor'd give you.'

Moist sniffed at the pot. 'What's it made of?'

'Arsenic, sir,' said Groat calmly.

'*Arsenic?*'

'Very natural, sir,' said Groat. 'And green.'

So, Moist thought, as he put the pot back with extreme care, inside the Post Office normality clearly does not have a one-to-one relationship with the outside world. I might miss the cues. He decided that the role of keen but bewildered manager was the one to play here. Besides, apart from the 'keen' aspect it didn't need any effort.

'Can you help me, Mr Groat?' he said. 'I don't know *anything* about the post!'

'Well, sir . . . what did you use to do?'

Rob. Trick. Forge. Embezzle. But never – and this was important – using any kind of violence. Never. Moist had always been very careful about that. He tried not to sneak, either, if he could avoid it. Being caught at 1 a.m. in a bank's deposit vault while wearing a black suit with lots of little pockets in it could be considered suspicious, so why do it? With careful planning, the right suit, the right papers and, above all, the right manner, you could walk into the place at midday and the manager would hold the door open for you when you left. Palming rings and exploiting the cupidity of the rural stupid was just a way of keeping his hand in.

It was the face, that was what it was. He had an honest face. And he loved those people who looked him firmly in the eye to see his inner self, because he had a whole set of inner selves, one for every occasion. As for firm handshakes, practice had given him one to which you could moor boats. It was people skills, that's what it was. Special people skills. Before you could sell glass as diamonds you had to make people really want *to see diamonds. That was* the *trick, the trick of all tricks. You changed the way people saw the world. You let them see it the way* they *wanted it to be . . .*

How the hell had Vetinari known his name? The man had cracked von Lipwig like an egg! And the Watch here were . . . demonic! As for setting a golem on a man . . .

'I was a clerk,' said Moist.

'What, paperwork, that sort of thing?' said Groat, looking at him intently.

'Yes, pretty much all paperwork.' That was honest, if you included playing cards, cheques, letters of accreditation, bank drafts and deeds.

'Oh, another one,' said Groat. 'Well, there's not a lot to do. We can shove up and make room for you in here, no problem.'

'But I am supposed to make it work again as it used to, Mr Groat.'

'Yeah, right,' said the old man. 'You just come along with me, then, Postmaster. I reckon there's one or two things you ain't bin tole!'

He led the way out, back into the dingy main hall, a little trail of yellow powder leaking from his boots.

'My dad used to bring me here when I were a lad,' he said. 'A lot of families were Post Office families in those days. They had them big glass drippy tinkling things up in the ceiling, right? For lights?'

'Chandeliers?' Moist suggested.

'Yep, prob'ly,' said Groat. 'Two of 'em. And there was brass an' copper everywhere, polished up like gold. There was balconies, sir, all round the big hall on every floor, made of iron, like lace! And all the counters was made of rare wood, my dad said. And people? This place was packed! The doors never stopped swinging! Even at night . . . oh, at *night*, sir, out in the big back yard, you should've been there! The lights! The coaches, coming and going, the horses steamin' . . . oh, sir, you should've seen it, sir! The men running the teams out . . . they had this thing, sir, this device, you could get a coach in and out of the yard in one minute, sir, *one minute!* The bustle, sir, the bustle and fuss! They said you could come here from Dolly Sisters or even down in the Shambles, and post a letter to yourself, and you'd have to run like the blazes, sir, the very *blazes*, sir, to beat the postman to your door! And the uniforms, sir, royal blue with brass buttons! You should've *seen* them! And—'

Moist looked over the babbling man's shoulder to the nearest mountain of pigeon guano, where Mr Pump had paused in his digging. The golem had been prodding at the fetid horrible mess and, as Moist watched him, he straightened up and headed towards them with something in his hand.

'—and when the big coaches came in, sir, all the way from the mountains, you could hear the horns miles away! You should've *heard* them, sir! And if any bandits tried anything, there was men we had, who went out and—'

'Yes, Mr Pump?' said Moist, halting Groat in mid-history.

'A Surprising Discovery, Postmaster. The Mounds Are Not, As I Surmised, Made Of Pigeon Dung. No Pigeons Could Achieve That Amount In Thousands Of Years, Sir.'

'Well, what are they made of, then?'

'Letters, Sir,' said the golem.

Moist looked down at Groat, who shifted uneasily.

'Ah, yes,' said the old man. 'I was coming to that.'

Letters . . .

. . . there was no end to them. They filled every room of the building and spilled out into the corridors. It was, technically, true that the postmaster's office was unusable because of the state of the floor: it was twelve feet deep in letters. Whole corridors were blocked off with them. Cupboards had been stuffed full of them; to open a door incautiously was to be buried in an avalanche of yellowing envelopes. Floorboards bulged suspiciously upwards. Through cracks in the sagging ceiling plaster, paper protruded.

The sorting room, almost as big as the main hall, had drifts reaching to twenty feet in places. Here and there, filing cabinets rose out of the paper sea like icebergs.

After half an hour of exploration Moist wanted a bath. It was like walking through desert tombs. He felt he was choking on the smell of old paper, as though his throat was filled with yellow dust.

'I was told I had an apartment here,' he croaked.

'Yes, sir,' said Groat. 'Me and the lad had a look for it the other day. I heard that it was the other side of your office. So the lad went in on the end of a rope, sir. He said he felt a door, sir, but he'd sunk six feet under the mail by then and he was suffering, sir, *suffering* . . . so I pulled him out.'

'The whole *place* is full of undelivered mail?'

They were back in the locker room. Groat had topped up the black kettle from a pan of water, and it was steaming. At the far end of the room, sitting at his neat little table, Stanley was counting his pins.

'Pretty much, sir, except in the basement and the stables,' said the old man, washing a couple of tin mugs in a bowl of not very clean water.

'You mean even the postm— *my* office is full of old mail but they never filled the basement? Where's the sense in that?'

'Oh, you couldn't use the basement, sir, oh, not the basement,' said Groat, looking shocked. 'It's far too damp down here. The letters'd be destroyed in no time.'

'Destroyed,' said Moist flatly.

'Nothing like damp for destroying things, sir,' said Groat, nodding sagely.

'Destroying mail from dead people to dead people,' said Moist, in the same flat voice.

'We don't *know* that, sir,' said the old man. 'I mean, we've got no actual proof.'

'Well, no. After all, some of those envelopes are only a hundred years old!' said Moist. He had a headache from the dust and a sore throat from the dryness, and there was something about the old man that was grating on his raw nerves. He was keeping something back. 'That's no time at all to *some* people. I bet the zombie and vampire population are still waiting by the letter box every day, right?'

'No need to be like that, sir,' said Groat levelly, 'no need to be like that. You can't *destroy* the letters. You just can't do it, sir. That's Tampering with the Mail, sir. That's not just a crime, sir. That's, a, a—'

'Sin?' said Moist.

'Oh, worse'n a *sin*,' said Groat, almost sneering. 'For sins you're only in trouble with a god, but in my day if you interfered with the mail you'd be up against Chief Postal Inspector Rumbelow. Hah! And there's a *big* difference. Gods *forgive*.'

Moist sought for sanity in the wrinkled face opposite him. The unkempt beard was streaked with different colours, either of dirt, tea or random celestial pigment. Like some hermit, he thought. Only a hermit could wear a wig like that.

'Sorry?' he said. 'And you mean that shoving someone's letter under the floorboards for a hundred years *isn't* tampering with it?'

Groat suddenly looked wretched. The beard quivered. Then he started to cough, great hacking, wooden, crackling lumps of cough, that made the jars shake and caused a yellow mist to rise from his trouser bottoms. ''scuse me a moment, sir,' he wheezed, between hacks, and he fumbled in his pocket for a scratched and battered tin. 'You suck at all, sir?' he said, tears rolling down his cheeks. He proffered the tin to Moist. 'They're Number Threes, sir. Very mild. I make 'em meself, sir. Nat'ral remedies from nat'ral ingredients, that's my style, sir. Got to keep the tubes clear, sir, otherwise they turn against you.'

Moist took a large, violet lozenge from the box and sniffed it. It smelled faintly of aniseed.

'Thank you, Mr Groat,' he said, but in case this counted as an attempt at bribery, he added sternly: 'The mail, Mr Groat? Sticking undelivered mail wherever there's a space isn't tampering with it?'

'That's more . . . *delaying* the mail, sir. Just, er . . . slowing it down. A bit. It's not like there's any intention of *never* delivering it, sir.'

Moist stared at Groat's worried expression. He felt that sense of shifting ground you experience when you realize that you're dealing with someone whose world is connected with your own only by their fingertips. Not a hermit, he thought, more like a shipwrecked mariner, living in this dry desert island of a building while the world outside moves on and all sanity evaporates.

'Mr Groat, I don't want to, you know, *upset* you or anything, but there's thousands of letters out there under a thick layer of pigeon guano . . .' he said slowly.

'Actually, on that score, sir, things aren't as bad as they seem,' Groat said, and paused to suck noisily on his natural cough lozenge. 'It's very dry stuff, pigeon doings, and forms quite a hard protective crust on the envelopes . . .'

'Why are they all *here*, Mr Groat?' said Moist. People skills, he remembered. You're not allowed to shake him.

The Junior Postman avoided his gaze. 'Well, you know how it is . . .' he tried.

'No, Mr Groat. I don't think I do.'

'Well . . . maybe a man's busy, got a full round, maybe it's Hogswatch, lots of cards, see, and the inspector is after him about his timekeeping, and so maybe he just shoves half a bag of letters somewhere safe . . . but he *will* deliver 'em, right? I mean, it's not his fault if they keeps pushing, sir, *pushing* him all the time. Then it's tomorrow and he's got an even bigger bag, 'cos they're *pushing* all the time, so he reckons, I'll just drop a few off today, too, 'cos it's my day off on Thursday and I can catch up then, but you see by Thursday he's behind by more'n a day's work because they keeps on *pushing*, and he's tired anyway, tired as a dog, so he says to himself, got some leave coming up soon, but he gets his leave and by then – well, it all got very nasty towards the end. There was . . . unpleasantness. We'd gone too far, sir, that's what it was, we'd tried too hard. Sometimes things smash so bad it's better to leave it alone than try to pick up the pieces. I mean, where would you start?'

'I think I get the picture,' said Moist. *You're lying, Mr Groat. You're lying by omission. You're not telling me everything. And what you're not telling me is very important, isn't it? I've turned lying into an art, Mr Groat, and you're just a talented amateur.*

Groat's face, unaware of the internal monologue, managed a smile.

'But the trouble is – what's your first name, Mr Groat?' Moist asked.

'Tolliver, sir.'

'Nice name . . . the thing *is*, Tolliver, that the picture I see in your description is what I might refer to for the purposes of the analogy as a *cameo*, whereas all *this*' – Moist waved his hand to include the building and everything it contained – 'is a full-sized triptych showing scenes from history, the creation of the world and the disposition of the gods, with a matching chapel ceiling portraying the glorious firmament and a sketch of a lady with a weird smile thrown in for good measure! Tolliver, I think you are not being frank with me.'

'Sorry about that, sir,' said Groat, eyeing him with a sort of nervous defiance.

'I could have you sacked, you know,' said Moist, knowing that this was a stupid thing to say.

'You could, sir, you could try doin' that,' said Groat, quietly and slowly. 'But I'm all you got, apart from the lad. And you don't know nuffin' about the Post Office, sir. You don't know nuffin' about the Regulations, neither. I'm the only one that knows what needs doing round here. You wouldn't last five minutes without me, sir. You wouldn't even see that the inkwells get filled every day!'

'Inkwells? Filling inkwells?' said Moist. 'This is just an old building full of . . . of . . . of dead paper! We have *no customers*!'

'Got to keep the inkwells filled, sir. Post Office Regulations,' said Groat in a steely voice. 'Got to follow Regulations, sir.'

'For what? It appears we don't accept any mail or deliver any mail! We just sit here!'

'No, sir, we don't just sit here,' said Groat patiently. 'We follow the Post Office Regulations. Fill the inkwells, polish the brass—'

'You don't sweep up the pigeon shit!'

'Oddly enough, that's not in the Regulations, sir,' said the old man. 'Truth is, sir, no one wants us any more. It's all the clacks now, the damn clacks, clack clack clack. Everyone's got a clacks tower now, sir. That's the fashion. Fast as the speed of light, they say. Ha! It's got no soul, sir, no heart. I hates 'em. But we're ready, sir. If there was any mail, we'd deal with it, sir. We'd spring into action, sir, *spring* into action. But there ain't.'

'Of course there isn't! It's clearly sunk into this town long ago that you might as well throw your letters away as give them to the Post Office!'

'No, sir, wrong again. They're all kept, sir. That's what we do, sir. We keep things as they are. We try not to disturb things, sir,' said Groat quietly. 'We try not to disturb *anything*.'

The way he said it made Moist hesitate.

'What kind of anything?' he said.

'Oh, nothing, sir. We just . . . go carefully.'

Moist looked around the room. Did it appear smaller? Did the shadows deepen and lengthen? Was there a sudden cold sensation in the air?

No, there wasn't. But an opportunity had definitely been missed, Moist felt. The hairs on the back of his neck were rising. Moist had heard that this was because men had been made out of monkeys, and it meant that there was a tiger behind you.

In fact Mr Pump was behind him, just standing there, eyes burning more brightly than any tiger had ever managed. That was worse. Tigers couldn't follow you across the sea, and they had to sleep.

He gave up. Mr Groat was in some strange, musty little world of his own. 'Do you call this a life?' he said.

For the first time in this conversation, Mr Groat looked him squarely in the eye. 'Much better than a death, sir,' he said.

Mr Pump followed Moist across the main hall and out of the main doors, at which point Moist turned on him.

'All right, what are the rules here?' he demanded. 'Are you going to follow me *everywhere*? You know I can't run!'

'You Are Allowed Autonomous Movement Within The City And Environs,' the golem rumbled. 'But Until You Are Settled In I Am Also Instructed To Accompany You For Your Own Protection.'

'Against who? Someone annoyed that their great-granddaddy's mail didn't turn up?'

'I Couldn't Say, Sir.'

'I need some fresh air. What happened in there? Why is it so . . . creepy? What *happened* to the Post Office?'

'I Couldn't Say, Sir,' said Mr Pump placidly.

'You don't know? But it's *your* city,' said Moist sarcastically. 'Have you been stuck at the bottom of a hole in the ground for the last hundred years?'

'No, Mr Lipvig,' said the golem.

'Well, why can't—' Moist began.

'It Was Two Hundred And Forty Years, Mr Lipvig,' said the golem.

'What was?'

'The Time I Spent At The Bottom Of The Hole In The Ground, Mr Lipvig.'

'What are you *talking* about?' said Moist.

'Why, The Time I Spent At The Bottom Of The Hole In The Ground, Mr Lipvig. Pump Is Not My Name, Mr Lipvig. It Is My Description. Pump. Pump 19, To Be Precise. I Stood At The Bottom Of A Hole A Hundred Feet Deep And Pumped Water. For Two Hundred And Forty Years, Mr Lipvig. But Now I Am Ambulating In The Sunlight. This Is Better, Mr Lipvig. This Is Better!'

That night, Moist lay staring at the ceiling. It was three feet from him. Hanging from it, a little distance away, was a candle in a safety lantern. Stanley had been insistent about that, and no wonder. This place would go up like a bomb. It was the boy who'd showed him up here; Groat was sulking somewhere. He'd been right, damn him. He needed Groat. Groat practically *was* the Post Office.

It had been a long day and Moist hadn't slept well last night, what with being upside down over Mr Pump's shoulder and occasionally kicked by the frantic horse.

He didn't want to sleep here either, heavens knew, but he didn't have lodgings he could use any more, and they were at a premium in this hive of a city in any case. The locker room did not appeal, no, not at all. So he'd simply scrambled on to the pile of dead letters in what was in theory his office. It was no great hardship. A man of affairs such as he had to learn to sleep in all kinds of situations, often while mobs were looking for him a wall's thickness away. At least the heaps of letters were dry and warm and weren't carrying edged weapons.

Paper crackled underneath him as he tried to get comfortable. Idly, he picked up a letter at random; it was addressed to someone called Antimony Parker at 1 Lobbin Clout, and on the back, in capitals, was S.W.A.L.K. He eased it open with a fingernail; the paper inside all but crumbled at his touch.

My Very Dearest Timony,

Yes! Why should a Woman, Sensible of the Great Honour that a Man is Doing her, play the Coy Minx at such a time! I know you have spoken to Papa, and of course I consent to becoming the Wife of the Kindest, Most Wonderfu—

Moist glanced at the date on the letter. It had been written forty-one years ago.

He was not as a rule given to introspection, it being a major drawback in his line of work, but he couldn't help wondering if – he glanced back at the letter – 'Your loving Agnathea' had ever married Antimony, or whether the romance had died right here in this graveyard of paper.

He shivered, and tucked the envelope into his jacket. He'd have to ask Groat what S.W.A.L.K. meant.

'Mr Pump!' he shouted.

There was a faint rumble from the corner of the room where the golem stood, waist-deep in mail.

'Yes, Mr Lipvig?'

'Is there no way you can shut your eyes? I can't sleep with two red glowing eyes watching me. It's a . . . well, it's a childhood thing.'

'Sorry, Mr Lipvig. I Could Turn My Back.'

'That won't work. I'd still know they're there. Anyway, the glow reflects off the wall. Look, where would I run to?'

The golem gave this some thought. 'I Will Go And Stand In The Corridor, Mr Lipvig,' he decided, and began to wade towards the door.

'You do that,' said Moist. 'And in the morning I want you to find my bedroom, okay? Some of the offices still have space near the ceiling; you can move the letters into there.'

'Mr Groat Does Not Like The Mail To Be Moved, Mr Lipvig,' the golem rumbled.

'Mr Groat is not the postmaster, Mr Pump. I am.'

Good gods, the madness is catching, Moist thought, as the golem's glow disappeared into the darkness outside. I am *not* the postmaster, I'm some poor bastard who's the victim of some stupid . . . experiment. What a place! What a situation! What kind of man would put a known criminal in charge of a major branch of government? Apart from, say, the average voter.

He tried to find the angle, the way out . . . but all the time a conversation kept bouncing off the insides of his brain.

Imagine a hole, a hundred feet deep and full of water.

Imagine the darkness. Imagine, at the bottom of the hole, a figure roughly of human shape, turning in that swirling darkness a massive handle once every eight seconds.

Pump . . . Pump . . . Pump . . .

For two hundred and forty years.

'You didn't mind?' Moist had asked.

'You Mean Did I Harbour Resentment, Mr Lipvig? But I Was Doing Useful And Necessary Work! Besides, There Was Much For Me To Think About.'

'At the bottom of a hundred feet of dirty water? What the hell did you find to think about?'

'Pumping, Mr Lipvig.'

And then, the golem said, had come cessation, and dim light, a lowering of levels, a locking of chains, movement upwards, emergence into a world of light and colour . . . and other golems.

Moist knew *something* about golems. They used to be baked out of clay, thousands of years ago, and brought to life by some kind of scroll put inside their heads, and they never wore out and they worked, all the time. You saw them pushing brooms, or doing heavy work in timber yards and foundries. Most of them you never saw at all. They made the hidden wheels go round, down in the dark. And that was more or less the limit of his interest in them. They were, almost by definition, honest.

But now the golems were freeing themselves. It was the quietest, most socially responsible revolution in history. They were property, and so they saved up and *bought* themselves.

Mr Pump was buying his freedom by seriously limiting the freedom of Moist. A man could get quite upset about that. Surely that wasn't how freedom was supposed to work?

Ye gods, thought Moist, back in the here-and-now, no wonder Groat sucked cough sweets all the time, the dust in this place could choke you!

He rummaged in his pocket and pulled out the diamond-shaped cough lozenge the old man had given him. It looked harmless enough.

One minute later, after Mr Pump had lurched into the room and slapped him heavily on the back, the steaming lozenge was stuck to the wall on the far side of the room where, by morning, it had dissolved quite a lot of the plaster.

Mr Groat took a measured spoonful of tincture of rhubarb and cayenne pepper, to keep the tubes open, and checked that he still had the dead mole round his neck, to ward off any sudden attack of doctors. Everyone knew doctors made you ill, it stood to reason. Nature's remedies were the trick every time, not some hellish potion made of gods knew what.

He smacked his lips appreciatively. He'd put fresh sulphur in his socks tonight, too, and he could feel it doing him good.

Two candle lanterns glowed in the velvet, papery darkness of the main sorting office. The light was shining through the outer glass, filled with water so that the candle would go out if it was dropped; it made the lanterns look like the lights of some abyssal fish from the squiddy, iron-hard depths.

There was a little glugging noise in the dark. Groat corked his bottle of elixir and got on with business.

'Be the inkwells filled, Apprentice Postman Stanley?' he intoned.

'Aye, Junior Postman Groat, full to a depth of one-third of one inch from the top as per Post Office Counter Regulations, Daily Observances, Rule C18,' said Stanley.

There was a rustle as Groat turned the pages of a huge book on the lectern in front of him.

'Can I see the picture, Mr Groat?' said Stanley eagerly.

Groat smiled. It had become part of the ceremony, and he gave the reply he gave every time.

'Very well, but this is the last time. It's not good to look too often on the face of a god,' he said. 'Or any other part.'

'But you said there used to be a gold statue of him in the big hall, Mr Groat. People must've looked on it all the time.'

Groat hesitated. But Stanley was a growing lad. He'd have to know sooner or later.

'Mind you, I don't reckon people used to look on the face much,' he said. 'They looked more on the . . . wings.'

'On his hat and his ankles,' said Stanley. 'So he could fly the messages at the speed of . . . messages.'

A little bead of sweat dripped off Groat's forehead. 'Mostly on his hat and ankles, yes,' he said. 'Er . . . but not *only* there.'

Stanley peered at the picture. 'Oh, yes. I never noticed them before. He's got wings on—'

'The fig leaf,' said Groat quickly. 'That's what we call it.'

'Why's he got a leaf there?' said Stanley.

'Oh, they all had 'em in the olden days, 'cos of being Classical,' said

Groat, relieved to be shifting away from the heart of the matter. 'It's a fig leaf. Off a fig tree.'

'Haha, the joke's on them, there's no fig trees round here!' said Stanley, in the manner of one exposing the flaw in a long-held dogma.

'Yes, lad, very good, but it was a tin one anyway,' said Groat, with patience.

'And the wings?' said the boy.

'We-ell, I s'pose they thought that the more wings, the better,' said Groat.

'Yes, but s'posing his hat wings and his ankle wings stopped work-ing, he'd be held up by—'

'Stanley! It's just a statue! Don't get excited! Calm down! You don't want to upset . . . *them*.'

Stanley hung his head. 'They've been . . . whispering to me again, Mr Groat,' he confided in a low voice.

'Yes, Stanley. They whisper to me, too.'

'I remember 'em last time, talking in the night, Mr Groat,' said Stanley, his voice trembling. 'I shut my eyes and I keep seeing the writin' . . .'

'Yes, Stanley. Don't worry about it. Try not to think about it. It's Mr Lipstick's fault, stirring them up. Leave well alone, I say. They never listen, and then what happens? They find out the hard way.'

'It seems like only yesterday, those watchmen drawing that chalk outline round Mr Mutable,' said Stanley, beginning to tremble. '*He* found out the hard way!'

'Calm down, now, calm down,' said Groat, patting him gently on the shoulder. 'You'll set 'em off. Think about pins.'

'But it's a cruel shame, Mr Groat, them never being alive long enough to make you Senior Postman!'

Groat sniffed. 'Oh, that's enough of that. That's not important, Stanley,' he said, his face like thunder.

'Yes, Mr Groat, but you're an old, old man and you're still only a Junior Postm—' Stanley persisted.

'I said that's *enough*, Stanley! Now, just raise that lamp again, will

you? Good. That's better. I'll read a page of the Regulations, that
always quietens them down.' Groat cleared his throat. 'I shall now read
from the Book of Regulations, Delivery Times (Metropolitan)
(Sundays and Octedays excepted),' he announced to the air. 'As
follows: "The hours by which letters should be put into the receiving
houses in town for each delivery within the city walls of Ankh-
Morpork are as the following: overnight by eight o'clock in the
evening, for the first delivery. Morning by eight o'clock, for the second
delivery. Morning by ten o'clock, for the third delivery. Morning by
twelve o'clock, for the fourth delivery. Afternoon by two o'clock, for
the fifth delivery. Afternoon by four o'clock, for the sixth delivery.
Afternoon by six o'clock, for the seventh delivery." These are the
hours, and I have read them.' Groat hung his head for a moment, and
then he closed the book with a snap.

'Why are we doing this, Mr Groat?' said Stanley meekly.

' 'Cos of hub-riss,' said Mr Groat. 'That's what it was. Hub-riss
killed the Post Office. Hub-riss and greed and Bloody Stupid Johnson
and the New Pie.'

'A pie, Mr Groat? How could a pie—'

'Don't ask, Stanley. It gets complicated and there's nothing in it
about pins.'

They put out the candles, and left.

When they had gone, a faint whispering started.

CHAPTER THREE

Our Own Hand, Or None

In which our hero discovers the world of pins – The Greengrocer's Apos'trophe – S.W.A.L.K. – The path of Fate – The Golem Lady – The Business of Business and the Nature of Freedom Once Again Discussed – Clerk Brian shows enthusiasm

'RISE AND SHINE, Mr Lipvig. Your Second Day As Postmaster!'
Moist opened one crusted eye and glared at the golem.

'Oh, so you're an alarm clock too?' he said. 'Aargh. My tongue. It feels like it was caught in a mousetrap.'

He half crawled, half rolled across the bed of letters and managed to stand up just outside the door.

'I need new clothes,' he said. 'And food. And a toothbrush. I'm going out, Mr Pump. *You* are to stay here. Do something. Tidy the place up. Get rid of the graffiti on the walls, will you? At least we can make the place look clean!'

'Anything You Say, Mr Lipvig.'

'Right!' said Moist, and strode off, for one stride, and then yelped.

'Be Careful Of Your Ankle, Mr Lipvig,' said Mr Pump.

'And another thing!' said Moist, hopping on one leg. '*How* can you follow me? How can you possibly know where I am?'

'Karmic Signature, Mr Lipvig,' said the golem.

'And that means what, exactly?' Moist demanded.

'It Means I Know Exactly Where You Are, Mr Lipvig.'

The pottery face was impassive. Moist gave up.

He limped out into what, for this city, was a fresh new morning. There had been a touch of frost overnight, just enough to put some zest into the air and give him an appetite. The leg still hurt, but at least he didn't need the crutch today.

Here was Moist von Lipwig walking through the city. He'd never done that before. The late Albert Spangler had, and so had Mundo Smith and Edwin Streep and half a dozen other personas that he'd donned and discarded. Oh, he'd been Moist inside (what a name, yes, he'd heard every possible joke), but *they* had been on the outside, between him and the world.

Edwin Streep had been a work of art. He'd been a lack-of-confidence trickster, and *needed* to be noticed. He was so patently, obviously *bad* at running a bent Find The Lady game and other street scams that people positively queued up to trick the dumb trickster and walked away grinning . . . right up to the point when they tried to spend the coins they'd scooped up so quickly.

There's a secret art to forgery, and Moist had discovered it: in a hurry, or when excited, people will complete the forgery by their own cupidity. They'll be so keen to snatch the money from the obvious idiot that *their own eyes* fill in all the little details that aren't quite there on the coins they so quickly pocket. All you needed to do was hint at them.

But that was just for starters. Some customers never even discovered that they'd put fake coins in their purse, thus revealing to the incompetent Streep in which pocket they kept it. Later on they learned that Streep might be rubbish with a deck of cards but also that this lack was more than made up for by his exceptional skill as a pickpocket.

Now Moist felt like a peeled prawn. He felt as though he'd stepped out naked. *And yet, still, no one was taking any notice.* There were no cries of 'Hey, you', no shouts of 'That's him!' He was just another face in the crowd. It was a strange new feeling. He'd never really had to be himself before.

He celebrated by buying a street directory from the Guild of Merchants, and had a coffee and a bacon sandwich while he thumbed, greasily, through it for the list of bars. He didn't find what he was looking for there but he did find it in the list of hairdressers, and grinned when he did so. It was nice to be right.

He also found a mention of Dave's Pin Exchange, up in Dolly Sisters, in an alley between a house of negotiable affection and a massage parlour. It bought and sold pins to pin fanciers.

Moist finished his coffee with a look on his face which those who knew him well, a group consisting in fact of absolutely nobody, would have recognized as the formation of a plan. Ultimately, everything was all about people. If he was going to be staying here for a while, he'd make himself comfortable.

He went for a walk to the self-styled 'Home of Acuphilia!!!'

It was like lifting an unregarded stone and finding a whole new world. Dave's Pin Exchange was the kind of small shop where the owner knows every single one of his customers by name. It was a wonderful world, the world of pins. It was a hobby that could last you a lifetime. Moist knew this because he expended one dollar on *Pins* by J. Lanugo Owlsbury, apparently the last word on the subject. Everyone had their funny little ways, Moist conceded, but he wasn't entirely at home among people who, if they saw a pin-up, would pay attention to the pins. Some of the customers browsing the book racks (*Misdraws, Double Pointers and Flaws, Pins of Uberwald and Genua, First Steps in Pins, Adventures in Acuphilia* . . .) and staring covetously at the rack of pins laid out under glass had an intensity of expression that frightened him. They looked a bit like Stanley. They were all male. Clearly, women weren't natural 'pinheads'.

He found *Total Pins* on the bottom rack. It had a smudgy, home-produced look, and the print was small and dense and lacked such subtleties as paragraphs and, in many cases, punctuation. The common comma had looked at Stanley's expression and decided not to disturb him.

When Moist put the little magazine on the counter the shop's owner, a huge bearded man with dreadlocks, a pin through his nose, a beer belly belonging to three other people and the words 'Death or Pins' tattooed on a bicep, picked it up and tossed it back down dismissively.

'Sure about that, sir?' he said. 'We've got *Pins Monthly, New Pins, Practical Pins, Modern Pins, Pins Extra, Pins International, Talking Pins, Pins World, World Pins, World of Pins, Pins and Pinneries* . . .' Moist's attention wandered off for a while but came back in time to catch '. . . the *Acuphile Digest*, *Extreme Pins*, **Stifte!** – that's from Uberwald, very good if you collect foreign pins – *Beginning Pins* – that's a part-work, sir, with a new pin every week – *Pin Times* and' – here the big man winked – '*Back Alley Pins.*'

'I noticed that one,' said Moist. 'It has lots of pictures of young women in leather.'

'Yes, sir. But, to be fair, they're generally holding pins. So, then . . . it's still *Total Pins* for you, is it?' he added, as if giving a fool one last chance to repent of his folly.

'Yes,' said Moist. 'What's wrong with it?'

'Oh, nothing. Nothing at all.' Dave scratched his stomach thoughtfully. 'It's just that the editor is a bit . . . a bit . . .'

'A bit what?' said Moist.

'Well, we think he's a bit weird about pins, to tell you the truth.'

Moist looked around the shop. 'Really?' he said.

Moist went to a nearby café and leafed through the magazine. One of the skills of his previous life had been an ability to pick up just enough about anything to sound like an expert, at least to non-experts. Then he returned to the shop.

Everyone had their levers. Often it was greed. Greed was a reliable old standby. Sometimes it was pride. That was Groat's lever. He desperately wanted promotion; you could see it in his eyes. Find the lever, and then it was plain sailing.

Stanley, now, Stanley . . . would be easy.

Big Dave was examining a pin under a microscope when Moist returned to the shop. The rush hour for pin buying must have been nearly over, because there were only a few laggards ogling the pins under glass, or thumbing through the racks.

Moist sidled over to the counter and coughed.

'Yes, sir?' said Big Dave, looking up from his work. 'Back again, eh? They get to you, don't they? Seen anything you like?'

'A packet of pre-perforated pin papers and a tenpenny lucky dip bag, please,' said Moist loudly. The other customers looked up for a moment as Dave pulled the packets off their rack, and then looked down again.

Moist leaned over the counter. 'I was wondering,' he whispered hoarsely, 'if you'd got anything a bit . . . you know . . . sharper?'

The big man gave him a carefully blank look. 'How d'you mean, sharper?' he said.

'You know,' said Moist. He cleared his throat. 'More . . . pointed.'

The doorbell jangled as the last of the customers, sated on pins for one day, stepped out. Dave watched them go and then turned his attention back to Moist.

'A bit of a connoisseur, are we, sir?' he said, winking.

'A serious student,' said Moist. 'Most of the stuff here, well . . .'

'I don't touch nails,' said Dave sharply. 'Won't have 'em in the shop! I've got a reputation to think about! Little kids come in here, you know!'

'Oh no! Strictly pins, that's me!' said Moist hastily.

'Good,' said Dave, relaxing. 'As it happens, I might have one or two items for the genuine collector.' He nodded towards a beaded curtain at the back of the shop. 'Can't put everything on display, not with youngsters around, you know how it is . . .'

Moist followed him through the clashing curtain and into the crowded little room behind, where Dave, after looking around conspiratorially, pulled a small black box off a shelf and flipped it open under Moist's nose.

'Not something you find every day, eh?' said Dave.

Gosh, it's a pin, thought Moist, but said 'Wow!' in a tone of well-crafted genuine surprise.

A few minutes later he stepped out of the shop, fighting an impulse to turn his collar up. That was the problem with certain kinds of insanity. They could strike at any time. After all, he'd just spent AM$70 on a damn *pin*!

He stared at the little packets in his hand and sighed. As he carefully put them in his jacket pocket, his hand touched something papery.

Oh, yes. The S.W.A.L.K. letter. He was about to shove it back when his eye caught sight of the ancient street sign opposite: Lobbin Clout. And as his gaze moved down it also saw, over the first shop in the narrow street:

NO.1   A. PARKER & SON'S
GREENGROCER'S
HIGH CLAS'S FRUIT AND VEGETABLE'S

Well, why not deliver it? Hah! He *was* the postmaster, wasn't he? What harm could it do?

He slipped into the shop. A middle-aged man was introducing fresh carrots, or possibly carrot's, into the life of a bulky woman with a big shopping bag and hairy warts.

'Mr Antimony Parker?' said Moist urgently.

'Be with you in ju'st one moment, s'ir, I'm ju'st—' the man began.

'I just need to know if you *are* Mr Antimony Parker, that's all,' said Moist. The woman turned to glare at the intruder, and Moist gave her a smile so winning that she blushed and wished just for a moment she'd worn make-up today.

'Thats' father,' said the greengrocer. 'He's out the back, tackling a difficult cabbage—'

'This is his,' said Moist. 'Postal delivery.' He put the envelope on the counter and walked quickly out of the shop.

Shopkeeper and customer stared down at the pink envelope.

'S'.W.A.L.K?' said Mr Parker.

'Ooh, that takes me back, Mr Parker,' said the woman. 'In my day we used to put that on our letters when we were courting. Didn't you? Sealed With A Loving Kiss. There was S.W.A.L.K., and L.A.N.C.R.E. and . . .' she lowered her voice and giggled, 'K.L.A.T.C.H., of course. Remember?'

'All that pas'sed me by, Mrs Goodbody,' said the greengrocer stiffly. 'And if it mean's young men are s'ending our dad pink envelope's with 'swalk on them, I'm thankful for that. Modern time's, eh?' He turned and raised his voice. 'Father!'

*   *   *

Well, that was a good deed for the day, Moist thought. Or *a* deed, in any case.

It looked as though Mr Parker had managed to acquire some sons, one way or another. Still, it was . . . odd to think of all those letters heaped in that old building. You could imagine them as little packets of history. Deliver them, and history went one way. But if you dropped them in the gap between the floorboards, it went the other.

Ha. He shook his head. As if one tiny choice by someone un-important could make that much difference! History had to be a bit tougher than that. It all sprang back eventually, didn't it? He was sure he'd read something, somewhere. If it wasn't like that, no one would ever dare do *anything*.

He stood in the little square where eight roads met, and chose to go home via Market Street. It was as good a way as any other.

When he was sure that both Stanley and the golem were busy on the mail mountains, Mr Groat crept away through the labyrinth of corridors. Bundles of letters were stacked so high and tightly that it was all he could do to squeeze through, but at last he reached the shaft of the old hydraulic elevator, long disused. The shaft had been filled up with letters.

However, the engineer's ladder was still clear, and *that* at least went up to the roof. Of course, there was the fire escape outside, but that was *outside*, and Groat was not over-keen on going outside at the best of times. He inhabited the Post Office like a very small snail in a very large shell. He was used to gloom.

Now, slowly and painfully, his legs shaking, he climbed up through the floors of mail and forced open the trapdoor at the top.

He blinked and shuddered in the unfamiliar sunlight, and hauled himself out on to the flat roof.

He'd never really liked doing this, but what else could he have done? Stanley ate like a bird and Groat mostly got by on tea and biscuits, but it all cost money, even if you went round the markets just as they closed up, and somewhere in the past, decades ago, the pay had stopped arriving. Groat had been too frightened to go up to the palace to find out why. He was afraid that if he asked for money he'd be sacked. So he'd taken to renting out the old pigeon loft. Where was the harm in that? All the pigeons had joined their feral brethren years ago, and a decent shed was not to be sneezed at in this city, even if it did whiff a bit. There was an outside fire escape and everything. It was a little palace compared to most lodgings.

Besides, these lads didn't mind the smell, they said. They were pigeon fanciers. Groat wasn't sure what that entailed, except that they had to use a little clacks tower to fancy them properly. But they paid up, that was the important thing.

He skirted the big rainwater tank for the defunct lift and sidled around the rooftops to the shed, where he knocked politely.

'It's me, lads. Just come about the rent,' he said.

The door was opened and he heard a snatch of conversation: '. . . the linkages won't stand it for more than thirty seconds . . .'

'Oh, Mr Groat, come on in,' said the man who had opened the door. This was Mr Carlton, the one with the beard a dwarf would be proud of, no, *two* dwarfs would be proud of. He seemed more sensible than the other two, although this was not hard.

Groat removed his hat. 'Come about the rent, sir,' he repeated, peering around the man. 'Got a bit o' news, too. Just thought I'd better mention, lads, we've got a new postmaster. If you could be a bit careful for a while? A nod's as good as a wink, eh?'

'How long's this one going to last, then?' said a man who was sitting on the floor, working on a big metal drum full of what, to Mr Groat, appeared to be very complicated clockwork. 'You'll push him off the roof by Saturday, right?'

'Now, now, Mr Winton, there's no call to make fun of me like that,' said Groat nervously. 'Once he's been here a few weeks and got settled in I'll kind of . . . *hint* that you're here, all right? Pigeons getting on okay, are they?' He peered around the loft. Only one pigeon was visible, hunched up high in a corner.

'They're out for exercise right now,' said Winton.

'Ah, right, that'd be it, then,' said Groat.

'Anyway, we're a bit more interested in woodpeckers at the moment,' said Winton, pulling a bent metal bar out of the drum. 'See, Alex? I told you, it's bent. And two gears are stripped bare . . .'

'Woodpeckers?' said Groat.

There was a certain lowering of the temperature, as if he'd said the wrong thing.

'That's right, woodpeckers,' said a third voice.

'Woodpeckers, Mr Emery?' The third pigeon fancier always made Groat nervous. It was the way his eyes were always on the move, as if he was trying to see everything at once. And he was always holding a tube with smoke coming out of it, or another piece of machinery. They all seemed very interested in tubes and cogwheels, if it came to that. Oddly enough, Groat had never seen them holding a pigeon. He didn't know how pigeons were fancied, but he'd assumed that it had to be close up.

'Yes, woodpeckers,' said the man, while the tube in his hand changed colour from red to blue. 'Because . . .' and here he appeared to stop and think for a moment, 'we're seeing if they can be taught to . . . oh, yes, tap out the message when they get there, see? Much better than messenger pigeons.'

'Why?' said Groat.

Mr Emery stared at the whole world for a moment. 'Because . . . they can deliver messages in the dark?' he said.

'Well done,' murmured the man dismantling the drum.

'Ah, could be a lifesaver, I can see that,' said Groat. 'Can't see it beating the clacks, though!'

'That's what we want to find out,' said Winton.

'But we'd be very grateful if you didn't tell anyone about this,' said Carlton quickly. 'Here's your three dollars, Mr Groat. We wouldn't want other people stealing our idea, you see.'

'Lips are sealed, lads,' said Groat. 'Don't you worry about it. You can rely on Groat.'

Carlton was holding the door open. 'We know we can. Goodbye, Mr Groat.'

Groat heard the door shut behind him as he walked back across the roof. Inside the shed, there seemed to be an argument starting; he heard someone say, 'What did you have to go and tell him that for?'

That was a bit hurtful, someone thinking that he couldn't be trusted. And, as he eased his way down the long ladder, Groat wondered if he ought to have pointed out that woodpeckers wouldn't fly in the dark. It was amazing that bright lads like them hadn't spotted this flaw. They were, he thought, a bit gullible.

A hundred feet down and a quarter of a mile away as the woodpecker flies during daylight, Moist followed the path of destiny.

Currently, it was leading him through a neighbourhood that was on the downside of whatever curve you hoped you'd bought your property on the upside of. Graffiti and rubbish were everywhere here. They were everywhere in the city, if it came to that, but elsewhere the garbage was better quality rubbish and the graffiti were close to being correctly spelled. The whole area was waiting for something to happen, like a really bad fire.

And then he saw it. It was one of those hopeless little shop fronts that house enterprises with a lifetime measured in days, like Giant Clearance Sale!!! of socks with two heels each, tights with three legs and shirts with one sleeve, four feet long. The window was boarded over, but just visible behind the graffiti above it were the words: **The Golem Trust**.

Moist pushed open the door. Glass crunched under his feet.

A voice said, 'Hands where I can see them, mister!'

He raised his hands cautiously, while peering into the gloom. There was definitely a crossbow being wielded by a dim figure. Such light as had managed to get round the boards glinted off the tip of the bolt.

'Oh,' said the voice in the dark, as if mildly annoyed that there was no excuse to shoot anybody. 'All right, then. We had visitors last night.'

'The window?' said Moist.

'It happens about once a month. I was just sweeping it up.' There was the scratch of a match, and a lamp was lit. 'They don't generally attack the golems themselves, not now there's free ones around. But glass doesn't fight back.'

The lamp was turned up, revealing a tall young woman in a tight grey woollen dress, with coal-black hair plastered down so that she looked like a peg doll and forced into a tight bun at the back. There was a slight redness to her eyes that suggested she had been crying.

'You're lucky to have caught me,' she said. 'I'd only come in to make sure nothing's been taken. Are you here to sell or to hire? You can put your hands down now,' she added, placing the crossbow under the counter.

'Sell or hire?' said Moist, lowering his hands with care.

'A golem,' she said, in a talking-to-the-hard-of-thinking voice. 'We are the Go-lem Trust. We buy or hire go-lems. Do you want to sell a go-lem or hire a go-lem?'

'Nei-ther,' said Moist. 'I've got a go-lem. I mean, one is work-ing for me.'

'Really? Where?' said the woman. 'And we can probably speed up a little, I think.'

'At the Post Office.'

'Oh, Pump 19,' said the woman. 'He said it was government service.'

'We call him *Mister* Pump,' said Moist primly.

'Really? And do you get a wonderful warm charitable feeling when you do?'

'Pardon? What?' said Moist, bewildered. He wasn't sure if she was managing the trick of laughing at him behind her frown.

The woman sighed. 'Sorry, I'm a bit snappish this morning. A brick landing on your desk does that to you. Let's just say they don't see the world in the same way as we do, okay? They've got feelings, in their own way, but they're not like ours. Anyway . . . how can I help you, Mr . . .?'

'Von Lipwig,' said Moist, and added: '*Moist* von Lipwig,' to get the worst over with. But the woman didn't even smile.

'Lipwig, small town in Near Uberwald,' she said, picking up a brick from the broken glass and debris on her desk, regarding it critically, and then turning to the ancient filing cabinet behind her and filing it under B. 'Chief export: its famous dogs, of course, second most important export its beer, except during the two weeks of Sektoberfest, when it exports . . . second-hand beer, probably?'

'I don't know. We left when I was a kid,' said Moist. 'As far as I'm concerned, it's just a funny name.'

'Try Adora Belle Dearheart some time,' said the woman.

'Ah. That's *not* a funny name,' said Moist.

'Quite,' said Adora Belle Dearheart. 'I now have no sense of humour whatsoever. Well, now that we've been appropriately human towards one another, what exactly *was* it you wanted?'

'Look, Vetinari has sort of lumbered me with Mr— with Pump 19 as an . . . an assistant, but I don't know how to treat . . .' Moist sought in the woman's eyes for some clue as to the politically correct term, and plumped for 'him.'

'Huh? Just treat him normally.'

'You mean normally for a human being, or normally for a pottery man filled with fire?'

To Moist's astonishment Adora Belle Dearheart took a packet of cigarettes out of a desk drawer and lit one. She mistook his expression, and proffered the pack.

'No, thanks,' he said, waving it away. Apart from the occasional old lady with a pipe, he'd never seen a woman smoke before. It was . . . strangely attractive, especially since, as it turned out, she smoked a cigarette as if she had a grudge against it, sucking the smoke down and blowing it out almost immediately.

'You're getting hung up about it all, right?' she said. When Ms Dearheart wasn't smoking she held the cigarette at shoulder height, the elbow of her left arm cupped in her right hand. There was a definite feel about Adora Belle Dearheart that a lid was only barely holding down an entire womanful of anger.

'Yes! I mean—' Moist began.

'Hah! It's just like the Campaign for Equal Heights and all that patronizing stuff they spout about dwarfs and why we shouldn't use terms like "small talk" and "feeling small". Golems don't have any of our baggage about "who am I, why am I here", okay? Because they *know*. They were made to be tools, to be property, to work. Work is what they do. In a way, it's what they *are*. End of existential angst.'

Ms Dearheart inhaled and then blew out the smoke in one nervous movement. 'And then stupid people go around calling them "persons of clay" and "Mr Spanner" and so on, which they find rather strange. They *understand* about free will. They also understand that they don't have it. Mind you, once a golem *owns* himself, it's a different matter.'

'Own? How does property own itself?' said Moist. 'You said they were—'

'They save up and *buy* themselves, of course! Freehold is the only path to freedom they'll accept. Actually, what happens is that the free golems support the Trust, the Trust buys golems whenever it can, and the new golems then buy themselves from the Trust at cost. It's working well. The free golems earn twenty-four/eight and there's more and more of them. They don't eat, sleep, wear clothes or understand the concept of leisure. The occasional tube of ceramic cement doesn't cost much. They're buying more golems every month now, and paying my wages, and the iniquitous rent the landlord of this dump is charging because he knows he's renting to golems. They never complain, you know. They pay whatever's asked. They're so *patient* it could drive you nuts.'

Tube of ceramic cement, thought Moist. He tried to fix that thought in case it came in useful, but some mental processes were fully occupied with the growing realization of how well some women could look in a severely plain dress.

'Surely they can't be damaged, can they?' he managed.

'Certainly they can! A sledgehammer on the right spot would really mess one up. Owned golems will just stand there and take it. But the Trust golems are allowed to defend themselves, and when someone weighing a ton snatches a hammer out of your hand you have to let go *really* quickly.'

'I think Mr Pump is allowed to hit people,' said Moist.

'Quite possibly. A lot of the frees are against that, but others say a tool can't be blamed for the use to which it's put,' said Ms Dearheart. 'They debate it a lot. For days and days.'

No rings on her fingers, Moist noted. What kind of attractive girl works for a bunch of clay men?

'This is all *fascinating*,' he said. 'Where can I find out more?'

'We do a pamphlet,' said almost-certainly-Miss Dearheart, pulling open a drawer and flipping a thin booklet on to the desk. 'It's five pence.'

The title on the cover was *Common Clay*.

Moist put down a dollar. 'Keep the change,' he said.

'No!' said Miss Dearheart, fumbling for coins in the drawer. 'Didn't you read what it said over the door?'

'Yes. It said "SmasH The Barstuds"', said Moist.

Miss Dearheart put a hand to her forehead wearily. 'Oh, yes. The painter hasn't been yet. But underneath that . . . look, it's on the back of the pamphlet . . .'

V꒱ ⅃ꙜꙘ ⅃ꙀꙘ ꙀꚈꙖꙀ ⅃Ꙓ Ꙁ⅃Ꙅꙡ, Moist read, or at least looked at.

'It's one of their own languages,' she said. 'It's all a bit . . . mystic. Said to be spoken by angels. It translates as "By Our Own Hand, Or None". They're fiercely independent. You've no idea.'

She admires them, Moist thought. Whoo-ee. And . . . angels?

'Well, thank you,' he said. 'I'd better be going. I'll definitely . . . well, thank you, anyway.'

'What are you doing at the Post Office, Mr von Lipwig?' said the woman, as he opened the door.

'Call me Moist,' said Moist, and a bit of his inner self shuddered. 'I'm the new postmaster.'

'No kidding?' said Miss Dearheart. 'Then I'm glad you've got Pump 19 with you. The last few postmasters didn't last long, I gather.'

'I think I heard something about that,' said Moist cheerfully. 'It sounds as though things were pretty bad in the olden days.'

Miss Dearheart's brow wrinkled. 'Olden days?' she said. 'Last month was *olden days*?'

Lord Vetinari stood looking out of his window. His office had once had a wonderful view of the city and, technically, it still did, although now the roofline was a forest of clacks towers, winking and twinkling in the sunlight. On the Tump, the old castle mound across the river, the big tower, one end of the Grand Trunk that wound more than two thousand miles across the continent to Genua, glittered with semaphore.

It was good to see the lifeblood of trade and commerce and diplomacy pumping so steadily, especially when you employed clerks who were exceptionally good at decryption. White and black by day, light and dark by night, the shutters stopped only for fog and snow.

At least, until the last few months. He sighed, and went back to his desk.

There was a file open. It contained a report from Commander Vimes of the City Watch, with a lot of exclamation marks. It also contained a more measured report from clerk Alfred, and Lord Vetinari had circled the section headed 'The Smoking Gnu'.

There was a gentle knock at the door and the clerk Drumknott came in like a ghost.

'The gentlemen from the Grand Trunk semaphore company are all here now, sir,' he said. He laid down several sheets of paper covered in tiny, intricate lines. Vetinari gave the shorthand a cursory glance.

'Idle chitchat?' he said.

'Yes, my lord. One might say *excessively* so. But I am certain that the mouth of the speaking tube is quite invisible in the plasterwork, my lord. It's hidden in a gilt cherub most cunningly, sir. Clerk Brian has built it into its cornucopia, which apparently collects more sounds and can be swivelled to face whoever—'

'One does not have to see something to know that it is there, Drumknott.' Vetinari tapped the paper. 'These are not stupid men. Well, some of them, at least. You have the files?'

Drumknott's pale face bore for a moment the pained expression of a man forced to betray the high principles of filing.

'In a manner of speaking, my lord. We actually have nothing substantial about any of the allegations, we really haven't. We're running a Concludium in the Long Gallery, but it's all hearsay, sir, I'm afraid.

There's . . . hints, here and there, but really we need something more solid . . .'

'There will be an opportunity,' said Vetinari. Being an absolute ruler today was not as simple as people thought. At least, it was not simple if your ambitions included being an absolute ruler tomorrow. There were subtleties. Oh, you could order men to smash down doors and drag people off to dungeons without trial, but too much of that sort of thing lacked style and anyway was bad for business, habit-forming and very, very dangerous for your health. A thinking tyrant, it seemed to Vetinari, had a much harder job than a ruler raised to power by some idiot vote-yourself-rich system like democracy. At least *they* could tell the people he was their fault.

'. . . we would not normally have started individual folders at this time,' Drumknott was agonizing. 'You see, I'd merely have referenced them on the daily—'

'Your concern is, as ever, exemplary,' said Vetinari. 'I see, however, that you *have* prepared some folders.'

'Yes, my lord. I have bulked some of them out with copies of clerk Harold's analysis of pig production in Genua, sir.' Drumknott looked unhappy as he handed over the card folders. Deliberate misfiling ran fingernails down the blackboard of his very soul.

'Very good,' said Vetinari. He put them on his desk, pulled another folder out of a desk drawer to place on top of them, and moved some other papers to cover the small pile. 'Now please show our visitors in.'

'Mr Slant is with them, my lord,' said the clerk.

Vetinari smiled his mirthless smile. 'How surprising.'

'And Mr Reacher Gilt,' Drumknott added, watching his master carefully.

'Of course,' said Vetinari.

When the financiers filed in a few minutes later the conference table at one end of the room was clear and gleaming, except for a paper pad and the pile of files. Vetinari himself was standing at the window again.

'Ah, gentlemen. So kind of you to come for this little chat,' he said. 'I was enjoying the view.'

He turned round sharply, and confronted a row of puzzled faces, except for two. One was grey and belonged to Mr Slant, who was the most renowned, expensive and certainly the oldest lawyer in the city. He had been a zombie for many years, although apparently the change in habits between life and death had not been marked. The other face belonged to a man with one eye and one black eye-patch, and it smiled like a tiger.

'It's particularly refreshing to see the Grand Trunk back in operation,' said Vetinari, ignoring that face. 'I believe it was shut down all day yesterday. I was only thinking to myself that it was such a shame, the Grand Trunk being so vital to us all, and so regrettable that there's only one of it. Sadly, I understand the backers of the New Trunk are now in disarray, which, of course, leaves the Grand Trunk operating in solitary splendour and your company, gentlemen, unchallenged. Oh, what am I thinking of? *Do* be seated, gentlemen.'

He gave Mr Slant another friendly smile as he took his seat.

'I don't believe I know *all* these gentlemen,' he said.

Mr Slant sighed. 'My lord, let me present Mr Greenyham of Ankh-Sto Associates, who is the Grand Trunk Company's treasurer, Mr Nutmeg of Sto Plains Holdings, Mr Horsefry of the Ankh-Morpork Mercantile Credit Bank, Mr Stowley of Ankh Futures (Financial Advisers) and Mr Gilt—'

'—all by himself,' said the one-eyed man calmly.

'Ah, Mr Reacher Gilt,' said Vetinari, looking directly at him. 'I'm so . . . *pleased* to meet you at last.'

'You don't come to my parties, my lord,' said Gilt.

'Do excuse me. Affairs of state take up so much of my time,' said Lord Vetinari brusquely.

'We should all make time to unwind, my lord. All work and no play makes Jack a dull boy, as they say.'

Several of the assembly paused in their breathing when they heard this, but Vetinari merely looked blank.

'Interesting,' he said.

He riffled through the files and opened one of them. 'Now, my staff have prepared some notes for me, from information publicly available down at the Barbican,' he said to the lawyer. 'Directorships, for example. Of course, the mysterious world of finance is a closed, aha, ledger to me, but it seems to me that some of your clients work, as it were, for each other?'

'Yes, my lord?' said Slant.

'Is that normal?'

'Oh, it is quite common for people with particular expertise to be on the board of several companies, my lord.'

'Even if the companies are rivals?' said Vetinari.

There were smiles from around the table. Most of the financiers settled a little more easily in their chairs. The man was clearly a fool about business matters. What did he know about compound interest, eh? He'd been classically educated. And then they remembered his education had been at the Assassins' Guild School, and stopped smiling. But Mr Gilt stared intently at Vetinari.

'There are ways – extremely honourable ways – of assuring confidentiality and avoiding conflicts of interest, my lord,' said Mr Slant.

'Ah, this would be . . . what is it now . . . the glass ceiling?' said Lord Vetinari brightly.

'No, my lord. That is something else. I believe you may be thinking about the "Agatean Wall",' said Mr Slant smoothly. 'This carefully and successfully ensures that there will be no breach of confidentiality should, for example, one part of an organization come into possession of privileged information which could conceivably be used by another department for unethical gain.'

'This is fascinating! How does it work, exactly?' said Vetinari.

'People agree not to do it,' said Mr Slant.

'I'm sorry? I thought you said there is a wall—' said Vetinari.

'That's just a name, my lord. For agreeing not to do it.'

'Ah? And they do? How wonderful. Even though in this case the invisible wall must pass through the middle of their brains?'

'We have a Code of Conduct, you know!' said a voice.

All eyes except those belonging to Mr Slant turned to the speaker, who had been fidgeting in his chair. Mr Slant was a long-time student of the Patrician, and when his subject appeared to be a confused civil servant asking innocent questions it was time to watch him closely.

'I'm very glad to hear it, Mr . . . ?' Vetinari began.

'Crispin Horsefry, my lord, and I don't like the tone of your questioning!'

For a moment it seemed that even the chairs themselves edged away from him. Mr Horsefry was a youngish man, not simply running to fat but vaulting, leaping and diving towards obesity. He had acquired at thirty an impressive selection of chins, and now they wobbled with angry pride.*

'I do have a number of other tones,' said Lord Vetinari calmly.

Mr Horsefry looked around at his colleagues, who were somehow, suddenly, on the distant horizon.

'I just wanted to make it clear that we've done nothing wrong,' he muttered. 'That's all. There is a Code of Conduct.'

'I'm sure I've not suggested that you have done anything wrong,' said Lord Vetinari. 'However, I shall make a note of what you tell me.'

He pulled a sheet of paper towards him and wrote, in a careful copperplate hand, 'Code of Conduct'. The shifting of the paper exposed a file marked 'Embezzlement'. The title was of course upside down to the rest of the group and, since presumably it was not intended to be read by them, they read it. Horsefry even twisted his head for a better view.

'However,' Vetinari went on, 'since the question of wrongdoing has been raised by Mr Horsefry,' and he gave the young man a brief smile, 'I am sure you are aware of talk suggesting a conspiracy amongst yourselves to keep rates high and competition non-existent.' The sentence came out fast and smooth, like a snake's tongue, and the swift flick on the end of it was: 'And, indeed, some rumours about the death of young Mr Dearheart last month.'

A stir among the semicircle of men said that the shoe had been

---

* It is wrong to judge by appearances. Despite his expression, which was that of a piglet having a bright idea, and his mode of speech, which might put you in mind of a small, breathless, neurotic but ridiculously expensive dog, Mr Horsefry might well have been a kind, generous and pious man. In the same way, the man climbing out of your window in a stripy jumper, a mask and a great hurry might merely be lost on the way to a fancy-dress party, and the man in the wig and robes at the focus of the courtroom might only be a transvestite who wandered in out of the rain. Snap judgements can be so unfair.

dropped. It wasn't a welcome shoe, but it was a shoe they had been expecting and it had just gone thud.

'An actionable falsehood,' said Slant.

'On the contrary, Mr Slant,' said Vetinari, 'merely mentioning to you the existence of a rumour is not actionable, as I am sure you are aware.'

'There is no proof that we had anything to do with the boy's murder,' snapped Horsefry.

'Ah, so you too have heard people saying he was murdered?' said Vetinari, his eyes on Reacher Gilt's face. 'These rumours just *fly* around, don't they . . .'

'My lord, people talk,' said Slant wearily. 'But the facts are that Mr Dearheart was alone in the tower. No one else went up or down. His safety line was apparently not clipped to anything. It was an accident, such as happens often. Yes, we know people say his fingers were broken, but with a fall of that distance, hitting the tower on the way, can that really be surprising? Alas, the Grand Trunk Company is not popular at the moment and so these scurrilous and baseless accusations are made. As Mr Horsefry pointed out, there is no evidence whatsoever that what happened was anything more than a tragic accident. And, if I may speak frankly, what *exactly* is the purpose of calling us here? My clients are busy men.'

Vetinari leaned back and placed his fingers together.

'Let us consider a situation in which some keen and highly inventive men devise a remarkable system of communication,' he said. 'What they have is a kind of passionate ingenuity, in large amounts. What they don't have is money. They are not *used* to money. So they meet some . . . people, who introduce them to other people, friendly people, who for, oh, a forty per cent stake in the enterprise *give* them the much-needed cash and, very important, much fatherly advice and an introduction to a really *good* firm of accountants. And so they proceed, and soon money is coming in and money is going out but somehow, they learn, they're not quite as financially stable as they think and really do need *more* money. Well, this is all fine because it's clear to all that the basic enterprise is going to be a money tree one day, and does it matter if they sign over another fifteen per cent? It's just money. It's not *important* in the way that shutter mechanisms are, is it? And then they find out that *yes*, it is. It is *everything*. Suddenly the world's turned upside down, suddenly those nice people aren't so friendly any more, suddenly it turns out that those bits of paper they signed in a hurry, were *advised* to sign by people who smiled all the time, mean that they don't actually own anything at all, not patents, not property, nothing. Not even the contents of their own heads, indeed. Even any ideas they have now don't belong to them, apparently. And somehow they're *still* in trouble about money. Well, some run and some hide and some try to fight, which is foolish in the extreme, because it turns out that everything is legal, it really is. Some accept low-level jobs in the enterprise, because one has to live and in any case the enterprise even owns their dreams at night. And yet actual illegality, it would appear, has not taken place. Business is business.'

Lord Vetinari opened his eyes. The men around the table were staring at him.

'Just thinking aloud,' he said. 'I am sure you will point out that this is not the business of the government. I *know* Mr Gilt will. However, since you acquired the Grand Trunk at a fraction of its value, I note that breakdowns are increasing, the speed of messages has slowed down and the cost to customers has risen. Last week the Grand Trunk was closed for almost three days. We could not even talk to Sto Lat! Hardly "As Fast as Light", gentlemen.'

'That was for essential maintenance—' Mr Slant began.

'No, it was for repairs,' snapped Vetinari. 'Under the previous management the system shut down for an hour every day. *That* was for maintenance. Now the towers run until they break down. What do you think you are doing, gentlemen?'

'That, my lord, and with respect, is none of your business.'

Lord Vetinari smiled. For the first time that morning, it was a smile of genuine pleasure.

'Ah, Mr Reacher Gilt, I was wondering when we'd hear from you. You have been so uncharacteristically silent. I read your recent article in the

Times with great interest. You are passionate about freedom, I gather. You used the word "tyranny" three times and the word "tyrant" once.'

'Don't patronize me, my lord,' said Gilt. 'We own the Trunk. It is our *property*. You understand that? Property is the foundation of freedom. Oh, customers complain about the service and the cost, but customers always complain about such things. We have no shortage of customers at whatever cost. Before the semaphore, news from Genua took months to get here, now it takes less than a day. It is affordable magic. We are answerable to our shareholders, my lord. Not, with respect, to you. It is not your business. It is our business, and we will run it according to the market. I hope there are no tyrannies here. This is, with respect, a free city.'

'Such a lot of respect is gratifying,' said the Patrician. 'But the only *choice* your customers have is between you and nothing.'

'Exactly,' said Reacher Gilt calmly. 'There is always a choice. They can ride a horse a few thousand miles, or they can wait patiently until we can send their message.'

Vetinari gave him a smile that lasted as long as a lightning flash.

'Or fund and build another system,' he said. 'Although I note that every other company that has lately tried to run a clacks system in opposition has failed quite quickly, sometimes in distressing circumstances. Falls from the tops of clacks towers, and so on.'

'Accidents do happen. It is most unfortunate,' said Mr Slant stiffly.

'Most unfortunate,' Vetinari echoed. He pulled the paper towards him once again, dislodging the files slightly, so that a few more names were visible, and wrote 'Most unfortunate'.

'Well, I believe that covers everything,' he said. 'In fact, the purpose of this meeting was to tell you formally that I am, at last, reopening the Post Office as planned. This is just a courtesy announcement, but I felt I should tell you because you are, after all, in the same business. I believe the recent string of accidents is now at an en—'

Reacher Gilt chuckled. 'Sorry, my lord? Did I understand you correctly? You really intend to continue with this folly, in the face of everything? The *Post Office*? When we all know that it was a lumbering, smug, overstaffed, overweight monster of a place? It barely earned its keep! It was the very essence and exemplar of public enterprise!'

'It never made much of a profit, it is true, but in the business areas of this city there were seven deliveries a day,' said Vetinari, cold as the depths of the sea.

'Hah! Not at the end!' said Mr Horsefry. 'It was bloody useless!'

'Indeed. A classic example of a corroded government organization dragging on the public purse,' Gilt added.

'Too true!' said Mr Horsefry. 'They used to say that if you wanted to get rid of a dead body you should take it to the Post Office and it'd never be seen again!'

'And was it?' said Lord Vetinari, raising an eyebrow.

'Was what?'

'Was it seen again?'

There was a sudden hunted look in Mr Horsefry's eyes. 'What? How would I know?'

'Oh, I see,' said Lord Vetinari. 'It was a joke. Ah, well.' He shuffled the papers. 'Unfortunately the Post Office came to be seen not as a system for moving the mail efficiently, to the benefit and profit of all, but as a money box. And so it collapsed, losing both mail and money. A lesson for us all, perhaps. Anyway, I have high hopes of Mr Lipwig, a young man full of fresh ideas. A good head for heights, too, although I imagine he will not be climbing any towers.'

'I do hope this resurrection will not prove to be a drain on our taxes,' said Mr Slant.

'I assure you, Mr Slant, that apart from the modest sum necessary to, as it were, prime the pump, the postal service will be self-supporting as, indeed, it used to be. We cannot have a drag on the public purse, can we? And now, gentlemen, I am conscious that I am keeping you from your very important business. I do trust that the Trunk will be back in commission very shortly.'

As they stood up, Reacher Gilt leaned across the table and said: 'May I congratulate you, my lord?'

'I am delighted that you feel inclined to congratulate me on anything, Mr Gilt,' said Vetinari. 'To what do we owe this unique occurrence?'

'This, my lord,' said Gilt, gesturing to the little side table on which had been set the rough-hewn piece of stone. 'Is this not an original Hnaflbaflsniflwhifltafl slab? Llamedos bluestone, isn't it? And the pieces look like basalt, which is the very devil to carve. A valuable antique, I think.'

'It was a present to me from the Low King of the Dwarfs,' said Vetinari. 'It is, indeed, very old.'

'And you have a game in progress, I see. You're playing the dwarf side, yes?'

'Yes. I play by clacks against an old friend in Uberwald,' said Vetinari. 'Happily for me, your breakdown yesterday has given me an extra day to think of my next move.'

Their eyes met. Reacher Gilt laughed hugely. Vetinari smiled. The other men, who badly needed to laugh, laughed too. See, we're all friends, we're like colleagues really, nothing *bad* is going to happen.

The laughter died away, a little uneasily. Gilt and Vetinari maintained smiles, maintained eye contact.

'We should play a game,' said Gilt. 'I have a rather nice board myself. I play the troll side, for preference.'

'Ruthless, initially outnumbered, inevitably defeated in the hands of the careless player?' said Vetinari.

'Indeed. Just as the dwarfs rely on guile, feint and swift changes of position. A man can learn all of an opponent's weaknesses on that board,' said Gilt.

'Really?' said Vetinari, raising his eyebrows. 'Should he not be trying to learn his own?'

'Oh, that's just Thud! That's *easy!*' yapped a voice.

Both men turned to look at Horsefry, who had been made perky by sheer relief.

'I used to play it when I was a kid,' he burbled. 'It's *boring*. The dwarfs always win!'

Gilt and Vetinari shared a look. It said: while I loathe you and every aspect of your personal philosophy to a depth unplumbable by any line, I'll credit you at least with not being Crispin Horsefry.

'Appearances are deceptive, Crispin,' said Gilt jovially. 'A troll player need never lose, if he puts his mind to it.'

'I know I once got a dwarf stuck up my nose and Mummy had to get it out with a hairpin,' said Horsefry, as if this was a source of immense pride.

Gilt put his arm round the man's shoulders. 'That's very interesting, Crispin,' he said. 'Do you think it's likely to happen again?'

Vetinari stood at the window after they had left, watching the city below. After a few minutes, Drumknott drifted in.

'There was a brief exchange in the ante-room, my lord,' he said.

Vetinari didn't turn round, but held up a hand. 'Let me see . . . I imagine one of them started saying something like "Do you think he—" and Slant very quickly shushed him? Mr Horsefry, I suspect.'

Drumknott glanced at the paper in his hand. 'Almost to the word, my lord.'

'It takes no great leap of the imagination,' sighed Lord Vetinari. 'Dear Mr Slant. He's so . . . dependable. Sometimes I really think that if he was not already a zombie it would be necessary to have him turned into one.'

'Shall I order a Number One Investigation on Mr Gilt, my lord?'

'Good heavens, no. He is far too clever. Order it on Mr Horsefry.'

'Really, sir? But you did say yesterday that you believed him to be no more than a greedy fool.'

'A nervous fool, which is useful. He's a venal coward and a glutton. I've watched him sit down to a meal of *pot au feu* with white beans, and that was an impressive sight, Drumknott, which I will not easily forget. The sauce went *everywhere*. Those pink shirts he wears cost more than a hundred dollars, too. Oh, he acquires other people's money, in a safe and secret and not very clever way. Send . . . yes, send clerk Brian.'

'Brian, sir?' said Drumknott. 'Are you sure? He's wonderful at devices, but quite inept on the street. He'll be seen.'

'Yes, Drumknott. I know. I would like Mr Horsefry to become a little . . . *more* nervous.'

'Ah, I see, sir.'

Vetinari turned back to the window. 'Tell me, Drumknott,' he said, 'would *you* say I'm a tyrant?'

'Most certainly not, my lord,' said Drumknott, tidying the desk.

'But of course that's the problem, is it not? Who will tell the tyrant he *is* a tyrant?'

'That's a tricky one, my lord, certainly,' said Drumknott, squaring up the files.

'In his *Thoughts*, which I have always considered fare badly in translation, Bouffant says that intervening in order to prevent a murder is to curtail the freedom of the murderer and yet that freedom, by definition, is natural and universal, without condition,' said Vetinari. 'You may recall his famous dictum: "If any man is not free, then I too am a small pie made of chicken", which has led to a considerable amount of debate. Thus we might consider, for example, that taking a bottle from a man killing himself with drink is a charitable, nay, praiseworthy act, and yet freedom is curtailed once more. Mr Gilt has studied his Bouffant but, I fear, failed to understand him. Freedom may be mankind's natural state, but so is sitting in a tree eating your dinner while it is still wriggling. On the other hand, Freidegger, in *Modal Contextities*, claims that all freedom is limited, artificial and therefore illusory, a shared hallucination at best. No sane mortal is truly free, because true freedom is so terrible that only the mad or the divine can face it with open eyes. It over-whelms the soul, very much like the state he elsewhere describes as *Vonallesvolkommenunverstandlichdasdaskeit*. What position would you take here, Drumknott?'

'I've always thought, my lord, that what the world really needs are filing boxes which are not so flimsy,' said Drumknott, after a moment's pause.

'Hmm,' said Lord Vetinari. 'A point to think about, certainly.'

He stopped. On the carven decorations over the room's fireplace a small cherub began to turn, with a faint squeaking noise. Vetinari raised an eyebrow at Drumknott.

'I shall have a word with clerk Brian immediately, my lord,' said the clerk.

'Good. Tell him it's time he got out into the fresh air more.'

CHAPTER FOUR

A Sign

Dark Clerks and dead Postmasters – A Werewolf in the Watch – The wonderful pin – Mr Lipwig reads letters that are not there – Hugo the hairdresser is surprised – Mr Parker buys fripperies – The Nature of Social Untruths – Princess in the Tower – 'A man is not dead while his name is still spoken.'

'NOW THEN, MR LIPVIG, What Good Will Violence Do?' Mr Pump rumbled. He rocked on his huge feet as Moist struggled in his grip.

Groat and Stanley were huddled at the far end of the locker room. One of Mr Groat's natural remedies was bubbling over on to the floor, where the boards were staining purple.

'They were all accidents, Mr Lipwig! All accidents!' Groat babbled. 'The Watch was all over the place by the fourth one! They were all accidents, they said!'

'Oh, *yes*!' screamed Moist. 'Four in five weeks, eh? I bet that happens all the time around here! Ye gods, I've been done up good and brown! I'm dead, right? Just not lying down yet! Vetinari? There's a man who knows how to save the price of a rope! I'm done for!'

'You'll feel better for a nice cup o' bismuth and brimstone tea, sir,' Groat quavered. 'I've got the kettle boiling—'

'A cup of tea is not going to be sufficient!' Moist got a grip on himself, or at least began to act as if he had, and took a deep, theatrical breath. 'Okay, okay, Mr Pump, you can let go now.'

The golem released his grip. Moist straightened up. 'Well, Mr Groat?' he said.

'Looks like you're genuine after all, then,' the old man said. 'One of the dark clerks wouldn't have gone bursar like that. We thought you was one of his lordship's special gentlemen, see.' Groat fussed around the kettle. 'No offence, but you've got a bit more colour than the average penpusher.'

'Dark clerks?' said Moist, and then recollection dawned. 'Oh . . . do you mean those stocky little men in black suits and bowler hats?'

'The very same. Scholarship boys at the Assassins' Guild, some of 'em. I heard that they can do some nasty things when they've a mind.'

'I thought you called them penpushers?'

'Yeah, but I didn't say where, heehee.' Groat caught Moist's expression and coughed. 'Sorry, didn't mean it, just my little joke. We reckon the last new postmaster we had, Mr Whobblebury, he was a dark clerk. Can't hardly blame him, with a name like that. He was always snooping around.'

'And why do you think that was?' said Moist.

'Well, Mr Mutable, he was the first, decent chap, he fell down into the big hall from the fifth floor, smack, sir, *smack* on to the marble. Head first. It was a bit . . . splashy, sir.'

Moist glanced at Stanley, who was starting to tremble.

'Then there was Mr Sideburn. He fell down the back stairs and broke his neck, sir. Excuse me, sir, it's eleven forty-three.' Groat walked over to the door and opened it, Tiddles walked through, Groat shut the door again. 'At three in the morning, it was. Right down five flights. Broke just about every bone you could break, sir.'

'You mean he was wandering around without a light?'

'Dunno, sir. But I know about the stairs. The stairs have lamps burning all night, sir. Stanley fills them every day, regular as Tiddles.'

'Use those stairs a lot, then, do you?' said Moist.

'Never, sir, except for the lamps. Nearly everywhere on that side is bunged up with mail. But it's a Post Office Regulation, sir.'

'And the next man?' said Moist, a little hoarsely. 'Another accidental fall?'

'Oh, no, sir. Mr Ignavia, that was his name. They said it was his heart. He was just lyin' dead on the fifth floor, dead as a doorknob, face all contorted like he'd seen a ghost. Natural causes, they said. Werrrl, the Watch was all over the place by then, you may depend on it. No one had been near him, they said, and there was not a mark on him. Surprised you didn't know about all this, sir. It was in the paper.'

Except you don't get much chance to keep up with the news in a condemned cell, Moist thought.

'Oh yes?' he said. 'And how would they know no one had been near him?'

Groat leaned forward and lowered his voice conspiratorially. 'Everyone knows there's a werewolf in the Watch and one of *them* could bloody nearly smell what colour clothes someone was wearing.'

'A werewolf,' said Moist, flatly.

'Yes. Anyway, the one before him—'

'A werewolf.'

'That's what I said, sir,' said Groat.

'A damn *werewolf*.'

'Takes all sorts to make a world, sir. Anyway—'

'A werewolf.' Moist awoke from the horror. 'And they don't tell visitors?'

'Now, how'd they do that, sir?' said Groat, in a kindly voice. 'Put it on a sign outside? "Welcome To Ankh-Morpork, We Have A Werewolf", sir? The Watch's got loads of dwarfs and trolls and a golem – a free golem, savin' your presence, Mr Pump – and a couple of gnomes and a zombie . . . even a Nobbs.'

'Nobbs? What's a Nobbs?'

'Corporal Nobby Nobbs, sir. Not met him yet? They *say* he's got an official chitty saying he's human, and who needs one of those, eh? Fortunately there's only one of him so he can't breed. Anyway, we've got a bit of everything, sir. Very cosmopolitan. You don't like werewolves?'

They know who you are by your smell, thought Moist. They're as bright as a human and can track you better than any wolf. They can follow a trail that's days old, even if you cover yourself with scent – *especially* if you cover yourself with scent. Oh, there's ways around, *if* you know there is going to be a werewolf on your tail. No wonder they caught up with me. There should be a law!

'Not a lot,' he said aloud, and glanced at Stanley again. It was useful to watch Stanley when Groat was talking. Now the boy had his eyes turned up so much that they were practically all whites.

'And Mr Whobblebury?' he said. 'He was investigating for Vetinari, eh? What happened to him?'

Stanley was shaking like a bush in a high wind.

'Er, you did get given the big keyring, sir?' Groat enquired, his voice trembling with innocence.

'Yes, of course.'

'I bet there is one key missing,' said Groat. 'The Watch took it. It was the only one. Some doors ought to stay closed, sir. It's all over and done with, sir. Mr Whobblebury died of an industrial accident, they said. Nobody near him. You don't want to go there, sir. Sometimes things get so broke it's best to walk away, sir.'

'I can't,' said Moist. 'I *am* the Postmaster General. And this is my building, isn't it? I'll decide where I go, Junior Postman Groat.'

Stanley shut his eyes.

'Yes, sir,' said Groat, as if talking to a child. 'But you don't want to go *there*, sir.'

'*His head was all over the wall!*' Stanley quavered.

'Oh dear, now you've set him off, sir,' said Groat, scuttling across to the boy. 'It's all right, lad, I'll just get you your pills—'

'What is the most expensive pin ever made commercially, Stanley?' said Moist quickly.

It was like pulling a lever. Stanley's expression went from agonized grief to scholarly cogitation in an instant.

'Commercially? Leaving aside those special pins made for exhibitions and trade shows, including the Great Pin of 1899, then probably it is the Number Three Broad-headed "Chicken" Extra Long made for the lace-making market by the noted pinner Josiah Doldrum, I would say. They were hand-drawn and had his trademark silver head with a microscopic engraving of a cockerel. It's believed that fewer than a hundred were made before his death, sir. According to Hubert Spider's Pin Catalogue, examples can fetch between fifty and sixty-five dollars, depending on condition. A Number Three Broad-headed Extra Long would grace any true pinhead's collection.'

'Only . . . I spotted this in the street,' said Moist, extracting one of that morning's purchases from his lapel. 'I was walking down Market Street and there it was, between two cobblestones. I thought it looked unusual. For a pin.'

Stanley pushed away the fussing Groat and carefully took the pin from Moist's fingers. A very large magnifying glass appeared as if by magic in his other hand.

The room held its breath as the pin was subjected to serious scrutiny. Then Stanley looked up at Moist in amazement.

'You *knew*?' he said. 'And you spotted this in the *street*? I thought you didn't know anything about pins!'

'Oh, not really, but I dabbled a bit as a boy,' said Moist, waving a hand deprecatingly to suggest that he had been too foolish to turn a schoolboy hobby into a lifetime's obsession. 'You know . . . a few of the old brass Imperials, one or two oddities like an unbroken pair or a double-header, the occasional cheap packet of mixed pins on approval . . .' Thank the gods, he thought, for the skill of speed-reading.

'Oh, there's never anything worthwhile in those,' said Stanley, and slid again into the voice of the academic: 'While most pinheads do indeed begin with a casually acquired flashy novelty pin, followed by the contents of their grandmothers' pincushions, haha, the path to a truly worthwhile collection lies not in the simple disbursement of money in the nearest pin emporium, oh no. Any dilettante can become "king pin" with enough expenditure, but for the true pinhead the real pleasure is in the joy of the chase, the pin fairs, the house clearances and, who knows, a casual glint in the gutter that turns out to be a well-preserved Doublefast or an unbroken two-pointer. Well is it said: "See a pin and pick it up, and all day long you'll have a pin".'

Moist nearly applauded. It was word for word what J. Lanugo Owlsbury had written in the introduction to his work. And, much more important, he now had an unshakable friend in Stanley. That was to say, his darker regions added, Stanley was friends with *him*. The boy, his panic subsumed by the joy of pins, was holding his new acquisition up to the light.

'Magnificent,' he breathed, all terrors fled. 'Clean as a new pin! I have a place ready and waiting for this in my pin folder, sir!'

'Yes, I thought you might.'

His head was all over the wall . . .

Somewhere there was a locked door, and Moist didn't have the key. Four of his predecessors had predeceased in this very building. And there was *no escape*. Being Postmaster General was a job for life – one way or the other. *That* was why Vetinari had put him here. He needed a man who *couldn't* walk away, and who was incidentally completely expendable. It didn't matter if Moist von Lipwig died. He was already dead.

And then he tried not to think about Mr Pump.

How many other golems had worked their way to freedom in the service of the city? Had there been a Mr Saw, fresh from a hundred years in a pit of sawdust? Or Mr Shovel? Mr Axe, maybe?

And had there been one here when the last poor guy had found the key to the locked door, or a good lockpick, and was about to open it when behind him someone called maybe Mr Hammer, *yes, oh gods, yes,* raised his fist for one sudden, terminal blow?

No one had been near him? But they weren't people, were they . . . they were tools. It'd be an industrial accident.

His head was all over the wall . . .

I'm going to find out about this. I have to, otherwise it'll lie in wait for me. And everyone will tell me lies. But I am the fibbermeister.

'Hmm?' he said, aware that he'd missed something.

'I said, could I go and put this in my collection, Postmaster?' said Stanley.

'What? Oh. Yes. Fine. Yes. Give it a really good polish, too.'

As the boy gangled off to his end of the locker room, and he did gangle, Moist caught Groat looking at him shrewdly.

'Well done, Mr Lipwig,' he said. 'Well done.'

'Thank you, Mr Groat.'

'Good eyesight you've got there,' the old man went on.

'Well, the light was shining off it—'

'Nah, I meant to see cobbles in Market Street, it being all brick paving up there.'

Moist returned his blank stare with one even blanker. 'Bricks, cobbles, who cares?' he said.

'Yeah, right. Not important, really,' said Groat.

'And now,' said Moist, feeling the need for some fresh air, 'there's a little errand I have to run. I'd like you to come with me, Mr Groat. Can you find a crowbar anywhere? Bring it, please. And I'll need you, too, Mr Pump.'

Werewolves and golems, golems and werewolves, Moist thought. I'm stuck here. I might as well take it seriously.

I will show them a sign.

'There's a little habit I have,' said Moist, as he led the way through the streets. 'It's to do with signs.'

'Signs, sir?' said Groat, trying to keep close to the walls.

'Yes, Junior Postman Groat, signs,' said Moist, noticing the way the man winced at 'Junior'. 'Particularly signs with missing letters. When I see one, I automatically read what the missing letters say.'

'And how can you do that, sir, when they're missing?' said Groat.

Ah, so there's a clue as to why you're still sitting in a run-down old building making tea from rocks and weeds all day, Moist thought. Aloud he said: 'It's a knack. Now, I could be wrong, of course, but— Ah, we turn left here . . .'

This was quite a busy street, and the shop was in front of them. It was everything that Moist had hoped.

'Voilà,' he said and, remembering his audience, he added: 'That is to say, there we have it.'

'It's a barber's shop,' said Groat uncertainly. 'For ladies.'

'Ah, you're a man of the world, Tolliver, there's no fooling you,' said Moist. 'And the name over the window, in those large, blue-green letters, is . . . ?'

'Hugos,' said Groat. 'And?'

'Yes, Hugo's,' said Moist. 'No apostrophe present in fact, and the reason for this is . . . you could work *with* me a little here, perhaps . . . ?'

'Er . . .' Groat stared frantically at the letters, defying them to reveal their meaning.

'Close enough,' said Moist. 'There is no apostrophe there because
there was and is no apostrophe in the uplifting slogan that adorns
our beloved Post Office, Mr Groat.' He waited for light to dawn.
'Those big metal letters were stolen from our façade, Mr Groat. I
mean, the front of the building. They're the reason for Glom of Nit,
Mr Groat.'

It took a little time for Mr Groat's mental sunrise to take place, but
Moist was ready when it did.

'No, no, no!' he said, grabbing the old man's greasy collar as he
lurched forward, and almost pulling Groat off his feet. 'That's not
how we deal with this, is it?'

'That's Post Office property! That's worse'n stealing, that is! That's
treason!' Groat yelled.

'Quite so,' said Moist. 'Mr Pump, if you would just hold on to our
friend here, I will go and . . . discuss the matter.' Moist handed over
the furious Junior Postman and brushed himself off. He looked a bit
rumpled but it would have to do.

'What are you going to do, then?' said Groat.

Moist smiled his sunshine smile. 'Something I'm good at, Mr
Groat. I'm going to talk to people.'

He crossed the road and opened the shop door. The bell jangled.

Inside the hairdresser's shop was an array of little booths, and the
air smelled sweet and cloying and, somehow, pink; right by the door
was a little desk with a big open diary. There were lots of flowers
around, and the young woman at the desk gave him a haughty look
that was going to cost her employer a lot of money.

She waited for Moist to speak.

Moist put on a grave expression, leaned down and said in a voice
that had all the characteristics of a whisper but also seemed to be able
to carry quite a long way, 'Can I see Mr Hugo, please? It is very
important.'

'On what business would that be?'

'Well . . . it's a little delicate . . .' said Moist. He could see the tops of
permed heads turning. 'But you can tell him it's good news.'

'Well, if it's good news . . .'

'Tell him I think I can persuade Lord Vetinari that this can be settled without charges being brought. Probably,' said Moist, lowering his voice just enough to increase the curiosity of the customers while not so much as to be inaudible.

The woman stared at him in horror.

'You can? Er . . .' She groped for an ornate speaking tube, but Moist took it gently from her hand, whistled expertly down it, lifted it to his ear and flashed her a smile.

'Thank you,' he said. For *what* did not matter; smile, say the right kinds of words in the right kind of voice, and always, always radiate confidence like a supernova.

A voice in his ear, faint as a spider trapped in a matchbox, said: 'Scitich wabble nabnab?'

'Hugo?' said Moist. 'It's good of you to make time for me. It's Moist, Moist von Lipwig. Postmaster General.' He glanced at the speaking tube. It disappeared into the ceiling. 'So kind of you to assist us, Hugo. It's these missing letters. *Five* missing letters, to be exact.'

'Scrik? Shabadatwik? Scritch vit bottofix!'

'Don't really carry that kind of thing, Hugo, but if you'd care to look out of your window you'll see my personal assistant, Mr Pump. He's standing on the other side of the street.'

And he's eight feet tall and carrying a huge crowbar, Moist added mentally. He winked at the lady sitting at the desk, who was watching him in a kind of awe. You had to keep people skills polished at all times.

He heard the muffled expletive through the floor. Via the speaking tube it became 'Vugrs nickbibble!'

'Yes,' said Moist. 'Perhaps I should come up and speak to you directly . . .'

Ten minutes later Moist crossed the road with care and smiled at his staff. 'Mr Pump, if you would be so good as to step over there and pry out our letters, please?' he said. 'Try not to damage anything. Mr Hugo has been very co-operative. And Tolliver, you've lived here a long time, haven't you? You'll know where to hire men with ropes, steeplejacks, that sort of thing? I want those letters back on our building by midday, okay?'

'That'll cost a lot of money, Mr Lipwig,' said Groat, staring at him in amazement. Moist pulled a bag out of his pocket, and jingled it.

'One hundred dollars should more than cover it?' he said. 'Mr Hugo was very apologetic and very, very inclined to be helpful. Says he bought them years ago off a man in a pub and is only too happy to pay for them to be returned. It's amazing how nice people can be, if approached in the right way.'

There was a clang from the other side of the street. Mr Pump had already removed the H, without any apparent effort.

Speak softly and employ a huge man with a crowbar, thought Moist. This might be bearable after all.

The weak sunlight glinted on the S as it was swung into position. There was quite a crowd. People in Ankh-Morpork always paid attention to people on rooftops, in case there was a chance of an interesting suicide. There was a cheer, just on general principles, when the last letter was hammered back into place.

Four dead men, Moist thought, looking up at the roof. I wonder if the Watch would talk to me? Do they *know* about me? Do they think I'm dead? Do I *want* to speak to policemen? No! Damn! The only way I can get out of this is by running forward, not going back. Bloody, bloody Vetinari. But there's a way to win.

He could make money!

He was part of the government, wasn't he? Governments took money off people. That's what they were *for*.

He had people skills, hadn't he? He could persuade people that brass was gold that had got a bit tarnished, that glass was diamond, that tomorrow there was going to be free beer.

He'd outfox them all! He *wouldn't* try to escape, not yet! If a golem could buy its freedom, then so could he! He'd buckle down and bustle and look busy and he'd send all the bills to Vetinari, because this was *government work*! How could the man object?

And if Moist von Lipwig couldn't cream a little somethi— a *big* something off the top, and the bottom, and maybe a little off the sides, then he didn't deserve to! And then, when it was all going well and the cash was rolling in . . . well, then there'd be time to make plans for the big one. Enough money bought a lot of men with sledgehammers.

The workmen pulled themselves back on to the flat roof. There was another ragged cheer from a crowd that reckoned it hadn't been bad entertainment even if no one had fallen off.

'What do you think, Mr Groat?' he said.

'Looks nice, sir, looks nice,' said Groat, as the crowd dispersed and they walked back to the Post Office building.

'Not disturbing anything, then?' said Moist.

Groat patted the surprised Moist on the arm. 'I don't know why his lordship sent you, sir, really I don't,' he whispered. 'You mean well, I can see. But take my advice, sir, and get out of here.'

Moist glanced towards the building's doors. Mr Pump was standing beside them. Just standing, with his arms hanging down. The fire in his eyes was a banked glow.

'I can't do that,' he said.

'Nice of you to say so, sir, but this place isn't for a young man with a future,' said Groat. 'Now, Stanley, he's all right if he's got his pins, but you, sir, you could go far.'

'No-o, I don't think I can,' said Moist. 'Honestly. My place, Mr Groat, is here.'

'Gods *bless* you for saying that, sir, gods *bless* you,' said Groat. Tears were beginning to roll down his face. 'We used to be heroes,' he said. 'People *wanted* us. Everyone watched out for us. Everyone knew us. This was a great place, once. Once, we were *postmen*.'

'Mister!'

Moist turned. Three people were hurrying towards him, and he had to quell an automatic urge to turn and run, especially when one of them shouted, 'Yes, that's him!'

He recognized the greengrocer from this morning. An elderly

couple were trailing behind him. The older man, who had the determined face and upright bearing of a man who subdued cabbages
daily, stopped an inch in front of Moist and bellowed: 'Are you the
po'stman, young man?'

'Yes, sir, I suppose I am,' said Moist. 'How can I—'

'You delivered me this letter from Aggie here! I'm Tim Parker!' the
man roared. 'Now, there's s'ome people'd say it wa's a little bit on
the late side!'

'Oh,' said Moist. 'Well, I—'

'That took a bit of nerve, young man!'

'I'm very sorry that—' Moist began. People skills weren't much
good in the face of Mr Parker. He was one of the impervious people,
whose grasp of volume control was about as good as his understanding of personal space.

'S'orry?' Parker shouted. 'What've you got to be s'orry about? Not
your fault, lad. You weren't even born! More fool me for thinking she
didn't care, eh? Hah, I wa's so downhearted, lad, I went right out and
joined the . . .' His red face wrinkled. 'You know . . . camel's, funny
hat's, sand, where you go to forget . . .'

'The Klatchian Foreign Legion?' said Moist.

'That wa's it! And when I came back I met Sadie, and Aggie had met
her Frederick, and we both got s'ettled and forgot the other one was
alive and then blow me down if this letter didn't arrive from Aggie!
Me and my lad have s'pent half the morning tracking her down! And
to cut a long s'tory short, lad, we're getting married Sat'day! 'co's of
you, boy!'

Mr Parker was one of those men who turn into teak with age.
When he slapped Moist on the back it was like being hit with a chair.

'Won't Frederick and Aggie object—' Moist wheezed.

'I doubt it! Frederick pas'sed away ten years ago and Sadie's been
buried up in S'mall God's for the last five!' Mr Barker bellowed cheerfully. 'And we were s'orry to see them go but, as Aggie say's, it was all
meant to be and you wa's sent by a higher power. And I say it took a
man with real backbone to come and deliver that letter after all this
time. There's many that would have tos'sed it aside like it was of no

account! You'd do me and the future second Mrs Parker a great favour if you wa's to be a guest of honour at our wedding, and I for one won't take no for an ans'wer! I'm Grand Ma'ster of the Guild of Merchant's this year, too! We might not be posh like the Assassins or the Alchemists but there's a lot of us and I shall put in a word on your behalf, you can depend on that! My lad George here will be down later on with the invitation's for you to deliver, now you're back in busines's! It will be a great honour for me, my boy, if you would shake me by the hand . . .'

He thrust out a huge hand. Moist took it, and old habits died hard. Firm grip, steady gaze . . .

'Ah, you're an honest man, all right,' said Parker. 'I'm never mis'taken!' He clapped his hand on Moist's shoulder, causing a knee joint to crunch. 'What's your name, lad?'

'Lipwig, sir. Moist von Lipwig,' Moist said. He was afraid he'd gone deaf in one ear.

'A von, eh,' said Parker. 'Well, you're doing damn well for a foreigner, and I don't care who know's it! Got to be going now. Aggie want's to buy fripperie's!'

The woman came up to Moist, stood on tiptoe and kissed him on the cheek. 'And I know a good man when I see one,' she said. 'Do you have a young lady?'

'What? No! Not at all! Er . . . no!' said Moist.

'I'm sure you shall,' she said, smiling sweetly. 'And while we're very grateful to you, I would advise you to propose in person. We do so much look forward to seeing you on Saturday!'

Moist watched her scurry away after her long-lost swain.

'You delivered a letter?' said Groat, horrified.

'Yes, Mr Groat. I didn't mean to, but I just happened to be—'

'You took one of the old letters and you *delivered* it?' said Groat, as if the concept was something he could not fit into his head—

His head was all over the wall . . .

Moist blinked.

'We are *supposed* to deliver the mail, man! That's our job! Remember?'

'You delivered a letter . . .' breathed Groat. 'What was the date on it?'

'I can't remember! More than forty years ago?'

'What was it like? Was it in good condition?' Groat insisted.

Moist glared at the little postman. A small crowd was forming around them, as was the Ankh-Morpork way.

'It was a forty-year-old letter in a cheap envelope!' he snarled. 'And that's what it looked like! It never got delivered and it upset the lives of two people. I delivered it and it's made two people very happy. What is the *problem*, Mr Groat— Yes, what is it?'

This was to a woman who was tugging at his sleeve.

'I said is it true you're opening the old place again?' she repeated. 'My grandad used to work there!'

'Well done him,' said Moist.

'He said there was a curse!' said the woman, as if the idea was rather pleasing.

'Really?' said Moist. 'Well, I could do with a good curse right now, as a matter of fact.'

'It lives under the floor and drives you maaad!' she went on, enjoying the syllable so much that she seemed loath to let it go. 'Maaad!'

'Really,' said Moist. 'Well, we do not believe in going crazy in the postal service, do we, Mr Gro—' He stopped. Mr Groat had the expression of one who did believe in going crazy.

'You daft old woman!' Groat yelled. 'What did you have to tell him that for?'

'Mr Groat!' snapped Moist. 'I wish to speak to you inside!'

He grabbed the old man by the shoulder and very nearly carried him through the amused crowd, dragged him into the building and slammed the door.

'I've had enough of this!' he said. 'Enough of dark comments and mutterings, do you understand? No more secrets. What's going on here? What went on here? You tell me right now or—'

The little man's eyes were full of fear. This is not me, Moist thought. This is not the way. People skills, eh?

'You tell me right now, *Senior* Postman Groat!' he snapped.

The old man's eyes widened. 'Senior Postman?'

'I *am* the postmaster in this vicinity, yes?' said Moist. 'That means I can promote, yes? Senior Postman, indeed. On probation, of course. Now, will you tell me what—'

'Don't you hurt Mr Groat, sir!' said a ringing voice behind Moist.

Groat looked past Moist into the gloom and said: 'It's all right, Stanley, there's no need for that, we don't want a Little Moment.' To Moist he whispered: 'Best you put me down gently, sir . . .'

Moist did so, with exaggerated care, and turned round.

The boy was standing behind him with a glazed look on his face and the big kettle raised. It was a *heavy* kettle.

'You mustn't hurt Mr Groat, sir,' he said hoarsely.

Moist pulled a pin out of his lapel. 'Of course not, Stanley. By the way, is this a genuine Clayfeather Medium Sharp?'

Stanley dropped the kettle, suddenly oblivious of everything but the inch of silvery steel between Moist's fingers. One hand was already pulling out his magnifying glass.

'Let me see, let me see,' he said, in a level, thoughtful voice. 'Oh, yes. Ha. No, sorry. It's an easy mistake to make. Look at the marks on the shoulder, here. See? And the head was never coiled. This is machine-made. Probably by one of the Happily brothers. Short run, I imagine. Hasn't got their sigil, though. Could have been done by a creative apprentice. Not worth much, I'm afraid, unless you find someone who specializes in the minutiae of the Happily pinnery.'

'I'll, er, just make a cup of tea, shall I?' said Groat, picking up the kettle as it rolled backwards and forwards on the floor. 'Well done again, Mr Lipwig. Er . . . *Senior* Postman Groat, right?'

'Off you go with, yes, *probationary* Senior Postman Groat, Stanley,' said Moist, as kindly as he could manage. He looked up and added sharply: 'I just want to talk to Mr Pump here.'

Stanley looked round at the golem, who was right behind him. It was astonishing how quietly a golem could move; he'd crossed the floor like a shadow and now stood with one still fist raised like the wrath of gods.

'Oh, I didn't see you standing there, Mr Pump,' said Stanley cheerfully. 'Why is your hand up?'

The holes in the golem's face bathed the boy in red light. 'I . . . Wanted To Ask The Postmaster A Question?' said the golem slowly.

'Oh. All right,' said Stanley, as if he hadn't been about to brain Moist a moment before. 'Do you want your pin back, Mr Lipwig?' he added, and when Moist waved him away he went on, 'All right, I'll put it in next month's charity pin auction.'

When the door had shut behind him, Moist looked up at the golem's impassive face.

'You lied to him. Are you *allowed* to lie, Mr Pump?' he said. 'And you can lower that arm, by the way.'

'I Have Been Instructed As To The Nature Of Social Untruths, Yes.'

'You were going to smash his brains out!' said Moist.

'I Would Have Endeavoured Not To,' the golem rumbled. 'However, I Cannot Allow You To Come To Inappropriate Harm. It Was A Heavy Kettle.'

'You can't do that, you idiot!' said Moist, who'd noticed the use of 'inappropriate'.

'I Should Have Let Him Kill You?' said the golem. 'It Would Not Have Been His Fault. His Head Is Not Right.'

'It would be even less right if you walloped it. Look, I sorted it out!'

'Yes,' Pump said. 'You Have A Talent. It Is A Pity You Misuse It.'

'Do you understand anything I'm saying?' shouted Moist. 'You can't just go around killing people!'

'Why Not? You Do.' The golem lowered his arm.

'What?' snapped Moist. 'I do not! Who told you that?'

'I Worked It Out. You Have Killed Two Point Three Three Eight People,' said the golem calmly.

'I have never laid a finger on anyone in my life, Mr Pump. I may be— all the things you know I am, but I am *not* a killer! I have never so much as drawn a sword!'

'No, You Have Not. But You Have Stolen, Embezzled, Defrauded And Swindled Without Discrimination, Mr Lipwig. You Have Ruined Businesses And Destroyed Jobs. When Banks Fail, It Is Seldom Bankers Who Starve. Your Actions Have Taken Money From Those Who Had Little Enough To Begin With. In A Myriad Small Ways You

Have *Hastened* The Deaths Of Many. You Do Not Know Them. You Did Not See Them Bleed. But You Snatched Bread From Their Mouths And Tore Clothes From Their Backs. For Sport, Mr Lipvig. For Sport. For The Joy Of The Game.'

Moist's mouth had dropped open. It shut. It opened again. It shut again. You can never find repartee when you need it.

'You're nothing but a walking flowerpot, Pump 19,' he snapped. 'Where did *that* come from?'

'I Have Read The Details Of Your Many Crimes, Mr Lipvig. And Pumping Water Teaches One The Value Of Rational Thought. You Took From Others Because You Were Clever And They Were Stupid.'

'Hold on, most of the time they thought they were swindling me!'

'You Set Out To Trap Them, Mr Lipvig,' said Mr Pump.

Moist went to prod the golem meaningfully, but decided against it just in time. A man could break a finger that way.

'Well, think about this,' he said. 'I'm paying for all that! I was nearly hanged, godsdammit!'

'Yes. But Even Now You Harbour Thoughts Of Escape, Of Somehow Turning The Situation To Your Advantage. They Say The Leopard Does Not Change His Shorts.'

'But you have to obey my orders, yes?' snarled Moist.

'Yes.'

'Then screw your damn head off!'

For a moment the red eyes flickered. When Pump spoke next, it was in the voice of Lord Vetinari.

'Ah, Lipwig. Despite everything, you do not pay attention. Mr Pump cannot be instructed to destroy himself. I would have thought you at least could have worked this out. If you instruct him to do so again, punitive action will be taken.'

The golem blinked again.

'How did you—' Moist began.

'I Have Perfect Recall Of Legal Verbal Instructions,' said the golem, in his normal rumbling tone. 'I Surmise That Lord Vetinari, Mindful Of Your Way Of Thinking, Left That Message Because—'

'I meant the *voice*!'

'*Perfect* Recall, Mr Lipvig,' Pump replied. 'I Can Speak With All The Voices Of Men.'

'Really? How nice for you.' Moist stared up at Mr Pump. There was never any animation in that face. There was a nose, of sorts, but it was just a lump in the clay. The mouth moved when he spoke, and the gods knew how baked clay could move like that – indeed, they probably *did* know. The eyes never closed, they merely dimmed.

'Can you really read my thoughts?' he said.

'No, I Merely Extrapolate From Past Behaviour.'

'Well . . .' Moist, most unusually, was stuck for words. He glared up at the expressionless face, which nevertheless contrived to be disapproving. He was used to looks of anger, indignation and hatred. They were part of the job. But what was a golem? Just . . . dirt. Fired earth. People looking at you as though you were less than the dust beneath their feet was one thing, but it was strangely unpleasant when even the dust did that too.

'. . . don't,' he finished lamely. 'Go and . . . work. Yes! Go on! That's what you do! That's what you're for!'

It was called the lucky clacks tower, Tower 181. It was close enough to the town of Bonk for a man to be able to go and get a hot bath and a good bed on his days off, but since this was Uberwald there wasn't too much local traffic and – this was important – it was way, way up in the mountains and management didn't like to go that far. In the good old days of last year, when the Hour of the Dead took place every night, it was a happy tower because both the up-line and the down-line got the Hour at the same time, so there was an extra pair of hands for maintenance. Now Tower 181 did maintenance on the fly or not at all, just like all the others, but it was still, proverbially, a good tower to man.

Mostly man, anyway. Back down on the plains it was a standing joke that 181 was staffed by vampires and werewolves. In fact, like a lot of towers, it was often manned by kids.

Everyone knew it happened. Actually, the new management

probably didn't, but wouldn't have done anything about it if they'd found out, apart from carefully forgetting that they'd known. Kids didn't need to be paid.

The – mostly – young men on the towers worked hard in all weathers for just enough money. They were loners, hard dreamers, fugitives from the law that the law had forgotten, or just from everybody else. They had a special kind of directed madness; they said the rattle of the clacks got into your head and your thoughts beat time with it so that sooner or later you could tell what messages were going through by listening to the rattle of the shutters. In their towers they drank hot tea out of strange tin mugs, much wider at the bottom so that they didn't fall over when gales banged into the tower. On leave, they drank alcohol out of anything. And they talked a gibberish of their own, of donkey and nondonkey, system overhead and packet space, of drumming it and hotfooting, of a 181 (which was good) or flock (which was bad) or totally flocked (really not good at all) and plug-code and hog-code and jacquard . . .

And they liked kids, who reminded them of the ones they'd left behind or would never have, and kids loved the towers. They'd come and hang around and do odd jobs and maybe pick up the craft of semaphore just by watching. They tended to be bright, they mastered the keyboard and levers as if by magic, they usually had good eyesight and what they were doing, most of them, was running away from home without actually leaving.

Because, up on the towers, you might believe you could see to the rim of the world. You could certainly see several other towers, on a good clear day. You pretended that you too could read messages by listening to the rattle of the shutters, while under your fingers flowed the names of faraway places you'd never see but, on the tower, were somehow connected to . . .

She was known as Princess to the men on Tower 181, although she was really Alice. She was thirteen, could run a line for hours on end without needing help, and later on would have an interesting career which . . . but anyway, she remembered this one conversation, on this day, because it was strange.

Not all the signals were messages. Some were instructions to towers. Some, as you operated your levers to follow the distant signal, made things happen in your own tower. Princess knew all about this. A lot of what travelled on the Grand Trunk was called the Overhead. It was instructions to towers, reports, messages about messages, even chatter between operators, although this was strictly forbidden these days. It was all in code. It was very rare you got Plain in the Overhead. But now . . .

'There it goes again,' she said. 'It must be wrong. It's got no origin code and no address. It's Overhead, but it's in Plain.'

On the other side of the tower, sitting in a seat facing the opposite direction because he was operating the up-line, was Roger, who was seventeen and already working for his tower-master certificate.

His hand didn't stop moving as he said: 'What did it say?'

'There was GNU, and I know that's a code, and then just a name. It was John Dearheart. Was it a—'

'You sent it on?' said Grandad. Grandad had been hunched in the corner, repairing a shutter box in this cramped shed halfway up the tower. Grandad was the tower-master and had been everywhere and knew everything. Everyone called him Grandad. He was twenty-six. He was always doing something in the tower when she was working the line, even though there was always a boy in the other chair. She didn't work out why until later.

'Yes, because it was a G code,' said Princess.

'Then you did right. Don't worry about it.'

'Yes, but I've sent that name before. Several times. Upline and downline. Just a name, no message or anything!'

She had a sense that something was wrong, but she went on: 'I know a U at the end means it has to be turned round at the end of the line, and an N means Not Logged.' This was showing off, but she'd spent hours reading the cypher book. 'So it's just a name, going up and down all the time! Where's the sense in that?'

Something was really wrong. Roger was still working his line, but he was staring ahead with a thunderous expression.

Then Grandad said: 'Very clever, Princess. You're dead right.'

'Hah!' said Roger.

'I'm sorry if I did something wrong,' said the girl meekly. 'I just thought it was strange. Who's John Dearheart?'

'He . . . fell off a tower,' said Grandad.

'Hah!' said Roger, working his shutters as if he suddenly hated them.

'He's *dead*?' said Princess.

'Well, some people say—' Roger began.

'Roger!' snapped Grandad. It sounded like a warning.

'I know about Sending Home,' said Princess. 'And I know the souls of dead linesmen stay on the Trunk.'

'Who told you that?' said Grandad.

Princess was bright enough to know that someone would get into trouble if she was too specific.

'Oh, I just heard it,' she said airily. 'Somewhere.'

'Someone was trying to scare you,' said Grandad, looking at Roger's reddening ears.

It hadn't sounded scary to Princess. If you had to be dead, it seemed a lot better to spend your time flying between the towers than lying underground. But she was bright enough, too, to know when to drop a subject.

It was Grandad who spoke next, after a long pause broken only by the squeaking of the new shutter bars. When he did speak, it was as if something was on his mind. 'We keep that name moving in the Overhead,' he said, and it seemed to Princess that the wind in the shutter arrays above her blew more forlornly, and the everlasting clicking of the shutters grew more urgent. 'He'd never have wanted to go home. He was a *real* linesman. His name is in the code, in the wind in the rigging and the shutters. Haven't you ever heard the saying "A man's not dead while his name is still spoken"?'

CHAPTER FIVE

Lost in the Post

In which Stanley experiences the joy of sacks – Mr Groat's ancestral fears – Horsefry is worried – Reacher Gilt, a man of Society – The Stairway of Letters – Mailslide! – Mr Lipwig Sees It – Hoodwinked – The Postman's Walk – The Hat

S TANLEY POLISHED HIS PINS. He did so with a look of beatific con-
centration, like a man dreaming with his eyes open.

The collection sparkled on the folded strips of brown paper and the rolls of black felt that made up the landscape of the true pinhead's world. Beside him was his large desktop magnifying glass and, by his feet, a sack of miscellaneous pins bought last week from a retiring needlewoman.

He was putting off the moment of opening it to savour it all the more. Of course, it'd almost certainly turn out to be full of everyday brassers, with maybe the occasional flathead or line flaw, but the thing was, *you never knew.* That was the joy of sacks. You never knew. Non-collectors were woefully unconcerned about pins, treating them as if they were no more than thin pointy bits of metal for sticking things to other things. Many a wonderful pin of great worth had been found in a sack of brassers.

And now he had a No. 3 Broad-headed 'Chicken' Extra Long, thanks to kind Mr Lipwig. The world shone like the pins so neatly ranged on the felt rolled out in front of him. He might smell faintly of cheese, and have athlete's foot extending to the knee, but just now Stanley soared through glittering skies on wings of silver.

Groat sat by the stove, chewing his fingernails and muttering to himself. Stanley paid no attention, since pins were not the subject.

'. . . appointed, right? Never mind what the Order says! He can promote anyone, right? That means I get the extra gold button on m'sleeve *and* the pay, right? None of the others called me *Senior* Postman! And when all's said and done, he delivered a letter. Had the letter, saw the address, delivered it just like that! Maybe he *has* got postman's blood! *And* he got them metal letters put back! Letters again, see? That's a sign, sure enough. Hah, he can read words that ain't there!' Groat spat out a fragment of fingernail, and frowned. 'But . . . then he'll want to know about the New Pie. Oh yeah. But . . . it'd be like scratching at a scab. Could be bad. Very bad. But . . . hah, the way he got them letters back for us . . . very good. Maybe it's true that one day we'll get a true postmaster again, just like they say. "Yea, he will tread the Abandoned Roller Skates beneath his Boots, and Lo! the Dogs of the World will Break their Teeth upon Him." And he did show us a sign, right? Okay, it was over a posh haircut shop for ladies, but it was a sign, you can't argue with that. I mean, if it was *obvious*, anyone could show it to us.' Another sliver of fingernail hit the side of the glowing stove, where it sizzled. 'And I ain't getting any younger, that's a fact. Probationary, though, that's not good, *that's not good*. What'd happen if I popped my clogs tomorrow, eh? I'd stand there before my forefathers, and they'd say "Art thou Senior Postal Inspector Groat?" and I'd say no, and they'd say "Art thou then Postal Inspector Groat?" and I'd say not as such, and they'd say "Then surely thou art Senior Postman Groat?" and I'd say not in point of fact, and they'd say "Stone the crows, Tolliver, are you telling us you never got further than Junior Postman? What kind of Groat are you?" and my face will be red and I will be knee deep in the ignominy. Dun't matter that I've been runnin' this place for *years*, oh no. You got to have that gold button!'

He stared at the fire, and somewhere in his matted beard a smile struggled to get out.

'He can try walking the Walk,' he said. 'No one can argue if he walks the Walk. An' then I can tell him everything! So it'll be all right! An' if he don't walk to the end, then he ain't postmaster material anyway! Stanley? *Stanley!*'

Stanley awoke from a dream of pins. 'Yes, Mr Groat?'

'Got a few errands for you to run, lad.' And if he ain't postmaster material, Groat added in the privacy of his creaking brain, I'll die a junior postman . . .

It was hard to knock at a door whilst trying desperately not to make a sound, and in the end Crispin Horsefry gave up on the second aim and just swung on the doorknocker.

The noise echoed through the empty street, but no one came to their window. No one in this select street would have come to the window even if a murder was going on. At least in the poorer districts people would have come out to watch, or join in.

The door opened.

'Good evening, thur—'

Horsefry pushed past the stumpy figure and into the dark hallway, waving frantically to the servant to close the door.

'Shut it, man, shut it! I may have been followed— Good grief, you're an Igor, aren't you? Gilt can afford an Igor?'

'Well done, thur!' said the Igor. He peered out into the early evening darkness. 'All clear, thur.'

'Shut the door, for gods' sakes!' moaned Horsefry. 'I must see Mr Gilt!'

'The marthter ith having one of hith little thoireeth, thur,' said Igor. 'I will thee if he can be dithturbed.'

'Are any of the others here? Have they— What's a thwawreath?'

'A little get-together, thur,' said Igor, sniffing. The man reeked of drink.

'A soiree?'

'Exactly tho, thur,' said Igor impassively. 'May I take your highly notitheable long hooded cloak, thur? And be tho kind ath to follow me into the withdrawing room . . .'

And suddenly Horsefry was alone in a big room full of shadows and candlelight and staring eyes, with the door closing behind him.

The eyes belonged to the portraits in the big dusty frames that filled the walls, edge to edge. Rumour was that Gilt had bought them out-right, and not only the pictures; it was said that he'd bought all the rights in the long dead as well, deed-polled their names, and thus equipped himself with a proud pedigree overnight. That was slightly worrying, even for Horsefry. Everyone lied about their ancestors, and that was fair enough. Buying them was slightly disconcerting, but in its dark, original stylishness it was so very Reacher Gilt.

A lot of rumours had begun concerning Reacher Gilt, just as soon as people had noticed him and started asking, 'Who is Reacher Gilt? What kind of a name is Reacher, anyway?' He threw big parties, that was certain. They were the kind of parties that entered urban mythology (Was it true about the chopped liver? Were you there? What about the time when he brought in a troll stripper and three people jumped out of the window? Were you there? And that story about the bowl of sweets? Were you there? Did you see it? Was it true? *Were you there?*) Half of Ankh-Morpork had been, it seemed, drifting from table to buffet to dance floor to gaming tables, every guest seemingly followed by a silent and obliging waiter with a laden drinks tray. Some said he owned a gold mine, others swore that he was a pirate. And he certainly looked like a pirate, with his long curly black hair, pointed beard and eyepatch. He was even said to have a parrot. Certainly the piracy rumour might explain the apparently bottomless fortune and the fact that no one, absolutely no one, knew anything about him prior to his arrival in the city. Perhaps he'd sold his past, people joked, just like he'd bought himself a new one.

He was certainly piratical in his business dealing, Horsefry knew. Some of the things—

'*Twelve and a half per cent! Twelve and a half per cent!*'

When he was sure that he hadn't in fact had the heart attack he had been expecting all day, Horsefry crossed the room, swaying just like a man who's had a little drink or two to steady his nerves, and lifted the dark red cloth that, it turned out, concealed the parrot cage. It was in fact a cockatoo, and danced frantically up and down its perch.

'*Twelve and a half per cent! Twelve and a half per cent!*'

Horsefry grinned.

'Ah, you've met Alphonse,' said Reacher Gilt. 'And to what do I owe this unexpected pleasure, Crispin?' The door swung slowly behind him into its felt-lined frame, shutting out the sound of distant music.

Horsefry turned, the brief moment of amusement evaporating instantly into the fearful turmoil of his soul. Gilt, one hand in the pocket of a beautiful smoking jacket, gave him a quizzical look.

'I'm being spied on, Reacher!' Horsefry burst out. 'Vetinari sent one of—'

'Please! Sit down, Crispin. I think you require a large brandy.' He wrinkled his nose. 'Another large brandy, should I say?'

'I wouldn't say no! Had to have a little snifter, you know, just to calm m'nerves! What a day I've had!' Horsefry plumped down into a leather armchair. 'Did you know there was a watchman on duty outside the bank almost all afternoon?'

'A fat man? A sergeant?' said Gilt, handing him a glass.

'Fat, yes. I didn't notice his rank.' Horsefry sniffed. 'I've never had anything to do with the Watch.'

'I, on the other hand, have,' said Gilt, wincing to see very fine brandy drunk in the way Horsefry was drinking it. 'And I gather that Sergeant Colon is in the habit of loitering near large buildings not in case they are stolen, but in fact simply because he enjoys a quiet smoke out of the wind. He is a clown, and not to be feared.'

'Yes, but this morning one of the revenue officers came to see that old fool Cheeseborough—'

'Is that unusual, Crispin?' said Gilt soothingly. 'Let me top up your glass there . . .'

'Well, they come once or twice a month,' Horsefry conceded, thrusting out the empty brandy glass. 'But—'

'Not unusual, then. You're shying at flies, my dear Crispin.'

'Vetinari is spying on me!' Horsefry burst out. 'There was a man in black spying on the house this evening! I heard a noise and I looked out and I could see him standing in the corner of the garden!'

'A thief, perhaps?'

'No, I'm fully paid up with the Guild! I'm sure someone was in the house this afternoon, too. Things were moving in my study. I'm worried, Reacher! I'm the one who stands to lose here! If there's an audit—'

'You know there won't be, Crispin.' Gilt's voice was like honey.

'Yes, but I can't get my hands on all the paperwork, not yet, not until old Cheeseborough retires. And Vetinari's got lots of little, you know, what are they called . . . clerks, you know, who do nothing but look at li'l bits of paper! They'll work it out, they will! We bought the Grand Trunk wi' its own money!'

Gilt patted him on the shoulder. 'Calm yourself, Crispin. Nothing is going to go wrong. You think about money in the old-fashioned way. Money is not a thing, it is not even a process. It is a kind of shared dream. We dream that a small disc of common metal is worth the price of a substantial meal. Once you wake up from that dream, you can swim in a sea of money.'

The voice was almost hypnotic, but Horsefry's terror was driving him on. His forehead glistened.

'Then Greenyham's pissing in it!' he snapped, his little eyes aglint with desperate malice. 'You know that tower widdershins of Lancre that was giving all that trouble a coupla months ago? When we were tol' it was all due to witches flying into the towers? Hah! It w's only a witch the firs' time! Then Greenyham bribed a couple of the new men in the tower to call in a breakdown, and one of them rode like hell for the downstream tower and sen' him the Genua market figures a good two hours before everyone else got them! That's how he cornered dried prawns, you know. *And* dried fish maw and dried ground shrimp. It's not the firs' time he's done it, either! The man is coining it!'

Gilt looked at Horsefry, and wondered whether killing him now would be the best option. Vetinari was clever. You didn't stay ruler of a fermenting mess of a city like this one by being silly. If you saw his spy, it was a spy he wanted you to see. The way you'd know that Vetinari was keeping an eye on you would be by turning round very quickly and seeing no one at all.

Godsdamn Greenyham, too. Some people had no grasp, no grasp at all. They were so . . . *small*.

Using the clacks like that was stupid, but allowing a bottom-feeder like Horsefry to find out about it was indefensible. It was *silly*. Silly small people with the arrogance of kings, running their little swindles, smiling at the people they stole from, and not understanding money at all.

And stupid, pig-like Horsefry had come running here. That made it a little tricky. The door was soundproofed, the carpet was easily replaceable and, of course, Igors were renowned for their discretion, but almost certainly someone unseen had watched the man walk in and therefore it was prudent to ensure that he walked out.

'Y'r a goo' man, Reacher Gilt,' Horsefry hiccuped, waving the brandy glass unsteadily now that it was almost empty again. He put it down on a small table with the exaggerated care of a drunk, but since it was the wrong one of three images of the table sliding back and forth across his vision the glass smashed on the carpet.

'Sor' 'bout that,' he slurred. 'Y'r a goo' man, so I'm goin' to gi' you this. Can't keep it inna house, can't keep it, not wi' Vetininararari's spies on to me. Can't burn it neither, 'sgot everything in it. All the little . . . transactions. Ver' important. Can't trust the others, they hate me. You take care of it, eh?'

He pulled out a battered red journal and proffered it unsteadily. Gilt took it, and flicked it open. His eye ran down the entries.

'You wrote *everything* down, Crispin?' he said. 'Why?'

Crispin looked appalled. 'Got to keep records, Reacher,' he said. 'Can't cover y'tracks if you don't know where y'left 'em. Then . . . can put it all back, see, hardly a crime at all.' He tried to tap the side of his nose, and missed.

'I shall look after it with great care, Crispin,' said Gilt. 'You were very wise to bring it to me.'

'That means a lot t'me, Reacher,' said Crispin, now heading for the maudlin stage. 'You take me serioussoussly, not like Greenyham and his pals. I take the risks, then they treat me like drit. I mean dirt. Bloody goo' chap, you are. 'sfunny, y'know, you havin' an Igor, bloody goo' chap like you, 'cos—' He belched hugely. ' 'cos I heard that Igors only worked for mad chaps. Tot'ly bonkers chaps, y'know, and vampires and whatnot, people who're a few pennies short of a picnic. Nothing against your man, mark you, he looks a bloody fine fellow, hahaha, several bloody fine fellows . . .'

Reacher Gilt pulled him up gently. 'You're drunk, Crispin,' he said. 'And too talkative. Now, what I'm going to do is call Igor—'

'Yeth, thur?' said Igor behind him. It was the kind of service few could afford.

'—and he'll take you home in my coach. Make sure you deliver him safely to his valet, Igor. Oh, and when you've done that could you locate my colleague Mr Gryle? Tell him I have a little errand for him. Goodnight, Crispin.' Gilt patted the man on a wobbly cheek. 'And don't *worry*. Tomorrow you'll find all these little anxieties will have just . . . disappeared.'

'Ver' good chap,' Horsefry mumbled happily. 'F'r a foreigner . . .'

Igor took Crispin home. By that time the man had reached the 'jolly drunk' stage and was singing the kind of song that's hilarious to rugby players and children under the age of eleven, and getting him into his house must have awoken the neighbours, especially when he kept repeating the verse about the camel.

Then Igor drove back home, put the coach away, saw to the horse, and went to the little pigeon loft behind the house. These were big, plump pigeons, not the diseased roof rats of the city, and he selected a fat one, expertly slipped a silver message ring round its leg, and tossed it up into the night.

Ankh-Morpork pigeons were quite bright, for pigeons. Stupidity had a limited life in this city. This one would soon find Mr Gryle's rooftop lodgings, but it annoyed Igor that he never got his pigeons back.

Old envelopes rose up in drifts as Moist strode angrily, and sometimes waded angrily, through the abandoned rooms of the Post Office. He was in the mood to kick holes in walls. He was trapped. Trapped. He'd done his best, hadn't he? Perhaps there really was a curse on this place. Groat would be a good name for it—

He pushed open a door and found himself in the big coachyard round which the Post Office was bent like the letter U. It was still in use. When the postal service had collapsed the coach part had survived, Groat had said. It was useful and established and, besides, it owned scores of horses. You couldn't squash horses under the floor or bag them up in the attic. They had to be fed. More or less seamlessly, the coachmen had taken it over and run it as a passenger service.

Moist watched a laden coach roll out of the yard, and then movement up above caught his eye.

He had got used to the clacks towers now. Sometimes it seemed as though every roof sprouted one. Most were the new shutter boxes installed by the Grand Trunk Company, but old-fashioned arm semaphores and even signal flags were still well in evidence. Those, though, only worked slowly and by line-of-sight, and there was precious little space for that in the thrusting forest of towers. If you wanted more than the basic service, you went to one of the little clacks companies, and rented a small shutter tower with resident gargoyle to spot incoming messages and access to the bounce towers and, if you were really rich, a trained operator as well. And you *paid*. Moist had no grasp of or interest in technology, but as he understood it the price was something like an arm or a leg or both.

But these observations orbited his brain, as it were, like planetary thoughts around one central, solar thought: why the hell have *we* got a tower?

It was definitely on the roof. He could see it and he could hear the distant rattle of the shutters. And he was sure he'd seen a head, before it ducked out of sight.

Why have we got a tower up there, and who is using it?

He ran back inside. He'd never spotted a staircase to the roof, but then, who knew what was hidden behind some pile of letters at the end of some blocked corridor . . .

He squeezed his way along yet another passage lined with mail sacks, and came out into a space where big, bolted double doors led back to the yard. There were stairs there, leading upwards. Little safety lamps bled little pools of light into the blackness above. That was the

Post Office for you, Moist thought – the Regulations said the stairs must be lit and lit they were, decades after anyone ever used them except for Stanley, the lamplighter.

There was an old freight elevator here, too, one of those dangerous ones that worked by pumping water in and out of a big rainwater tank on the roof, but he couldn't work out how to make it go and wouldn't have trusted it if he could. Groat had said it was broken.

At the foot of the stairs, scuffed but still recognizable, was a chalk outline. The arms and legs were not in comfortable positions.

Moist swallowed, but gripped the banister.

He climbed.

There was a door on the first floor. It opened easily. It *burst* open at the mere touch of the handle, spilling pent-up mail out into the stairwell like some leaping monster. Moist swayed and whimpered as the letters slithered past him, shoal after shoal, and cascaded down the stairs.

Woodenly, he climbed up another flight, and found another dimly lit door, but this time he stood to one side as he opened it. The force of the letters still rammed it against his legs, and the noise of the dead letters was a dry whispering as they poured away into the gloom. Like bats, perhaps. This whole building full of dead letters, whispering to one another in the dark as a man fell to his death—

Any more of this and he'd end up like Groat, mad as a spoon. But there was more to this place. Somewhere there had to be a door—

His head was all over the wall . . .

Look, he said to his imagination, if this is how you're going to behave, I shan't bring you again.

But, with its usual treachery, it went on working. He'd never, ever, laid a finger on anyone. He'd always run rather than fight. And murder, now, surely murder was an absolute? You couldn't commit 0.021 of a murder, could you? But Pump seemed to think you could murder with a ruler. Okay, perhaps somewhere downstream people were . . . inconvenienced by a crime, but . . . what about bankers, landlords, even barmen? 'Here's your double brandy, sir, and I've 0.0003 killed you'? Everything everyone did affected everyone, sooner or later.

Besides, a lot of his crimes weren't even crimes. Take the ring trick, now. He never *said* it was a diamond ring. Besides, it was depressing how quickly honest citizens warmed to an opportunity to take advantage of a poor benighted traveller. It could ruin a man's faith in human nature, if he had one. Besides . . .

The third floor yielded another avalanche of letters, but when they subsided there was still a wall of paper plugging the corridor beyond. One or two rustling envelopes fell out, threatening a further fall as Moist advanced.

In fact it was retreat that was at the top of his mind, but the stairs were now layered with sliding envelopes and this was not the time to learn dry-slope skiing.

Well, the fifth floor would have to be clear, wouldn't it? How else could Sideburn have got to the stairs in order to meet his appointment with eternity? And, yes, there was still a piece of black and yellow rope on the fourth-floor landing, on a drift of letters. The Watch had been here. Nevertheless, Moist opened the door with care, as a watchman must have done.

One or two letters fell out, but the main slide had already taken place. A few feet beyond there was the familiar wall of letters, packed as tight as rock strata. A watchman had been in here, too. Someone had tried to break through the wordface, and Moist could see the hole. They'd put in their arm, full length, just as Moist was doing. Just like his, their fingertips had brushed against yet more compacted envelopes.

No one had got on to the stairs here. They would have had to walk through a wall of envelopes at least six feet thick . . .

There was one more flight. Moist climbed the stairs, cautiously, and was halfway up when he heard the slide begin, below him.

He must have disturbed the wall of letters on the floor below, somehow. It was emerging from the corridor with the unstoppability of a glacier. As the leading edge reached the stairwell, chunks of mail broke off and plunged into the depths. Far below, wood creaked and snapped. The stairway shivered.

Moist ran up the last few steps to the fifth floor, grabbed the door there, pulled it open and hung on as another mailslide poured past him. Everything was shaking now. There was a sudden crack as the rest of the staircase gave way and left Moist swinging from the handle, letters brushing past.

He swung there, eyes shut, until the noise and movement had more or less died away, although there was still the occasional creak from below.

The stairs had gone.

With great care, Moist brought his feet up until he could feel the edge of the new corridor. Without doing anything so provocative as breathing, he changed his grip on the door so that now he had hold of the handle on both sides. Slowly, he walked his heels through the drift of letters on the corridor floor, thus pulling the door closed, while at the same time getting *both* hands on to the inner handle.

Then he took a deep breath of the stale, dry air, scrabbled madly with his feet, bent his body like a hooked salmon and ended up with just enough of himself on the corridor floor to prevent a fall through sixty feet of letters and broken woodwork.

Barely thinking, he unhooked the lamp from the doorpost and turned to survey the task ahead.

The corridor was brightly lit, richly carpeted and completely free of mail. Moist stared.

There *had* been letters in there, wedged tight from floor to ceiling. He'd seen them, and felt them fall past him into the stairwell. They hadn't been a hallucination; they'd been solid, musty, dusty and real. To believe anything else now would be madness.

He turned back to look at the wreckage of the stairs and saw no doorway, no stairs. The carpeted floor extended all the way to the far wall.

Moist realized that there had to be an explanation for this, but the only one he could think of now was: it's strange. He reached down gingerly to touch the carpet where the stairwell should be, and felt a chill on his fingertips as they passed through it.

And he wondered: did one of the other new postmasters stand

here, just where I am? And did he walk out over what looked like solid floor and end up rolling down five flights of pain?

Moist inched his way along the corridor in the opposite direction, and sound began to grow. It was vague and generalized, the noise of a big building hard at work, shouts, conversations, the rattle of machinery, the crowded susurrus of a thousand voices and wheels and footfalls and stampings and scribblings and slammings all woven together in a huge space to become the pure audible texture of commerce.

The corridor opened out ahead of him, where it met a T-junction. The noise was coming from the brightly lit space beyond. Moist walked towards the shining brass railing of the balcony ahead—

—and stopped.

All right, the brain has been carried all the way up here at great expense; now it's time for it to do some work.

The hall of the Post Office was a dark cavern filled with mountains of mail. There were no balconies, no shining brasswork, no bustling staff and as sure as hell there were no customers.

The only time the Post Office could have looked like this was in the past, yes?

There was balconies, sir, all round the big hall on every floor, made of iron, like lace!

But they weren't in the present, not in the here and now. But he wasn't in the past, not exactly. His fingers had felt a stairwell when his eyes had seen carpeted floor.

Moist decided that he was standing in the here and now but seeing in the here and then. Of course, you'd have to be mad to believe it, but this *was* the Post Office.

Poor Mr Sideburn had stepped out on to a floor that wasn't there any more.

Moist stopped before stepping out on to the balcony, reached down, and felt the chill on his fingertips once again as they went through the carpet. Who was it – oh, yes, Mr Mutable. He'd stood here, rushed to look down and—

—*smack, sir, smack on to the marble.*

Moist stood up carefully, steadied himself against the wall, and peered gingerly into the big hall.

Chandeliers hung from the ceiling, but they were unlit because sunlight was pouring through the sparkling dome on to a scene innocent of pigeon droppings but alive with people, scuttling across the chequerboard floor or hard at work behind the long polished counters *made of rare wood, my dad said*. Moist stood and stared.

It was a scene made up of a hundred purposeful activities that fused happily into a great anarchy. Below him big wire baskets on wheels were being manhandled across the floor, sacks of letters were being tipped on moving belts, clerks were feverishly filling the pigeon-holes. It was a machine, made of people, *sir, you should've seen it!*

Away to Moist's left, at the far end of the hall, was a golden statue three or four times life size. It was of a slim young man, obviously a god, wearing nothing more than a hat with wings on, sandals with wings on and – Moist squinted – a fig leaf with wings on? He'd been caught by the sculptor as he was about to leap into the air, carrying an envelope and wearing an expression of noble purpose.

It dominated the hall. It wasn't there in the present day; the dais was unoccupied. If the counters and the chandeliers had gone, a statue that even *looked* like gold must've stood no chance. It had probably been *The Spirit of the Post*, or something.

Meanwhile, the mail down there was moving more prosaically.

Right under the dome was a clock with a face pointing in each of the four directions. As Moist watched it, the big hand clanked to the top of the hour.

A horn blew. The frantic ballet ceased as, somewhere below Moist, some doors opened and two lines of men in *the uniforms, sir, royal blue with brass buttons! You should've* seen *them!* marched into the hall in two lines and stood to attention in front of the big doors. A large man, in a rather grander version of the uniform and with a face like toothache, was waiting there for them; he wore a large hourglass hanging in a gimballed brass cage at his belt, and he looked at the waiting men as if he had seen worse sights but not often and even then only on the soles of his enormous boots.

He held up the hourglass with an air of evil satisfaction, and took a deep breath before roaring: 'Numbahhh Four Delivereeee . . . stand!'

The words reached Moist's ears slightly muffled, as though he was hearing them through cardboard. The postmen, already at attention, contrived to look even more alert. The big man glared at them and took another huge gulp of air.

'Numbahhh Four Delivereeee *wait for it, wait for it!* . . . DELIVAAAAAAAAH!'

The two lines marched past him and out into the day.

Once, we were postmen . . .

I've got to find a real stairway, Moist thought, pushing himself away from the edge. I'm . . . hallucinating the past. But I'm standing in the present. It's like sleepwalking. I don't want to walk out on to fresh air and end up as one more chalk outline.

He turned round, and someone walked right through him.

The sensation was unpleasant, like a sudden snap of fever. But that wasn't the worst part. The worst part is seeing someone's head walk through yours. The view is mostly grey, with traces of red and hollow hints of sinus. You would not wish to know about the eyeballs.

. . . face all contorted like he'd seen a ghost . . .

Moist's stomach heaved, and as he turned with his hand over his mouth he saw a young postman looking in his general direction with a look of horror that probably reflected the one on the unseen Moist's face. Then the boy shivered, and hurried away.

So Mr Ignavia had got this far, too. He'd been smart enough to work out the floor but seeing another head going through your own, well, that could take you the wrong way . . .

Moist ran after the boy. Up here, he was lost; he must have toured less than a tenth of the building with Groat, the way constantly being blocked by glaciers of mail. There were other stairs, he knew, and they still existed in the present. Ground level, that was the goal: a floor you could rely on.

The boy went through a door and into what looked like a room full of parcels, but Moist could see an open doorway at the far end, and a hint of banister. He speeded up, and the floor disappeared from under his feet.

The light vanished. He was briefly and horribly aware of dry letters all around him, falling with him. He landed on more letters, choking as dry, ancient mail piled up about him. For a moment, through the rain of paper, he caught a glimpse of a dusty window half covered with letters, and then he was submerged again. The heap under him began to move, slipping down and sideways. There was the crack of what could have been a door being burst off its hinges and the sideways flow increased noticeably. He struck out madly for the surface in time for his head to hit the top of a door jamb and then the current dragged him under.

Helpless now, tumbling in the river of paper, Moist dimly felt the jolt as a floor gave way. The mail poured through, taking him with it and slamming him into another drift of envelopes. Sight disappeared as thousands of letters thudded down on top of him, and then sound died, too.

Darkness and silence squeezed him in a fist.

Moist von Lipwig knelt with his head resting on his arms. There was air here but it was warm and stale and wouldn't last long. He couldn't move more than a finger.

He could die here. He *would* die here. There must be tons of mail around him.

'I commend my soul to any god who can find it,' he mumbled, in the stifling air.

A line of blue danced across his inner vision.

It was handwriting. But it spoke.

'Dear Mother, I have arrived safely and found good lodgings at...'

The voice sounded like a country boy but it had a . . . a *scritchy* quality to it. If a letter could talk, it would sound like that. The words rambled on, the characters curving and slanting awkwardly under the pen of a reluctant writer—

—and as it ran on another line also began to write across the dark, crisply and neatly:

Dear Sir, I have the honour to inform you that I am the sole executor of the estate of the late Sir Davie Thrills, of The Manor, Mixed Blessings, and it appears that you are the sole . . .'

The voice continued in words so clipped that you could *hear* the shelves full of legal books behind the desk, but a third line was beginning.

'Dear Mrs Clark, I much regret to inform you that in an engagement with the enemy yesterday your husband, C. Clark, fought valiantly but was . . .'

And then they all wrote at once. Voices in their dozens, their hundreds, their thousands, filled his ears and squiggled across his inner vision. They didn't shout, they just unrolled the words until his head was full of sound, which formed *new* words, just as all the instruments of an orchestra tinkle and scrape and blast to produce one climax—

Moist tried to scream, but envelopes filled his mouth.

And then a hand closed on his leg and he was in the air and upside down.

'Ah, Mr Lipvig!' boomed the voice of Mr Pump. 'You Have Been Exploring! Welcome To Your New Office!'

Moist spat out paper and sucked air into stinging lungs.

'They're . . . alive!' he gasped. 'They're all *alive*! And angry! They talk! It was *not* a hallucination! I've had hallucinations and they don't hurt! I know how the others died!'

'I Am Happy For You, Mr Lipvig,' said Pump, turning him the right way up and wading waist deep across the room, while behind them more mail trickled through a hole in the ceiling.

'You don't understand! They talk! They want . . .' Moist hesitated. He could still hear the whispering in his head. He said, as much to himself as for the benefit of the golem, 'It's as though they want to be . . . read.'

'That Is The Function Of A Letter,' said Pump calmly. 'You Will See That I Have Almost Cleared Your Apartment.'

'Listen, they're just paper! And they *talked*!'

'Yes,' rumbled the golem ponderously. 'This Place Is A Tomb Of Unheard Words. They Strive To Be Heard.'

'Oh, come on! Letters are just paper. They can't *speak*!'

'I Am Just Clay, And I Listen,' said Pump, with the same infuriating calm.

'Yes, but you've got added mumbo-jumbo—'

The red fire rose behind Pump's eyes as he turned to stare at Moist.

'I went . . . backwards in time, I think,' Moist mumbled, backing away. 'In . . . my head. That's how Sideburn died. He fell down stairs that weren't there in the past. And Mr Ignavia died of fright. I'm sure of it! But I was inside the letters! And there must have been a . . . a hole in the floor, or something, and that . . . I fell, and I . . .' He stopped. 'This place needs a priest, or a wizard. Someone who understands this kind of stuff. Not me!'

The golem scooped up two armfuls of the mail that had so recently entombed his client.

'You Are The Postmaster, Mr Lipwig,' he said.

'That's just Vetinari's trick! I'm no postman, I'm just a fraud—'

'Mr Lipwig?' said a nervous voice from the doorway behind him. He turned and saw the boy Stanley, who flinched at his expression.

'Yes?' snapped Moist. 'What the hell do you— What do you want, Stanley? I'm a little busy right now.'

'There's some men,' said Stanley, grinning uncertainly. 'They're downstairs. Some men.'

Moist glared at him, but Stanley seemed to have finished for now.

'And these men want . . . ?' he prompted.

'They want you, Mr Lipwig,' said Stanley. 'They said they want to see the man who wants to be postmaster.'

'I don't *want* to be—' Moist began, but gave up. There was no point in taking it out on the boy.

'Excuse Me, Postmaster,' said the golem behind him. 'I Wish To Complete My Allotted Task.'

Moist stood aside as the clay man walked out into the corridor, the old boards groaning under his enormous feet. Outside, you could see how he'd managed to clean out the office. The walls of other rooms were bowed out almost to the point of exploding. When a golem pushes things into a room, they stay pushed.

The sight of the plodding figure calmed Moist down a little. There was something intensely . . . well, down-to-earth about Mr Pump.

What he needed now was normality, normal people to talk to, normal things to do to drive the voices out of his head. He brushed fragments of paper off his increasingly greasy suit.

'All right,' he said, trying to find his tie, which had ended up hanging down his back. 'I shall see what they want.'

They were waiting on the half-landing on the big staircase. They were old men, thin and bowed, like slightly older copies of Groat. They had the same ancient uniform, but there was something odd about them.

Each man had the skeleton of a pigeon wired on to the top of his peaked hat.

'Be you the Unfranked Man?' growled one of them, as he approached.

'What? Who? Am I?' said Moist. Suddenly, the idea of normality was ebbing again.

'Yes, you are, sir,' whispered Stanley beside him. 'You have to say yes, sir. Gosh, sir, I wish it was me doing this.'

'Doing what?'

'For the second time: be you the Unfranked Man?' said the old man, looking angry. Moist noticed that he was missing the top joints on the middle fingers of his right hand.

'I suppose so. If you insist,' he said. This didn't meet with any approval at all.

'For the last time: be you the Unfranked Man?' This time there was real menace in the voice.

'Yes, all right! For the purposes of this conversation, yes! I *am* the Unfranked Man!' Moist shouted. 'Now can we—'

Something black was dropped over his head from behind and he felt strings pulled tightly round his neck.

'The Unfranked Man is tardy,' crackled another elderly voice, in his ear, and unseen but tough hands took hold of him. 'No postman *he*!'

'You'll be fine, sir,' said the voice of Stanley, as Moist struggled. 'Don't worry. Mr Groat will guide you. You'll do it easily, sir.'

'Do what?' said Moist. 'Let go of me, you daft old devils!'

'The Unfranked Man dreads the Walk,' one assailant hissed.

'Aye, the Unfranked Man will be Returned to Sender in no short order,' said another.

'The Unfranked Man must be weighed in the balance,' said a third.

'Stanley, fetch Mr Pump right now!' shouted Moist, but the hood was thick and clinging.

'Mustn't do that, sir,' said Stanley. 'Mustn't do that at all, sir. It will be all right, sir. It's just a . . . a test, sir. It's the Order of the Post, sir.'

Funny hats, Moist thought, and began to relax. Hoodwinks and threats . . . I *know* this stuff. It's mysticism for tradesmen. There's not a city in the world without its Loyal and Ancient and Justified and Hermetic Order of little men who think they can reap the secrets of the ancients for a couple of hours every Thursday night and don't realize what prats they look in a robe. I should know – I must have joined a dozen of 'em myself. I bet there's a secret handshake. I know more secret handshakes than the gods. I'm in about as much danger as I would be in a class of five-year-olds. Less, probably. Unfranked Man . . . good grief.

He relaxed. He let himself be led down the stairs, and turned round. Ah, yes, that's right. You've got to make the initiate fear, but everyone knows it's just a party game. It'll *sound* bad, it might even *feel* bad, but it won't *be* bad. He remembered joining – what was it?

Oh yes – the Men of the Furrow, in some town out in the stalks.* He had been blindfolded, of course, and the Men had made all the horrific noises they could imagine, and then a voice in the darkness had said, 'Shake hands with the Old Master!' and Moist had reached out and shaken a goat's foot. Those who got out of there with clean pants won.

Next day he'd swindled three of his trusting new Brothers out of eighty dollars. That didn't seem quite so funny now.

The old postmen were taking him into the big hall. He could tell by the echoes. And there were other people there, according to those little hairs on the back of his neck. Not just people, maybe; he thought he heard a muffled growl. But that was how it went, right? Things had to sound worrying. The key was to be bold, to act brave and forthright.

His escorts left him. Moist stood in darkness for a moment, and then felt a hand grasp his elbow.

'It's me, sir. Probationary Senior Postman Groat, sir. Don't you worry about a thing, sir. I'm your Temporary Deacon for tonight, sir.'

'Is this necessary, Mr Groat?' sighed Moist. 'I *was* appointed postmaster, you know.'

'Appointed, yes. Accepted, not yet, sir. Proof of posting is not proof of delivery, sir.'

'What *are* you talking about?'

'Can't tell secrets to an Unfranked Man, sir,' said Groat piously. 'You've done well to get this far, sir.'

'Oh, all right,' said Moist, trying to sound jovial. 'What's the worst that can happen, eh?'

Groat was silent.

'I said—' Moist began.

'I was just working that out, sir,' said Groat. 'Let's see . . . yes, sir. The worst that can happen is you lose all your fingers on one hand, are crippled for life, and break half the bones in your body. Oh, and then they don't let you join. But don't you worry about a thing, sir, not a thing!'

---

* In areas more wooded, areas less dominated by the cabbage and general brassica industry, it would of course have been in the sticks.

Up ahead, a voice boomed: 'Who brings the Unfranked Man?'

Beside Moist, Groat cleared his throat and, when he spoke, his voice actually shook.

'I, probationary Senior Postman Tolliver Groat, do bring the Unfranked Man.'

'You did say that about the bones to frighten me, right?' hissed Moist.

'And does he stand in the Gloom of Night?' the voice demanded.

'He does now, Worshipful Master!' shouted Groat happily, and whispered to the hooded Moist, 'Some of the old boys are really happy about you getting the sign back.'

'Good. Now, these broken bones you mentioned—'

'Then let him walk the Walk!' the unseen voice commanded.

'We're just going to walk forward, sir. Easy does it,' Groat whispered urgently. 'That's it. Stop here.'

'Look,' said Moist, 'all that stuff . . . that *was* just to scare me, right?'

'You leave it to me, sir,' Groat whispered.

'But listen, the—' Moist began, and had a mouthful of hood.

'Let him don the Boots!' the voice went on.

Amazing how you can *hear* the capital letters, Moist thought, trying not to choke on the cloth.

'Pair of boots right in front of you, sir,' came Groat's hoarse whisper. 'Put 'em on. No problem, sir.'

'Pff! Yes, but listen—'

'The boots, sir, please!'

Moist removed his shoes, very clumsily, and slid his feet into the invisible boots. They turned out to be as heavy as lead.

'The Walk of the Unfranked Man is Heavy,' the booming voice intoned. 'Let him continue!'

Moist took another step forward, trod on something which rolled, stumbled headlong and felt a stab of agony as his shins hit metal.

'Postmen,' the booming voice demanded again, 'what is the First Oath?'

Voices sang out from the darkness, in chorus: '*Strewth, would you bleedin' credit it? Toys, prams, garden tools . . . they don't care what they leaves out on the path on these dark mornings!'*

'Did the Unfranked Man cry out?' the voice said.

I think I've broken my chin, Moist thought, as Groat dragged him to his feet. I think I've broken my *chin*! The old man hissed: 'Well done, sir,' and then raised his voice to add for the benefit of the unseen watchers: 'He crydeth out not, Worshipful Master, but was resolute!'

'Then give unto him the Bag!' boomed the distant voice. Moist was beginning to loathe it.

Unseen hands put a strap round Moist's neck. When they let go, the weight on it bent him double.

'The Postman's Bag is Heavy, but soon it shall be Light!' echoed off the walls. No one had said anything about pain, Moist thought. Well, actually they had, but they didn't say they *meant* it—

'On we go, sir,' Groat urged, invisible at his side. 'This is the Postman's Walk, remember!'

Moist edged forward, very carefully, and felt something rattle away.

'He trod not upon the Roller Skate, Worshipful Master!' Groat reported to the invisible watchers.

Moist, aching but heartened, tried two more hesitant steps, and there was another rattle as something bounced off his boot.

'The Carelessly Abandoned Beer Bottle impeded him not!' Groat yelled triumphantly.

Emboldened, Moist essayed a further step, trod on something slippery, and felt his foot head off and up without him. He landed heavily on his back, his head thumping on the floor. He was sure he heard his own skull crack.

'Postmen, what is the Second Oath?' the echoing voice commanded.

'*Dogs! I tell you, there's no such thing as a good one! If they don't bite they all crap! It's as bad as stepping on machine oil!*'

Moist got to his knees, head spinning.

'That's right, that's right, you keeps goin'!' hissed Groat, grabbing his elbow. 'You get through, come rain or shine!' He lowered his voice even further. 'Remember what it says on the building!'

'Mrs Cake?' Moist mumbled, and then thought: was it rain or snow? Or sleet? He heard movement and hunched over the heavy bag as the water drenched him and an over-enthusiastic bucket bounced off his head.

Rain, then. He straightened up just in time to feel biting coldness slither down the back of the neck, and nearly screamed.

'That was ice cubes,' Groat whispered. 'Got 'em from the mortuary but don't you worry, sir, they was hardly used . . . best we can do for snow, this time of year. Sorry! Don't you worry about a thing, sir!'

'Let the Mail be tested!' bellowed the all-commanding voice.

Groat's hand plunged into the bag while Moist staggered in a circle, and he raised a letter triumphantly.

'I, probationary Senior— Oh, excuse me just a tick, Worshipful Master . . .' Moist felt his head being pulled down to the level of Groat's mouth, and the old man whispered: 'Was that probationary or *full* Senior Postman, sir?'

'What? Oh, full, yes, full!' said Moist, as iced water filled his shoes. 'Definitely!'

'I, *Senior* Postman Groat, do declare the mail to be as dry as a bone, Worshipful Master!' shouted Groat triumphantly.

This time the cracked voice of authority held a hint of gleeful menace.

'*Then let him . . . deliver it.*'

In the stifling gloom of the hood, Moist's sense of danger barred the door and hid in the cellar. This was where the unseen chanters leaned forward. This was where it stopped being a game.

'I haven't actually written anything down, mark you,' he began, swaying.

'Careful now, careful,' hissed Groat, ignoring him. 'Nearly there! There's a door right in front of you, there's a letter box— Could he take a breather, Worshipful Master? He caught his head a nasty crack—'

'A breather, Brother Groat? So's you can give him another hint or two, maybe?' said the presiding voice, with scorn.

'Worshipful Master, the rituals says that the Unfranked Man is allowed a—' Groat protested.

'This Unfranked Man walketh alone! On his tod, Tolliver Groat! He doesn't want to be a Junior Postman, oh no, nor even a Senior Postman, not him! He wants to achieve the rank of Postmaster all in one go! We're not playing Postman's Knock here, Junior Postman Groat! You talked us into this! We are *not* mucking about! He's got to show he's worth it!'

'That's *Senior* Postman Groat, thank you so very much!' Groat yelled.

'You ain't a proper Senior Postman, Tolliver Groat, not if he fails the test!'

'Yeah? And who says you're Worshipful Master, George Aggy? You're only Worshipful Master 'cos you got first crack at the robes!'

The Worshipful Master's voice become a little less commanding. 'You're a decent bloke, Tolliver, I'll give you that, but all this stuff you spout about a real postmaster turning up one day and making it all better is just . . . silly! Look at this place, will you? It's had its day. We all have. But if you're going to be pig-headed, we'll do it according to the book of rules!'

'Right, then!' said Groat.

'Right, then!' echoed the Worshipful Master.

A secret society of *postmen*, Moist thought. I mean, *why?*

Groat sighed, and leaned closer. 'There's going to be a bloody row after we're finished,' he hissed to Moist. 'Sorry about this, sir. Just post the letter. I *believe* in you, sir!'

He stepped back.

In the dark night of the hood, stunned and bleeding, Moist shuffled forward, arms outstretched. His hands found the door, and ran across it in a vain search for the slot. Eventually they found it a foot above the ground.

Okay, okay, ram a damn letter in there and get this stupid pantomime over with.

But it wasn't a game. This wasn't one of those events where everyone knew that old Harry just had to mouth the right words to be the latest member of the Loyal Order of Chair Stuffers. There were people out there taking it *seriously*.

Well, he just had to post a letter through a slot, didn't he? How hard could that b— Hold on, hold on . . . wasn't one of the men who'd led him down here missing the tips of his fingers on one hand?

Suddenly, Moist was angry. It even sheared through the pain from his chin. He didn't have to do this! At least, he didn't have to do it *like* this. It would be a poor lookout if he wasn't a better player of *les buggeures risibles* than this bunch of old fools!

He straightened up, stifling a groan, and pulled off the hood. There was still darkness all around him, but it was punctuated by the glow from the doors of a dozen or so dark lanterns.

' 'ere, 'e's taken the hood off!' someone shouted.

'The Unfranked Man may choose to remain in darkness,' said Moist. 'But the Postman loves the Light.'

He pitched the voice right. It was the key to a thousand frauds. You had to sound right, sound like you knew what you were doing, sound like you were in charge. And, while he'd spoken gibberish, it was authentic gibberish.

The door of a lantern opened a little wider and a plaintive voice said, ' 'ere, I can't find that in the book. Where's he supposed to say that?'

You had to move quickly, too. Moist wrapped the hood round his hand and levered up the flap of the letter box. With his other hand he grabbed a random letter out of the bag, flicked it through the slot and then pulled his makeshift glove away. It ripped as though cut by shears.

'Postmen, what is the Third Oath?' shouted Groat triumphantly. 'All together, lads: *Strewth, what do they make these flaps out of, razor blades?*'

There was a resentful silence.

'He never had 'is 'ood on,' muttered a robed figure.

'Yes he did! He wrapped it round his hand! Tell me where it says he can't do that!' screamed Groat. 'I told you! He's the One we've been waiting for!'

'There's still the final test,' said the Worshipful Master.

'What final test are you goin' on about, George Aggy? He delivered the mail!' Groat protested. 'Lord Vetinari appointed him postmaster and he's walked the Walk!'

'Vetinari? He's only been around five minutes! Who's he to say who's postmaster? Was his father a postman? No! Or his grandfather? Look at the men he's been sending! You said they were sneaky devils who didn't have a drop of Post Office ink in their blood!'

'I think this one might be able to—' Groat began.

'He can take the ultimate test,' said the Worshipful Master sternly. 'You know what that is.'

'It'll be murder!' said Groat. 'You can't—'

'I ain't telling you again, young Tolly, you just shut your mouth! Well, Mister Postmaster? Will you face the postman's greatest challenge? Will you face . . .' the voice paused for effect and just in case there might be a few bars of portentous music, 'the Enemy at the Gate?'

'Face it and o'ercome it, if you demand it!' said Moist. The fool had called him Postmaster! It was working! Sound as if you're in charge and they start to believe it! Oh, and 'o'er' had been a good touch, too.

'We do! Oh yes, we do!' chorused the robed postmen.

Groat, a bearded shadow in the gloom, took Moist's hand and, to his amazement, shook it.

'Sorry about this, Mr Lipwig,' he said. 'Din't expect this at all. They're cheating. But you'll be fine. You just rely on *Senior Postman* Groat, sir.'

He drew his hand away, and Moist felt something small and cold in his palm. He closed his fist over it. Didn't expect it at *all*?

'Right, *Postmaster*,' said the Worshipful Master. 'This is a simple test. All *you* have to do, right, is still be standing here, on your feet, in one minute's time, all right? Run for it, lads!'

There was a swishing of robes and scurrying of feet and a distant door slammed. Moist was left standing in silent, pigeon-smelling gloom.

What other test could there be? He tried to remember all the words on the front of the building. Trolls? Dragons? Green things with teeth? He opened his hand to see what it was that Groat had slipped him.

It looked very much like a whistle.

Somewhere in the darkness a door opened, and shut again. It was followed by the distant sound of paws moving purposefully.

Dogs.

Moist turned and ran down the hall to the plinth, and scrambled on to it. It wouldn't be much of a problem for large dogs, but at least it would put their heads at kicking height.

Then there was a bark, and Moist's face broke into a smile. You only ever needed to hear that bark once. It wasn't a particularly aggressive one, because it was made by a mouth capable of crushing a skull. You didn't need too much extra advertising when you could do that. News got around.

This was going to be … ironic. They'd actually got hold of Lipwigzers!

Moist waited until he could see the eyes in the lantern light before he said, 'Schlat!'

The dogs stopped, and stared at Moist. Clearly, they were thinking, something is wrong here. He sighed, and slipped down off the pedestal.

'Look,' he said, placing a hand on each rump and exerting downward pressure. 'One fact everyone knows is that no female Lipwigzers have ever been let out of the country. That keeps the breed price high … Schlat! I said! … and every puppy is trained to Lipwigzian commands! This is the old country talking, boys! Schlat!'

The dogs sat down instantly.

'Good boys,' said Moist. It was true what people like his grandfather said: once you got past their ability to bite through a whole leg in one go, they were very nice animals.

He cupped his hands and shouted: 'Gentlemen? It's safe for you to come in now!' The postmen would be listening, that was certain. They'd be waiting for snarls and screams.

The distant door opened.

'Come forward!' snapped Moist. The dogs turned to look at the huddle of approaching postmen. They growled, too, in one long, uninterrupted rumble.

Now he could see the mysterious Order clearly. They were robed, of course, because you couldn't have a secret order without robes. They had pushed the hoods back now, and each man* was wearing a peaked cap with a bird skeleton wired to it.

'Now, sir, we *knew* Tolliver'd slip you the dog whistle—' one of them began, looking nervously at the Lipwigzers.

'This?' said Moist, opening his hand. 'I didn't use it. It only makes 'em angry.'

The postmen stared at the sitting dogs.

'But you got 'em to sit—' one began.

'I can get them to do other things,' said Moist levelly. 'I just have to say the word.'

'Er ... there's a couple of lads outside with muzzles, if it's all the same to you, sir,' said Groat, as the Order backed away. 'We're heridititerrilyly wary of dogs. It's a postman thing.'

'I can assure you that the control my voice has over them at the moment is stronger than steel,' said Moist. This was probably garbage, but it was *good* garbage.

The growl from one of the dogs had taken on the edge it tended to get just before the creature became a tooth-tipped projectile.

'Vodit!' shouted Moist. 'Sorry about this, gentlemen,' he added. 'I think you make them nervous. They can smell fear, as you probably know.'

'Look, we're really sorry, all right?' said the one whose voice suggested to Moist that he had been the Worshipful Master. 'We had to be sure, all right?'

'I'm the postmaster, then?' said Moist.

'Absolutely, sir. No problem at all. Welcome, O Postmaster!'

Quick learner, Moist thought.

'I think I'll just—' he began, as the double doors opened at the other end of the hall.

Mr Pump entered, carrying a large box. It should be quite hard to open a big pair of doors while carrying something in both hands, but not if you're a golem. They just walk at them. The doors can choose to open or try to stay shut, it's up to them.

---

* Women are always significantly under-represented in secret orders.

The dogs took off like fireworks. The postmen took off in the opposite direction, climbing on to the dais behind Moist with commendable speed for such elderly men.

Mr Pump plodded forward, crushing underfoot the debris of the Walk. He rocked as the creatures struck him, and then patiently put down the box and picked up the dogs by the scruff of their necks.

'There Are Some Gentlemen Outside With Nets And Gloves And Extremely Thick Clothing, Mr Lipvig,' he said. 'They Say They Work For A Mr Harry King. They Want To Know If You Have Finished With These Dogs.'

'Harry King?' said Moist.

'He's a big scrap merchant, sir,' said Groat. 'I expect the dogs was borrowed off of him. He turns 'em loose in his yards at night.'

'No burglar gets in, eh?'

'I think he's quite happy if they get *in*, sir. Saves having to feed the dogs.'

'Hah! Please take them away, Mr Pump,' said Moist. Lipwigzers! It had been so *easy*.

As they watched the golem turn round with a whimpering dog under each arm, he added: 'Mr King must be doing well, then, to run Lipwigzers as common guard dogs!'

'Lipwigzers? Harry King? Bless you, sir, old Harry wouldn't buy posh foreign dogs when he can buy crossbreeds, not him!' said Groat. 'Probably a *bit* of Lipwigzer in 'em, I dare say, probably the worst bits. Hah, a purebred Lipwigzer prob'ly wouldn't last five minutes against some of the mongrels in *our* alleys. Some of 'em has got *crocodile* in 'em.'

There was a moment of silence and then Moist said, in a faraway voice: 'So . . . definitely not imported purebreds, you think?'

'Bet your life on it, sir,' said Groat cheerfully. 'Is there a problem, sir?'

'What? Um . . . no. Not at all.'

'You sounded a bit disappointed, sir. Or something.'

'No. I'm fine. No problem.' Moist added, thoughtfully: 'You know, I really have *got* to get some laundry done. And perhaps some new shoes . . .'

The doors swung open again to reveal, not the return of the dogs, but Mr Pump once more. He picked up the box he'd left and headed on towards Moist.

'Well, we'll be off,' said the Worshipful Master. 'Nice to have met you, Mr Lipwig.'

'That's it?' said Moist. 'Isn't there a ceremony or something?'

'Oh, that's Tolliver, that is,' said the Worshipful Master. 'I like to see the old place still standing, really I do, but it's all about the clacks these days, isn't it? Young Tolliver thinks it can all be got going again, but he was just a lad when it all broke down. You can't fix some things, Mr Lipwig. Oh, you can call yourself postmaster, but where'd you start to get this lot back working? It's an old fossil, sir, just like us.'

'Your Hat, Sir,' said Pump.

'What?' said Moist, and turned to where the golem was standing by the dais, patiently, with a hat in his hands.

It was a postman's peaked hat, in gold, with golden wings. Moist took it, and saw how the gold was just paint, cracked and peeling, and the wings were real dried pigeon wings and almost crumbled to the touch. As the golem had held it up in the light it had gleamed like something from some ancient tomb. In Moist's hands, it crackled and smelled of attics and shed golden flakes. Inside the brim, on a stained label, were the words 'Boult & Locke, Military and Ceremonial Outfitters, Peach Pie Street, A-M. Size: 7¼'

'There Is A Pair Of Boots With Wings, Too,' said Mr Pump, 'And Some Sort Of Elasticated—'

'Don't bother about that bit!' said Groat excitedly. 'Where did you find that stuff? We've been looking everywhere! For *years*!'

'It Was Under The Mail In The Postmaster's Office, Mr Groat.'

'Couldn't have been, couldn't have been!' Groat protested. 'We've sifted through there dozens of times! I seen every inch o' carpet in there!'

'A lot of mail, er, moved about today,' said Moist.

'That Is Correct,' said the golem. 'Mr Lipvig Came Through The Ceiling.'

'Ah, so he found it, eh?' said Groat triumphantly. 'See? It's all coming true! The prophecy!'

'There is no prophecy, Tolliver,' said the Worshipful Master, shaking his head sadly. 'I know you think there is, but wishing that someone will come along and sort this mess out one day is not the same as a prophecy. Not really.'

'We've been hearing the letters talking again!' said Groat. 'They whisper in the night. We have to read them the Regulations to keep 'em quiet. Just like the wizard said!'

'Yes, well, you know what we used to say: you *do* have to be mad to work here!' said the Worshipful Master. 'It's all over, Tolliver. It really is. The city doesn't even *need* us any more.'

'You put that hat on, Mr Lipwig!' said Groat. 'It's fate, that turning up like this. You just put it on and see what happens!'

'Well, if everyone's happy about it . . .' Moist mumbled. He held the hat above his head, but hesitated.

'Nothing is going to happen, is it?' he said. 'Only I've had a very strange day . . .'

'No, nothing's going to happen,' said the Worshipful Master. 'It never does. Oh, we all thought it would, once. Every time someone said they'd put the chandeliers back or deliver the mail we thought, maybe it's ended, maybe it really *is* going to work this time. And young Tolliver there, you made him happy when you put the sign back. Got him excited. Made *him* think it'd work this time. It never does, though, 'cos this place is cursèd.'

'That's cursed with an extra ed?'

'Yes, sir. The worst kind. No, put your hat on, sir. It'll keep the rain off, at least.'

Moist prepared to lower the hat, but as he did so he was aware that the old postmen were drawing back.

'You're not sure!' Moist yelled, waving a finger. 'You're not *actually* sure, are you! All of you! You're thinking, hmm, maybe this time it *will* work, right? You're holding your breath! I can tell! Hope is a terrible thing, gentlemen!'

He lowered the hat.

'Feeling anything?' said Groat, after a while.

'It's a bit . . . scratchy,' said Moist.

'Ah, that'd be some amazing mystic force leakin' out, eh?' said Groat desperately.

'I don't think so,' said Moist. 'Sorry.'

'Most of the postmasters I served under hated wearing that thing,' said the Worshipful Master, as everyone relaxed. 'Mind you, you've got the height to carry it off. Postmaster Atkinson was only five feet one, and it made him look broody.' He patted Moist on the shoulder. 'Never mind, lad, you did your best.'

An envelope bounced off his head. As he brushed it away another one landed on his shoulder, and slid off.

Around the group, letters started to land on the floor like fish dropped by a passing tornado.

Moist looked up. The letters were falling down from the darkness, and the drizzle was turning into a torrent.

'Stanley? Are you . . . messing about up there?' Groat ventured, almost invisible in the paper sleet.

'I always said those attics didn't have strong enough floors,' moaned the Worshipful Master. 'It's just a mailstorm again. We made too much noise, that's all. C'mon, let's get out while we can, eh?'

'Then put those lanterns out! They ain't safety lights!' shouted Groat.

'We'll be groping around in the dark, lad!'

'Oh, you'd rather see by the light of a burning roof, would you?'

The lanterns winked out . . . and by the darkness they now shed Moist von Lipwig saw the writing on the wall or, at least, hanging in the air just in front of it. The hidden pen swooped through the air in loops and curves, drawing its glowing blue letters behind it.

Moist von Lipwig? it wrote.

'Er . . . yes?'

You are the Postmaster!

'Look, I'm not the One you're looking for!'

Moist von Lipwig, at a time like this any One will do!

'But . . . but . . . I am not worthy!'

Acquire worth with speed, Moist von Lipwig!

Bring back the light! Open the doors! Stay not the messengers about their business!

Moist looked down at the golden light coming up from around his feet. It sparkled off his fingertips and began to fill him up from inside, like fine wine. He felt his feet leave the dais as the words lifted him up and spun him gently.

In the beginning was a Word, but what is a word without its messenger, Moist von Lipwig? You are the Postmaster!

'I *am* the Postmaster!' Moist shouted.

The mail must move, Moist von Lipwig! Too long have we been bound here.

'I will move the mail!'

You will move the mail?

'I will! I will!

Moist von Lipwig?

'Yes?'

The words came like a gale, whirling the envelopes in the sparkling light, shaking the building to its foundations.

Deliver us!

CHAPTER SIX

Little Pictures

The Postmen Unmasked – A terrible Engine – The New Pie – Mr Lipwig thinks about stamps – the Messenger from the Dawn of Time

'MR LIPVIG?' SAID MR PUMP.

Moist looked up into the golem's glowing eyes. There had to be a better way of waking up in the morning. Some people managed with a clock, for heavens' sake.

He was lying on a bare mattress under a musty blanket in his newly excavated apartment, which smelled of ancient paper, and every bit of him ached.

In a clouded kind of way, he was aware of Pump saying: 'The Postmen Are Waiting, Sir. Postal Inspector Groat Said That You Would Probably Wish To Send Them Out Properly On This Day.'

Moist blinked at the ceiling. 'Postal Inspector? I promoted him all the way to Postal Inspector?'

'Yes, Sir. You Were Very Ebullient.'

Memories of last night flocked treacherously to tap-dance their speciality acts on the famous stage of the Grand Old Embarrassing Recollection.

'Postmen?' he said.

'The Brotherhood Of The Order Of The Post. They're Old Men, Sir, But Wiry. They're Pensioners Now, But They All Volunteered. They've Been Here For Hours, Sorting The Mail.'

I hired a bunch of men even older than Groat . . .

'Did I do anything else?'

'You Gave A Very Inspirational Speech, Sir. I Was Particularly Impressed When You Pointed Out That "Angel" Is Just A Word For Messenger. Not Many People Know That.'

On the bed, Moist slowly tried to cram his fist into his mouth.

'Oh, And You Promised To Bring Back The Big Chandeliers And The Fine Polished Counter, Sir. They Were Very Impressed. No One Knows Where They Got To.'

Oh, gods, thought Moist.

'And The Statue Of The God, Sir. That Impressed Them Even More, I Would Say, Because Apparently It Was Melted Down Many Years Ago.'

'Did I do anything last night that suggested I was *sane*?'

'I Am Sorry, Sir?' said the golem.

But Moist remembered the light, and the whispering of the mail. It'd filled his mind with . . . knowledge, or memories that he didn't remember ever acquiring.

'Unfinished stories,' he said.

'Yes, Sir,' said the golem calmly. 'You Talked About Them At Length, Sir.'

'I did?'

'Yes, Sir. You Said—'

—that every undelivered message is a piece of space-time that lacks another end, a little bundle of effort and emotion floating freely. Pack millions of them together and they do what letters are meant to do. They communicate, and change the nature of events. When there's enough of them, they distort the universe around them.

It had all made sense to Moist. Or, at least, as much sense as anything else.

'And . . . did I actually rise up in the air, glowing gold?' said Moist.

'I Think I Must Have Missed That, Sir,' said Mr Pump.

'You mean I didn't, then.'

'In A Manner Of Speaking You Did, Sir,' said the golem.

'But in common, everyday reality I didn't?'

'You Were Lit, As It Were, By An Inner Fire, Sir. The Postmen Were Extremely Impressed.'

Moist's eye lit on the winged hat, which had been thrown carelessly on the desk.

'I'm never going to live up to all this, Mr Pump,' he said. 'They want a saint, not someone like me.'

'Perhaps A Saint Is Not What They *Need*, Sir,' said the golem.

Moist sat up, and the blanket dropped away. 'What happened to my clothes?' he said. 'I'm sure I hung them neatly on the floor.'

'I Did In Fact Try To Clean Your Suit With Spot Remover, Sir,' said Mr Pump. 'But Since It Was Effectively Just One Large Spot, It Removed The Whole Suit.'

'I liked that suit! At least you could have saved it for dusters, or something.'

'I'm Sorry, Sir, I'd Assumed That Dusters Had Been Saved For Your Suit. But In Any Case, I Obeyed Your Order, Sir.'

Moist paused. 'What order?' he said suspiciously.

'Last Night You Asked Me To Obtain A Suit Fit For A Postmaster, Sir. You Gave Me Very Precise Instructions,' said the golem. 'Fortunately My Colleague Stitcher 22 Was Working At The Theatrical Costumiers. It Is Hanging On The Door.'

And the golem had even found a mirror. It wasn't very big, but it was big enough to show Moist that if he were dressed any sharper he'd cut himself as he walked.

'Wow,' he breathed. 'El Dorado or what?'

The suit was cloth of gold, or whatever actors used instead. Moist was about to protest, but second thoughts intervened quickly.

Good suits helped. A smooth tongue was not much use in rough trousers. And people would notice the suit, not him. He'd certainly be noticed in this suit; it'd light up the street. People would have to shade their eyes to look at him. And apparently he'd *asked* for this.

'It's very . . .' He hesitated. The only word was '. . . fast. I mean, it looks as if it's about to speed away at any moment!'

'Yes, Sir. Stitcher 22 Has A Skill. Note Also The Gold Shirt And Tie. To Match The Hat, Sir.'

'Er, you couldn't get him to knock up something a little more sombre, could you?' said Moist, covering his eyes to stop himself being blinded by his own lapels. 'For me to wear when I don't want to illuminate distant objects?'

'I Shall Do So Immediately, Sir.'

'Well,' Moist said, blinking in the light of his sleeves. 'Let's speed the mail, then, shall we?'

The formerly retired postmen were waiting in the hall, in a space cleared from last night's maildrop. They all wore uniforms, although since no two uniforms were exactly alike they were not, in fact, uniform and therefore not technically uniforms. The caps all had peaks, but some were high-domed and some were soft and the old men themselves had ingrown their clothes, too, so that jackets hung like drape coats and trousers looked like concertinas. And, as is the wont of old men, they wore their medals and the determined looks of those ready for the final combat.

'Delivery ready for inspection, sah!' said Postal Inspector Groat, standing at attention so hard that sheer pride had lifted his feet a full inch off the floor.

'Thank you. Er . . . right.'

Moist wasn't sure what he was inspecting, but he did his best. Wrinkled face after wrinkled face stared back at him.

The medals, he realized, weren't all for military service. The Post Office had medals of its own. One was a golden dog's head, worn by a little man with a face like a packet of weasels.

'What's this, er . . .' he began.

'Senior Postman George Aggy, sir. The badge? Fifteen bites and still standin', sir!' said the man proudly.

'Well, that is a . . . a . . . a lot of bites, isn't it . . .'

'Ah, but I foxed 'em after number nine, sir, and got meself a tin leg, sir!'

'You lost your leg?' said Moist, horrified.

'No, sir. Bought a bit of ol' armour, didn't I?' said the wizened man, grinning artfully. 'Does m'heart good to hear their teeth squeaking, sir!'

'Aggy, Aggy . . .' Moist mused, and then memory sparked. 'Weren't you—'

'I'm the Worshipful Master, sir,' said Aggy. 'I hope you won't take last night the wrong way, sir. We all used to be like young Tolliver, sir, but we gave up hope, sir. No hard feelings?'

'No, no,' said Moist, rubbing the back of his head.

'And I'd like to add my own message of congratulations as chairman of the Ankh-Morpork Order of Postal Workers Benevolent and Friendly Society,' Aggy went on.

'Er . . . thank you,' said Moist. 'And who are they, exactly?'

'That was us last night, sir,' said Aggy, beaming.

'But I thought you were a secret society!'

'Not secret, sir. Not *exactly* secret. More . . . ignored, you might say. These days it's just about pensions and making sure your ol' mates get a proper funeral when they're Returned to Sender, really.'

'Well done,' said Moist vaguely, which seemed to cover everything. He stood back, and cleared his throat. 'Gentlemen, this is it. If we want the Post Office back in business, we must start by delivering the old mail. It is a sacred trust. The mail gets through. It may take fifty years, but we get there in the end. You know your walks. Take it steady. Remember, if you can't deliver it, if the house has gone . . . well, it comes back here and we'll put it into the Dead Letter office and at least we'll have tried. We just want people to know the Post Office is back again, understand?'

A postman raised a hand.

'Yes?' Moist's skill at remembering names was better than his skill at remembering anything else about last night. 'Senior Postman Thompson, isn't it?'

'Yes, sir! So what do we do when people give us letters, sir?'

Moist's brow wrinkled. 'Sorry? I thought you *deliver* the mail, don't you?'

'No, Bill's right, sir,' said Groat. 'What do we do if people give us new mail?'

'Er . . . what did you use to do?' said Moist.

The postmen looked at one another.

'Get one penny off 'em for the stamping, bring it back here to be stamped with the official stamp,' said Groat promptly. 'Then it gets sorted and delivered.'

'So . . . people have to wait until they see a postman? That seems rather—'

'Oh, in the old days there was dozens of smaller offices, see?' Groat added. 'But when it all started going bad we lost 'em.'

'Well, let's get the mail moving again and we can work things out as we go along,' said Moist. 'I'm sure ideas will occur. And now, Mr Groat, you have a secret to share . . .'

Groat's key ring jingled as he led Moist through the Post Office's cellars and eventually to a metal door. Moist noted a length of black and yellow rope on the floor: the Watch had been here, too.

The door clicked open. There was a blue glow inside, just faint enough to be annoying, leave purple shadows on the edge of vision and make the eyes water.

'Voil-ah,' said Groat.

'It's a . . . is it some kind of theatre organ?' said Moist. It was hard to see the outlines of the machine in the middle of the floor, but it stood there with all the charm of a torturer's rack. The blue glow was coming from somewhere in the middle of it. Moist's eyes were streaming already.

'Good try, sir! Actually it is the Sorting Engine,' said Groat. 'It's the curse of the Post Office, sir. It had imps in it for the actual reading of the envelopes, but they all evaporated years ago. Just as well, too.'

Moist's gaze took in the wire racks that occupied a whole wall of the big room. It also found the chalk outlines on the floor. The chalk glowed in the strange light. The outlines were quite small. One of them had five fingers.

'Industrial accident,' he muttered. 'All right, Mr Groat. Tell me.'

'Don't go near the glow, sir,' said Groat. 'That's what I said to Mr Whobblebury. But he snuck down here all by hisself, later on. Oh, dear, sir, it was poor young Stanley that went and found him, sir, after he saw poor little Tiddles dragging something along the passage. A scene of carnage met his eyes. You just can't imagine what it was like in here, sir.'

'I think I can,' said Moist.

'I doubt if you can, sir.'

'I can, really.'

'I'm sure you can't, sir.'

'I can! All right?' shouted Moist. 'Do you think I can't see all those little chalk outlines? Now can we get on with it before I throw up?'

'Er . . . right you are, sir,' said Groat. 'Ever heard of Bloody Stupid Johnson? Quite famous in this city.'

'Didn't he build things? Wasn't there always something wrong with them? I'm sure I read something about him—'

'That's the man, sir. He built all kinds of things, but, sad to say, there was always some major flaw.'

In Moist's brain, a memory kicked a neuron. 'Wasn't he the man who specified quicksand as a building material because he wanted a house finished fast?' he said.

'That's right, sir. Usually the major flaw was that the designer was Bloody Stupid Johnson. Flaw, you might say, was part of the whole thing. Actually, to be fair, a lot of the things he designed worked quite well, it was just that they didn't do the job they were supposed to. This thing, sir, did indeed begin life as an organ, but it ended up as a machine for sorting letters. The idea was that you tipped the mail sack in that hopper, and the letters were speedily sorted into those racks. Postmaster Cowerby meant well, they say. He was a stickler for speed and efficiency, that man. My grandad told me the Post Office spent a fortune on getting it to work.'

'And lost their money, eh?' said Moist.

'Oh no, sir. It worked. Oh yes, it worked very well. So well that people went mad, come the finish.'

'Let me guess,' said Moist. 'The postmen had to work too hard?'

'Oh, postmen always work too hard, sir,' said Groat, without blinking. 'No, what got people worried was finding letters in the sorting tray a year before they were due to be written.'

There was a silence. In that silence, Moist tried out a variety of responses, from 'Pull the other one, it's got bells on' to 'That's impossible', and decided they all sounded stupid. Groat looked deadly serious. So instead he said: 'How?'

The old postman pointed to the blue glow. 'Have a squint inside, sir. You can just see it. Don't get right above it, whatever you do.'

Moist moved a little closer to the machine and peered into the machinery. He could just make out, at the heart of the glow, a little wheel. It was turning, slowly.

'I was raised in the Post Office,' said Groat, behind him. 'Born in the sorting room, weighed on the official scales. Learned to read from envelopes, learned figuring from old ledgers, learned jography from looking at the maps of the city and history from the old men. Better than any school. Better than any school, sir. But never learned jommetry, sir. Bit of a hole in my understanding, all that stuff about angles and suchlike. But this, sir, is all about pie.'

'Like in food?' said Moist, drawing back from the sinister glow.

'No, no, sir. Pie like in jommetry.'

'Oh, you mean pi the number you get when . . .' Moist paused. He was erratically good at maths, which is to say he could calculate odds and currency very, very fast. There had been a geometry section in his book at school, but he'd never seen the point. He tried, anyway.

'It's all to do with . . . it's the number you get when the radius of a circle . . . no, the length of the rim of a wheel is three and a bit times the . . . er . . .'

'Something like that, sir, probably, something like that,' said Groat. 'Three and a bit, that's the ticket. Only Bloody Stupid Johnson said that was untidy, so he designed a wheel where the pie was exactly three. And that's it, in there.'

'But that's impossible!' said Moist. 'You can't do that! Pi is like . . . built in! You can't *change* it. You'd have to change the universe!'

'Yes, sir. They tell me that's what happened,' said Groat calmly. 'I'll do the party trick now. Stand back, sir.'

Groat wandered out into the other cellars and came back with a length of wood.

'Stand further back, sir,' he suggested, and tossed the piece of wood on top of the machine.

The noise wasn't loud. It was a sort of 'clop'. It seemed to Moist that something *happened* to the wood when it went over the light. There was a suggestion of curvature—

Several pieces of timber clattered on to the floor, along with a shower of splinters.

'They had a wizard in to look at it,' said Groat. 'He said the machine twists just a little bit of the universe so pie *could* be three, sir, but it plays hob with anything you put too near it. The bits that go missing get lost in the ... space-time-continuememememem, sir. But it doesn't happen to the letters because of the way they travel through the machine, you see. That's the long and short of it, sir. Some letters came out of that machine fifty years before they were posted!'

'Why didn't you switch it off?'

'Couldn't, sir. It kept on going like a siphon. Anyway, the wizard said if we did that terrible things might happen! 'cos of, er, quantum, I think.'

'Well, then, you could just stop feeding it mail, couldn't you?'

'Ah, well, sir, there it is,' said Groat, scratching his beard. 'You have positioned your digit right on the nub or crux, sir. We should've done that, sir, we should've, but we tried to make it work for us, you see. Oh, the management had schemes, sir. How about delivering a letter in Dolly Sisters thirty seconds after it had been posted in the city centre, eh? Of course, it wouldn't be polite to deliver mail before we'd actually got it, sir, but it could be a close run thing, eh? We were good, so we tried to be better . . .'

And, somehow, it was all familiar . . .

Moist listened glumly. Time travel was only a kind of magic, after all. That's why it always went wrong.

That's why there were postmen, with real feet. That's why the clacks was a string of expensive towers. Come to that, it was why farmers grew crops and fishermen trawled nets. Oh, you *could* do it all by magic, you certainly could. You could wave a wand and get twinkly stars and a fresh-baked loaf. You could make fish jump out of the sea ready cooked. And then, somewhere, somehow, magic would present its bill, which was always more than you could afford.

That's why it was left to wizards, who knew how to handle it safely. Not doing any magic at all was the chief task of wizards – not 'not doing magic' because they couldn't do magic, but not doing magic when they could do and didn't. Any ignorant fool can fail to turn someone else into a frog. You have to be clever to refrain from doing it when you know how easy it is. There were places in the world commemorating those times when wizards hadn't been quite as clever as that, and on many of them the grass would never grow again.

Anyway, there was a sense of inevitability about the whole business. People wanted to be fooled. They really believed that you found gold nuggets lying on the ground, that this time you could find the Lady, that just for once the glass ring might be real diamond.

Words spilled out of Mr Groat like stashed mail from a crack in the wall. Sometimes the machine had produced a thousand copies of the same letter, or filled the room with letters from next Tuesday, next month, next year. Sometimes they were letters that hadn't been written, or might have been written, or were meant to have been written, or letters which people had once sworn that they had written and hadn't really, but which nevertheless had a shadowy existence in some strange invisible letter world and were made real by the machine.

If, somewhere, any possible world can exist, then somewhere there is any letter that could possibly be written. Somewhere, all those cheques really are in the post.

They poured out – letters from the present day which turned out not to be from *this* present day, but ones that might have happened if only some small detail had been changed in the past. It didn't matter that the machine had been switched off, the wizards said. It existed in plenty of other presents and so worked here owing to . . . a lengthy sentence which the postmen didn't understand but had words like 'portal', 'multidimensional' and 'quantum' in it, quantum being in it twice. They didn't understand, but they had to *do* something. No one could deliver all that mail. And so the rooms began to fill up . . .

The wizards from Unseen University had been jolly interested in the problem, like doctors being really fascinated by some new virulent disease; the patient appreciates all the interest, but would very much prefer it if they either came up with a cure or stopped prodding.

The machine couldn't be stopped and certainly shouldn't be

destroyed, the wizards said. Destroying the machine might well cause this universe to stop existing, instantly.

On the other hand, the Post Office *was* filling up, so one day Chief Postal Inspector Rumbelow had gone into the room with a crowbar, had ordered all the wizards out, and belted the machine until things stopped whirring.

The letters ceased, at least. This came as a huge relief, but nevertheless the Post Office had its regulations and so the Chief Postal Inspector was brought before Postmaster Cowerby and asked why he had decided to risk destroying the whole universe in one go.

According to Post Office legend, Mr Rumbelow had replied: 'Firstly, sir, I reasoned that if I destroyed the universe all in one go no one would know; secondly, when I walloped the thing the first time the wizards ran away, so I surmised that unless they had another universe to run to they weren't really certain; and lastly, sir, the bloody thing was getting on my nerves. Never could stand machinery, sir.'

'And that was the end of it, sir,' said Mr Groat, as they left the room. 'Actually, I heard where the wizards were saying that the universe *was* destroyed all in one go but instantly came back all in one go. They said they could tell by lookin', sir. So that was okay and it let old Rumbelow off'f the hook, on account it's hard to discipline a man under Post Office Regulations for destroying the universe all in one go. Mind you – hah – there've been postmasters that would have given it a try. But it knocked the stuffing out of us, sir. It was all downhill after that. The men had lost heart. It broke us, to tell you the truth.'

'Look,' said Moist, 'the letters we've just given the lads, they're not from some other dimension or—'

'Don't worry, I checked 'em last night,' said Groat. 'They're just old. Mostly you can tell by the stamp. I'm good at telling which ones are prop'ly ours, sir. Had years to learn. It's a skill, sir.'

'Could you teach other people?'

'I dare say, yes,' said Groat.

'Mr Groat, the letters have talked to me,' Moist burst out.

To his surprise, the old man grabbed his hand and shook it. 'Well done, sir!' he said, tears rising in his eyes. 'I said it's a skill, didn't I?

Listen to the whispers, that's half the trick! They're alive, sir, *alive*. Not like people, but like . . . ships are alive, sir. I'll swear, all them letters pressed together in here, all the . . . the *passion* of 'em, sir, why, I do think this place has got something like a soul, sir, indeed I do . . .'

The tears coursed down Groat's cheeks. It's madness, of course, thought Moist. But now I've got it, too.

'Ah, I can see it in your eyes, sir, yes I can!' said Groat, grinning wetly. 'The Post Office has found you! It's enfolded you, sir, yes it has. You'll never leave it, sir. There's families that've worked here for hundreds and hundreds of years, sir. Once the postal service puts its stamp on you, sir, there's no turning back . . .'

Moist disentangled his hand as tactfully as he could.

'Yes,' he said. 'Do tell me about stamps.'

Thump.

Moist looked down at the piece of paper. Smudgy red letters, chipped and worn, spelled out: 'Ankh-Morpork Post Office.'

'That's right, sir,' said Groat, waving the heavy metal and wood stamper in the air. 'I bang the stamp on the ink pad here, then bang it, sir, *bang* it on the letter. There! See? Done it again. Same every time. Stamped.'

'And this is worth a penny?' said Moist. 'Good grief, man, a kid could forge this with half a potato!'

'That was always a bit of a problem, sir, yes,' said Groat.

'Why does a postman have to stamp the letters, anyway?' said Moist. 'Why don't we just sell people a stamp?'

'But they'd pay a penny and then go on stamping for ever, sir,' said Groat, reasonably.

In the machinery of the universe, the wheels of inevitability clicked into position . . .

'Well, then,' said Moist, staring thoughtfully at the paper, 'how about . . . how about a stamp you can use only once?'

'You mean, like, not much ink?' said Groat. His brow wrinkled, causing his toupee to slip sideways.

'I mean . . . if you stamped the stamper lots of times on paper, then cut out all the stampings . . .' Moist stared at an inner vision, if only to avoid the sight of the toupee slowly crawling back. 'The rate for delivery anywhere in the city is a penny, isn't it?'

'Except for the Shades, sir. That's five pence 'cos of the armed guard,' said Groat.

'Right. O-kay. I think I might have something here . . .' Moist looked up at Mr Pump, who was smouldering in the corner of the office. 'Mr Pump, would you be so good as to go along to the Goat and Spirit Level over at Hen-and-Chickens and ask the publican for "Mr Robinson's box", please? He may want a dollar. And while you're over there, there's a printing shop over that way, Teemer and Spools. Leave a message to say that the Postmaster General wishes to discuss a very large order.'

'Teemer and Spools? They're very expensive, sir,' said Groat. 'They do all the posh printing for the banks.'

'They're the very devil to forge, I know that,' said Moist. 'Or so I've been told,' he added quickly. 'Watermarks, special weaves in the paper, all kinds of tricks. Ahem. So . . . a penny stamping, and a fivepenny stamping . . . what about post to the other cities?'

'Five pence to Sto Lat,' said Groat. 'Ten or fifteen to the others. Hah, three dollars for all the way to Genua. We used to have to write those out.'

'We'll need a one-dollar stamp, then.' Moist started to scribble on the scrap of paper.

'A dollar stamp! Who'd buy one of those?' said Groat.

'Anyone who wants to send a letter to Genua,' said Moist. 'They'll buy three, eventually. But for now I'm dropping the price to one dollar.'

'One dollar! That's thousands of miles, sir!' Groat protested.

'Yep. Sounds like a bargain, right?'

Groat looked torn between exultation and despair. 'But we've only got a bunch of old men, sir! They're pretty spry, I'll grant you, but . . . well, you've got to learn to walk before you try to run, sir!'

'No!' Moist's fist thumped the table. 'Never say that, Tolliver! Never!

Run before you walk! Fly before you crawl! Keep moving forward! You think we should try to get a decent mail service in the city. *I* think we should try to send letters anywhere in the world! Because if we fail, I'd rather fail really hugely. All or nothing, Mr Groat!'

'Wow, sir!' said Groat.

Moist grinned his bright, sunny smile. It very nearly reflected off his suit.

'Let's get busy. We're going to need more staff, Postal Inspector Groat. A lot more staff. Smarten up, man. The Post Office is back!'

'Yessir!' said Groat, drunk on enthusiasm. 'We'll . . . we'll do things that are quite new, in interestin' ways!'

'You're getting the hang of it already,' said Moist, rolling his eyes.

Ten minutes later, the Post Office received its first delivery.

It was Senior Postman Bates, blood streaming down his face. He was helped into the office by two Watch officers, carrying a makeshift stretcher.

'Found him wandering in the street, sir,' said one of them. 'Sergeant Colon, sir, at your service.'

'What happened to him?' said Moist, horrified.

Bates opened his eyes. 'Sorry, sir,' he murmured. 'I held on tight, but they belted me over the bonce with a big thing!'

'Coupla toughs jumped him,' said Sergeant Colon. 'They threw his bag in the river, too.'

'Does that normally happen to postmen?' said Moist. 'I thought—Oh, no . . .'

The new, painfully slow arrival was Senior Postman Aggy, dragging one leg because it had a bulldog attached to it.

'Sorry about this, sir,' he said, limping forward. 'I think my official trousers is torn. I stunned the bugger with my bag, sir, but they're a devil to get to let go.' The bulldog's eyes were shut; it appeared to be thinking of something else.

'Good job you've got your armour, eh?' said Moist.

'Wrong leg, sir. But not to worry. I'm nat'rally imp-ervious around the calfy regions. It's all the scar tissue, sir, you could strike matches on it. Jimmy Tropes is in trouble, though. He's up a tree in Hide Park.'

Moist von Lipwig strode up Market Street, face set with grim purpose. The boards were still up on the Golem Trust, but had attracted another layer of graffiti. The paint on the door was burnt and bubbled, too.

He opened the door, and instinct made him duck. He felt the crossbow bolt zip between the wings of his hat.

Miss Dearheart lowered the bow. 'My gods, it's you! For a minute I thought a second sun had appeared in the sky!'

Moist rose cautiously as she laid the bow aside.

'We had a fire-bomb last night,' she said, by way of explanation for attempting to shoot him in the head.

'How many golems are for hire right now, Miss Dearheart?' said Moist.

'Huh? Oh . . . about . . . a dozen or so—'

'Fine. I'll take them. Don't bother to wrap them up. I want them down at the Post Office as soon as possible.'

'What?' Miss Dearheart's normal expression of perpetual annoyance returned. 'Look, you can't just walk in, snap your fingers and order a dozen *people* like this—'

'*They* think they're property!' said Moist. 'That's what you told me.'

They glared at one another. Then Miss Dearheart fumbled distractedly in a filing tray.

'I can let you ha— *employ* four right now,' she said. 'That'd be Doors 1, Saw 20, Campanile 2 and . . . Anghammarad. Only Anghammarad can talk at the moment; the frees haven't helped the others yet—'

'Helped?'

Miss Dearheart shrugged. 'A lot of the cultures that built golems thought tools shouldn't talk. They have no tongues.'

'And the Trust gives them some extra clay, eh?' said Moist cheerfully.

She gave him a look. 'It's a bit more mystical than that,' she said solemnly.

'Well, dumb is okay so long as they're not stupid,' said Moist, trying to look serious. 'This Anghammarad's got a name? Not just a description?'

'A lot of the very old ones have. Tell me, what do you want them to do?' said the woman.

'Be postmen,' said Moist.

'Working in public?'

'I don't think you can have secret postmen,' said Moist, briefly seeing shadowy figures skulking from door to door. 'Anything wrong with that?'

'Well . . . no. Certainly not! It's just that people get a bit nervous, and set fire to the shop. I'll bring them down as soon as possible.' She paused. 'You do understand that owned golems have to have a day off every week? You did read the pamphlet, didn't you?'

'Er . . . time off?' said Moist. 'What do they need time off for? A hammer doesn't get time off, does it?'

'In order to be golems. Don't ask what they do – I think just go and sit in a cellar somewhere. It's . . . it's a way to show they're *not* a hammer, Mr Lipwig. The buried ones forget. The free golems teach them. But don't worry, the rest of the time they won't even sleep.'

'So . . . Mr Pump has a day off coming?' said Moist.

'Of course,' said Miss Dearheart, and Moist filed this one under 'useful to know'.

'Good. Thank you,' he said. *Would you like to have dinner tonight?* Moist normally had no trouble with words, but these stuck to his tongue. There was something pineapple-prickly about Miss Dearheart. There was something about her expression, too, which said: there's no possible way you could surprise me. I know all about you.

'Is there anything else?' she said. 'Only you're standing there with your mouth open.'

'Er . . . no. That's fine. Thank you,' mumbled Moist.

She smiled at him, and bits of Moist tingled.

'Well, off you go then, Mr Lipwig,' she said. 'Brighten up the world like a little sunbeam.'

Four out of the five postmen were what Mr Groat called horse de combat and were brewing tea in the mail-stuffed cubbyhole that was laughingly called their Rest Room. Aggy had been sent home after the bulldog had been prised from his leg; Moist had a big basket of fruit sent round. You couldn't go wrong with a basket of fruit.

Well, they'd made an impression, at least. So had the bulldog. But some mail had been delivered, you had to admit it. You had to admit, too, that it was years and years late, but the post was *moving*. You could sense it in the air. The place didn't feel so much like a tomb. Now Moist had retired to his office, where he was getting creative.

'Cup of tea, Mr Lipwig?'

He looked up from his work into the slightly strange face of Stanley.

'Thank you, Stanley,' he said, laying down his pen. 'And I see you got nearly all of it in the cup this time! Nicely done!'

'What're you drawing, Mr Lipwig?' said the boy, craning his neck. 'It looks like the Post Office!'

'Well done. It's going to be on a stamp, Stanley. Here, what do you think of the others?' He passed over the other sketches.

'Coo, you're a good draw-er, Mr Lipwig. That looks just like Lord Vetinari!'

'That's the penny stamp,' said Moist. 'I copied the likeness off a penny. City coat-of-arms on the twopenny, Morporkia with her fork on the fivepenny, Tower of Art on the big one-dollar stamp. I was thinking of a tenpenny stamp, too.'

'They look *very* nice, Mr Lipwig,' said Stanley. 'All that detail. Like little paintings. What's all those tiny lines called?'

'Cross-hatching. Makes them hard to forge. And when the letter with the stamp on it comes into the Post Office, you see, we take one of the old rubber stamps and stamp over the new stamps so they can't be used again, and the—'

'Yes, 'cos they're like money, really,' said Stanley cheerfully.

'Pardon?' said Moist, tea halfway to his lips.

'Like money. These stamps'll be like money. 'cos a penny stamp *is* a penny, when you think about it. Are you all right, Mr Lipwig? Only you've gone all funny. Mr Lipwig?'

'Er . . . what?' said Moist, who was staring at the wall with a strange, faraway grin.

'Are you all right, sir?'

'What? Oh. Yes. Yes, indeed. Er . . . do we need a bigger stamp, do you think? Five dollars, perhaps?'

'Hah, I should think you could send a *big* letter all the way to Fourecks for that, Mr Lipwig!' said Stanley cheerfully.

'Worth thinking ahead, then,' said Moist. 'I mean, since we're designing the stamps and everything . . .'

But now Stanley was admiring Mr Robinson's box. It was an old friend to Moist. He never used 'Mr Robinson' as an alias except to get it stored by some halfway-honest merchant or publican, so that it'd be somewhere safe even if he had to leave town quickly. It was for a con-man and forger what a set of lock picks is to a burglar, but with the contents of this box you could open people's brains.

It was a work of art in its own right, the way all the little compartments lifted up and fanned out when you opened it. There were pens and inks, of course, but also little pots of paints and tints, stains and solvents. And, kept carefully flat, thirty-six different types of paper, some of them quite hard to obtain. Paper was important. Get the weight and translucence wrong, and no amount of skill would save you. You could get away with bad penmanship much more easily than you could with bad paper. In fact, rough penmanship often worked better than a week of industrious midnights spent getting every little thing right, because there was something in people's heads that spotted some little detail that wasn't *quite* right but at the same time would fill in details that had merely been suggested by a few careful strokes. Attitude, expectation and presentation were everything.

Just like me, he thought.

The door was knocked on and opened in one movement.

'Yes?' snapped Moist, not looking up. 'I'm busy designing mon—stamps here, you know!'

'There's a *lady*,' panted Groat. 'With *golems*!'

'Ah, that'll be Miss Dearheart,' said Moist, laying down his pen.

'Yessir. She said "Tell Mr Sunshine I've brought him his postmen", sir! You're going to use *golems* as postmen, sir?'

'Yes. Why not?' said Moist, giving Groat a severe look. 'You get on okay with Mr Pump, don't you?'

'Well, he's all right, sir,' the old man mumbled. 'I mean, he keeps the place tidy, he's always very respectful . . . I speak as I find, but people can be a bit odd about golems, sir, what with them glowing eyes and all, and the way they never *stops*. The lads might not take to 'em, sir, that's all I'm saying.'

Moist stared at him. Golems were thorough, reliable and by gods they took orders. *He'd get another chance to be smiled at by Miss Dearheart—* Think about golems! Golems, golems, golems!

He smiled, and said, 'Even if I can prove they're real postmen?'

Ten minutes later the fist of the golem called Anghammarad smashed through a letter box and several square inches of splintering wood.

'Mail Delivered,' it announced, and went still. The eyes dulled.

Moist turned to the cluster of human postmen and gestured towards the impromptu Postman's Walk he'd set up in the big hall.

'Note the flattened roller skate, gentlemen. Note the heap of ground glass where the beer bottle was. And Mr Anghammarad did it all with a hood on his head, I might add.'

'Yeah, but his eyes burned holes in it,' Groat pointed out.

'None of us can help the way we're made,' said Adora Belle Dearheart primly.

'I've got to admit, it did my heart good to see him punch through that door,' said Senior Postman Bates. 'That'll teach 'em to put 'em low and sharp.'

'And no problem with dogs, I expect,' said Jimmy Tropes. 'He'd never get the arse bitten out of *his* trousers.'

'So you all agree a golem is suitable to become a postman?' said Moist.

Suddenly all the faces twisted up as the postmen shuffled into a chorus.

'Well, it's not us, you understand . . .'

'. . . people can be a bit funny about, er, clay folk . . .'

'. . . all that stuff about taking jobs away from real people . . .'

'. . . nothing against him at all, but . . .'

They stopped, because the golem Anghammarad was beginning to speak again. Unlike Mr Pump, it took him some time to get up to speed. And when his voice arrived it seemed to be coming from long ago and far away, like the sound of surf in a fossil shell.

He said: 'What Is A Post Man?'

'A messenger, Anghammarad,' said Miss Dearheart. Moist noticed that she spoke to golems differently. There was actual *tenderness* in her voice.

'Gentlemen,' he said to the postmen, 'I know you feel—'

'I Was A Messenger,' Anghammarad rumbled.

His voice was not like Mr Pump's, and neither was his clay. He looked like a crude jigsaw puzzle of different clays, from almost black through red to light grey. Anghammarad's eyes, unlike the furnace glow of those of the other golems, burned a deep ruby red. He looked old. More than that, he *felt* old. The chill of time radiated off him.

On one arm, just above the elbow, was a metal box on a corroded band that had stained the clay.

'Running errands, eh?' said Groat nervously.

'Most Recently I Delivered The Decrees Of King Het Of Thut,' said Anghammarad.

'Never heard of any King Het,' said Jimmy Tropes.

'I Expect That Is Because The Land Of Thut Slid Under The Sea Nine Thousand Years Ago,' said the golem solemnly. 'So It Goes.'

'Blimey! You're nine thousand years old?' said Groat.

'No. I Am Almost Nineteen Thousand Years Old, Having Been Born In The Fire By The Priests Of Upsa In The Third Ning Of The

Shaving Of The Goat. They Gave Me A Voice That I Might Carry Messages. Of Such Things Is The World Made.'

'Never heard of them either,' said Tropes.

'Upsa Was Destroyed By The Explosion Of Mount Shiputu. I Spent Two Centuries Under A Mountain Of Pumice Before It Eroded, Whereupon I Became A Messenger For The Fishermen Kings Of The Holy Ult. It Could Have Been Worse.'

'You must've seen lots of things, sir!' said Stanley.

The glowing eyes turned to him, lighting up his face. 'Sea Urchins. I Have Seen Many Sea Urchins. And Sea Cucumbers. And The Dead Ships, Sailing. Once There Was An Anchor. All Things Pass.'

'How long were you under the sea?' said Moist.

'It Was Almost Nine Thousand Years.'

'You mean . . . you just sat there?' said Aggy.

'I Was Not Instructed To Do Otherwise. I Heard The Song Of The Whales Above Me. It Was Dark. Then There Was A Net, And Rising, And Light. These Things Happen.'

'Didn't you find it . . . well, dull?' said Groat. The postmen were staring.

'Dull,' said Anghammarad blankly, and turned to look at Miss Dearheart.

'He has no idea what you mean,' she said. 'None of them have. Not even the younger ones.'

'So I expect you'll be keen to deliver messages again, then!' said Moist, far more jovially than he'd intended. The golem's head turned towards Miss Dearheart again.

'Keen?' said Anghammarad.

She sighed. 'Another tough one, Mr Moist. It's as bad as "dull". The closest I can come is: you will satisfy the imperative to perform the directed action.'

'Yes,' said the golem. 'The Messages Must Be Delivered. That Is Written On My Chem.'

'And that's the scroll in his head that gives a golem his instructions,' said Miss Dearheart. 'In Anghammarad's case it's a clay tablet. They didn't have paper in those days.'

'You really used to deliver messages for kings?' said Groat.

'Many Kings,' said Anghammarad. 'Many Empires. Many Gods. Many Gods. All Gone. All Things Go.' The golem's voice got deeper, as if he was quoting from memory. 'Neither Deluge Nor Ice Storm Nor The Black Silence Of The Netherhells Shall Stay These Messengers About Their Sacred Business. Do Not Ask Us About Sabre-Tooth Tigers, Tar Pits, Big Green Things With Teeth Or The Goddess Czol.'

'You had big green things with teeth back then?' said Tropes.

'Bigger. Greener. More Teeth,' rumbled Anghammarad.

'And the goddess Czol?' said Moist.

'Do Not Ask.'

There was a thoughtful silence. Moist knew how to break it.

'And *you* will decide if *he* is a postman?' he said softly.

The postmen went into a brief huddle, and then Groat turned back to Moist.

'He's a postman and a half, Mr Lipwig. We never knew. The lads say – well, it'd be an honour, sir, an honour to work with him. I mean, it's like . . . it's like history, sir. It's like . . . well . . .'

'I always said the Order goes back a long way, didn't I?' said Jimmy Tropes, aglow with pride. 'There was postmen back inna dawn o' time! When they hears we've got a member who goes all that way back the other secret societies are gonna be as green as . . . as . . .'

'Something big with teeth?' Moist suggested.

'Right! And no problem with his chums neither, if they can take orders,' said Groat generously.

'Thank you, gentlemen,' said Moist. 'And now all that remains' – he nodded to Stanley, who held up two big tins of royal blue paint – 'is their uniform.'

By general agreement Anghammarad was given the unique rank of Extremely Senior Postman. It seemed . . . fair.

Half an hour later, still tacky to the touch, each one accompanied by a human postman, the golems took to the streets. Moist watched heads turn. The afternoon sunlight glinted off royal blue and Stanley, gods bless him, had found a small pot of gold paint too. Frankly, the golems were impressive. They gleamed.

You had to give people a show. Give them a show, and you were halfway to where you wanted to be.

A voice behind him said: '*The Postman came down like a wolf on the fold / His cohorts all gleaming in azure and gold . . .*'

Just for a moment, a flicker of time, Moist thought: I've been made, she knows. Somehow, she knows. Then his brain took over. He turned to Miss Dearheart.

'When I was a kid I always thought that a cohort was a piece of armour, Miss Dearheart,' he said, giving her a smile. 'I used to imagine the troops sitting up all night, polishing them.'

'Sweet,' said Miss Dearheart, lighting a cigarette. 'Look, I'll get you the rest of the golems as soon as possible. There may be trouble, of course. The Watch will be on your side, though. There's a free golem in the Watch and they rather like him, although here it doesn't much matter what you're made of when you join the Watch because Commander Vimes will see to it that you become solid copper through and through. He's the most cynical bastard that walks under the sun.'

'*You* think he's cynical?' said Moist.

'Yes,' she said, blowing smoke. 'As you suspect, that's practically a professional opinion. But thank you for hiring the boys. I'm not sure they understand what "liking" something means, but they like to work. And Pump 19 seems to hold you in some regard.'

'Thank you.'

'I personally think you are a phoney.'

'Yes, I expect you do,' said Moist. Ye gods, Miss Dearheart was hard work. He'd met women he couldn't charm, but they'd been foothills compared to the icy heights of Mount Dearheart. It was an act. It had to be. It was a game. It had to be.

He pulled out his packet of stamp designs. 'What do you think of these, Miss D— Look, what do your friends call you, Miss Dearheart?'

And in his head Moist said to himself *I don't know* just as the woman said: 'I don't know. What's this? You carry your etchings with you to save time?'

So it *was* a game, and he was invited to play.

'They will be copper-engraved, I hope,' he said meekly. 'They're my designs for the new stamps.' He explained about the stamps idea, while she looked at the pages.

'Good one of Vetinari,' she said. 'They say he dyes his hair, you know. What's this one? Oh, the Tower of Art . . . how like a man. A dollar, eh? Hmm. Yes, they're quite good. When will you start using them?'

'Actually, I was planning to slip along to Teemer and Spools while the lads are out now and discuss the engraving,' said Moist.

'Good. They're a decent firm,' she said. 'Sluice 23 is turning the machinery for them. They keep him clean and don't stick notices on him. I go and check on all the hired golems every week. The frees are very insistent on that.'

'To make sure they're not mistreated?' said Moist.

'To make sure they're not forgotten. You'd be amazed at how many businesses in the city have a golem working somewhere on the premises. Not the Grand Trunk, though,' she added. 'I won't let them work there.'

There was an edge to that statement.

'Er . . . why not?' said Moist.

'There's some shit not even a golem should work in,' said Miss Dearheart, in the same steel tone. 'They are moral creatures.'

O-kay, thought Moist, bit of a sore point there, then?

His mouth said: 'Would you like to have dinner tonight?' For just the skin of a second, Miss Dearheart was surprised, but not half as surprised as Moist. Then her natural cynicism reinflated.

'I like to have dinner every night. With you? No. I have things to do. Thank you for asking.'

'No problem,' said Moist, slightly relieved.

The woman looked around the echoing hall. 'Doesn't this place give you the creeps? You could perhaps do something with some floral wallpaper and a fire-bomb.'

'It's all going to be sorted out,' said Moist quickly. 'But it's best to get things moving as soon as possible. To show we're in business.'

They watched Stanley and Groat, who were patiently sorting at the edge of a pile, prospectors in the foothills of the postal mountain. They were dwarfed by the white hillocks.

'It will take you for ever to deliver them, you know,' said Miss Dearheart, turning to go.

'Yes, I know,' said Moist.

'But that's the thing about golems,' added Miss Dearheart, standing in the doorway. The light caught her face oddly. 'They're not frightened of "for ever". They're not frightened of *anything*.'

CHAPTER SEVEN

Tomb of Words

*The Invention of the Hole – Mr Lipwig Speaks Out – The Wizard in a
Jar – A discussion of Lord Vetinari's back side – A Promise to Deliver –
Mr Hobson's Boris*

M{R SPOOLS, IN HIS ANCIENT} office smelling of oil and ink, was
impressed by this strange young man in the golden suit and
wingèd hat.

'You certainly know your papers, Mr Lipwig,' he said, as Moist
thumbed through the samples. 'It's a pleasure to meet a customer who
does. Always use the right paper for the job, that's what I say.'

'The important thing is to make stamps hard to forge,' said Moist,
leafing through the samples. 'On the other hand, it mustn't cost us
anything like a penny to produce a penny stamp!'

'Watermarks are your friend there, Mr Lipwig,' said Mr
Spools.

'Not impossible to fake, though,' said Moist, and then added, 'so
I've been told.'

'Oh, we know all the tricks, Mr Lipwig, don't you worry about
that!' said Mr Spools. 'We're up to scratch, oh yes! Chemical voids,
thaumic shadows, timed inks, everything. We do paper and engraving
and even printing for some of the leading figures in the city, although
of course I am not at liberty to tell you who they are.'

He sat back in his worn leather chair and scribbled in a notebook
for a moment.

'Well, we could do you twenty thousand of the penny stamps,
uncoated stock, gummed, at two dollars a thousand plus setup,' said
Mr Spools. 'Ten pence less for ungummed. You'll have to find someone to cut them out, of course.'

'Can't you do that with some kind of machine?' said Moist.

'No. Wouldn't work, not with things as small as this. Sorry, Mr Lipwig.'

Moist pulled a scrap of brown paper out of his pocket and held it up. 'Do you recognize this, Mr Spools?'

'What, is that a pin paper?' Mr Spools beamed. 'Hah, that takes me back! Still got my old collection in the attic. I've always thought it must be worth a bob or two if only—'

'Watch this, Mr Spools,' said Moist, gripping the paper carefully. Stanley was almost painfully precise in placing his pins; a man with a micrometer couldn't have done it better.

Gently, the paper tore down the line of holes. Moist looked at Mr Spools and raised his eyebrows.

'It's all about holes,' he said. 'It ain't nothing if it ain't got a hole . . .'

Three hours went past. Foremen were sent for. Serious men in overalls turned things on lathes, other men soldered things together, tried them out, changed this, reamed that, then dismantled a small hand press and built it in a different way. Moist loitered on the periphery of all this, clearly bored, while the serious men fiddled, measured things, rebuilt things, tinkered, lowered things, raised things and, eventually, watched by Moist and Mr Spools, tried out the converted press officially—

Chonk . . .

It felt to Moist that everyone was holding their breath so hard that the windows were bending inwards. He reached down, eased the sheet of little perforated squares off the board, and lifted it up.

He tore off one stamp.

The windows snapped outwards. People breathed again. There wasn't a cheer. These weren't men to cheer and whoop at a job well done. Instead, they lit their pipes and nodded to one another.

Mr Spools and Moist von Lipwig shook hands over the perforated paper.

'The patent is yours, Mr Spools,' said Moist.

'You're very kind, Mr Lipwig. Very kind indeed. Oh, here's a little souvenir . . .'

An apprentice had bustled up with a sheet of paper. To Moist's astonishment, it was already covered with stamps – ungummed, unperforated, but perfect miniature copies of his drawing for the one penny stamp.

'Iconodiabolic engraving, Mr Lipwig!' said Spools, seeing his face. 'No one can say we're behind the times! Of course there'll be a few little flaws this time round, but by early next week we'll—'

'I want penny and twopenny ones tomorrow, Mr Spools, please,' said Moist firmly. 'I don't need perfect, I want quick.'

'My word, you're hot off the mark, Mr Lipwig!'

'Always move fast, Mr Spools. You never know who's catching up!'

'Hah! Yes! Er . . . good motto, Mr Lipwig. Nice one,' said Mr Spools, grinning uncertainly.

'And I want the fivepennies and one dollars the day after, please.'

'You'll scorch your boots, Mr Lipwig!' said Spools.

'Got to move, Mr Spools, got to fly!'

Moist hurried back to the Post Office as fast as decently possible, feeling slightly ashamed.

He liked Teemer and Spools. He liked the kind of business where you could actually speak to the man whose name was over the door; it meant it probably wasn't run by crooks. And he liked the big, solid, unflappable workmen, recognizing in them all the things he knew he lacked, like steadfastness, solidarity and honesty. You couldn't lie to a lathe or fool a hammer. They were good people, and quite unlike him . . .

One way in which they were quite unlike him was that none of them, right now, probably had wads of stolen paper stuffed into their jacket.

He really shouldn't have done it, he really shouldn't. It was just that Mr Spools was a kind and enthusiastic man and the desk had been covered with examples of his wonderful work, and when the perforation press was being made people had been bustling around and not really paying Moist much attention and he'd . . . tidied up. He couldn't help himself. He was a crook. What did Vetinari expect?

The postmen were arriving back as he walked into the building. Mr Groat was waiting for him with a worried smile on his face.

'How's it going, Postal Inspector?' said Moist cheerfully.

'Pretty well, sir, pretty well. There's good news, sir. People have been giving us letters to post, sir. Not many yet and some of them are a bit, er, jokey, but we got a penny off 'f them every time. That's seven pence, sir,' he added proudly, proffering the coins.

'Oh boy, we eat tonight!' said Moist, taking the coins and pocketing the letters.

'Sorry, sir?'

'Oh, nothing, Mr Groat. Well done. Er . . . you said there was good news. Is there any of the other sort, perhaps . . . ?'

'Um . . . some people didn't like getting their mail, sir.'

'Things got posted through the wrong doors?' said Moist.

'Oh, no, sir. But old letters ain't always welcome. Not when they're, as it might be, a will. A will. As in Last Will and Testament, sir,' the old man added meaningfully. 'As in, it turns out the wrong daughter got mum's jewellery twenty years ago. As it were.'

'Oh, dear,' said Moist.

'The Watch had to be called in, sir. There was what they call in the papers a "rumpus" in Weaver Street, sir. There's a lady waiting for you in your office, sir.'

'Oh gods, not one of the daughters?'

'No, sir. She's a writing lady from the *Times*. You can't trust 'em, sir, although they do a very reasonable crossword,' Groat added conspiratorially.

'What does she want *me* for?'

'Couldn't say, sir. I expect it's 'cos you're postmaster?'

'Go and . . . make her some tea or something, will you?' said Moist, patting his jacket. 'I'll just go and . . . pull myself together . . .'

Two minutes later, with the stolen paper tucked safely away, Moist strode into his office.

Mr Pump was standing by the door, fiery eyes banked, in the stance of a golem with no current task other than to exist, and a woman was sitting in the chair by Moist's desk.

Moist weighed her up. Attractive, certainly, but dressing apparently to play down the fact while artfully enhancing it. Bustles were back in

fashion in the city for some inexplicable reason, but her only con-
cession there was a bum-roll, which achieved a certain perkiness in
the rear without the need to wear twenty-seven pounds of dangerously spring-loaded underwear. She was blonde but wore her hair in
a bag net, another careful touch, while a small and quietly fashionable
hat perched on top of her head to no particular purpose. A large
shoulder bag was by her chair, a notebook was on her knee, and she
wore a wedding ring.

'Mr Lipwig?' she said brightly. 'I am Miss Cripslock. From the
Times.'

Okay, wedding ring but nevertheless 'Miss', thought Moist. Handle
with care. Probably has Views. Do not attempt to kiss hand.

'And how can I assist the *Times*?' he said, sitting down and giving
her a non-condescending smile.

'Do you intend to deliver all the backlog of mail, Mr Lipwig?'

'If at all possible, yes,' said Moist.

'Why?'

'It's my job. Rain, snow, gloom of night, just as it says over the
door.'

'Have you heard about the fracas in Weaver Street?'

'I heard it was a rumpus.'

'I'm afraid it's got worse. There was a house on fire when I left.
Doesn't that worry you?' Miss Cripslock's pencil was suddenly poised.

Moist's face remained expressionless as he thought furiously. 'Yes, it
does, of course,' he said. 'People shouldn't set fire to houses. But I also
know that Mr Parker of the Merchants' Guild is marrying his boy-
hood sweetheart on Saturday. Did *you* know that?'

Miss Cripslock hadn't, but she scribbled industriously as Moist told
her about the greengrocer's letter.

'That's very interesting,' she said. 'I will go and see him immediately. So you're saying that delivering the old mail is a good thing?'

'Delivering the mail is the *only* thing,' said Moist, and hesitated
again. Just on the edge of hearing was a whispering.

'Is there a problem?' said Miss Cripslock.

'What? No! What was I— Yes, it's the right thing. History is not to be denied, Miss Cripslock. And we are a communicating species, Miss Cripslock!' Moist raised his voice to drown out the whispering. 'The mail must get through! It *must* be delivered!'

'Er . . . you needn't shout, Mr Lipwig,' said the reporter, leaning backwards.

Moist tried to get a grip, and the whispering died down a little.

'I'm sorry,' he said, and cleared his throat. 'Yes, I intend to deliver all the mail. If people have moved, we will try to find them. If they have died, we'll try to deliver to their descendants. The post *will* be delivered. We are tasked to deliver it, and deliver it we will. What else should we do with it? Burn it? Throw it in the river? Open it to decide if it's important? No, the letters were entrusted to our care. Delivery is the only way.'

The whispering had almost died away now, so he went on: 'Besides, we need the space. The Post Office is being reborn!' He pulled out the sheet of stamps. 'With these!'

She peered at them, puzzled. 'Little pictures of Lord Vetinari?' she said.

'*Stamps*, Miss Cripslock. One of those stuck on a letter will ensure delivery anywhere within the city. These are early sheets, but to-morrow we will be selling them gummed and perforated for ease of use. I intend to make it *easy* to use the post. Obviously we are still finding our feet, but soon I intend that we should be capable of delivering a letter to anyone, anywhere in the world.'

It was a stupid thing to say, but his tongue had taken over.

'Aren't you being rather ambitious, Mr Lipwig?' she said.

'I'm sorry, I don't know any other way to be,' said Moist.

'I was thinking that we do have the clacks now.'

'The clacks?' said Moist. 'I dare say the clacks is wonderful if you wish to know the prawn market figures from Genua. But can you write S.W.A.L.K. on a clacks? Can you seal it with a loving kiss? Can you cry tears on to a clacks, can you smell it, can you enclose a pressed flower? A letter is more than just a message. And a clacks is so expensive in any case that the average man in the street can just about afford it in a time of crisis: GRANDADS DEAD FUNERAL TUES. A day's wages to send a message as warm and human as a thrown knife? But a letter is *real*.'

He stopped. Miss Cripslock was scribbling like mad, and it's always worrying to see a journalist take a sudden interest in what you're saying, especially when you half suspect it was a load of pigeon guano. And it's worse when they're smiling.

'People are complaining that the clacks is becoming expensive, slow and unreliable,' said Miss Cripslock. 'How do you feel about that?'

'All I can tell you is that today we've taken on a postman who is eighteen thousand years old,' said Moist. '*He* doesn't break down very easily.'

'Ah, yes. The golems. Some people say—'

'What is your first name, Miss Cripslock?' said Moist.

For a moment, the woman coloured. Then she said: 'It's Sacharissa.'

'Thank you. I'm Moist. Please don't laugh. The golems— You're laughing, aren't you . . .'

'It was just a cough, honestly,' said the reporter, raising a hand to her throat and coughing unconvincingly.

'Sorry. It sounded a bit like a laugh. Sacharissa, I need postmen, counter clerks, sorters – I need lots of people. The mail will move. I need people to help me move it. Any kind of people. Ah, thanks, Stanley.'

The boy had come in with two mismatched mugs of tea. One had an appealing little kitten on it, except that erratic collisions in the washing-up bowl had scratched it so that its expression was that of a creature in the final stages of rabies. The other had once hilariously informed the world that clinical insanity wasn't necessary for employment, but most of the words had faded, leaving:

YOU DON'T HAVE TO **BE MAD**

TO WORK HERE BUT **IT HELPS**

He put them down with care on Moist's desk; Stanley did everything carefully.

'Thank you,' Moist repeated. 'Er . . . you can go now, Stanley. Help with the sorting, eh?'

'There's a vampire in the hall, Mr Lipwig,' said Stanley.

'That will be Otto,' said Sacharissa quickly. 'You don't have a . . . a *thing* about vampires, do you?'

'Hey, if he's got a pair of hands and knows how to walk I'll give him a job!'

'He's already got one,' said Sacharissa, laughing. 'He's our chief iconographer. He's been taking pictures of your men at work. We'd very much like to have one of you. For the front page.'

'What? No!' said Moist. 'Please! No!'

'He's very good.'

'Yes, but . . . but . . . but . . .' Moist began, and in his head the sentence went on: but I don't think that even a talent for looking like half the men you see in the street would survive a picture.

What actually came out was: 'I don't want to be singled out from all the hard-working men and golems who are putting the Post Office back on its feet! After all, there's no "me" in team, eh?'

'Actually, there is,' said Sacharissa. 'Besides, you're the one wearing the wingèd hat and the golden suit. Come *on*, Mr Lipwig!'

'All right, all right, I really didn't want to go into this, but it's against my religion,' said Moist, who'd had time to think. 'We're forbidden to have any image made of us. It removes part of the soul, you know.'

'And you *believe* that?' said Sacharissa. 'Really?'

'Er, no. No. Of course not. Not as such. But . . . but you can't treat religion as a sort of buffet, can you? I mean, you can't say yes please, I'll have some of the Celestial Paradise and a helping of the Divine Plan but go easy on the kneeling and none of the Prohibition of Images, they give me wind. It's table d'hôte or nothing, otherwise . . . well, it would be silly.'

Miss Cripslock looked at him with her head on one side. 'You work for his lordship, don't you?' she said.

'Well, of course. This is an official job.'

'And I expect you'll tell me that your previous job was as a clerk, nothing special?'

'That's right.'

'Although your name probably *is* Moist von Lipwig, because I can't believe anyone would choose that as an assumed name,' she went on.

'Thank you very much!'

'It sounds to *me* as though you're issuing a challenge, Mr Lipwig. There's all sorts of problems with the clacks right now. There's been a big stink about the people they've been sacking and how the ones that're left are being worked to death, and up you pop, full of ideas.'

'I'm serious, Sacharissa. Look, people are already giving us *new* letters to post!'

He pulled them out of his pocket and fanned them out. 'See, there's one here to go to Dolly Sisters, another to Nap Hill, one for . . . Blind Io . . .'

'He's a god,' said the woman. 'Could be a problem.'

'No,' said Moist briskly, putting the letters back in his pocket. 'We'll deliver to the gods themselves. He has three temples in the city. It'll be easy.' And you've forgotten about the pictures, hooray . . .

'A man of resource, I see. Tell me, Mr Lipwig, do you know much about the history of this place?'

'Not too much. I'd certainly like to find out where the chandeliers went to!'

'You haven't spoken to Professor Pelc?'

'Who's he?'

'I'm amazed. He's at the University. He wrote a whole chapter on this place in his book on . . . oh, something to do with big masses of writing thinking for themselves. I suppose you do *know* about the people who died?'

'Oh, yes.'

'He said the place drove them mad in some way. Well, actually, we said that. What he said was a lot more complicated. I have to hand it to you, Mr Lipwig, taking on a job that has killed four men before you. It takes a special kind of man to do that.'

Yes, thought Moist. An *ignorant* one.

'You haven't noticed anything strange yourself?' she went on.

'Well, I *think* my body travelled in time but the soles of my feet didn't, but I'm not sure how much of it was hallucination; I was nearly killed in a mailslide and the letters keep talking to me,' were the words that Moist didn't say, because it's the kind of thing you don't say to an open notebook. What he did say was, 'Oh, no. It's a fine old building, and I fully intend to bring it back to its former glory.'

'Good. How old are you, Mr Lipwig?'

'Twenty-six. Is that important?'

'We like to be thorough.' Miss Cripslock gave him a sweet smile. 'Besides, it's useful if we have to write your obituary.'

Moist marched through the hall, with Groat sidling after him.

He pulled the new letters out of his pocket and thrust them into Groat's crabby hands. 'Get these delivered. Anything for a god goes to his or her or its temple. Any other strange ones put on my desk.'

'We picked up another fifteen just now, sir. People think it's funny!'

'Got the money?'

'Oh, yes, sir.'

'Then we're the ones who're laughing,' said Moist firmly. 'I won't be long. I'm off to see the wizard.'

By law and tradition the great Library of Unseen University is open to the public, although they aren't allowed as far as the magical shelves. They don't realize this, however, since the rules of time and space are twisted inside the Library and so hundreds of miles of shelving can easily be concealed inside a space roughly the thickness of paint.

People flock in, nevertheless, in search of answers to those questions only librarians are considered to be able to answer, such as 'Is this the laundry?' 'How do you spell surreptitious?' and, on a regular basis: 'Do you have a book I remember reading once? It had a red cover and it turned out they were twins.'

And, strictly speaking, the Library *will* have it . . . somewhere. Somewhere it has every book ever written, that ever will be written and, notably, every book that it is possible to write. These are not on the public shelves lest untrained handling cause the collapse of everything that it is possible to imagine.*

Moist, like everyone else who entered the Library, stared up at the dome. Everyone did. They always wondered why a library that was technically infinite in size was covered by a dome a few hundred feet across, and they were allowed to go on wondering.

Just below the dome, staring down from their niches, were statues of the Virtues: Patience, Chastity, Silence, Charity, Hope, Tubso, Bissonomy† and Fortitude.

Moist couldn't resist removing his hat and giving a little salute to Hope, to whom he owed so much. Then, as he wondered why the statue of Bissonomy was carrying a kettle and what looked like a bunch of parsnips, he collided with someone who grabbed him by the arm and hurried him across the floor.

'Don't say a word, don't say a word, but you are looking for a book, yes?'

'Well, actually—' He seemed to be in the clutches of a wizard.

'—you are not sure what book!' said the wizard. 'Exactly. It is the job of a librarian to find the right book for the right person. If you would just sit here, we can proceed. Thank you. Please excuse the straps. This will not take long. It is practically painless.'

'Practically?'

Moist was pushed, firmly, into a large and complex swivel chair. His captor, or helper or whatever he might turn out to be, gave him a reassuring smile. Other, shadowy figures helped him strap Moist into the chair which, while basically an old horseshoe-shaped one with a leather seat, was surrounded by . . . stuff. Some of it was clearly magical, being of the stars-and-skulls variety, but what about the jar of pickles, the pair of tongs and the live mouse in a cage made of—

Panic gripped Moist and, not at all coincidentally, so did a pair of padded paddles, which closed over his ears. Just before all sound was

---

* Again.

† Many cultures practise neither of these in the hustle and bustle of the modern world, because no one can remember what they are.

silenced, he heard: 'You may experience a taste of eggs and the sensation of being slapped in the face with some sort of fish. This is perfectly—'

And then thlabber happened. It was a traditional magic term, although Moist didn't know this. There was a moment in which everything, even the things that couldn't be stretched, felt stretched. And then there was the moment when everything suddenly went back to not being stretched, known as the moment of thlabber.

When Moist opened his eyes again, the chair was facing the other way. There was no sign of the pickles, the tongs or the mouse, but in their place was a bucket of clockwork pastry lobsters and a boxed set of novelty glass eyes.

Moist gulped, and muttered: 'Haddock.'

'Really? Most people say cod,' said someone. 'No accounting for taste, I suppose.' Hands unbuckled Moist and helped him to his feet. These hands belonged to an orang-utan, but Moist didn't pass comment. This was a university of wizards, after all.

The man who had shoved him into the chair was now standing by a desk staring at some wizardly device.

'Any moment now,' he said. 'Any moment. Any moment now. Any second . . .'

A bundle of what appeared to be hosepipes led from the desk into the wall. Moist was certain they bulged for a moment, like a snake eating in a hurry; the machine stuttered, and a piece of paper dropped out of a slot.

'Ah . . . here we are,' said the wizard, snatching it up. 'Yes, the book you were after was *A History of Hats*, by F. G. Smallfinger, am I right?'

'No. I'm not after a book, in fact—' Moist began.

'Are you sure? We have lots.'

There were two striking things about this wizard. One was . . . well, Grandfather Lipwig had always said that you could tell the honesty of a man by the size of his ears, and this was a very honest wizard. The other was that the beard he was wearing was clearly false.

'I was looking for a wizard called Pelc,' Moist ventured.

The beard parted slightly to reveal a wide smile.

'I *knew* the machine would work!' said the wizard. 'You are looking, in fact, for me.'

The sign on the outside of the office door said: Ladislav Pelc, D.M.Phil, Prehumous Professor of Morbid Bibliomancy.

On the inside of the door was a hook, on which the wizard hung his beard.

It was a wizard's study, so of course had the skull with a candle in it and a stuffed crocodile hanging from the ceiling. No one, least of all wizards, knows why this is, but you have to have them.

It was also a room full of books and made of books. There was no actual furniture; that is to say, the desk and chairs were shaped out of books. It looked as though many of them were frequently referred to, because they lay open with other books used as bookmarks.

'You want to know about your Post Office, I expect?' said Pelc, as Moist settled on to a chair carefully put together from volumes 1 to 41 of *Synonyms for the word 'Plimsoll'*.

'Yes, please,' said Moist.

'Voices? Strange events?'

'Yes!'

'How can I put this . . .' mused Pelc. 'Words have power, you understand? It is in the nature of our universe. Our Library itself distorts time and space on quite a grand scale. Well, when the Post Office started accumulating letters it was storing words. In fact what was being created was what we call a *gevaisa*, a tomb of living words. Are you of a literary persuasion, Mr Lipwig?'

'Not as such.' Books were a closed book to Moist.

'Would you burn a book?' said Pelc. 'An old book, say, battered, almost spineless, found in a box of rubbish?'

'Well . . . probably not,' Moist admitted.

'Why not? Would the thought make you uncomfortable?'

'Yes, I suppose it would. Books are . . . well, you just don't do that. Er . . . why do you wear a *false* beard? I thought wizards had real ones.'

'It's not compulsory, you know, but when we go outside the public expect beards,' said Pelc. 'It's like having stars on your robes. Besides, they're far too hot in the summer. Where was I? Gevaisas. Yes. All words have *some* power. We feel it instinctively. Some, like magical spells and the true names of the gods, have a great deal. They must be treated with respect. In Klatch there is a mountain with many caves, and in those caves are entombed more than a hundred thousand old books, mostly religious, each one in a white linen shroud. That is perhaps an extreme approach, but intelligent people have always known that some words at least should be disposed of with care and respect.'

'Not just shoved in sacks in the attic,' said Moist. 'Hold on . . . a golem called the Post Office "a tomb of unheard words".'

'I'm not at all surprised,' said Professor Pelc calmly. 'The old gevaisas and libraries used to employ golems, because the only words that have the power to influence them are the ones in their heads. Words are *important*. And when there is a critical mass of them, they change the nature of the universe. Did you have what seemed to be hallucinations?'

'Yes! I was back in time! But *also* in the present!'

'Ah, yes. That's quite common,' said the wizard. 'Enough words crammed together can affect time and space.'

'And they spoke to me!'

'I told the Watch the letters wanted to be delivered,' said Professor Pelc. 'Until a letter is read, it's not complete. They *will* try anything to be delivered. But they don't think, as you understand it, and they're not clever. They just reach out into any available mind. I see you've already been turned into an avatar.'

'I can't fly!'

'Avatar: the living likeness of a god,' said the professor patiently. 'The hat with wings. The golden suit.'

'No, they happened by accident—'

'Are you sure?'

The room went quiet.

'Um . . . I was until right now,' said Moist.

'They're not trying to hurt anyone, Mr Lipwig,' said Pelc. 'They just want deliverance.'

'We'll never be able to deliver them all,' said Moist. 'That'd take years.'

'The mere fact you're delivering any will help, I'm sure,' said Professor Pelc, smiling like a doctor telling a man not to worry, the disease is only fatal in 87 per cent of cases. 'Is there anything else I can help you with?' He stood up, to indicate that a wizard's time is valuable.

'Well, I'd quite like to know where the chandeliers went,' said Moist. 'It'd be nice to get them back. Symbolic, you could say.'

'I can't help you, but I'm sure Professor Goitre can. He's the *Post*humous Professor of Morbid Bibliomancy. We could drop in and see him on the way out, if you like. He's in the Wizards' Pantry.'

'Why's he "posthumous"?' Moist asked, as they stepped out into the corridor.

'He's dead,' said Pelc.

'Ah . . . I was kind of hoping that it was going to be a little more metaphorical than that,' said Moist.

'Don't worry, he decided to take Early Death. It was a very good package.'

'Oh,' said Moist. The important thing at a time like this was to spot the right moment to run, but they'd got here through a maze of dark passages and this was not a place you'd want to get lost in. Something might find you.

They stopped outside a door, through which came the muffled sound of voices and the occasional clink of glassware. The noise stopped as soon as the professor pushed the door open, and it was hard to see where it could have come from. This was, indeed, a pantry, quite empty of people, its walls lined with shelves, the shelves filled with little jars. There was a wizard in each one.

Now would be the right time to run, Moist's hindbrain thought, as Pelc reached for a jar, unscrewed the lid and rummaged around in it for the tiny wizard.

'Oh, this isn't him,' said the professor cheerfully, seeing Moist's expression. 'The housekeeper puts these little knitted wizard dolls in just to remind the kitchen staff that the jars shouldn't be used for anything else. There was an incident with some peanut butter, I believe. I just have to take it out so that he doesn't sound muffled.'

'So . . . er, where is the professor, in fact?'

'Oh, in the jar, for a certain value of "in", said Professor Pelc. 'It's very hard to explain to the layman. He's only dead for—'

'—a given value of dead?' said Moist.

'Exactly! And he can come back at a week's notice. A lot of the older wizards are opting for it now. Very refreshing, they say, just like a sabbatical. Only longer.'

'Where do they go?'

'No one's sure, exactly, but you can hear the sounds of cutlery,' said Pelc, and raised the jar to his mouth.

'Excuse me, Professor Goitre? Can you by any chance recall what happened to the chandeliers in the Post Office?'

Moist was expecting a tinny little voice to reply, but a sprightly if elderly voice a few inches away from his ear said: 'What? Oh! Yes indeed! One ended up in the Opera House and the other was acquired by the Assassins' Guild. Here comes the pudding trolley! Goodbye!'

'Thank you, Professor,' said Pelc solemnly. 'All is well here—'

'Fat lot I care!' said the disembodied voice. 'Be off, please, we're eating!'

'There you have it, then,' said Pelc, putting the wizard doll back in the jar and screwing the lid on. 'The Opera House and the Assassins' Guild. Might be quite hard to get them back, I fancy.'

'Yes, I think I shall put that off for a day or two,' said Moist, stepping out of the door. 'Dangerous people to tangle with.'

'Indeed,' said the professor, shutting the door behind them, which was the signal for the buzz of conversation to start up again. 'I understand some of those sopranos can kick like a mule.'

Moist dreamed of bottled wizards, all shouting his name.

In the best traditions of awaking from a nightmare, the voices gradually became one voice, which turned out to be that of Mr Pump, who was shaking him.

'Some of them were covered in jam!' Moist shouted, and then focused. 'What?'

'Mr Lipwig, You Have An Appointment With Lord Vetinari.'

This sank in, and sounded worse than wizards in jars. 'I don't have any appointment with Vetinari! Er . . . do I?'

'He Says You Do, Mr Lipwig,' said the golem. 'Therefore, You Do. We'll Leave By The Coach Yard. There Is A Big Crowd Outside The Front Doors.'

Moist stopped with his trousers halfway on. 'Are they angry? Are any of them carrying buckets of tar? Feathers of any kind?'

'I Do Not Know. I Have Been Given Instructions. I Am Carrying Them Out. I Advise You To Do The Same.'

Moist was hustled out into the back streets, where some shreds of mist were still floating. 'What time is this, for heavens' sake?' he complained.

'A Quarter To Seven, Mr Lipwig.'

'That's still night time! Doesn't the man ever sleep? What's so important that I've got to be dragged off my nice warm pile of letters?'

The clock in Lord Vetinari's ante-room didn't tick right. Sometimes the tick was just a fraction late, sometimes the tock was early. Occasionally, one or the other didn't happen at all. This wasn't really noticeable until you'd been in there for five minutes, by which time small but significant parts of the brain were going crazy.

Moist was not good at early mornings in any case. That was one of the advantages of a life of crime: you didn't have to get up until other people had got the streets aired.

The clerk Drumknott glided in on hushed feet, so soundlessly that he came as a shock. He was one of the most silent people Moist had ever encountered.

'Would you like some coffee, Postmaster?' he said quietly.

'Am I in trouble, Mr Drumknott?'

'I wouldn't care to say, sir. Have you read the *Times* this morning?'

'The paper? No. Oh . . .' Moist's mind ran back furiously over yesterday's interview. He hadn't said anything wrong, had he? It had all been good, positive stuff, hadn't it? Vetinari wanted people to use the post, didn't he?

'We always get a few copies straight off the press,' said Drumknott. 'I shall fetch you one.'

He returned with the paper. Moist unfolded it, took in the front page in one moment of agony, read a few sentences, put his hand over his eyes and said, 'Oh, gods.'

'Did you notice the cartoon, Postmaster?' said Drumknott innocently. 'It may be thought quite droll.'

Moist risked another glance at the terrible page. Perhaps in unconscious self-defence his gaze had skipped over the cartoon, which showed two ragged street urchins. One of them was holding a strip of penny stamps. The text below read:

First urchin (having acquired some of the newly minted 'Stampings'): ' 'ere, 'ave you seen Lord Vetinari's back side?'

Second urchin: 'Nah, and I wouldn't lick it for a penny, neiver!'

Moist's face went waxen. 'He's seen this?' he croaked.

'Oh, *yes*, sir.'

Moist stood up quickly. 'It's still early,' he said. 'Mr Trooper is probably still on duty. If I run he can probably fit me in. I'll go right away. That will be okay, won't it? It'll cut out the paperwork. I don't want to be a burden to anyone. I'll even—'

'Now, now, Postmaster,' said Drumknott, pushing him gently back into his chair, 'don't distress yourself unduly. In my experience, his lordship is a . . . *complex* man. It is not wise to anticipate his reactions.'

'You mean you think I'm going to *live*?'

Drumknott screwed up his face in thought, and stared at the ceiling for a moment. 'Hmm, yes. Yes, I think you might,' he said.

'I mean, in the fresh air? With everything attached?'

'Quite probably, sir. You may go in now, sir.'

Moist tiptoed into the Patrician's office.

Only Lord Vetinari's hands were visible on either side of the *Times*. Moist reread the headlines with dull horror.

WE DON'T BREAK DOWN, POSTMASTER VOWS

Amazing Attack On Clacks

Pledges: We'll Deliver Anywhere

Using Remarkable New 'Stamps'

That was the main story. It was alongside a smaller story which nevertheless drew the eye. The headline was:

Grand Trunk Down Again: Continent Cut Off

. . . and at the bottom, in a heavier typeface to show it was meant to be light-hearted, and under the headline:

History Cannot Be Denied

. . . were a dozen stories about the things that had happened when the ancient post turned up. There was the rumpus that had turned into a fracas, Mr Parker and his bride-to-be and others too. The post had changed unremarkable lives in small ways. It was like cutting a window into History and seeing what might have been.

That seemed to be the entirety of the front page, except for a story about the Watch hunting for the 'mystery killer' who had mauled some banker to death in his house. They were baffled, it said. That cheered Moist up a little; if their infamous werewolf officer couldn't sniff out a bloody murderer, then maybe they wouldn't find Moist, when the time came. A brain could surely beat a nose.

Lord Vetinari seemed oblivious of Moist's presence, and Moist wondered what effect a polite cough might have.

At which point, the newspaper rustled.

'It says here in the Letters column,' said the voice of the Patrician, 'that the phrase "stick it up your jumper" is based on an ancient Ephebian saying that is at least two thousand years old, thus clearly pre-dating jumpers but not, presumably, the act of sticking.' He lowered the paper and looked at Moist over the top of it. 'I don't know if you have been following this interesting little etymological debate?'

'No, sir,' said Moist. 'If you remember, I spent the past six weeks in a condemned cell.'

His lordship put down the paper, steepled his fingers, and looked at Moist over the top of them.

'Ah, yes. So you did, Mr Lipwig. Well, well, well.'

'Look, I'm really sorr—' Moist began.

'Anywhere in the world? Even to the gods? Our postmen don't break down so easily? History is not to be denied? Very impressive, Mr Lipwig. You have made quite a splash,' Vetinari smiled, 'as the fish said to the man with the lead weight tied to his feet.'

'I didn't exactly say—'

'In my experience Miss Cripslock tends to write down *exactly* what one says,' Vetinari observed. 'It's a terrible thing when journalists do that. It spoils the fun. One feels instinctively that it's cheating, somehow. And I gather you are selling promissory notes, too?'

'What?'

'The *stamps*, Mr Lipwig. A promise to carry a penny's worth of mail. A promise that must be kept. Do come and look at this.' He stood up and walked across to the window, where he beckoned. 'Do come, Mr Lipwig.'

Fearing that he might be hurled down on to the cobbles, Moist nevertheless did so.

'See the big clacks tower over there on the Tump?' said Vetinari, gesturing. 'Not much activity on the Grand Trunk this morning. Problems with a tower out on the plains, I gather. Nothing is getting to Sto Lat and beyond. But now, if you look down . . .'

It took Moist a moment to understand what he was seeing, and then—

'That's a *queue* outside the Post Office?' he said.

'*Yes*, Mr Lipwig,' said Vetinari, with dark glee. 'For stamps, as advertised. Ankh-Morpork citizens have an instinct for, you might say, joining in the fun. Go to it, Mr Lipwig. I'm sure you're full of ideas. Don't let me detain you.'

Lord Vetinari returned to his desk and picked up the paper.

It's right there on the front page, Moist thought, he can't have not seen it . . .

'Er . . . about the other thing . . .' he ventured, staring at the cartoon.

'What other thing would that be?' said Lord Vetinari.

There was a moment's silence.

'Er . . . nothing, really,' said Moist. 'I'll be off, then.'

'Indeed you will, Postmaster. The mail must get through, must it not?'

Vetinari listened to distant doors shut, and then went and stood at the window until he saw a golden figure hurry across the courtyard.

Drumknott came and tidied up the 'Out' tray. 'Well done, sir,' he said quietly.

'Thank you, Drumknott.'

'I see Mr Horsefry has passed away, sir.'

'So I understand, Drumknott.'

There was a stir in the crowd as Moist crossed the street. To his unspeakable relief he saw Mr Spools, standing with one of the serious men from his printery. Spools hurried over to him.

'I, er, have several thousand of both of the, er, items,' he whispered, pulling out a package from under his coat. 'Pennies and twopennies. They're not the best we can do but I thought you might be in want of them. We heard the clacks was down again.'

'You're a life saver, Mr Spools. If you could just take them inside. By the way, how much is a clacks message to Sto Lat?'

'Even a very short message would be at least thirty pence, I think,' said the engraver.

'Thank you.' Moist stood back and cupped his hands. 'Ladies and gentlemen!' he shouted. 'The Post Office will be open in five minutes for the sale of penny and twopenny stamps! In addition, we will be taking mail for Sto Lat! First express delivery to Sto Lat leaves on the hour, ladies and gentlemen, to arrive *this morning*. The cost will be ten pence per standard envelope! I repeat, ten pence! The Royal Mail, ladies and gentlemen! Accept no substitutes! Thank you!'

There was a stir from the crowd, and several people hurried away.

Moist led Mr Spools into the building, politely closing the door in the face of the crowd. He felt the tingle he always felt when the game was afoot. Life should be made of moments like this, he decided. With his heart singing, he poured out orders.

'Stanley!'

'Yes, Mr Lipwig?' said the boy, behind him.

'Run along to Hobson's Livery Stable and tell them I want a good fast horse, right? Something with a bit of fizz in its blood! Not some feagued-up old screw, and I know the difference! I want it here in half an hour! Off you go! Mr Groat?'

'Yessir!' Groat actually saluted.

'Rig up some kind of table for a counter, will you?' said Moist. 'In five minutes, we open to accept mail and sell stamps! I'm taking letters to Sto Lat while the clacks is down and you're Acting Postmaster while I'm gone! Mr Spools!'

'I'm right here, Mr Lipwig. You really don't have to shout,' said the engraver reproachfully.

'Sorry, Mr Spools. More stamps, please. I'll need some to take with me, in case there's mail to come back. Can you do that? And I'll need the fives and the dollar stamps as soon as— Are you all right, Mr Groat?'

The old man was swaying, his lips moving soundlessly.

'Mr Groat?' Moist repeated.

'Acting Postmaster . . .' mumbled Groat.

'That's right, Mr Groat.'

'No Groat has ever been Acting Postmaster . . .' Suddenly Groat dropped to his knees and gripped Moist round the legs. 'Oh, thank you, sir! I won't let you down, Mr Lipwig! You can rely on me, sir! Neither rain nor snow nor glom of—'

'Yes, yes, thank you, Acting Postmaster, thank you, that's enough, thank you,' said Moist, trying to pull away. 'Please get *up*, Mr Groat. Mr Groat, please!'

'Can I wear the wingèd hat while you're gone, sir?' Groat pleaded. 'It'd mean such a lot, sir—'

'I'm sure it would, Mr Groat, but not today. Today, the hat flies to Sto Lat.'

Groat stood up. 'Should it really be you that takes the mail, sir?'

'Who else? Golems can't move fast enough, Stanley is . . . well, Stanley, and the rest of you gentlemen are ol— rich in years.' Moist rubbed his hands together. 'No argument, Acting Postmaster Groat! Now – let's sell some stamps!'

The doors were opened, and the crowd flocked in. Vetinari had been right. If there was any action, the people of Ankh-Morpork liked to be a part of it. Penny stamps flowed over the makeshift counter. After all, the reasoning went, for a penny you got something worth a penny, right? After all, even if it was a joke it was as safe as buying money! And envelopes came the other way. People were actually writing letters in the Post Office. Moist made a mental note: envelopes with a stamp already on them and a sheet of folded paper inside them: Instant Letter Kit, Just Add Ink! That was an important rule of any game: always make it easy for people to give you money.

To his surprise, although he realized it shouldn't have been, Drumknott elbowed his way through the crowd with a small but heavy leather package, sealed with a heavy wax seal bearing the city crest and a heavy V. It was addressed to the mayor of Sto Lat.

'Government business,' he announced pointedly, as he handed it over.

'Do you want to buy any stamps for it?' said Moist, taking the packet.

'What do *you* think, Postmaster?' said the clerk.

'I definitely think government business travels free,' said Moist.

'Thank you, Mr Lipwig. The lord likes a fast learner.'

Other mail for Sto Lat did get stamped, though. A lot of people had friends or business there. Moist looked around. People were scribbling everywhere, even holding the notepaper up against walls. The stamps, penny and twopenny, were shifting fast. At the other end of the hall, the golems were sorting the endless mail mountains . . .

In fact, in a small way, the place was bustling.

You should've seen it, sir, you should've seen it!

'Lipwig, are yer?'

He snapped out of a dream of chandeliers to see a thickset man in front of him. Recognition took a moment, and then said that this was the owner of Hobson's Livery Stable, at once the most famous and the most notorious such enterprise in the city. It was probably not the hive of criminal activity that popular rumour suggested, although the huge establishment often seemed to contain grubby-looking men with not much to do apart from sit around and squint at people. And he was employing an Igor, everyone knew, which *of course* was sensible when you had such a high veterinary overhead, but you heard stories . . .*

'Oh, hello, Mr Hobson,' said Moist.

'Seems yer think I hire tired old horses, sir, do you?' said Willie Hobson. His smile was not entirely friendly. A nervous Stanley stood behind him. Hobson was big and heavy-set but not exactly fat; he was probably what you'd get if you shaved a bear.

'I have ridden some that—' Moist began, but Hobson raised a hand.

'Seems yer want fizz,' said Hobson. His smile widened. 'Well, I always give the customer what I want, you know that. So I've brought yer Boris.'

'Oh, yes?' said Moist. 'And he'll get me to Sto Lat, will he?'

'Oh, at the very least, sir,' said Hobson. 'Good horseman, are yer?'

'When it comes to riding out of town, Mr Hobson, there's no one faster.'

---

* That, for example, stolen horses got dismantled at dead of night and might well turn up with a dye job and two different legs. And it was said that there was one horse in Ankh-Morpork that had a longitudinal seam from head to tail, being sewn together from what was left of two horses that had been involved in a particularly nasty accident.

'That's good, sir, that's good,' said Hobson, in the slow voice of someone carefully urging the prey towards the trap. 'Boris does have a few faults, but I can see a skilled horseman like you should have no trouble. Ready, then? He's right outside. Got a man holding him.'

It turned out that there were in fact four men holding the huge black stallion in a network of ropes, while it danced and lunged and kicked and tried to bite. A fifth man was lying on the ground. Boris was a killer.

'Like I said, sir, he's got a few faults, but no one could call him a . . . now what was it . . . oh, yeah, a feagued-up old screw. Still want a horse with fizz?' Hobson's grin said it all: this is what I do to snooty buggers who try to mess me around. Let's see you try to ride this one, Mister-I-Know-All-About-Horses!

Moist looked at Boris, who was trying to trample the fallen man, and at the watching crowd. Damn the gold suit. If you were Moist von Lipwig, there was only one thing to do now, and that was raise the stakes.

'Take his saddle off,' he said.

'You what?' said Hobson.

'Take his saddle off, Mr Hobson,' said Moist firmly. 'This bag's quite heavy, so let's lose the saddle.'

Hobson's smile remained, but the rest of his face tried to sidle away from it. 'Had all the kids you want, have yer?' he said.

'Just give me a blanket and a bellyband, Mr Hobson.'

Now Hobson's smile vanished completely. This was going to look too much like murder. 'You might want to think again, sir,' he said. 'Boris took a couple of fingers off a man last year. He's a trampler, too, and a snaffler and a scraper and he'll horlock if he can get away with it. He's got demons in him, and that's a fact.'

'Will he run?'

'Not so much run as bolt, sir. Born evil, that one,' said Hobson. 'You need a crowbar to get him round corners, too. Look, sir, fair play to yer for a game 'un, but I've got plenty of other—'

Hobson flinched as Moist gave him a special grin. '*You* chose him, Mr Hobson. I'll ride him. I'd be grateful if you could get your gentlemen to point him up Broadway for me while I go and conclude a few items of business.'

Moist went into the building, ran up the stairs to his office, shut the door, crammed his handkerchief in his mouth and whimpered gently for a few seconds, until he felt better. He'd ridden bareback a few times, when things had been really hot, but Boris had the eyes of a crazy thing.

But back off now and he'd be . . . just a fool in a shiny suit. You had to give them a show, an image, something to remember. All he had to do was stay on until he left the city and then find a suitable bush to jump off into. Yes, that'd do. And then stagger into Sto Lat hours later, still with the mail, having valiantly fought off bandits. He'd be believed, because it would feel right . . . because people wanted to believe things, because it'd make a good tale, because if you made it glitter sufficiently glass could appear more like a diamond than a diamond did.

There was a cheer when he strode out on to the steps again. The sun, on cue, decided to appear from the mists, and sparkled off his wings.

Boris was looking apparently docile now, chewing his bit. This didn't fool Moist; if a horse like Boris was quiet it was because he was planning something.

'Mr Pump, I shall need you to give me a leg up,' he said, slinging the post bag round his neck.

'Yes, Mr Lipvig,' said the golem.

'Mr Lipwig!'

Moist turned round to see Sacharissa Cripslock hurrying up the street, notebook in hand.

'Always a pleasure to see you, Sacharissa,' said Moist, 'but I am a little busy right now—'

'You are aware that the Grand Trunk is shut again?' she said.

'Yes, it was in the paper. Now I must—'

'So you *are* challenging the clacks company?' The pencil hung poised over her notebook.

'Simply delivering the mail, Miss Cripslock, just like I said I'd do,' said Moist in firm, manly tones.

'But it's rather strange, is it not, that a man on horseback is more reliable than a—'

'Please, Miss Cripslock! We are the Post Office!' said Moist, in his best high-minded voice. 'We don't go in for petty rivalry. We're sorry to hear that our colleagues in the clacks company are experiencing temporary difficulties with their machinery, we fully sympathize with their plight, and if they would like us to deliver their messages for them we would *of course* be happy to sell them some stamps – soon to be available in penny, twopenny, fivepenny, tenpenny and one dollar values, available here at your Post Office, ready gummed. Incidentally, we intend eventually to flavour the gum in liquorice, orange, cinnamon and banana flavours, but not strawberry because I hate strawberries.'

He could see her smile as she wrote this down. Then she said: 'I did hear you correctly, did I? *You* are offering to carry *clacks messages?*'

'Certainly. Ongoing messages can be put on the Trunk in Sto Lat. Helpfulness is our middle name.'

'Are you sure it's not "cheekiness"?' said Sacharissa, to laughter from the crowd.

'I don't understand you, I'm sure,' said Moist. 'Now, if you will—'

'You're cocking a snook at the clacks people again, aren't you?' said the journalist.

'Ah, that must be a journalistic term,' said Moist. 'I've never owned a snook, and even if I did I wouldn't know how to cock it. And now, if you *will* excuse me, I have the mail to deliver and ought to leave before Boris eats somebody. Again.'

'Can I ask you just one last thing? Will your soul be unduly diminished if Otto takes a picture of you departing?'

'I suppose I can't stop you out here, provided my face isn't very clear,' said Moist, as Mr Pump cupped his pottery hands to make a step. 'The priest is very hot on that, you know.'

'Yes, I expect "the priest" is,' said Miss Cripslock, making sure the inverted commas clanged with irony. 'Besides, by the look of that creature, it may be the last chance we get. It looks like death on four legs, Mr Lipwig.'

The crowd fell silent as Moist mounted. Boris merely shifted his weight a little.

Look at it like this, Moist thought, what have you got to lose? Your life? You've already been hanged. You're into angel time. And you're impressing the hell out of everybody. Why are they buying stamps? Because you're giving them a show—

'Just say the word, mister,' said one of Hobson's men, hauling on the end of a rope. 'When we let him go, we ain't hanging around!'

'Wait a moment—' said Moist quickly.

He'd seen a figure at the front of the crowd. It was wearing a figure-hugging grey dress and, as he watched, it blew a neurotic cloud of smoke at the sky, gave him a look, and shrugged.

'Dinner *tonight*, Miss Dearheart?' he shouted.

Heads turned. There was a ripple of laughter, and a few cheers. For a moment she flashed him a look that should have left his shadow on the smoking remains of the wall opposite, and then she gave a curt nod.

Who knows, it could be peaches underneath . . .

'Let him go, boys!' said Moist, his heart soaring.

The men dived away. The world was still for a breath, and then Boris sprang from docility into a mad rearing dance, back legs clattering across the flagstones, hooves pawing at the air.

'Vunderful! Hold it!'

The world went white. Boris went mad.

Chapter Seven A

Post Haste

*The Nature of Boris the Horse – Foreboding Tower – Mr Lipwig
cools off – The Lady with Buns on Her Ears – Invitation Accepted –
Mr Robinson's Box – A mysterious stranger*

HOBSON HAD TRIED BORIS as a racehorse and he would have been a very good one were it not for his unbreakable habit, at the off, of attacking the horse next to him and jumping the railings at the first bend. Moist clapped one hand on to his hat, wedged his toes into the belly band and hung on to the reins as Broadway came at him all at once, carts and people blurring past, his eyeballs pressing into his head.

There was a cart across the street but there was no possibility of steering Boris. Huge muscles bunched and there was a long, slow, silent moment as he *drifted* over the cart.

Hooves slid over the cobbles ahead of a trail of sparks when he landed again, but he recovered by sheer momentum and *accelerated*.

The usual crowd around the Hubwards Gate scattered and there, filling the horizon, were the plains. They did something to Boris's mad horse brain. All that space, nice and flat with only a few easily jumped obstacles, like trees . . .

He found extra muscle and speeded up again, bushes and trees and carts flying towards him.

Moist cursed the bravado with which he'd ordered the saddle taken away. Every part of his body already hated him. But in truth Boris, once you got past the pineapple, wasn't too bad a ride. He'd hit his rhythm, a natural single-footed gait, and his burning eyes were focused on the blueness. His hatred of everything was for the moment subsumed in the sheer joy of space. Hobson was right, you couldn't steer him with a mallet, but at least he was headed in the right direction, which was away from his stable. Boris didn't want to spend the days kicking the bricks out of his wall while waiting to throw the next bumptious idiot. He wanted to bite the horizon. He wanted to run.

Moist carefully removed his hat and gripped it in his mouth. He didn't dare imagine what'd happen if he lost it, and he'd need to have it on his head at the end of the journey. It was important. It was all about style.

One of the towers of the Grand Trunk was ahead and slightly to the left. There were two in the twenty miles between Ankh-Morpork and Sto Lat, because they were taking almost all the traffic of lines that stretched right across the continent. Beyond Sto Lat the Trunk began to split into tributaries, but here, flashing overhead, the words of the world were flowing—

—should be flowing. But the shutters were still. As he drew level, Moist saw men working high up on the open wooden tower; by the look of it, a whole section had broken off.

Ha! So long, suckers! That'd take some repairing! Worth an overnight attempt at a delivery to Pseudopolis, maybe? He'd talk to the coachmen. It wasn't as if they'd ever paid the Post Office for their damn coaches. And it wouldn't matter if the clacks got repaired in time, either, because the Post Office would have *made the effort*. The clacks company was a big bully, sacking people, racking up the charges, demanding lots of money for bad service. The Post Office was the underdog, and an underdog can always find somewhere soft to bite.

Carefully, he eased more of the blanket under him. Various organs were going numb.

The towering fumes of Ankh-Morpork were falling far behind. Sto Lat was visible between Boris's ears, a plume of lesser smokes. The tower disappeared astern and already Moist could see the next one. He'd ridden more than a third of the way in twenty minutes, and Boris was still eating up the ground.

About halfway between the cities was an old stone tower, all that remained of a heap of ruins surrounded by woodland. It was almost as high as a clacks tower and Moist wondered why they hadn't simply used it as one. It was probably too derelict to survive in a gale under the weight of the shutters, he thought. The area looked bleak, a piece of weedy wilderness in the endless fields.

If he'd had spurs, Moist would have spurred Boris on at this point, and would probably have been thrown, trampled and eaten for his pains.* Instead, he lay low over the horse's back and tried not to think about what this ride was doing to his kidneys.

Time passed.

The second tower went by, and Boris dropped into a canter. Sto Lat was clearly visible now; Moist could make out the city walls and the turrets of the castle.

He'd have to jump off; there was no other way. Moist had tried out half a dozen scenarios as the walls loomed, but nearly all of them involved haystacks. The one that didn't was the one where he broke his neck.

But it didn't seem to occur to Boris to turn aside. He was on a road, the road was straight, it went through this gateway and Boris had no problem with that. Besides, he wanted a drink.

The city streets were crowded with things that couldn't be jumped or trampled, but there *was* a horse trough. He was only vaguely aware of something falling off his back.

Sto Lat wasn't a big city. Moist had once spent a happy week there, passing a few dud bills, pulling off the Indigent Heir trick twice and selling a glass ring on the way out, not so much for the money as out of a permanent fascination with human deviousness and gullibility.

Now he staggered up the steps of the town hall, watched by a crowd. He pushed open the doors and slammed the mailbag on the desk of the first clerk he saw.

'Mail from Ankh-Morpork,' he growled. 'Started out at nine, so it's fresh, okay?'

'But it's only just struck a quarter past ten! What mail?'

Moist tried not to get angry. He was sore enough as it was.

---

* Which would have been agonizing.

'See this hat?' he said, pointing. 'You see it? That means I'm the Postmaster General of Ankh-Morpork! *This* is your mail! In an hour I'm going back again, understand? If you want mail de-liv-ered to the big city by two p.m.— Ouch. Make that three p.m. – then put it in this bag. *These*,' he waved a wad of stamps under the young man's nose, 'are stamps! Red ones tuppence, black ones a penny. It'll cost ten – ow – eleven pence per letter, got it? You sell the stamps, you give me the money, you lick the stamps and put them on the letters! Express Delivery guaranteed! I'm making you Acting Postmaster for an hour. There's an inn next door. I've going to find a bath. I want a cold bath. Really cold. Got an ice house here? As cold as that. Colder. Ooooh, colder. And a drink and a sandwich and by the way there's a big black horse outside. If your people can catch him, please put a saddle on him and a cushion and drag him round to face Ankh-Morpork. Do it!'

It was only a hip bath, but at least there was an ice house in the city. Moist sat in a state of bliss amongst the floating ice, drinking a brandy, and listened to the commotion outside.

After a while there was a knock at the door, and a male voice enquired: 'Are you decent, Mr Postmaster?'

'Thoroughly decent, but not dressed,' said Moist. He reached down beside him and put his wingèd hat on again. 'Do come in.'

The mayor of Sto Lat was a short, bird-like man, who'd either become mayor very recently and immediately after the post had been held by a big fat man, or thought that a robe that trailed several feet behind you and a chain that reached to the waist was *the* look for civic dignitaries this year.

'Er . . . Joe Camels, sir,' he said nervously. 'I'm the mayor here . . .'

'Really? Good to meet you, Joe,' said Moist, raising his glass. 'Excuse me if I don't get up.'

'Your horse, er, has run away after kicking three men, I'm sorry to say.'

'Really? He never usually does that,' said Moist.

'Don't worry, sir, we'll catch him, and anyway we can let you have a horse to get back on. Not as fast, though, I dare say.'

'Oh dear,' said Moist, easing himself into a new position amongst the floating ice. 'That's a shame.'

'Oh, I know all about *you*, Mr Lipwig,' said the mayor, winking conspiratorially. 'There were some copies of the *Times* in the mailbag! A man who wants to be up and doing, you are. A man full of vim, you are! A man after my own heart, you are! You aim for the moon, you do! You see your target and you go for it hell for leather, you do! That's how I does business, too! You're a go-getter, just like me! I'd like you to put it here, sir!'

'What where?' said Moist, stirring uneasily in his rapidly-becoming-lukewarm tub. 'Oh.' He shook the proffered hand. 'What *is* your business, Mr Camels?'

'I make parasols,' said the mayor. 'And it's about time that clacks company was told what's what! It was all fine up until a few months ago – I mean, they made you pay through the nose but at least stuff got where it was going fast as an arrow, but now it's all these breakdowns and repairs and they charge even more, mark you! And they never tell you how long you're going to be waiting, it's always "very shortly". They're always "sorry for the inconvenience" – they even got that written on a sign they hang up on the office! As warm and human as a thrown knife, just like you said. So you know what we just done? We went round to the clacks tower in the city and had a serious word with young Davey, who's a decent lad, and he gave us back all the overnight clacks for the big city that never got sent. How about that, eh?'

'Won't he get into trouble?'

'He says he's quitting anyway. None of the boys like the way the company's run now. They've all been stamped for you, just like you said. Well, I'll let you get dressed, Mr Lipwig. Your horse is ready.' He stopped at the door. 'Oh, just one thing, sir, about them stamps . . .'

'Yes? Is there a problem, Mr Camels?' said Moist.

'Not as such, sir. I wouldn't say anything against Lord Vetinari, sir, or Ankh-Morpork' – said a man living within twenty miles of a proud and touchy citizenry – 'but, er, it doesn't seem right, licking . . . well, licking Ankh-Morpork stamps. Couldn't you print up a few for us? We've got a Queen, nice girl. She'd look good on a stamp. We're an important city, you know!'

'I'll see what I can do, Mr Camels. Got a picture of her, by any chance?'

They'll all want one, he thought, as he got dressed. Having your own stamps could be like having your own flag, your own crest. It could be big! And I bet I could do a deal with my friend Mr Spools, oh yes. Doesn't matter if you haven't got your own post office, you've got to have your own stamp . . .

An enthusiastic crowd saw him off on a horse which, while no Boris, did his best and seemed to know what reins were for. Moist gratefully accepted the cushion on the saddle, too. That added more glitter to the glass: *he'd ridden so hard he needed a cushion!*

He set off with a full mailbag. Amazingly, once again, people had bought stamps just to own them. The *Times* had got around. Here was something new, so people wanted to be part of it.

Once he was cantering over the fields, though, he felt the fizz die away. He was employing Stanley, a bunch of game but creaky old men, and some golems. He couldn't keep this up.

But the thing was, you added sparkle. You told people what you intended to do and they believed you *could* do it. Anyone could have done this ride. No one had. They kept waiting for the clacks to be repaired.

He took things gently along the road, speeding up as he passed the clacks tower that had been under repair. It was still under repair, in fact, but he could see more men around it and high up on the tower. There was a definite suggestion that repair work was suddenly going a lot faster.

As he watched, he was sure he saw someone fall off. It probably wouldn't be a good idea to go over there and see if he could help, though, not if he wanted to continue to go through life with his own teeth. Besides, it was a long, long drop all the way down to the cabbage fields, handily combining death and burial at the same time.

He speeded up again when he reached the city. Somehow trotting up to the Post Office steps was not an option. The queue – *still* a queue – cheered when he cantered up.

Mr Groat came running out, insofar as a crab can run.

'Can you make another delivery to Sto Lat, sir?' he shouted. 'Got a full bag already! And everyone's asking when you'll be taking 'em to Pseudopolis and Quirm! Got one here for Lancre, too!'

'What? That's five hundred damn miles, man!' Moist dismounted, although the state of his legs turned the action into more of a drop.

'It's all got a bit busy since you were away,' said Groat, steadying him. 'Oh, yes indeed! Ain't got enough people! But there's people wanting jobs, too, sir, since the paper came out! People from the old postal families, just like me! Even some more workers out of retirement! I took the liberty of taking them on pro tem for the time being, seeing as I'm Acting Postmaster. I hope that's all right with you, sir? And Mr Spools is running off more stamps! I've twice had to send Stanley up for more. I hear we'll have the early fivepennies and the dollars out tonight! Great times, eh, sir?'

'Er . . . yes,' said Moist. Suddenly the whole world had turned into a kind of Boris – moving fast, inclined to bite and impossible to steer. The only way not to be ground down was to stay on top.

Inside the hall extra makeshift tables had been set up. They were crowded with people.

'We're selling them the envelopes and paper,' said Groat. 'The ink is free gratis.'

'Did you think that up yourself?' said Moist.

'No, it's what we used to do,' said Groat. 'Miss Maccalariat got a load of cheap paper from Spools.'

'Miss Maccalariat?' said Moist. 'Who is Miss Maccalariat?'

'Very old Post Office family, sir,' said Groat. 'She's decided to work for you.' He looked a little nervous.

'Sorry?' said Moist. '*She* has decided to work for *me*?'

'Well, you know what it's like with Post Office people, sir,' said Groat. 'We don't like to—'

'Are you the postmaster?' said a withering voice behind Moist.

The voice went into his head, bored down through his memories, riffled through his fears, found the right levers, battened on to them and pulled. In Moist's case, it found Frau Shambers. In the second year at school you were precipitated out of the warm, easy-going kindergarten of Frau Tissel, smelling of finger paint, salt dough and inadequate toilet training, and on to the cold benches governed by Frau Shambers, smelling of Education. It was as bad as being born, with the added disadvantage that your mother wasn't there.

Moist automatically turned and looked down. Yes, there they were, the sensible shoes, the thick black stockings that were slightly hairy, the baggy cardigan – oh, yes, arrgh, the cardigan; Frau Shambers used to stuff the sleeves with handkerchiefs, arrgh, arrgh – and the glasses and the expression like an early frost. And her hair was plaited and coiled up on either side of her head in those discs that back home in Uberwald had been called 'snails' but in Ankh-Morpork put people in mind of a woman with a curly iced bun clamped to each ear.

'Now look here, Miss Maccalariat,' he said firmly. 'I am the postmaster here, and I am in charge, and I do not intend to be browbeaten by a member of the counter staff just because their ancestors worked here. I do not fear your clumpy shoes, Miss Maccalariat, I smile happily in the teeth of your icy stare. Fie on you! Now I am a grown man, Frau Shambers, I will quake not at your sharp voice and will control my bladder perfectly however hard you look at me, oh yes indeed! For I am the Postmaster and my word here is law!'

That was the sentence his brain said. Unfortunately it got routed through his trembling backbone on the way to his mouth and issued from his lips as: 'Er, yes!' which came out as a squeak.

'*Mr* Lipwig, I ask you: I have nothing against them, but are these golems you are employing in my Post Office gentlemen or ladies?' the terrible woman demanded.

This was sufficiently unexpected to jolt Moist back into something like reality. 'What?' he said. 'I don't know! What's the difference? A bit more clay . . . less clay? Why?'

Miss Maccalariat folded her arms, causing both Moist and Mr Groat to shy backwards.

'I hope you're not funning with me, Mr Lipwig?' she demanded.

'What? Funning? I never fun!' Moist tried to pull himself together. Whatever happened next, he could not be made to stand in the corner. 'I do not fun, Miss Maccalariat, and have no history of funning, and even if I were inclined to funning, Miss Maccalariat, I would not dream of funning with you. What is the problem?'

'One of them was in the ladies' . . . rest room, Mr Lipwig,' said Miss Maccalariat.

'Doing what? I mean, they don't eat, so—'

'Cleaning it, *apparently*,' said Miss Maccalariat, contriving to suggest that she had dark suspicions on this point. 'But I have heard them referred to as "Mister".'

'Well, they do odd jobs all the time, because they don't like to stop working,' said Moist. 'And we prefer to give them Mister as an honorific because, er, "it" seems wrong and there are some people, yes, some people for whom the word "Miss" is not appropriate, Miss Maccalariat.'

'It is the *principle* of the thing, Mr Lipwig,' said the woman firmly. 'Anyone called Mister is *not* allowed in the Ladies. That sort of thing can only lead to hanky-panky. I will not stand for it, Mr Lipwig.'

Moist stared at her. Then he looked up at Mr Pump, who was never far away.

'Mr Pump, is there any reason why one of the golems can't have a new name?' he asked. 'In the interest of hanky-panky avoidance?'

'No, Mr Lipvig,' the golem rumbled.

Moist turned back to Miss Maccalariat. 'Would "Gladys" do, Miss Maccalariat?'

'Gladys will be sufficient, Mr Lipwig,' said Miss Maccalariat, more than a hint of triumph in her voice. 'She must be properly clothed, of course.'

'Clothed?' said Moist weakly. 'But a golem isn't— it doesn't— they don't have . . .' He quailed under the glare, and gave up. 'Yes, Miss Maccalariat. Something gingham, I think, Mr Pump?'

'I Shall Arrange It, Postmaster,' said the golem.

'Will that be all right, Miss Maccalariat?' said Moist meekly.

'For the present,' said Miss Maccalariat, as if she regretted that there were currently no further things to complain of. 'Mr Groat knows my particulars, Postmaster. I will now return to the proper execution of my duties, otherwise people will try to steal the pens again. You have to watch them like hawks, you know.'

'A good woman, that,' said Groat, as she strode away. 'Fifth generation of Miss Maccalariats. Maiden name kept for professional purposes, o' course.'

'They get *married*?' From the mob around the makeshift counter came the ringing command: 'Put that pen back this minute! Do you think I'm made of pens?'

'Yessir,' said Groat.

'Do they bite their husbands' heads off on their wedding night?' said Moist.

'I wouldn't know about that sort of thing, sir,' said Groat, blushing.

'But she's even got a bit of a moustache!'

'Yessir. There's someone for everyone in this wonderful world, sir.'

'And we've got other people looking for work, you say?'

Groat beamed. 'That's right, sir. 'cos of the bit in the paper, sir.'

'You mean this morning?'

'I expect that helped, sir,' said Groat. 'But I reckon it was the lunchtime edition that did it.'

'*What lunchtime edition?*'

'We're all over the front page!' said Groat proudly. 'I put a copy on your desk upstairs—'

Moist pushed the Sto Lat mailbag into the man's arms. 'Get this . . . sorted,' he said. 'If there's enough mail for another delivery to go, find some kid who's mad for a job and put him on a horse and get him to take it. Doesn't have to be fast; we'll call it the overnight delivery. Tell him to see the mayor and come back in the morning with any fresh mail.'

'Right you are, sir,' said Groat. 'We could do an overnight to Quirm and Pseudopolis too, sir, if we could change horses like the mail coaches do—'

'Hang on . . . why *can't* the mail coaches take it?' said Moist. 'Hell, they're still *called* mail coaches, right? We know they take stuff from anyone, on the quiet. Well, the Post Office is back in business. They take our mail. Go and find whoever runs them and tell him so!'

'Yessir,' said Groat, beaming. 'Thought about how we're going to send post to the moon yet, sir?'

'One thing at a time, Mr Groat!'

'That's not like you, sir,' said Groat cheerfully. 'All at once is more your style, sir!'

I wish it wasn't, Moist thought, as he eased his way upstairs. But you had to move fast. He always moved fast. His whole life had been movement. Move fast, because you never know what's trying to catch you up—

He paused on the stairs.

Not Mr Pump!

The golem hadn't left the Post Office! He hadn't tried to catch him up! Was it that he'd been on postal business? How *long* could he be away on postal business? Could he fake his death, maybe? The old pile-of-clothes-on-the-seashore trick? Worth remembering. All he needed was a long enough start. How did a golem's mind actually work? He'd have to ask Miss—

Miss Dearheart! He'd been flying so high that he'd asked her out! That might be a problem now, because most of the lower part of his body was on fire, not especially for Miss Dearheart. Oh, well, he thought as he entered the office, perhaps he could find a restaurant with really soft seats—

FASTER THAN THE 'SPEED OF LIGHT'

'Old-fashioned' Mail Beats Clacks

Postmaster delivers, says: Snook Not Cocked

Amazing Scenes at Post Office

The headlines screamed at him as soon as he saw the paper. He almost screamed back.

Of course he'd said all that. But he'd said it to the innocent smiling face of Miss Sacharissa Cripslock, not to the whole world! And then she'd written it down all truthfully, and suddenly . . . you got this.

Moist had never much bothered with newspapers. He was an artist. He wasn't interested in big schemes. You swindled the man in front of you, looking him sincerely in the eyes.

The picture was good, though, he had to admit. The rearing horse, the wingèd hat and above all the slight blurring with speed. It was impressive.

He relaxed a little. The place was *operating*, after all. Letters were being posted. Mail was being delivered. Okay, so a major part of it all was that the clacks wasn't working properly, but maybe in time people would see that a letter to your sister in Sto Lat didn't need to cost thirty pence to *maybe* get there in an hour but might as well cost a mere five pence to be there in the morning.

Stanley knocked at the door and then pushed it open.

'Cup of tea, Mr Lipwig?' he said. 'And a bun, sir.'

'You're an angel in heavy disguise, Stanley,' said Moist, sitting back with care, and wincing.

'Yes, thank you, sir,' said Stanley solemnly. 'Got some messages for you, sir.'

'Thank you, Stanley,' said Moist. There was a lengthy pause until he remembered that this was Stanley he was talking to and added: 'Please tell me what they are, Stanley.'

'Er . . . the golem lady came in and said . . .' Stanley closed his eyes, ' "Tell the Streak of Lightning he'll have another eight golems in the morning and if he's not too busy working miracles I'll accept his invitation to dine at eight at Le Foie Heureux, meeting at the Mended Drum at seven." '

'The Happy Liver? Are you sure?' But of course it would be correct. This was Stanley. 'Ha, even the damn soup there is fifteen dollars!' said Moist. 'And you have to wait three weeks for an appointment to be considered for a booking! They weigh your wallet! How does she think I—'

His eye fell on 'Mr Robinson's box', sitting innocently in the corner of the office. He *liked* Miss Dearheart. Most people were . . . accessible. Sooner or later you could find the springs that worked them; even Miss Maccalariat would have a lever somewhere, although it was a horrible thought. But Adora Belle fought back, and to make sure fought back even before she was attacked. She was a challenge, and therefore fascinating. She was so cynical, so defensive, so *spiky*. And he had a feeling she could read him much, much better than he read her. All in all, she was intriguing. And looked good in a severely plain dress, don't forget that bit.

'Okay. Thank you, Stanley,' he said. 'Anything else?'

The boy put a sheet of slightly damp greeny-grey stamps on the desk. 'The first dollar stamps, sir!' he announced.

'My word, Mr Spools has done a good job here!' said Moist, staring at the hundreds of little green pictures of the university's Tower of Art. 'It even *looks* worth a dollar!'

'Yes, sir. You hardly notice the little man jumping from the top,' said Stanley.

Moist snatched the sheet from the boy's hand. 'What? Where?'

'You need a magnifying glass, sir. And it's only on a few of them. In some of them he's in the water. Mr Spools is very sorry, sir. He says it may be some kind of induced magic. You know, sir? Like, even a picture of a wizards' tower might be a bit magical itself? There's a few faults on some of the others, too. The printing went wrong on some of the black penny ones and Lord Vetinari's got grey hair, sir. Some haven't got gum on, but they're all right because some people have asked for them that way.'

'Why?'

'They say they're as good as real pennies and a whole lot lighter, sir.'

'Do you like stamps, Stanley?' said Moist kindly. He was feeling a lot better in a seat that didn't go up and down.

Stanley's face lit up. 'Oh, *yes*, sir. Really, sir. They're wonderful, sir! Amazing, sir!'

Moist raised his eyebrows. 'As good as that, eh?'

'It's like . . . well, it's like being there when they invented the first pin, sir!' Stanley's face glowed.

'Really? The first pin, eh?' said Moist. 'Outstanding! Well, in that case, Stanley, you are Head of Stamps. The whole department. Which is, in fact, you. How do you like that? I imagine you already know more about them than anyone else.'

'Oh, I do, sir! For example, on the very first run of the penny stamps they used a different type of—'

'Good!' said Moist hurriedly. 'Well done! Can I keep this first sheet? As a souvenir?'

'Of course, sir,' said Stanley. 'Head of Stamps, sir? Wow! Er . . . is there a hat?'

'If you like,' said Moist generously, folding up the sheet of stamps and putting them in his inside pocket. So much more convenient than dollars. Wow, indeed. 'Or perhaps a shirt?' he added. 'You know . . . "Ask Me About Stamps"?'

'Good idea, sir! Can I go and tell Mr Groat, sir? He'd be so proud of me!'

'Off you go, Stanley,' said Moist. 'But come back in ten minutes, will you? I'll have a letter for you to deliver – personally.'

Stanley ran off.

Moist opened the wooden box, which fanned out its trays obediently, and flexed his fingers.

Hmm. It seemed that anyone who was, well, anyone in the city had their paper printed by Teemer and Spools. Moist thumbed through his recently acquired paper samples, and spotted:

THE GRAND TRUNK COMPANY
'As Fast As Light'

From the Office of the Chairman

It was tempting. Very tempting. They were rich, very rich. Even with the current trouble, they were still very big. And

Moist had never met a head waiter who hated money.

He found a copy of yesterday's *Times*. There'd been a picture . . . yes, here. There was a picture of Reacher Gilt, chairman of the Grand Trunk, at some function. He looked like a better class of pirate, a buccaneer maybe, but one who took the time to polish his plank. That flowing black hair, that beard, that eyepatch and, oh gods, that cockatoo . . . that was a Look, wasn't it?

Moist hadn't paid much attention to the Grand Trunk Company. It was too big, and from what he'd heard it practically employed its own army. Things could be tough in the mountains, where you were often a long way from anything that resembled a watchman. It wasn't a good idea to steal things from people who did their own law enforcement. They tended to be very definite.

But what he was intending wouldn't be stealing. It might not even be breaking the law. Fooling a maître d' was practically a public service.

He looked at the picture again. Now, how would a man like that sign his name?

Hmm . . . flowing yet small, that would be the handwriting of Reacher Gilt. He was so florid, so sociable, so huge a *personality* that one who was good at this sort of thing might wonder if another shard of glass was trying to sparkle like a diamond. And the essence of forgery is to make, by misdirection and careful timing, the glass look so much more like a diamond than a diamond does.

Well, it was worth a try. It was not as though he was going to swindle anyone, as such.

Hmm. Small yet flowing, yes . . . but someone who'd never seen the man's writing would expect it to be extravagantly big and curly, just like him . . .

Moist poised the pen over the headed paper, and then wrote:

Maître d',
Le Foie Heureux
 I would be most grateful if you could find a table for

my good friend Mr Lipwig and his lady at eight o'clock
tonight.
   Reacher Gilt

Most grateful, that was good. The Reacher Gilt persona probably tipped like a drunken sailor.

He folded the letter, and was addressing the envelope when Stanley and Groat came in.

'You've got a letter, Mr Lipwig,' said Stanley proudly.

'Yes, here it is,' said Moist.

'No, I mean here's one for you,' said the boy. They exchanged envelopes. Moist glanced cursorily at the envelope, and opened it with a thumb.

'I've got bad news, sir,' said Groat, as Stanley left.

'Hmm?' said Moist, looking at the letter.

Postmaster,
   The Pseudopolis clacks line will break down at 9 a.m.
tomorrow.
   The Smoking Gnu

'Yessir. I went round to the coach office,' Groat went on, 'and told them what you said and they said you stick to your business, thank you very much, and they'll stick to theirs.'

'Hmm,' said Moist, still staring at the letter. 'Well, well. Have you heard of someone called "The Smoking Gnu", Mr Groat?'

'What's a gernue, sir?'

'A bit like a dangerous cow, I think,' said Moist. 'Er . . . what were you saying about the coach people?'

'They give me *lip*, sir, that's what they give me,' said Groat. 'I *told* 'em, I *told* 'em I was the Assistant Head Postmaster and they said "so what?" sir. Then I said I'd tell you, sir, and they said— you want to know what they said, sir?'

'Hmm. Oh, yes. I'm agog, Tolliver.' Moist's eyes were scanning the strange letter over and over again.

'They said "yeah, right",' said Groat, a beacon of righteous indignation.

'I wonder if Mr Trooper can still fit me in . . .' mused Moist, staring at the ceiling.

'Sorry, sir?'

'Oh, nothing. I suppose I'd better go and talk to them. Go and find Mr Pump, will you? And tell him to bring a couple of the other golems, will you? I want to . . . impress people.'

Igor opened the front door in answer to the knock.

There was no one there. He stepped outside and looked up and down the street.

There was no one there.

He stepped back inside, closing the door behind him – and no one was standing in the hall, his black cloak dripping rain, removing his wide, flat-brimmed hat.

'Ah, Mithter Gryle, thur,' Igor said to the tall figure, 'I thould have known it wath you.'

'Reacher Gilt asked for me,' said Gryle. It was more a breath than a voice.

The clan of the Igors had had any tendency to shuddering bred out of it generations ago, which was just as well. Igor felt uneasy in the presence of Gryle and his kind.

'The marthter ith expecting—' he began.

But there was no one there.

It wasn't magic, and Gryle wasn't a vampire. Igors could spot these things. It was just that there was nothing *spare* about him – spare flesh, spare time, or spare words. It was impossible to imagine Gryle collecting pins, or savouring wine or even throwing up after a bad pork pie. The picture of him cleaning his teeth or sleeping completely failed to form in the mind. He gave the impression of restraining himself, with difficulty, from killing you.

Thoughtfully, Igor went down to his room off the kitchen and checked that his little leather bag was packed, just in case.

In his study, Reacher Gilt poured a small brandy. Gryle looked around him with eyes that seemed not at home with the limited vistas of a room.

'And for yourself?' said Gilt.

'Water,' said Gryle.

'I expect you know what this is about?'

'No.' Gryle was not a man for small talk or, if it came to it, any talk at all.

'You've read the newspapers?'

'Do not read.'

'You know about the Post Office.'

'Yes.'

'How, may I ask?'

'There is talk.'

Gilt accepted that. Mr Gryle had a special talent, and if that came as a package with funny little ways then so be it. Besides, he was trustworthy; a man without middle grounds. He'd never blackmail you, because such an attempt would be the first move in a game that would almost certainly end in death for *somebody*; if Mr Gryle found himself in such a game he'd kill right now, without further thought, in order to save time, and assumed that anyone else would, too. Presumably he was insane, by the usual human standards, but it was hard to tell; the phrase 'differently normal' might do instead. After all, Gryle could probably defeat a vampire within ten seconds, and had none of a vampire's vulnerabilities, except perhaps an inordinate fondness for pigeons. He'd been a real find.

'And you have discovered nothing about Mr Lipwig?' Gilt said.

'No. Father dead. Mother dead. Raised by grandfather. Sent away to school. Bullied. Ran away. Vanished,' said the tall figure.

'Hmm. I wonder where he's been all this time? Or *who* he has been?'

Gryle didn't waste breath on rhetorical questions.

'He is . . . a nuisance.'

'Understood.' And that was the charm. Gryle *did* understand. He seldom needed an order, you just had to state the problem. The fact that it was Gryle that you were stating it to went a long way towards ensuring what the solution was likely to be.

'The Post Office building is old and full of paper. Very *dry* paper,' said Gilt. 'It would be regrettable if the fine old place caught fire.'

'Understood.'

And that was another thing about Gryle. He really did not talk much. He especially did not talk about old times, and all the other little solutions he had provided for Reacher Gilt. And he never said things like 'What do you mean?' He understood.

'Require one thousand, three hundred dollars,' he said.

'Of course,' said Gilt. 'I will clacks it to your account in—'

'Will take cash,' said Gryle.

'Gold? I don't keep that much around,' said Gilt. 'I can get it in a few days, of course, but I thought you preferred—'

'I do not trust the semaphore now.'

'But our ciphers are very well—'

'I do not trust the semaphore now,' Gryle repeated.

'Very well.'

'Description,' said Gryle.

'No one seems to remember what he looks like,' said Gilt. 'But he always wears a big golden hat, with wings, and he has an apartment in the building.'

For a moment something flickered around Gryle's thin lips. It was a smile panicking at finding itself in such an unfamiliar place.

'Can he fly?' he said.

'Alas, he doesn't seem inclined to venture into high places,' said Gilt.

Gryle stood up. 'I will do this tonight.'

'Good man. Or, rather—'

'Understood,' said Gryle.

CHAPTER NINE

Bonfire

*Slugger and Leadpipe – Gladys Pulls It Off – The Hour of the Dead –
Irrational Fear of Dental Spinach – 'A proper brawl doesn't just happen'
– How the Trunk Was Stolen – Stanley's Little Moment – The etiquette
of knives – Face to Face – Fire*

THE MAIL COACHES HAD SURVIVED the decline and fall of the Post
Office because they had to. Horses needed to be fed. But in any
case, the coaches had always carried passengers. The halls went silent,
the chandeliers disappeared along with everything else, even things
that were nailed down, but out back in the big yard the coach service
flourished. The coaches weren't exactly stolen, and weren't exactly
inherited . . . they just drifted into the possession of the coach people.

Then, according to Groat, who regarded himself as the custodian of
all Post Office knowledge, the other coach drivers had been bought
out by Big Jim 'Still Standing' Upwright with the money he'd won
betting on himself in a bare knuckle contest against Harold 'The Hog'
Boots, and the coach business was now run by his sons Harry
'Slugger' Upwright and Little Jim 'Leadpipe' Upwright.

Moist could see that a careful approach was going to be required.

The hub or nerve centre of the coach business was a big shed next
to the stable. It smelled – no, it stank – no, it *fugged* of horses, leather,
veterinary medicine, bad coal, brandy and cheap cigars. That's what a
fug was. You could have cut cubes out of the air and sold it for cheap
building material.

When Moist entered, a huge man, made practically spherical by
multiple layers of waistcoats and overcoats, was warming his backside
in front of the roaring stove. Another man of very much the same
shape was leaning over the shoulder of a clerk, both of them
concentrating on some paper.

Some staffing debate had obviously been in progress, because the man by the fire was saying '. . . well, then, if he's sick put young Alfred on the evening run and—'

He stopped when he saw Moist, and then said, 'Yes, sir? What can we do for you?'

'Carry my mailbags,' said Moist.

They stared at him, and then the man who'd been toasting his bottom broke into a grin. Jim and Harry Upwright might have been twins. They were *big* men, who looked as though they'd been built out of pork and fat bacon.

'Are you this shiny new postmaster we've been hearing about?'

'That's right.'

'Yeah, well, your man was already here,' said the toaster. 'Went on and on about how we should do this and do that, never said anything about the price!'

'A price?' said Moist, spreading out his hands and beaming. 'Is that all this is about? Easily done. Easily done.'

He turned, opened the door and shouted: 'Okay, Gladys!'

There was some shouting in the darkness of the yard, and then the creak of timber.

'What the hell did you do?' said the spherical man.

'My price is this,' said Moist. 'You agree to carry my mail, and you won't have another wheel dragged off that mail coach out there. I can't say fairer than that, okay?'

The man lumbered forward, growling, but the other coachman grabbed his coat.

'Steady there, Jim,' he said. 'He's gov'ment and he's got golems working for 'im.'

On cue, Mr Pump stepped into the room, bending to get through the doorway. Jim scowled at him.

'That don't frighten me!' said Jim. 'They ain't allowed to hurt folks!'

'Wrong,' said Moist. 'Probably dead wrong.'

'Then we'll call the Watch on yer,' said Harry Upwright, still holding back his brother. 'All proper and official. How d'you like that?'

'Good, call the Watch,' said Moist. 'And I shall tell them I'm recovering stolen property.' He raised his voice. 'Gladys!'

There was another crash from outside.

'Stolen? Those coaches are ours!' said Harry Upwright.

'Wrong again, I'm afraid,' said Moist. 'Mr Pump?'

'The Mail Coaches Were Never Sold Off,' the golem rumbled. 'They Are The Property Of The Post Office. No Rent Has Been Paid For The Use Of Post Office Property.'

'Right, that's it!' Jim roared, shaking his brother away. Mr Pump's fists rose, instantly.

The world paused.

'Hold on, Jim, hold on just one minute,' said Harry Upwright carefully. 'What's your game, Mr Postman? The coaches always used to carry passengers too, right? And then there was no mail to take but people still wanted to travel, and the coaches were just standing around and the horses were needing to be fed, so our dad paid for the fodder and the vet's bills and no one—'

'Just take my mail,' said Moist. 'That's all. Every coach takes the mailbags and drops them off where I say. That's all. Tell me where you'll get a better deal tonight, eh? You could try your luck pleading finders keepers to Vetinari but that'd take a while to sort out and in the meantime you'd lose all that lovely revenue . . . No? Okay. Glady—'

'No! No! Wait a minute,' said Harry. 'Just the mailbags? That's all?'

'What?' said Jim. 'You want to negotiate? Why? They say possession's nine points of the law, right?'

'And I possess a lot of golems, Mr Upwright,' said Moist. 'And you don't possess any deeds, mortgages or bills of sale.'

'Yeah? And you won't possess any teeth, mister!' said Jim, rolling forward.

'Now, now,' said Moist, stepping quickly in front of Mr Pump and raising a hand. 'Don't kill me again, Mr Upwright.'

Both the brothers looked puzzled.

'I'll swear Jim never laid a finger on you, and that's the truth,' said Harry. 'What's your game?'

'Oh, he did, Harry,' said Moist. 'Lost his temper, took a swing, I went over, hit my head on that old bench there, got up not knowing where the hell I was, you tried to hold Jim back, he hit me with that chair, the one just there, and down I went for keeps. The golems got you, Harry, but Jim went on the run, only to be tracked down by the Watch in Sto Lat. Oh, what scenes, what chases, and you both ended up in the Tanty, the charge against the pair of you being murder—'

'Here, *I* didn't hit you with the chair!' said Harry, eyes wide. 'It was Ji— Here, hang on a minute . . .'

'—and this morning Mr Trooper measured you up for the last necktie and there you were, standing in that room under the gallows, knowing that you'd lost your business, you'd lost your coaches, you'd lost your fine horses, and in two minutes—'

Moist let the sentence hang in the air.

'And?' said Harry. Both brothers were watching him with expressions of horrified confusion which would coalesce into violence inside five seconds if this didn't work. Keeping them off balance was the ticket.

Moist counted to four in his head, while smiling beatifically. 'And then an angel appeared,' he said.

Ten minutes can change a lot. It was enough to brew two cups of tea thick enough to spread on bread.

The brothers Upwright probably didn't believe in angels. But they believed in bullshit, and were the type to admire it when it was delivered with panache. There's a kind of big, outdoor sort of man who's got no patience at all with prevaricators and fibbers, but will applaud any man who can tell an outrageous whopper with a gleam in his eye.

'Funny you should turn up tonight,' said Harry.

'Oh? Why?'

''cos a man from the Grand Trunk came round this afternoon and offered us big money for the business. Too much money, you could say.'

Oh, thought Moist, something's starting . . .

'But *you*, Mr Lipwig, is giving us nothing but attitude and threats,' said Jim. 'Care to raise your offer?'

'Okay. Bigger threats,' said Moist. 'But I'll throw in a new paint job on every coach, gratis. Be *sensible*, gentlemen. You've had an easy ride, but now we're back in business. All you have to do is what you've always done, but you'll carry my mail. Come *on*, there's a lady waiting for me and you know you shouldn't keep a lady waiting. What do you say?'

'Is she an angel?' said Harry.

'He probably hopes not, hur, hur.' Jim had a laugh like a bull clearing its throat.

'Hur, hur,' said Moist solemnly. 'Just carry the bags, gents. The Post Office is going places and you could be in the driving seat.'

The brothers exchanged a glance. Then they grinned. It was as if one grin spread across two glistening red faces.

'Our dad would've liked you,' said Jim.

'He sure as hell wouldn't like the Grand Trunk devils,' said Harry. 'They need cutting down to size, Mr Lipwig, and people are saying you're the man to do it.'

'People die on them towers,' said Jim. 'We see, you know. Damn right! The towers follows the coach roads. We used to have the contract to haul lads out to the towers and we heard 'em talking. They used to have an hour a day when they shut the whole Trunk down for maint'nance.'

'The Hour of the Dead, they called it,' said Harry. 'Just before dawn. That's when people die.'

Across a continent, the line of light, beads on the pre-dawn darkness. And, then, the Hour of the Dead begins, at either end of the Grand Trunk, as the upline and downline shutters clear their messages and stop moving, one after the other.

The men of the towers had prided themselves on the speed with which they could switch their towers from black and white daylight transmission to the light and dark mode of the night. On a good day

they could do it with barely a break in transmission, clinging to swaying ladders high above the ground while around them the shutters
rattled and chattered. There were heroes who'd lit all sixteen lamps on
a big tower in less than a minute, sliding down ladders, swinging
on ropes, keeping their tower alive. 'Alive' was the word they used. No
one wanted a dark tower, not even for a minute.

The Hour of the Dead was different. That was one hour for repairs,
replacements, maybe even some paperwork. It was mostly replacements. It was fiddly to repair a shutter high up on the tower with the
wind making it tremble and freezing the blood in your fingers, and
always better to swing it out and down to the ground and slot another
one in place. But when you were running out of time, it was tempting
to brave the wind and try to free the bloody shutters by hand.

Sometimes the wind won. The Hour of the Dead was when men
died.

And when a man died, they sent him home by clacks.

Moist's mouth dropped open. 'Huh?'

'That's what they call it,' said Harry. 'Not lit'rally, o' course. But they
send his name from one end of the Trunk to the other, ending up at
the tower nearest his home.'

'Yeah, but they say sometimes the person stays on in the towers,
somehow,' said Jim. ' "Living in the Overhead", they call it.'

'But they're mostly pissed when they say that,' said Harry.

'Oh, yes, mostly pissed, I'll grant you,' said his brother. 'They get
worked too hard. There's no Hour of the Dead now; they only get
twenty minutes. They cut the staff, too. They used to run a slow
service on Octedays; now it's high speed all the time, except towers
keep breaking down. We seen lads come down from them towers with
their eyes spinning and their hands shaking and no idea if it's bum or
breakfast time. It drives 'em mad. Eh? Damn right!'

'Except that they're already mad,' said Harry. 'You'd have to be mad
to work up in them things.'

'They get so mad even ordinary mad people think they're mad.'

'That's right. But they still go back up there. The clacks drives them back. The clacks owns them, gets into their souls,' said Harry. 'They get paid practically nothing but I'll swear they'd go up those towers for free.'

'The Grand Trunk runs on blood now, since the new gang took over. It's killin' men for money,' said Jim.

Harry drained his mug. 'We won't have none of it,' he said. 'We'll run your mail for you, Mr Lipwig, for all that you wear a damn silly hat.'

'Tell me,' said Moist, 'have you ever heard of something called the Smoking Gnu?'

'Dunno much,' said Jim. 'A couple of the boys mentioned them once. Some kind of outlaw signallers, or something. Something to do with the Overhead.'

'What *is* the Overhead? Er . . . dead people live in it?'

'Look, Mr Lipwig, we just listen, okay,' said Jim. 'We chat to 'em nice and easy, 'cos when they come down from the towers they're so dozy they'll walk under your coach wheels—'

'It's the rocking in the wind,' said Harry. 'They walk like sailors.'

'Right. The Overhead? Well, they say a lot of the messages the clacks carries is *about* the clacks, okay? Orders from the company, house-keeping messages, messages *about* messages—'

'—dead men's names—' said Moist.

'Yeah, them too. Well, the Smoking Gnu is in there somewhere,' Jim went on. 'That's all I know. I drive coaches, Mr Lipwig. I ain't a clever man like them up on the towers. Hah, I'm stupid enough to keep my feet on the ground!'

'Tell Mr Lipwig about Tower 93, Jim,' said Harry. 'Make 'is flesh creep!'

'Yeah, heard about that one?' said Jim, looking slyly at Moist.

'No. What happened?'

'Only two lads were up there, where there should've been three. One of them went out in a gale to budge a stuck shutter, which he shouldn't've done, and fell off and got his safety rope tangled round his neck. So the other bloke rushed out to get him, without *his* safety rope – which he shouldn't've done – and they reckon he got blown right off the tower.'

'That's horrible,' said Moist. 'Not creepy, though. As such.'

'Oh, you want the creepy bit? Ten minutes after they was both dead the tower sent a message for help. Sent by a dead man's hand.' Jim stood up and put his tricorn hat on. 'Got to take a coach out in twenty minutes. Nice to meet you, Mr Lipwig.' He pulled open a drawer in the battered desk and pulled out a length of lead pipe. 'That's for highwaymen,' he said, and then took out a big silver brandy flask. 'And this is for me,' he added with rather more satisfaction. 'Eh? Damn right!'

And I thought the Post Office was full of crazy people, Moist thought.

'Thank you,' he said, standing. Then he remembered the strange letter in his pocket, for whatever use it was, and added: 'Have you got a coach stopping at Pseudopolis tomorrow?'

'Yeah, at ten o'clock,' said Harry.

'We'll have a bag for it,' said Moist.

'Is is worth it?' said Jim. 'It's more'n fifty miles, and I heard they've got the Trunk repaired. It's a stoppin' coach, won't get there 'til nearly dark.'

'Got to make the effort, Jim,' said Moist.

The coachman gave him a look with a little glint that indicated he thought Moist was up to something, but said: 'Well, you're game, I'll say that for you. We'll wait for your bag, Mr Lipwig, and the best of luck to you. Must rush, sir.'

'What coach are you taking out?' said Moist.

'I'll take the first two stages of the overnight flyer to Quirm, leaving at seven,' said Jim. 'If it's still got all its wheels.'

'It's nearly seven?'

'Twenty to, sir.'

'I'll be late!'

The coachmen watched him run back across the yard, with Mr Pump and Gladys trailing slowly behind.

Jim pulled on his thick leather gauntlets, thoughtfully, and then said to his brother: 'You know how you get them funny feelings?'

'I reckon I do, Jim.'

'And would you reckon there'll be a clacks failure between here and Pseudopolis tomorrow?'

'Funny you should mention that. Mind you, it'd be a two to one bet anyway, the way things have been going. Maybe he's just a betting man, Jim.'

'Yeah,' said Jim. 'Yeah. Eh? Damn right!'

Moist struggled out of the golden suit. It was good advertising, no doubt about it, and when he wore it he felt he had style coming out of his ears, but wearing something like that to the Mended Drum meant that he wanted to be hit over the head with a stool and what would come out of his ears wouldn't bear thinking about.

He threw the wingèd hat on the bed and struggled into his second golem-made suit. Sombre, he'd said. You had to hand it to golem tailoring. The suit was so black that if it had been sprinkled with stars the owls would have collided with it. He needed more time but Adora Belle Dearheart was not someone you felt you should keep waiting.

'You look fine, sir,' said Groat.

'Thanks, thanks,' said Moist, struggling with his tie. 'You're in charge, Mr Groat. Should all be quiet this evening. Remember, first thing tomorrow, all mail for Pseudopolis ten pence a go, okay?'

'Right you are, sir. Can I wear the hat now?' Groat pleaded.

'What? What?' said Moist, staring into the mirror. 'Look, have I got spinach between my teeth?'

'Have You Eaten Spinach Today, Sir?' said Mr Pump.

'I haven't eaten spinach since I was old enough to spit,' said Moist. 'But people always worry about that at a time like this, don't they? I thought it just turned up somehow. You know . . . like moss? What was it you asked me, Tolliver?'

'Can I wear the hat, sir?' said Groat patiently. 'Bein' as I'm your deputy and you're going out, sir.'

'But we're closed, Groat.'

'Yes, but . . . it's . . . I'd just like to wear the hat. For a while, sir. Just for a while, sir. If it's all right with you.' Groat shifted from one foot to the other. 'I mean, I *will* be in charge.'

Moist sighed. 'Yes, of course, Mr Groat. You may wear the hat. Mr Pump?'

'Yes, Sir?'

'Mr Groat is in charge for the evening. You will *not* follow me, please.'

'No, I Will Not. My Day Off Begins Now. For All Of Us. We Will Return At Sunset Tomorrow,' said the golem.

'Oh . . . yes.' One day off every week, Miss Dearheart said. It was part of what distinguished golems from hammers. 'I wish you'd given me more warning, you know? We're going to be a bit short-staffed.'

'You Were Told, Mr Lipvig.'

'Yes, yes. It is a rule. It's just that tomorrow is going to be—'

'Don't you worry about a thing, sir,' said Groat. 'Some of the lads I hired today, sir, they're postmen's sons, sir, and grandsons. No problem, sir. They'll be out delivering tomorrow.'

'Oh. Good. That's fine, then.' Moist adjusted the tie again. A black tie on a black shirt under a black jacket isn't easy even to find. 'All right, Mr Pump? Still no attack of spinach? I'm going to see a lady.'

'Yes, Mr Lipvig. Miss Dearheart,' said the golem calmly.

'How did you know that?' said Moist.

'You Shouted It Out In Front Of Approximately A Hundred People, Mr Lipvig,' said Mr Pump. 'We – That Is To Say, Mr Lipvig, All The Golems – We Wish Miss Dearheart Was A Happier Lady. She Has Had Much Trouble. She Is Looking For Someone With—'

'—a cigarette lighter?' said Moist quickly. 'Stop right there, Mr Pump, please! Cupids are these . . . little overweight kids in nappies, all right? Not big clay people.'

'Anghammarad Said She Reminded Him Of Lela The Volcano Goddess, Who Smokes All The Time Because The God Of Rain Has Rained On Her Lava,' the golem went on.

'Yes, but women always complain about that sort of thing,' said Moist. 'I look all right, Mr Groat, do I?'

'Oh, sir,' said Groat, 'I shouldn't think Mr Moist von Lipwig ever has to worry when he's off to meet a young lady, eh?'

Come to think of it, Moist came to think as he hurried through the crowded streets, he never has been off to meet a young lady. Not in all these years. Oh, Albert and all the rest of them had met hundreds, and had all kinds of fun, including once getting his jaw dislocated which was only fun in a no-fun-at-all kind of way. But Moist, never. He'd always been behind the false moustache or glasses or, really, just the false person. He had that naked feeling again, and began to wish he hadn't left his golden suit behind.

When he reached the Mended Drum he remembered why he had.

People kept telling him that Ankh-Morpork was a lot more civilized these days, that between them the Watch and the Guilds had settled things down enough to ensure that actually being attacked while going about your lawful business in Ankh-Morpork was now merely a possibility instead of, as it once was, a matter of course. And the streets were so clean now that you could sometimes even *see* the street.

But the Mended Drum could be depended upon. If someone didn't come out of the door backwards and fall down in the street just as you passed, then there was something wrong with the world.

And there was a fight going on. More or less. But in some ways at least time had moved on. You couldn't just haul off and belt someone with an axe these days. People *expected* things of a bar brawl. As he went in Moist passed a large group of men of the broken-nosed, one-eared persuasion, bent in anxious conclave.

'Look, Bob, what part of this don't you understand, eh? It's a matter of style, okay? A proper brawl doesn't just *happen*. You don't just pile in, not any more. Now, Oyster Dave here – put your helmet back on, Dave – will be the enemy in front and Basalt who, as we know, don't need a helmet, he'll be the enemy coming up behind you. Okay, it's well past knuckles time, let's say Gravy there has done his thing with the Bench Swipe, there's a bit of knifeplay, we've done the whole Chandelier Swing number, blah blah blah, then Second Chair – that's *you*, Bob – you step smartly between their Number Five man and a

Bottler, swing the chair *back* over your head like this – sorry, Pointy – and then swing it right back on to Number Five, bang, crash, and there's a cushy six points in your pocket. If they're playing a dwarf at Number Five then a chair won't even slow him down but don't fret, hang on to the bits that stay in your hand, pause one moment as he comes at you and then belt him across both ears. They hate that, as Stronginthearm here will tell you. Another three points. It's probably going to be freestyle after that but I want all of you, including Mucky Mick and Crispo, to try for a Double Andrew when it gets down to the fist-fighting again. Remember? You back into each other, turn round to give the other guy a thumping, cue moment of humorous recognition, then link left arms, swing round and see to the other fellow's attacker, foot or fist, it's your choice. Fifteen points right there if you get it to flow just right. Oh, and remember we'll have an Igor standing by, so if your arm gets taken off do pick it up and hit the other bugger with it – it gets a laugh and twenty points. On that subject, *do* remember what I said about getting everything tattooed with your name, all right? Igors do their best, but you'll be on your feet much quicker if you make life easier for him and, what's more, it's *your* feet you'll be on. Okay, positions everyone, let's run through it again . . .'

Moist sidled past the group and scanned the huge room. The important thing was not to slow down. Slowing down attracted people.

He saw a thin plume of blue smoke rise above the crowd, and forced his way through.

Miss Dearheart was sitting alone at a very small table with a very small drink in front of her. She couldn't have been there long; the only other stool was unoccupied.

'Do you come in here often?' said Moist, slipping on to it quickly.

Miss Dearheart raised her eyebrows at him. 'Yes. Why not?'

'Well, I . . . I imagine it's not very safe for a woman on her own.'

'What, with all these big strong men here to protect me? Why don't you go and get your drink?'

Moist got to the bar eventually, by dropping a handful of small change on the floor. That usually cleared the crush a little.

When he returned, his seat was occupied by a Currently Friendly

Drunk. Moist recognized the type, and the operative word was 'currently'. Miss Dearheart was leaning back to avoid his attentions and more probably his breath.

Moist heard the familiar cry of the generously sloshed.

'What ... right? What I'm saying is, right, what I'm saying, narhmean, why won't you, right, gimme a kiss, right? All I'm saying is—'

Oh gods, I'm going to have to do something, Moist thought. He's big and he's got a sword like a butcher's cleaver and the moment I say anything he's going to go right into stage four, Violent Undirected Madman, and they can be surprisingly accurate before they fall over.

He put down his drink.

Miss Dearheart gave him a very brief look, and shook her head. There was movement under the table, a small fleshy kind of noise and the drunk suddenly bent forward, colour draining from his face. Probably only he and Moist heard Miss Dearheart purr: 'What is sticking in your foot is a Mitzy "Pretty Lucretia" four-inch heel, the most dangerous footwear in the world. Considered as pounds per square inch, it's like being trodden on by a very pointy elephant. Now, I know what you're thinking: you're thinking, "Could she press it all the way through to the floor?" And, you know, I'm not sure about that myself. The sole of your boot might give me a bit of trouble, but nothing else will. But that's not the worrying part. The worrying part is that I was forced practically at knifepoint to take ballet lessons as a child, which means I can kick like a mule; you are sitting in front of me; and *I have another shoe*. Good, I can see you have worked that out. I'm going to withdraw the heel now.'

There was a small 'pop' from under the table. With great care the man stood up, turned and, without a backward glance, lurched unsteadily away.

'Can *I* bother you?' said Moist. Miss Dearheart nodded, and he sat down, with his legs crossed. 'He was only a drunk,' he ventured.

'Yes, men say that sort of thing,' said Miss Dearheart. 'Anyway, tell me that if I hadn't done that you wouldn't now be trying to collect all your teeth in your hat. Which you are not wearing, I notice. This must be your secret identity. Sorry, was that the wrong thing to say? You spilled your drink.'

Moist wiped beer off his lapel. 'No, this is me,' he said. 'Pure and unadorned.'

'You hardly know me and yet you invited me out on a date,' said Miss Dearheart. 'Why?'

Because you called me a phoney, Moist thought. You saw through me straight away. Because you didn't nail my head to the door with your crossbow. Because you have no small talk. Because I'd like to get to know you better, even though it would be like smooching an ashtray. Because I wonder if you could put into the rest of your life the passion you put into smoking a cigarette. In defiance of Miss Maccalariat I'd like to commit hanky-panky with you, Miss Adora Belle Dearheart . . . well, certainly hanky, and possibly panky when we get to know one another better. I'd like to know as much about your soul as you know about mine . . .

He *said*: 'Because I hardly know you.'

'If it comes to that, I hardly know you, either,' said Miss Dearheart.

'I'm rather banking on that,' said Moist. This got a smile.

'Smooth answer. Slick. Where are we really eating tonight?'

'Le Foie Heureux, of course,' said Moist.

She looked genuinely surprised. 'You got a reservation?'

'Oh, yes.'

'You've got a relative that works there, then? You're blackmailing the maître d'?'

'No. But I've got a table for tonight,' said Moist.

'Then it's some sort of trick,' said Miss Dearheart. 'I'm impressed. But I'd better warn you, enjoy the meal. It may be your last.'

'What?'

'The Grand Trunk Company kills people, Mr Lipwig. In all kinds of ways. You must be getting on Reacher Gilt's nerves.'

'Oh, come *on*! I'm barely a wasp at their picnic!'

'And what do people do to wasps, do you think?' said Miss Dearheart. 'The Trunk is in trouble, Mr Lipwig. The company has been running it as a machine for making money. They thought repair would be cheaper than maintenance. They've cut everything to the bone – to the *bone*. They're people who can't take a joke. Do you think Reacher Gilt will hesitate for one minute to swat you?'

'But I'm being very—' Moist tried.

'Do you think you're playing a *game* with them? Ringing doorbells and running away? Gilt's aiming to become Patrician one day, everyone says so. And suddenly there's this . . . this *idiot* in a big gold hat reminding everyone what a mess the clacks is, poking fun at it, getting the Post Office working again—'

'Hang on, hang on,' Moist managed. 'This is a city, not some cow town somewhere! People don't kill business rivals just like that, do they?'

'In Ankh-Morpork? You really think so? Oh, *he* won't kill you. He won't even bother with the formality of going through the Guild of Assassins. You'll just die. Just like my brother. And he'll be behind it.'

'Your brother?' said Moist. On the far side of the huge room, the evening's fight began with a well-executed Looking-At-Me-In-A-Funny-Way, earning two points and a broken tooth.

'He and some of the people who used to work on the Trunk before it was pirated – *pirated*, Mr Lipwig – were going to start up a new Trunk,' said Miss Dearheart, leaning forward. 'They'd scraped up funding somehow for a few demonstration towers. It was going to be more than four times as fast as the old system, they were going to do all kinds of clever things with the coding, it was going to be wonderful. A lot of people gave them their savings, people who'd worked for my father. Most of the good engineers left when my father lost the Trunk, you see. They couldn't stand Gilt and his bunch of looters. My brother was going to get all our money back.'

'You've lost me there,' said Moist. An axe landed in the table, and juddered.

Miss Dearheart stared at Moist and blew a stream of smoke past his ear.

'My father was Robert Dearheart,' she said distantly. 'He was chairman of the original Grand Trunk Company. The clacks was his vision. Hell, he designed half of the mechanisms in the towers. And he got together with a group of other engineers, all serious men with slide rules, and they borrowed money and mortgaged their houses and built a local system and poured the money back in and started building the Trunk. There was a *lot* of money coming in; every city wanted to be in on it, everyone was going to be rich. We had stables. I had a horse. Admittedly I didn't like it much, but I used to feed it and watch it run about or whatever it is they do. Everything was going fine and suddenly he got this letter and there were meetings and they said he was lucky not to go to prison for, oh, I don't know, something complicated and legal. But the clacks was still making huge amounts. Can you understand that? Reacher Gilt and his gang acted friendly, oh yes, but they were buying up the mortgages and controlling banks and moving numbers around and they pulled the Grand Trunk out from under us like *thieves*. All they want to do is make money. They don't *care* about the Trunk. They'll run it into the ground and make more money by selling it. When Dad was in charge people were *proud* of what they did. And because they were engineers they made sure that the towers *worked* properly, all the time. They even had what they called "walking towers", prefabricated ones that packed on to a couple of big carts so that if a tower was having serious trouble they could set this one up alongside and start it up and take over the traffic without dropping a single code. They were *proud* of it, everyone was, they were proud to be a part of it!'

'*You should've been there. You should've seen it!*' Moist said to himself. He hadn't meant to say it out loud. Across the room, a man hit another man with his own leg and picked up seven points.

'Yes,' said Miss Dearheart. 'You should have. And three months ago my brother John raised enough to start a rival to the Trunk. That took some doing. Gilt has got tentacles everywhere. Well, John ended up dead in a field. They said he hadn't clipped his safety rope on. He always did. And now my father just sits and stares at the wall. He even lost his workshop when everything got taken away. We lost our house, of course. Now we live with my aunt in Dolly Sisters. That's what we've come to. When Reacher Gilt talks about freedom he means his, not anyone else's. And now *you* pop up, Mr Moist von Lipwig, all shiny and new, running around doing everything at once. Why?'

'Vetinari offered me the job, that's all,' said Moist.

'Why did you take it?'

'It was a job for life.'

She stared at Moist so hard that he began to feel uncomfortable. 'Well, you've managed to get a table at Le Foie Heureux at a few hours' notice,' she conceded, as a knife struck a beam behind her. 'Are you still going to lie if I ask you how?'

'Yes, I think so.'

'Good. Shall we go?'

A little pressure lamp burned in the stuffy snugness of the locker room, its glow a globe of unusual brilliance. In the centre of it, magnifying glass in hand, Stanley examined his stamps.

This was . . . heaven. Peas are known for their thoroughness, and Stanley was conscientious in the extreme. Mr Spools, slightly unnerved by his smile, had given him all the test sheets and faulty pages, and Stanley was carefully cataloguing them – how many of each, what the errors were, everything.

A little tendril of guilt was curling through his mind: this *was* better than pins, it really was. There could be no *end* to stamps. You could put anything on them. They were amazing. They could move letters around and then you could stick them in a book, all neat. You wouldn't get 'pinhead's thumb', either.

He'd read about this feeling in the pin magazines. They said you could come unpinned. Girls and marriage were sometimes mentioned in this context. Sometimes an ex-head would sell off his whole collection, just like that. Or at some pin-meet someone would suddenly throw all their pins in the air and run out shouting, 'Aargh, they're just pins!' Up until now, such a thing had been unthinkable to Stanley.

He picked up his little sack of unsorted pins, and stared at it. A few days ago, the mere thought of an evening with his pins would have given him a lovely warm, comfortable feeling inside. But now it was time to put away childish pins.

Something screamed.

It was harsh, guttural, it was malice and hunger given a voice. Small huddling shrew-like creatures had once heard sounds like that, circling over the swamps.

After a moment of ancient terror had subsided, Stanley crept over and opened the door.

'H-hello?' he called, into the cavernous darkness of the hall. 'Is there anyone there?'

There was fortunately no reply, but there was some scrabbling up near the roof.

'We're closed, you know,' he quavered. 'But we're open again at seven in the morning for a range of stamps and a wonderful deal on mail to Pseudopolis.' His voice slowed and his brow creased as he tried to remember everything Mr Lipwig had told them earlier. 'Remember, we may not be the fastest but we always get there. Why not write to your old granny?'

'I ate my grandmother,' growled a voice from high in the darkness. 'I gnawed her bones.'

Stanley coughed. He had not been trained in the art of salesmanship.

'Ah,' he said. 'Er . . . perhaps an aunt, then?'

He wrinkled his nose. Why was there the stink of lamp oil in the air?

'Hello?' he said again.

Something dropped out of the dark, bounced off his shoulder and landed on the floor with a wet thud. Stanley reached down, felt around and found a pigeon. At least, he found about half a pigeon. It was still warm, and very sticky.

Mr Gryle sat on a beam high above the hall. His stomach was on fire.

It was no good, old habits died too hard. They were bred in the bone. Something warm and feathery fluttered up in front of you and *of course* you snapped at it. Ankh-Morpork had pigeons roosting on every gutter, cornice and statue. Not even the resident gargoyles could keep them down. He'd had six before he sailed in through the broken dome, and then another huge warm feathery cloud had risen up and a red haze had simply dropped in front of his eyes.

They were so *tasty*. You couldn't stop at one! And five minutes later you remembered why you should have done.

These were feral, urban birds, that lived on what they could find on the streets. Ankh-Morpork streets, at that. They were bobbing, cooing plague pits. You might as well eat a dog turd burger and wash it down with a jumbo cup of septic tank.

Mr Gryle groaned. Best to finish the job, get out of here and go and throw up over a busy street. He dropped his oil bottle into the dark and fumbled for his matches. His species had come to fire late, because nests burned too easily, but it did have its uses . . .

Flame blossomed, high up at the far end of the hall. It dropped from the beams and landed on the stacks of letters. There was a whoomph as the oil caught fire; blue runnels of flame began to climb the walls.

Stanley looked down. A few feet away, lit by the fire crawling across the letters, was a figure curled up on the floor. The golden hat with wings lay next to it.

Stanley looked up, eyes glowing red in the firelight, as a figure swooped from the rafters and sped towards him, mouth open.

And that's when it all went wrong for Mr Gryle, because Stanley had one of his Little Moments.

Attitude was everything. Moist had studied attitude. Some of the old nobility had it. It was the total lack of any doubt that things would go the way they expected them to go.

The maître d' ushered them to their table without a moment's hesitation.

'Can you really afford this on a government salary, Mr Lipwig?' said Miss Dearheart as they sat down. 'Or are we going to exit via the kitchens?'

'I believe I have adequate funds,' said Moist.

He probably hadn't, he knew. A restaurant that has a waiter even for the mustard stacks up the prices. But right now Moist wasn't worrying about the bill. There were ways to deal with bills, and it was best to deal with them on a full stomach.

They ordered starters that probably cost more than the weekly food bill for an average man. There was no point in looking for the cheapest thing on the menu. The cheapest thing theoretically existed but somehow, no matter how hard you stared, didn't quite manage to be there. On the other hand, there were a lot of most expensive things.

'Are the boys settling in okay?' said Miss Dearheart.

The boys, Moist thought. 'Oh, yes. Anghammarad has really taken to it. A natural postman,' he said.

'Well, he's had practice.'

'What's that box he's got riveted to his arm?'

'That? A message he's got to deliver. Not the original baked clay tablet, I gather. He's had to make copies two or three times and the bronze lasts hardly any time at all, to a golem. It's a message to King Het of Thut from his astrologers on their holy mountain, telling him that the Goddess of the Sea was angry and what ceremonies he'd have to do to placate her.'

'Didn't Thut slide into the sea anyway? I thought he said—'

'Yeah, yeah, Anghammarad got there too late and was swept away by the ferocious tidal wave and the island sank.'

'So . . . ?' said Moist.

'So what?' said Miss Dearheart.

'So . . . he doesn't think that delivering it now might be a bit on the tardy side?'

'No. He doesn't. You're not seeing it like a golem. They believe the universe is doughnut-shaped.'

'Would that be a ring doughnut or a jam doughnut?' said Moist.

'Ring, definitely, but don't push for further culinary details, because I can see you'll try to make a joke of it. They think it has no start or finish. We just keep going round and round, but we don't have to make the same decisions every time.'

'Like getting an angel the hard way,' said Moist.

'What do you mean?' said Miss Dearheart.

'Er . . . he's waiting until the whole tidal wave business comes around again and this time he'll get there earlier and do it right?'

'Yes. Don't point out all the flaws in the idea. It works for him.'

'He's going to wait for millions and millions of years?' said Moist.

'*That's* not a flaw, not to a golem. That's only a matter of time. They don't get bored. They repair themselves and they're very hard to shatter. They survive under the sea or in red-hot lava. He might be able to do it, who knows? In the meantime, he keeps himself busy. Just like you, Mr Lipwig. You've been *very* busy—'

She froze, staring over his shoulder. He saw her right hand scrabble frantically among the cutlery and grab a knife.

'That bastard has just walked into the place!' she hissed. 'Reacher Gilt! I'll just kill him and join you for the pudding . . .'

'You can't do that!' hissed Moist.

'Oh? Why not?'

'You're using the wrong knife! That's for the fish! You'll get into trouble!'

She glared at him, but her hand relaxed and something like a smile appeared.

'They don't have a knife for stabbing rich murdering bastards?' she said.

'They bring it to the table when you order one,' said Moist urgently. 'Look, this isn't the Drum, they don't just throw the body on to the river! They'll call the Watch! Get a grip. Not on the knife! And get ready to run.'

'Why?'

'Because I forged his signature on Grand Trunk notepaper to get us in here, that's why.'

Moist turned round to look at the great man in the flesh for the first time. He *was* great, a bear-shaped man, in a frock coat big enough for two and a gold-braid waistcoat. And he had a cockatoo on his shoulder, although a waiter was hurrying forward with a shiny brass perch and, presumably, the seed-and-nut menu.

There was a party of well-dressed people with Gilt, and as they progressed across the room the whole place began to revolve around the big man, gold being very dense and having a gravity all of its own. Waiters bustled and grovelled and did unimportant things with an air of great importance, and it was probably only a matter of minutes before one of them told Gilt that his other guests had been seated. But Moist was scanning the rest of the room for the— Ah, there they were, two of them. What was it about hired muscle that made it impossible to get a suit to fit?

One was watching the door, one was watching the room, and without a shadow of a doubt there was at least one in the kitchen.

—and, yes, the maître d' was earning his tip by assuring the great man that his friends had been duly looked after—

—the big head, with its leonine mane, turned to stare at Moist's table—

—Miss Dearheart murmured, 'Oh gods, he's coming over!'—

—and Moist stood up. The hired fists had shifted position. They wouldn't actually do anything in here, but nor would anyone else be worried if he was escorted out with speed and firmness for a little discussion in some alley somewhere. Gilt was advancing between the tables, leaving his puzzled guests behind.

This was a job for people skills, or diving through the window. But Gilt would have to be at least marginally polite. People were listening.

'Mr Reacher Gilt?' said Moist.

'Indeed, sir,' said Gilt, grinning without a trace of humour. 'But you appear to have me at a disadvantage.'

'I do hope not, sir,' said Moist.

'It appears that I asked the restaurant to retain a table for you, Mr . . . Lipwig?'

'Did you, Mr Gilt?' said Moist, with what he knew was remarkably persuasive innocence. 'We arrived in the hope that there might be a spare table and were astonished to find there was!'

'Then at least one of us has been made a fool of, Mr Lipwig,' said Gilt. 'But tell me . . . are you truly Mr Moist von Lipwig the postmaster?'

'Yes, I am.'

'Without your hat?'

Moist coughed. 'It's not actually compulsory,' he said.

The big face observed him in silence, and then a hand like a steel-worker's glove was thrust forward.

'I am very pleased to meet you at last, Mr Lipwig. I trust your good luck will continue.'

Moist took the hand and, instead of the bone-crushing grip he was expecting, felt the firm handshake of an honourable man and looked into the steady, honest, one-eyed gaze of Reacher Gilt.

Moist had worked hard at his profession and considered himself pretty good at it but, if he had been wearing his hat, he would have taken it off right now. He was in the presence of a master. He could feel it in the hand, see it in that one commanding eye. Were things otherwise, he would have humbly begged to be taken on as an apprentice, scrub the man's floors, cook his food, just to sit at the feet of greatness and learn how to do the three card trick using whole banks. If Moist was any judge, any judge at all, the man in front of him was the biggest fraud he'd ever met. And he *advertised* it. That was ... style. The pirate curls, the eyepatch, even the damn parrot. Twelve and a half per cent, for heavens' sake, didn't anyone spot that? He told them what he was, and they laughed and loved him for it. It was breathtaking. If Moist von Lipwig had been a career killer, it would have been like meeting a man who'd devised a way to destroy civilizations.

All this came in an instant, in one bolt of understanding, in the glint of an eye. But something ran in front of it as fast as a little fish ahead of a shark.

Gilt was *shocked*, not surprised. That tiny moment was barely measurable on any clock but just for an instant the world had gone wrong for Reacher Gilt. That moment had been wiped out so competently that all that remained of it was Moist's certainty that it had happened, but the certainty was rigid.

He was loath to let go of the hand in case there was a flash that might broil him alive. After all, he had recognized the nature of Gilt, so the man must certainly have spotted him.

'Thank you, Mr Gilt,' he said.

'I gather you were kind enough to carry some of our messages today,' Gilt rumbled.

'It was a pleasure, sir. If ever you need our help, you only have to ask.'

'Hmm,' said Gilt. 'But the least I can do is buy you dinner, Postmaster. The bill will come to my table. Choose whatever you wish. And now, if you will excuse me, I must attend to my . . . *other* guests.'

He bowed to the simmering Miss Dearheart and walked back.

'The management would like to thank you for not killing the guests,' said Moist, sitting down. 'Now we should—'

He stopped, and stared.

Miss Dearheart, who had been saving up to hiss at him, took one look at his face and hesitated.

'Are you ill?' she said.

'They're . . . burning,' said Moist, his eyes widening.

'Ye gods, you've gone white!'

'The writing . . . they're screaming . . . I can smell burning!'

'Someone over there is having crêpes,' said Miss Dearheart. 'It's just—' She stopped, and sniffed. 'It smells like *paper*, though . . .'

People looked round as Moist's chair crashed backwards.

'The Post Office is on fire! I *know* it is!' he shouted, and turned and ran.

Miss Dearheart caught up just as he was in the hall, where one of Gilt's bodyguards had grabbed him. She tapped the man on the shoulder and, as he turned to push her away, stamped down heavily. While he screamed she dragged the bewildered Moist away.

'Water . . . we've got to get water,' he groaned. 'They're burning! They're all burning!'

CHAPTER TEN

The Burning of Words

In which Stanley remains Calm – Moist the Hero – Searching for a Cat, never a good idea – Something in the Dark – Mr Gryle is encountered – Fire and Water – Mr Lipwig Helps the Watch – Dancing on the edge – Mr Lipwig Gets Religion – Opportunity Time – Miss Maccalariat's hairgrip – The Miracle

THE LETTERS BURNED.

Part of the ceiling fell down, showering more letters on to the flames. The fire was already reaching for the upper floors. As Stanley dragged Mr Groat across the floor another slab of plaster smashed on the tiles and the old mail that poured down after it was already burning. Smoke, thick as soup, rolled across the distant ceiling.

Stanley pulled the old man into the locker room and laid him on his bed. He rescued the golden hat, too, because Mr Lipwig would be bound to be angry if he didn't. Then he shut the door and took down, from the shelf over Groat's desk, the Book of Regulations. He turned the pages methodically until he came to the bookmark he'd put in a minute ago, on the page What To Do In Case Of Fire.

Stanley always followed the rules. All sorts of things could go wrong if you didn't.

So far he'd done 1: Upon Discovery of the Fire, Remain Calm.

Now he came to 2: Shout 'Fire!' in a Loud, Clear Voice.

'Fire!' he shouted, and then ticked off 2 with his pencil.

Next was: 3: Endeavour to Extinguish Fire If Possible.

Stanley went to the door and opened it. Flames and smoke billowed in. He stared at them for a moment, shook his head, and shut the door.

Paragraph 4 said: If Trapped by Fire, Endeavour to Escape. Do Not Open Doors If Warm. Do Not Use Stairs If Burning. If No Exit

Presents Itself Remain Calm and Await a) Rescue or b) Death.

This seemed to cover it. The world of pins was simple and Stanley knew his way around it as a goldfish knows its tank, but everything else was very complicated and only worked if you followed the rules.

He glanced up at the grubby little windows. They were far too small to climb through and had been welded shut by many applications of official paint, so he broke one pane as neatly as possible to allow some fresh air in. He made a note of this in the breakages book.

Mr Groat was still breathing, although with an unpleasant bubbling sound. There was a First Aid kit in the locker room, because Regulations demanded it, but it contained only a small length of bandage, a bottle of something black and sticky, and Mr Groat's spare teeth. Mr Groat had told him never to touch his home-made medicines, and since it was not unusual for bottles to explode during the night Stanley had always observed this rule very carefully.

It did *not* say in the Regulations: If Attacked by Huge Swooping Screaming Creature Hit Hard in the Mouth with Sack of Pins, and Stanley wondered if he should pencil this in. But that would be Defacing Post Office Property, and he could get into trouble for that.

All avenues of further activity being therefore closed, Stanley remained calm.

It was a gentle snow of letters. Some landed still burning, fountaining out of the column of crackling fire that had already broken through the Post Office roof. Some were blackened ashes on which sparks travelled in mockery of the dying ink. Some – many – had sailed up and over the city unscathed, zigzagging down gently like communications from an excessively formal sort of god.

Moist tore off his jacket as he pushed through the crowd.

'The people probably got out,' said Miss Dearheart, clattering along beside him.

'Do you *really* think so?' said Moist.

'Really? No. Not if Gilt set this up. Sorry, I'm not very good at being comforting any more.'

Moist paused, and tried to think. The flames were coming out of the roof at one end of the building. The main door and the whole left side looked untouched. But fire was sneaky stuff, he knew. It sat there and smouldered until you opened the door to see how it was getting on, and then the fire caught its breath and your eyeballs got soldered to your skull.

'I'd better go in,' he said. 'Er . . . you wouldn't care to say "No, no, don't do it, you're being far too brave!" would you?' he added. Some people were organizing a bucket chain from a nearby fountain; it would be as effective as spitting at the sun.

Miss Dearheart caught a burning letter, lit a cigarette with it, and took a drag. 'No, no, don't do it, you're being far too brave!' she said. 'How was that for you? But if you do, the left side looks pretty clear. Watch out, though. There are rumours Gilt employs a vampire. One of the wild ones.'

'Ah. Fire kills them, doesn't it?' said Moist, desperate to look on the bright side.

'It kills everybody, Mr Lipwig,' said Miss Dearheart. 'It kills everybody.' She grabbed him by the ears and gave him a big kiss on the mouth. It was like being kissed by an ashtray, but in a good way.

'On the whole, I'd like you to come out of there,' she said quietly. 'Are you sure you won't wait? The boys will be here in a minute—'

'The golems? It's their day off!'

'They have to obey their chem, though. A fire means humans are in danger. They'll smell it and be here in minutes, believe me.'

Moist hesitated, looking at her face. And people were watching him. He *couldn't* not go in there, it wouldn't fit in with the persona. Gods damn Vetinari!

He shook his head, turned, and ran towards the doors. Best not to think about it. Best not to think about being so *dumb*. Just feel the front door . . . quite cool. Open it gently . . . a rush of air, but no explosion. The big hall, lit with flame . . . but it was all above him, and if he weaved and dodged he could make it to the door that led down to the locker room.

He kicked it open.

Stanley looked up from his stamps.

'Hello, Mr Lipwig,' he said. 'I kept calm. But I think Mr Groat is ill.'

The old man was lying on the bed, and ill was too jolly a word.

'What happened to him?' said Moist, lifting him gently. Mr Groat was no weight at all.

'It was like a big bird, but I frightened it off,' said Stanley. 'I hit it in the mouth with a sack of pins. I . . . had a Little Moment, sir.'

'Well, that ought to do it,' said Moist. 'Now, can you follow me?'

'I've got all the stamps,' said Stanley. 'And the cashbox. Mr Groat keeps them under his bed for safety.' The boy beamed. 'And your hat, too. I kept calm.'

'Well done, well done,' said Moist. 'Now, stick right behind me, okay?'

'What about Mr Tiddles, Mr Lipwig?' said Stanley, suddenly looking worried. Somewhere outside in the hall there was a crash, and the crackle of the fire grew distinctly louder.

'Who? Mr Tidd— the cat? To hell with—' Moist stopped, and readjusted his mouth. 'He'll be outside, you can bet on it, eating a toasted rat and grinning. Come on, will you?'

'But he's the Post Office cat!' said Stanley. 'He's never been outside!'

I'll bet he has now, thought Moist. But there was that edge in the boy's voice again.

'Let's get Mr Groat out of here, okay,' he said, easing his way through the door with the old man in his arms, 'and then I'll come back for Tidd—'

A burning beam dropped on to the floor halfway across the hall, and sent sparks and burning envelopes spiralling upwards into the main blaze. It roared, a wall of flame, a fiery waterfall in reverse, up through the other floors and out through the roof. It thundered. It was fire let loose and making the most of it.

Part of Moist von Lipwig was happy to let it happen. But a new and troublesome part was thinking: I was making it work. It was all moving forward. The stamps were really working. It was as good as being a criminal without the crime. It had been *fun*.

'Come *on*, Stanley!' Moist snapped, turning away from the horrible sight and the fascinating thought. The boy followed, reluctantly, call-ing for the damn cat all the way to the door.

The air outside struck like a knife, but there was a round of applause from the crowd and then a flash of light that Moist had come to associate with eventual trouble.

'Good eefning, Mr Lipvig!' said the cheery voice of Otto Chriek. 'My vord, if ve vant news, all ve have to do is follow you!'

Moist ignored him and shouldered his way to Miss Dearheart who, he noticed, was not beside herself with worry.

'Is there a hospice in this city?' he said. 'A decent doctor, even?'

'There's the Lady Sybil Free Hospital,' said Miss Dearheart.

'Is it any good?'

'Some people don't die.'

'That good, eh? Get him there right now! I've got to go back in for the cat!'

'*You* are going to go back in *there* for a *cat*?'

'It's Mr Tiddles,' said Stanley primly. 'He was born in the Post Office.'

'Best not to argue,' said Moist, turning to go. 'See to Mr Groat, will you?'

Miss Dearheart looked down at the old man's bloodstained shirt. 'But it looks as though some creature tried to—' she began.

'Something fell on him,' said Moist shortly.

'That couldn't cause—'

'*Something fell on him*,' said Moist. 'That's what happened.'

She looked at his face. 'All right,' she agreed. 'Something fell on him. Something with big claws.'

'No, a joist with lots of nails in it, something like that. Anyone can see that.'

'That's what happened, was it?' said Miss Dearheart.

'That's exactly what happened,' said Moist, and strode away before there were any more questions.

No point in getting the Watch involved in this, he thought, hurry-ing towards the doors. They'll clump around and there won't be any answers for them and in my experience watchmen always like to arrest *somebody*. What makes you think it was Reacher Gilt, Mr . . . Lipwig, wasn't it? Oh, you could *tell*, could you? That's a skill of yours, is it? Funny thing, we can tell sometimes, too. You've got a very familiar face, Mr Lipwig. Where are you from?

No, there was no point in getting friendly with the Watch. They might get in the way.

An upper window exploded outwards, and flames licked along the edge of the roof; Moist ducked into the doorway as glass rained down. As for Tiddles . . . well, he had to find the damn cat. If he didn't, it wouldn't be fun any more. If he didn't risk at least a tiny bit of life and a smidgen of limb, he just wouldn't be able to carry on being him.

Had he just thought that?

Oh, gods. He'd lost *it*. He'd never been sure how he'd got it, but it had gone. That's what happened if you took wages. And hadn't his grandfather warned him to keep away from women as neurotic as a shaved monkey? Actually he hadn't, his interest lying mainly with dogs and beer, but he should have done.

The vision of Mr Groat's chest kept bumping insistently against his imagination. It looked as though something with claws had taken a swipe at him, and only the thick uniform coat prevented him from being opened like a clam. But that didn't sound like a vampire. They weren't messy like that. It was a waste of good food. Nevertheless, he picked up a piece of smashed chair. It had splintered nicely. And the good thing about a stake through the heart was that it also worked on non-vampires.

More ceiling had come down in the hall, but he was able to dodge between the debris. The main staircase was at this end and completely untouched, although smoke lay on the floor like a carpet; at the other end of the hall, where the mountains of old mail had been, the blaze still roared.

He couldn't hear the letters any more. Sorry, he thought. I did my best. It wasn't my fault . . .

What now? At least he could get his box out of his office. He didn't want that to burn. Some of those chemicals would be quite hard to replace.

The office was full of smoke but he dragged the box out from under his desk and then spotted the golden suit on its hanger. He had to take it, didn't he? Something like that couldn't be allowed to burn. He could come back for the box, right? But the suit ... the suit was *necessary*. There was no sign of Tiddles. He *must* have got out, yes? Didn't cats leave sinking ships? Or was it rats? Wouldn't the cats follow the rats? Anyway, smoke was coming up between the floorboards and drifting down from the upper floors, and this wasn't the time to hang around. He'd looked everywhere sensible; there was *no* sense in being where a ton of burning paper could drop on your head.

It was a good plan and it was only spoiled when he spotted the cat, down in the hall. It was watching him with interest.

'Tiddles!' bellowed Moist. He wished he hadn't. It was such a stupid name to shout in a burning building.

The cat looked at him, and trotted away. Cursing, Moist hurried after it, and saw it disappear down into the cellars.

Cats were bright, weren't they? There was probably another way out ... bound to be ...

Moist didn't even look up when he heard the creaking of wood overhead, but ran forward and went down the steps five at a time. By the sound of it, a large amount of the entire building smashed on to the floor just behind him, and sparks roared down the cellar passage, burning his neck.

Well, there was no going back, at least. But cellars, now, they had trapdoors and coal shutes and things, didn't they? And they were cool and safe and—

—just the place where you'd go to lick your wounds after being smashed in the mouth with a sackful of pins, right?

An imagination is a terrible thing to bring along.

A vampire, she'd said. And Stanley had hit 'a big bird' with a sackful of pins. Stanley the Vampire Slayer, with a bag of pins. You wouldn't believe it, unless you'd seen him in one of what Mr Groat called his 'little moments'.

You probably couldn't *kill* a vampire with pins ...

And after a thought like that is when you realize that however hard you try to look behind you, there's a behind you, behind you, where you aren't looking. Moist flung his back to the cold stone wall, and slithered along it until he ran out of wall and acquired a doorframe.

The faint blue glow of the Sorting Engine was just visible.

As Moist peered into the machine's room, Tiddles was visible too. He was crouched under the engine.

'That's a very cat thing you're doing there, Tiddles,' said Moist, staring at the shadows. 'Come to Uncle Moist. Please?'

He sighed, and hung the suit on an old letter rack, and crouched down. How were you supposed to pick up a cat? He'd never done it. Cats never figured in grandfather's Lipwigzer kennels, except as an impromptu snack.

As his hand drew near Tiddles, the cat flattened its ears and hissed.

'Do you want to cook down here?' said Moist. 'No claws, please.'

The cat began to growl, and Moist realized that it wasn't looking directly at him.

'Good Tiddles,' he said, feeling the terror begin to rise. It was one of the prime rules of exploring in a hostile environment: do not bother about the cat. And, suddenly, the environment was a lot more hostile.

Another important rule was: don't turn round slowly to look. It's there all right. Not the cat. Damn the cat. It's something else.

He stood upright and took a two-handed grip on the wooden stake. It's right behind me, yes? he thought. Bloody well bloody right bloody behind me! Of *course* it is! How could things be otherwise?

The feeling of fear was almost the same as the feeling he got when, say, a mark was examining a glass diamond. Time slowed a little, every sense was heightened, and there was a taste of copper in his mouth.

Don't turn round slowly. Turn round fast.

He spun, screamed and thrust. The stake met resistance, which yielded only slightly.

A long pale face grinned at him in the blue light. It showed rows of pointy teeth.

'Missed *both* my hearts,' said Mr Gryle, spitting blood.

* * *

Moist jumped back as a thin clawed hand sliced through the air, but kept the stake in front of him, jabbing with it, holding the thing off . . .

Banshee, he thought. Oh, hell . . .

Only when he moved did Gryle's leathery black cape swing aside briefly to show the skeletal figure beneath; it helped if you knew that the black leather was wing. It helped if you thought of banshees as the only humanoid race that had evolved the ability to fly, in some lush jungle somewhere where they'd hunted flying squirrels. It didn't help, much, if you knew why the story had grown up that hearing the scream of the banshee meant that you were going to die.

It meant that the banshee was tracking you. No good looking behind you. It was overhead.

There weren't many of the feral ones, even in Uberwald, but Moist knew the advice passed on by people who'd survived them. Keep away from the mouth – those teeth are vicious. Don't attack the chest; the flight muscles there are like armour. They're not strong but they've got sinews like steel cables and the long reach of those arm bones'll mean it can slap your silly head right off—

Tiddles yowled and backed further under the Sorting Engine. Gryle slashed at Moist again, and came after him as he backed away.

—but their necks snap easily if you can get inside their reach, and they have to shut their eyes when they scream.

Gryle came forward, head bobbing as he strutted. There was nowhere else for Moist to go, so he tossed aside the wood and held up his hands.

'All right, I give in,' he said. 'Just make it quick, okay?'

The creature kept looking at the golden suit; they had a magpie's eye for glitter.

'I'm going somewhere afterwards,' said Moist helpfully.

Gryle hesitated. He was hurt, disorientated and had eaten pigeons that were effluent on wings. He wanted to get out of here and up into the cool sky. Everything was too complicated here. There were too many targets, too many smells.

For a banshee, everything was in the pounce, when teeth, claws and bodyweight all bore down at once. Now, bewildered, he strutted back and forth, trying to deal with the situation. There was no room to fly, nowhere else to go, the prey was standing there . . . instinct, emotion and some attempt at rational thought all banged together in Gryle's overheated head.

Instinct won. Leaping at things with your claws out had worked for a million years, so why stop now?

He threw his head back, screamed, and sprang.

So did Moist, ducking under the long arms. That wasn't programmed into the banshee's responses: the prey should be huddled, or running away. But Moist's shoulder caught him in the chest.

The creature was as light as a child.

Moist felt a claw slash into his arm as he hurled the thing on to the Sorting Engine, and flung himself to the floor. For one horrible moment he thought it was going to get up, that he'd missed the wheel, but as the enraged Mr Gryle shifted there was a sound like . . .

. . . gloop . . .

. . . followed by silence.

Moist lay on the cool flagstones until his heart slowed down to the point where he could make out individual beats. He was aware, as he lay there, that something sticky was dripping down the side of the machine.

He arose slowly, on unsteady legs, and stared at what had become of the creature. If he'd been a hero, he would have taken the opportunity to say, 'That's what *I* call sorted!' Since he wasn't a hero, he threw up. A body doesn't work properly when significant bits are not sharing the same space-time frame as the rest of it, but it does look more colourful.

Then, clutching at his bleeding arm, Moist knelt down and looked under the engine for Tiddles.

He had to come back with the cat, he thought muzzily. It was just something that had to happen. A man who rushes into a burning building to rescue a stupid cat and comes out carrying the cat is seen as a hero, even if he is a rather dumb one. If he comes out *sans* cat he's a twit.

A muffled thunder above them suggested that part of the building had fallen down. The air was roasting.

Tiddles backed away from Moist's hand.

'Listen,' Moist growled. 'The hero has to come out with the cat. The cat doesn't have to be alive—'

He lunged, grabbed Tiddles and dragged the cat out.

'Right,' he said, and picked up the suit hanger in his other hand. There were a few blobs of banshee on it, but, he thought light-headedly, he could probably find something to remove them.

He lurched out into the corridor. There was a wall of fire at both ends, and Tiddles chose this moment to sink all four sets of claws into his arm.

'Ah,' said Moist. 'Up until now it was going so well—'

'*Mr Lipvig! Are You All Right, Mr Lipvig?*'

What golems removed from a fire was, in fact, the fire. They took out of a burning property everything that was burning. It was curiously surgical. They assembled at the edge of the fire and deprived it of anything to burn, herded it, cornered it, and stamped it to death.

Golems could wade through lava and pour molten iron. Even if they knew what fear was, they wouldn't find it in a mere burning building.

Glowing rubble was hauled away from the steps by red-hot hands. Moist stared up into a landscape of flame but also, in front of it, Mr Pump. He was glowing orange. Specks of dust and dirt on his clay flashed and sparkled.

'Good To See You, Mr Lipvig!' he boomed cheerfully, tossing a crackling beam aside. 'We Have Cleared A Path To The Door! Move With Speed!'

'Er . . . thank you!' shouted Moist, above the roar of the flames. There *was* a path, dragged clear of debris, with the open door beckoning calmly and coolly at the end of it. Away towards the far end of the hall other golems, oblivious of the pillars of flame, were calmly throwing burning floorboards out through a hole in the wall.

The heat was intense. Moist lowered his head, clutched the terrified cat to his chest, felt the back of his neck begin to roast and scampered forward.

From then on, it became all one memory. The crashing noise high above. The metallic boom. The golem Anghammarad looking up, with his message glowing yellow on his cherry-red arm. Ten thousand tons of rainwater pouring down in deceptive slow motion. The cold hitting the glowing golem . . .

. . . the explosion . . .

Flames died. Sound died. Light died.

ANGHAMMARAD.

Anghammarad looked at his hands. There was nothing there except heat, furnace heat, blasting heat that nevertheless made the shapes of fingers.

ANGHAMMARAD, a hollow voice repeated.

'I Have Lost My Clay,' said the golem.

YES, said Death, THAT IS STANDARD. YOU ARE DEAD. SMASHED. EXPLODED INTO A MILLION PIECES.

'Then Who Is This Doing The Listening?'

EVERYTHING THERE WAS ABOUT YOU THAT ISN'T CLAY.

'Do You Have A Command For Me?' said the remains of Anghammarad, standing up.

NOT NOW. YOU HAVE REACHED THE PLACE WHERE THERE ARE NO MORE ORDERS.

'What Shall I Do?'

I BELIEVE YOU HAVE FAILED TO UNDERSTAND MY LAST COMMENT.

Anghammarad sat down again. Apart from the fact that there was sand rather than ooze underfoot, this place reminded him of the abyssal plain.

GENERALLY PEOPLE LIKE TO MOVE ON, Death hinted. THEY LOOK FORWARD TO AN AFTERLIFE.

'I Will Stay Here, Please.'

HERE? THERE'S NOTHING TO DO HERE, said Death.

'Yes, I Know,' said the ghost of the golem. 'It Is Perfect. I Am Free.'

At two in the morning it began to rain.

Things could have been worse. It could have rained snakes. It could have rained acid.

There was still some roof, and some walls. That meant there was still some building.

Moist and Miss Dearheart sat on some warm rubble outside the locker room, which was more or less the only room that could still be properly described as one. The golems had stamped out the last of the fire, shored things up and then, without a word, had gone back to not being a hammer until sunset.

Miss Dearheart held a half-melted bronze band in her hand, and turned it over and over.

'Eighteen thousand years,' she whispered.

'It was the rainwater tank,' mumbled Moist, staring at nothing.

'Fire and water,' muttered Miss Dearheart. 'But not both!'

'Can't you . . . rebake him, or something?' It sounded hopeless even as Moist said it. He'd seen the other golems scrabbling in the rubble.

'Not enough left. Just dust, mixed up with everything else,' said Miss Dearheart. 'All he wanted to do was be useful.'

Moist looked at the remains of the letters. The flood had washed the black slurry of their ashes into every corner.

All *they* wanted to do was be delivered, he thought. At a time like this, sitting on the sea bed for nine thousand years seemed quite attractive.

'He was going to wait until the universe comes round again. Did you know that?'

'You told me, yes,' said Moist.

There's no stink more sorrowful than the stink of wet, burnt paper, Moist thought. It means: the end.

'Vetinari won't rebuild this place, you know,' Miss Dearheart went on. 'Gilt will get people to make a fuss if he tries it. Waste of city funds. He's got friends. People who owe him money and favours. He's good at that sort of people.'

'It was Gilt who had this place torched,' said Moist. 'He was shocked to see me back in the restaurant. He thought I'd be here.'

'You'll never be able to prove it.'

Probably not, Moist agreed, in the sour, smoke-addled hollow of his head. The Watch had turned up with more speed than Moist had found usual amongst city policemen. They had a werewolf with them. Oh, probably most people would have thought it was just a handsome dog, but grow up in Uberwald with a grandfather who bred dogs and you learned to spot the signs. This one had a collar, and snuffled around while the embers were still smoking, and found something extra to scent in the pall of steaming ashes.

They'd dug down, and there had been an awkward interview. Moist had handled it as well as he could manage, in the circumstances. The key point was never to tell the truth. Coppers never believed what people told them in any case, so there was no point in giving them extra work.

'A winged skeleton?' Moist had said, with what surely sounded like genuine surprise.

'Yes, sir. About the size of a man, but very . . . damaged. I could even say mangled. I wonder if you know anything about it?' This watchman was a captain. Moist hadn't been able to make him out. His face gave nothing away that he didn't want to let go of. Something about him suggested that he already knew the answers but was asking the questions for the look of the thing.

'Perhaps it was an extra large pigeon? They're real pests in this building,' Moist had said.

'I doubt it, sir. We believe it to have been a banshee, Mr Lipwig,' said the captain patiently. 'They're very rare.'

'I thought they just screamed on the rooftops of people who are going to die,' said Moist.

'The civilized ones do, sir. The wild ones cut out the middle man. Your young man said he hit something?'

'Stanley did say something about, oh, something flying around,' said Moist. 'But I thought it was simply—'

'—an extra large pigeon. I see. And you've no idea how the fire started? I know you use safety lamps in here.'

'Probably spontaneous combustion in the letter piles, I'm afraid,' said Moist, who'd had time to think about this one.

'No one has been behaving oddly?'

'In the Post Office, captain, it's very hard to tell. Believe me.'

'No threats made, sir? By anyone you may have upset, perhaps?'

'None at all.'

The captain had sighed and put away his notebook.

'I'll have a couple of men watching the building overnight, nevertheless,' he'd said. 'Well done for saving the cat, sir. That was a big cheer you got when you came out. Just one thing, though, sir . . .'

'Yes, captain?'

'Why would a banshee – or possibly a giant pigeon – attack Mr Groat?'

And Moist thought: the hat . . .

'I have no idea,' he said.

'Yes, sir. I'm sure you haven't,' said the captain. 'I'm sure you haven't. I'm Captain Ironfoundersson, sir, although most people call me Captain Carrot. Don't hesitate to contact me, sir, if anything occurs to you. We are here for your protection.'

And what would you have done against a banshee? Moist had thought. You suspect Gilt. Well done. But people like Gilt don't bother with the law. They never break it, they just use people who do. And you'll never find anything written down, anywhere.

Just before the captain had turned to go Moist was sure that the werewolf had winked at him.

Now, with the rain drifting in and hissing where the stones were still warm, Moist looked around at the fires. There were still plenty of them, where the golems had dumped the rubble. This being Ankh-Morpork, people of the night had risen like the mists and gathered around them for warmth.

This place would need a fortune spent on it. Well? He knew where to lay his hands on plenty of money, didn't he? He didn't have much use for it. It had only ever been a way of keeping score. But then this would all end, because it had belonged to Albert Spangler and the rest of them, not to an innocent postmaster.

He took off his golden hat and looked at it. An avatar, Pelc had said. The human embodiment of a god. But he wasn't a god, he was just a conman in a golden suit, and the con was over. Where was the angel now? Where were the gods when you needed them?

The gods could help.

The hat glinted in the firelight, and parts of Moist's brain sparkled. He didn't breathe as the thought emerged, in case it took fright, but it was so *simple.* And something that no honest man would ever have thought of . . .

'What we need,' he said, 'is . . .'

'Is what?' said Miss Dearheart.

'Is music!' declared Moist. He stood up and cupped his hands. 'Hey, you people! Any banjo players out there? A fiddle, maybe? I'll give a one-dollar stamp, highly collectable, to anyone who can pick out a waltz tune. You know, one-two-three, one-two-three?'

'Have you gone *completely* mad?' said Miss Dearheart. 'You're clearly—'

She stopped, because a shabbily dressed man had tapped Moist on the shoulder.

'I can play the banjo,' he said, 'and my friend Humphrey here can blow the harmonica something cruel. The fee will be a dollar, sir. Coin, please, if it's all the same to you, on account of how I can't write and don't know anyone who can read.'

'My lovely Miss Dearheart,' said Moist, smiling madly at her. 'Do you have any other name? Some pet name or nickname, some delightful little diminutive you don't mind being called?'

'Are you drunk?' she demanded.

'Unfortunately, no,' said Moist. 'But I'd like to be. Well, Miss Dearheart? I even rescued my best suit!'

She was taken aback, but an answer escaped before natural cynicism could bar the door. 'My brother used to call me . . . er . . .'

'Yes?'

'Killer,' said Miss Dearheart. 'But he meant it in a nice way. Don't *you* even think about using it.'

'How about Spike?'

'*Spike?* We-ell, I could live with Spike,' said Miss Dearheart. 'So you will, too. But this is not the time for dancing—'

'On the contrary, Spike,' said Moist, beaming in the firelight, 'this is just the time. We'll dance, and then we'll get things cleaned up ready for opening time, get the mail delivery working again, order the rebuilding of the building and have everything back the way it was. Just watch me.'

'You know, perhaps it *is* true that working for the Post Office drives people mad,' said Miss Dearheart. 'Just where will you get the money to have this place rebuilt?'

'The gods will provide,' said Moist. 'Trust me on this.'

She peered at him. 'You're serious?'

'Deadly,' said Moist.

'You're going to *pray* for money?'

'Not exactly, Spike. They get thousands of prayers every day. I have other plans. We'll bring the Post Office back, Miss Dearheart. I don't have to think like a policeman, or a postman, or a clerk. I just have to do things *my* way. And then I'll bankrupt Reacher Gilt by the end of the week.'

Her mouth became a perfect O.

'How exactly will you do that?' she managed.

'I've no idea, but anything is possible if I can dance with you and still have ten toes left. Shall we dance, Miss Dearheart?'

She was amazed and surprised and bewildered, and Moist von Lipwig liked that in a person. For some reason, he felt immensely happy. He didn't know why, and he didn't know what he was going to do next, but it was going to be *fun*.

He could feel that old electric feeling, the one you got deep inside when you stood right there in front of a banker who was carefully examining an example of your very best work. The universe held its breath, and then the man would smile and say 'Very good, Mr

Assumed Name, I will have my clerk bring up the money right away.' It was the thrill not of the chase but of the standing still, of remaining so calm, composed and genuine that, for just long enough, you could fool the world and spin it on your finger. They were the moments he lived for, when he was *really* alive and his thoughts flowed like quicksilver and the very air sparkled. Later, that feeling would present its bill. For now, he flew.

He *was* back in the game. But, for now, by the light of the burning yesterdays, he waltzed with Miss Dearheart while the scratch band scratched away.

Then she went home to bed, puzzled but smiling oddly, and he went up to his office, which was missing the whole of one wall, and got religion as it had never been got before.

The young priest of Offler the Crocodile God was somewhat off-balance at 4 a.m., but the man in the wingèd hat and golden suit seemed to know what should be happening and so the priest went along with it. He was not hugely bright, which was why he was on this shift.

'You want to *deliver* this letter to Offler?' he said, yawning. An envelope had been placed in his hand.

'It's addressed to him,' said Moist. 'And correctly stamped. A smartly written letter always gets attention. I've also brought a pound of sausages, which I believe is customary. Crocodiles love sausages.'

'Strictly speaking, you see, it's prayers that go up to the gods,' said the priest doubtfully. The nave of the temple was deserted, except for a little old man in a grubby robe, dreamily sweeping the floor.

'As I understand it,' said Moist, 'the gift of sausages reaches Offler by being fried, yes? And the spirit of the sausages ascends unto Offler by means of the smell? And then you eat the sausages?'

'Ah, no. Not exactly. Not at all,' said the young priest, who knew this one. 'It might *look* like that to the uninitiated, but, as you say, the true sausagidity goes straight to Offler. He, of course, eats the spirit of the sausages. We eat the mere earthly shell, which believe me turns to dust and ashes in our mouths.'

'That would explain why the smell of sausages is always better than the actual sausage, then?' said Moist. 'I've often noticed that.'

The priest was impressed. 'Are you a theologian, sir?' he said.

'I'm in . . . a similar line of work,' said Moist. 'But what I'm getting at is this: if you were to read this letter it would be as though Offler himself was reading it, am I right? Through your eyeballs the *spirit* of the letter would ascend unto Offler? And then I could give you the sausages.'

The young priest looked desperately around the temple. It was too early in the morning. When your god, metaphorically, doesn't do much until the sandbanks have got nice and warm, the senior priests tend to lie in.

'I *suppose* so,' he said reluctantly. 'But would you rather wait until Deacon Jones gets—'

'I'm in rather a hurry,' said Moist. There was a pause. 'I've brought some honey mustard,' he added. 'The perfect accompaniment to sausages.'

Suddenly, the priest was all attention. 'What sort?' he said.

'Mrs Edith Leakall's Premium Reserve,' said Moist, holding up the jar.

The young man's face lit up. He was low in the hierarchy and got barely more sausage than Offler.

'God, that's the expensive stuff!' he breathed.

'Yes, it's the hint of wild garlic that does it,' said Moist. 'But perhaps I should wait until Deacon—'

The priest grabbed the letter and the jar. 'No, no, I can see you are in a hurry,' he said. 'I'll do it right away. It's probably a request for help, yes?'

'Yes. I'd like Offler to let the light of his eyes and the gleam of his teeth shine on my colleague Tolliver Groat, who is in the Lady Sybil Hospital,' said Moist.

'Oh, yes,' said the acolyte, relieved, 'we often do this sort of—'

'And I would also like one hundred and fifty thousand dollars,'

Moist went on. 'Ankh-Morpork dollars preferred, of course, but other reasonably hard currencies would be acceptable.'

There was a certain spring in his step as Moist walked back to the ruin of the Post Office. He'd sent letters to Offler, Om and Blind Io, all important gods, and also to Anoia, a minor goddess of Things That Stick In Drawers.* She had no temple and was handled by a jobbing priestess in Cable Street, but Moist had a feeling that by the end of the day Anoia was destined for higher things. He only picked her because he liked the name.

He'd leave it about an hour. Gods worked fast, didn't they?

The Post Office was no better by grey daylight. About half of the building was still standing. Even with tarpaulins, the area under cover was small and dank. People were milling around, uncertain of what to do.

He'd tell them.

The first person he saw was George Aggy, heading for him at a high-speed hobble.

'Terrible thing, sir, terrible thing. I came as soon as—' he began.

'Good to see you, George. How's the leg?'

'What? Oh, feels fine, sir. Glows in the dark, but on the other hand that's a great saving in candles. What are we—'

'You're my deputy while Mr Groat's in hospital,' said Moist. 'How many postmen can you muster?'

'About a dozen, sir, but what shall we—'

'Get the mail moving, Mr Aggy! That's what we do. Tell everyone that today's special is Pseudopolis for ten pence, guaranteed! Everyone else can get on with cleaning up. There's still some roof left. We're open as usual. *More* open than usual.'

'But . . .' Aggy's words failed him, and he waved at the debris. 'All this?'

---

* Often, but not uniquely, a ladle, but sometimes a metal spatula or, rarely, a mechanical egg-whisk that nobody in the house admits to ever buying. The desperate mad rattling and cries of 'How can it close on the damn thing but not open with it? Who bought this? Do we *ever* use it?' is as praise unto Anoia. She also eats corkscrews.

'Neither rain nor fire, Mr Aggy!' said Moist sharply.

'Doesn't say *that* on the motto, sir,' said Aggy.

'It will by tomorrow. Ah, Jim . . .'

The coachman bore down on Moist, his enormous driving cape flapping.

'It was bloody Gilt, wasn't it!' he growled. 'Arson around! What can we do for you, Mr Lipwig?'

'Can you still run a service to Pseudopolis today?' said Moist.

'Yes,' said Jim. 'Harry and the lads got all the horses out as soon as they smelled smoke, and only lost one coach. We'll help you, damn right about that, but the Trunk is running okay. You'll be wasting your time.'

'You provide the wheels, Jim, and I'll give them something to carry,' said Moist. 'We'll have a bag for you at ten.'

'You're very certain, Mr Lipwig,' said Jim, putting his head on one side.

'An angel came and told me in my sleep,' said Moist.

Jim grinned. 'Ah, that'd be it, then. An angel, eh? A very present help in times of trouble, or so I'm given to understand.'

'So I believe,' said Moist, and went up to the draughty, smoke-blackened, three-walled cave that was the wreckage of his office. He brushed off the ash from the chair, reached into his pocket, and put the Smoking Gnu's letter on his desk.

The only people who could *know* when a clacks tower would break down must work for the company, right? Or *used* to work for it, more likely. Hah. That's how things happened. That bank in Sto Lat, for example – he'd never have been able to forge those bills if that bent clerk hadn't sold him that old ledger with all the signatures in. That had been a good day.

The Grand Trunk mustn't just make enemies, it must mass-produce them. And now this Smoking Gnu wanted to help him. Outlaw signallers. Think of all the secrets they'd know . . .

He'd kept an ear open for clock chimes, and it was gone a quarter to nine now. What would they do? Blow up a tower? But people worked in the towers. Surely not . . .

'Oh, Mr Lipwig!'

It is not often that a wailing woman rushes into a room and throws herself at a man. It had never happened to Moist before. Now it happened, and it seemed such a waste that the woman was Miss Maccalariat.

She tottered forward and clung to the startled Moist, tears streaming down her face.

'Oh, Mr Lipwig!' she wailed. 'Oh, Mr Lipwig!'

Moist reeled under her weight. She was dragging at his collar so hard that he was likely to end up on the floor, and the thought of being found on the floor with Miss Maccalariat was— well, a thought that just couldn't be thought. The head would explode before entertaining it.

She had a pink hairgrip in her grey hair. It had little hand-painted violets on it. The sight of it, a few inches from Moist's eyes, was curiously disturbing.

'Now, now, steady on, Miss Maccalariat, steady on,' he muttered, trying to keep the balance for both of them.

'Oh, Mr Lipwig!'

'Yes indeed, Miss Maccalariat,' he said desperately. 'What can I do for—'

'Mr Aggy said the Post Office won't ever be rebuilt! He says Lord Vetinari will never release the money! Oh, Mr Lipwig! I dreamed all my life of working on the counter here! My grandmother taught me everything, she even made me practise sucking lemons to get the expression right! I've passed it all on to my daughter, too. She's got a voice that'd take the skin off paint! Oh, Mr Lipwig!'

Moist searched wildly for somewhere to pat the woman that wasn't soaked or out of bounds. He settled for her shoulder. He really, really needed Mr Groat. Mr Groat knew how to deal with things like this.

'It's all going to be all right, Miss Maccalariat,' he said soothingly.

'And poor Mr Groat!' the woman sobbed.

'I understand he's going to be fine, Miss Maccalariat. You know what they say about the Lady Sybil: some people come out alive.' I really, really hope he does, he added to himself. I'm lost without him.

'It's all so dreadful, Mr Lipwig!' said Miss Maccalariat, determined to drain the bitter cup of despair to the very dregs. 'We're all going to be walking the streets!'

Moist held her by her arms and pushed her gently away, while fighting against a mental picture of Miss Maccalariat walking the streets. 'Now you listen to me, Miss Mac— What is your first name, by the way?'

'It's Iodine, Mr Lipwig,' said Miss Maccalariat, snuffling into a handkerchief. 'My father liked the sound.'

'Well . . . Iodine, I firmly believe that I will have the money to rebuild by the end of the day,' said Moist. She's blown her nose on it and, yes, yes, aargh, she's going to put it back up the sleeve of her cardigan, oh, gods . . .

'Yes, Mr Aggy said that, and there's talk, sir. They say you sent the gods letters asking for money! Oh, sir! It's not my place to say so, sir, but gods don't send you money!'

'I have faith, Miss Maccalariat,' said Moist, drawing himself up.

'My family have been Anoians for five generations, sir,' said Miss Maccalariat. 'We rattle the drawers every day, and we've never got anything *solid*, as you might say, excepting my granny who got an egg beater she didn't remember putting there and we're sure that was an accident—'

'Mr Lipwig! Mr Lipwig!' someone yelled. 'They say the clacks— Oh, I'm *so* sorry . . .' The sentence ended in syrup.

Moist sighed, and turned to the grinning newcomer in the charcoal-rimmed doorway. '*Yes*, Mr Aggy?'

'We've heard the clacks has gone down again, sir! To Pseudopolis!' said Aggy.

'How unfortunate,' said Moist. 'Come, Miss Maccalariat, come, Mr Aggy – let's move the mail!'

There was a crowd in what remained of the hall. As Moist had remarked, the citizens had an enthusiasm for new things. The post was an old thing, of course, but it was so old that it had magically become new again.

A cheer greeted Moist when he came down the steps. Give them a show, always give them a show. Ankh-Morpork would applaud a show.

Moist commandeered a chair, stood on it and cupped his hands.

'Special today, ladies and gentlemen!' he shouted above the din. 'Mail to Pseudopolis, reduced to three pence only. Three pence! Coach goes at ten! And if anyone has clacks messages lodged with our unfortunate colleagues in the Grand Trunk Company, and would care to get them back, we will deliver them *for free*!'

This caused an additional stir, and a number of people peeled away from the crowd and hurried off.

'The Post Office, ladies and gentlemen!' yelled Moist. 'We deliver!' There was a cheer.

'Do you want to know something really interesting, Mr Lipwig?' said Stanley, hurrying up.

'And what's that, Stanley?' said Moist, climbing down off the chair.

'We're selling lots of the new one-dollar stamps this morning! And do you know what? People are sending letters to themselves!'

'What?' said Moist, mystified.

'Just so the stamps have been through the post, sir. That makes them real, you see! It proves they've been used. They're *collecting*, them, sir! And it gets better, sir!'

'How could it get better than that, Stanley?' said Moist. He looked down. Yes, the boy had a new shirt, showing a picture of the penny stamp and bearing the legend: Ask Me About Stamps.

'Sto Lat want Teemer and Spools to do them their own set! *And* the other cities are asking about it, too!'

Moist made a mental note: we'll change the stamps often. And offer stamp designs to every city and country we can think of. Everyone will want to have their own stamps rather than 'lick Vetinari's back side' and we'll honour them, too, if they'll deliver *our* mail, and Mr Spools will express his gratitude to us in very definite ways, I'll see to it.

'Sorry about your pins, Stanley.'

'Pins?' said the boy. 'Oh, *pins*. Pins are just pointy metal things, sir. Pins are *dead*.'

And so we progress, thought Moist. Aways keep moving. There may be something behind you.

All we need now is for the gods to smile on us.

Hmm. I think they'll smile a little broader outside.

Moist stepped out into the daylight. The difference between the inside and the outside of the Post Office was less marked than formerly, but there were still a lot of people. There were a couple of watchmen, too. They'd be useful. They were already watching him suspiciously.

Well, this was it. It was going to be a miracle. Actually, it bloody well *was* going to be a miracle!

Moist stared up into the sky, and listened to the voices of the gods.

CHAPTER ELEVEN

Mission Statement

In which Lord Vetinari Gives Advice – Mr Lipwig's Bad Memory – Evil Criminal Geniuses' difficulty with finding property – Mr Groat's Fear of Bathing, and a Discussion on Explosive Underwear – Mr Pony and his flimsies – The Board debates, Gilt decides – Moist von Lipwig Attempts the Impossible

THE CLOCKS WERE CHIMING seven o'clock.

'Ah, Mr Lipwig,' said Lord Vetinari, looking up. 'Thank you so much for dropping in. It has been such a busy day, has it not? Drumknott, do help Mr Lipwig to a chair. Prophecy can be very exhausting, I believe.'

Moist waved the clerk away and eased his aching body into a seat.

'I didn't exactly *decide* to drop in,' he said. 'A large troll watchman walked in and grabbed me by the arm.'

'Ah, to steady you, I have no doubt,' said Lord Vetinari, who was poring over the battle between the stone trolls and the stone dwarfs. 'You accompanied him of your own free will, did you not?'

'I'm very attached to my arm,' said Moist. 'I thought I'd better follow it. What can I do for you, my lord?'

Vetinari got up and went and sat in the chair behind his desk, where he regarded Moist with what almost looked like amusement.

'Commander Vimes has given me some succinct reports of today's events,' he said, putting down the troll figure he was holding and turning over a few sheets of paper. 'Beginning with the riot at the Grand Trunk offices this morning which, he says, you instigated . . . ?'

'All I did was volunteer to deliver such clacks messages as had been held up by the unfortunate breakdown,' said Moist. 'I didn't expect the idiots in their office to refuse to hand the messages back to their customers! People had paid in advance, after all. I was just helping everyone in a difficult time. And I certainly didn't "instigate" anyone to hit a clerk with a chair!'

'Of course not, of course not,' said Lord Vetinari. 'I am sure you acted quite innocently and from the best of intentions. But I am *agog* to hear about the gold, Mr Lipwig. One hundred and fifty *thousand* dollars, I believe.'

'Some of it I can't quite remember,' said Moist. 'It's all a bit unclear.'

'Yes, yes, I imagine it was. Perhaps I can clarify a few details?' said Lord Vetinari. 'Around mid-morning, Mr Lipwig, you were chatting to people outside your regrettably distressed building when' – here the Patrician glanced at his notes – 'you suddenly looked up, shielded your eyes, dropped to your knees and screamed, "Yes, yes, thank you, I am not worthy, glory be, may your teeth be picked clean by birds, halleluiah, rattle your drawers" and similar phrases, to the general concern of people nearby, and you then stood up with your hands outstretched and shouted "One hundred and fifty thousand dollars, buried in a field! Thank you, thank you, I shall fetch it immediately!" Whereupon you wrested a shovel from one of the men helping to clear the debris of the building and began to walk with some purpose out of the city.'

'Really?' said Moist. 'It's all a bit of a blank.'

'I'm sure it is,' said Vetinari happily. 'You will probably be quite surprised to know that a number of people followed you, Mr Lipwig? Including Mr Pump and two members of the City Watch?'

'Good heavens, did they?'

'Quite. For several hours. You stopped to pray on a number of occasions. We must assume it was for the guidance which led your footsteps, at last, to a small wood among the cabbage fields.'

'It did? I'm afraid it's all rather a blur,' said Moist.

'I understand you dug like a demon, according to the Watch. And I note that a number of reputable witnesses were there when your shovel struck the lid of the chest. I understand the *Times* will be carrying a picture in the next edition.'

Moist said nothing. It was the only way to be sure.

'Any comments, Mr Lipwig?'

'No, my lord, not really.'

'Hmm. About three hours ago I had the senior priests of three of the major religions in this office, along with a rather bewildered freelance priestess who I gather handles the worldly affairs of Anoia on an agency basis. They all claim that it was *their* god or goddess who told you where the gold was. You don't happen to *remember* which one it was, do you?'

'I sort of *felt* the voice rather than heard it,' said Moist carefully.

'Quite so,' said Vetinari. 'Incidentally, *they* all felt that their temples should get a tithe of the money,' he added. 'Each.'

'Sixty thousand dollars?' said Moist, sitting up. 'That's not right!'

'I commend the speed of your mental arithmetic in your shaken state. No lack of clarity *there*, I'm glad to see,' said Vetinari. 'I would advise you to donate fifty thousand, split four ways. It is, after all, in a very public and very *definite* and *incontrovertible* way, a gift from the gods. Is this not a time for reverential gratitude?'

There was a lengthy pause, and then Moist raised a finger and managed, against all the odds, a cheerful smile. 'Sound advice, my lord. Besides, a man never knows when he might need a prayer.'

'Exactly,' said Lord Vetinari. 'It is less than they demanded but more than they expect, and I did point out to them that the remainder of the money was all going to be used for the civic good. It *is* going to be used for the civic good, isn't it, Mr Lipwig?'

'Oh, yes. Indeed!'

'That is just as well, since currently it's sitting in Commander Vimes's cells.' Vetinari looked down at Moist's trousers. 'I see you still have mud all over your lovely golden suit, Postmaster. Fancy all that money being buried in a field. And you can *still* remember *nothing* about how you got there?'

Vetinari's expression was getting on Moist's nerves. You know, he thought. I know you know. You know I know you know. But I know you can't be certain, not *certain*. 'Well . . . there *was* an angel,' he said.

'Indeed? Any particular kind?'

'The kind you only get one of, I think,' said Moist.

'Ah, *good*. Well, then it all seems very clear to me,' said Vetinari, sitting back. 'It is not often a mortal man achieves such a moment of glorious epiphany, but I am assured by the priests that such a thing could happen, and who should know better than they? Anyone even *suggesting* that the money was in some way ... obtained in some wrong fashion will have to argue with some very turbulent priests and also, I assume, find their kitchen drawers quite impossible to shut. Besides, you are donating money to the city—' he held up his hand when Moist opened his mouth, and went on, 'that is, the Post Office, so the notion of private gain does not arise. There appears to be no owner for the money, although so far, of course, nine hundred and thirty-eight people would like me to believe it belongs to them. Such is life in Ankh-Morpork. So, Mr Lipwig, you are instructed to rebuild the Post Office as soon as possible. The bills will be met and, since the money is effectively a gift from the gods, there will be no drain on our taxes. Well done, Mr Lipwig. Very well done. Don't let me detain you.'

Moist actually had his hand on the door handle when the voice behind him said: 'Just one minor thing, Mr Lipwig.'

He stopped. 'Yes, sir?'

'It occurs to me that the sum which the gods so generously have seen fit to bestow upon us does, by pure happenstance, approximate to the estimated haul of a notorious criminal, which as far as I know has never been recovered.'

Moist stared at the woodwork in front of him. Why is this man ruling just one city? he thought. Why isn't he ruling the world? Is this how he treats other people? It's like being a puppet. The difference is, he arranges for you to pull your own strings.

He turned, face carefully deadpan. Lord Vetinari had walked over to his game.

'Really, sir? Who was that, then?' he said.

'One Albert Spangler, Mr Lipwig.'

'He's dead, sir,' said Moist.

'Are you sure?'

'Yes, sir. I was there when they hanged him.'

'Well remembered, Mr Lipwig,' said Vetinari, moving a dwarf all the way across the board.

Damn, damn, damn! Moist shouted, but only for internal consumption.

He'd worked hard for that mon— well, the banks and merchants had worked har— well, somewhere down the line *someone* had worked hard for that money, and now a third of it had been . . . well, *stolen*, that was the only word for it.

Moist experienced a certain amount of unrighteous indignation about this.

Of course he would have given *most* of it to the Post Office, that was the whole point, but you could construct a damn good building for a lot less than a hundred thousand dollars and Moist had been hoping for a little something for himself.

Still, he felt good. Perhaps this was that 'wonderful warm feeling' people talked about. And what would he have done with the money? He never had time to spend it in any case. After all, what could a master criminal buy? There was a shortage of seaside properties with real lava flows near a reliable source of piranhas, and the world sure as hell didn't need another Dark Lord, not with Gilt doing so well. Gilt didn't need a tower with ten thousand trolls camped outside. He just needed a ledger and a sharp mind. It worked better, was cheaper and he could go out and party at night.

Handing all that gold over to a copper had been a difficult thing to do, but there really was no choice. He'd got them by the short and curlies, anyway. No one was going to stand up and say the gods didn't do this sort of thing. True, they'd never done it so far, but you could never tell, with gods. Certainly there were queues outside the three temples, once the *Times* had put out its afternoon edition.

This had presented a philosophical problem to the priesthoods. They were officially against people laying up treasures on earth but, they had to admit, it was always good to get bums on pews, feet in sacred groves, hands rattling drawers and fingers being trailed in the baby crocodile pool. They settled therefore for a kind of twinkle-eyed denial that it could happen again, while hinting that, well, you never know, ineffable are the ways of gods, eh? Besides, petitioners standing in line with their letter asking for a big bag of cash were open to the suggestion that those most likely to receiveth were the ones who had already givethed, and got the message once you'd tapped them on the head with the collecting plate a few times.

Even Miss Extremelia Mume, whose small multi-purpose temple over a bookmakers' office in Cable Street handled the everyday affairs of several dozen minor gods, was doing good business among those prepared to back an outside chance. She'd hung a banner over the door. It read: It Could Be YOU.

It couldn't happen. It shouldn't happen. But, you never knew . . . this time it might.

Moist recognized that hope. It was how he'd made his living. You *knew* that the man running the Find The Lady game was going to win, you knew that people in distress didn't sell diamond rings for a fraction of their value, you knew that life generally handed you the sticky end of the stick, and you knew that the gods didn't pick some everyday undeserving tit out of the population and hand them a fortune.

Except that, this time, you might be wrong, right? It might just happen, yes?

And this was known as that greatest of treasures, which is Hope. It was a good way of getting poorer really very quickly, and staying poor. It could be you. But it wouldn't be.

Now Moist von Lipwig headed along Attic Bee Street, towards the Lady Sybil Free Hospital. Heads turned as he went past. He'd never been off the front page for days, after all. He just had to hope that the wingèd hat and golden suit were the ultimate in furniture; people saw the gold, not the face.

The hospital was still being built, as all hospitals are, but it had its own queue at the entrance. Moist dealt with that by ignoring it, and going straight in. There were, in the main hallway, people who looked like the kind of people whose job it is to say 'oi, you!' when other people just wander in, but Moist generated his personal 'I'm too important to be stopped' field and they never quite managed to frame the words.

And, of course, once you got past the doorway demons of any organization people just assumed you had a right to be there, and gave you directions.

Mr Groat was in a room by himself; a sign on the door said 'Do Not Enter', but Moist seldom bothered about that sort of thing.

The old man was sitting up in bed, looking gloomy, but he beamed as soon as he saw Moist.

'Mr Lipwig! You're a sight for sore eyes, sir! Can you find out where they've hid my trousers? I told them I was fit as a flea, sir, but they went and hid my trousers! Help me out of here before they carry me away to another bath, sir. A *bath*, sir!'

'They have to carry you?' said Moist. 'Can't you walk, Tolliver?'

'Yessir, but I fights 'em, *fights* 'em, sir. A bath, sir? From wimmin? Oggling at my trumpet-and-skittles? I call that shameless! Everyone knows soap kills the natural effulgences, sir! Oh, sir! They're holdin' me *pris'ner*, sir! They gived me a trouserectomy, sir!'

'Please calm down, Mr Groat,' said Moist urgently. The old man had gone quite red in the face. 'You're all right, then?'

'Just a scratch, sir, look . . .' Groat unfastened the buttons of his nightshirt. 'See?' he said triumphantly.

Moist nearly fainted. The banshee had tried to make a noughts-and-crosses board out of the man's chest. Someone else had stitched it neatly.

'Nice job of work, I'll give them that,' Groat said grudgingly. 'But I've got to be up and doing, sir, up and doing!'

'Are you sure you're all right?' said Moist, staring at the mess of scabs.

'Right as rain, sir. I *told* 'em, sir, if a banshee can't get at me through my chest protector, none of their damn invisible little biting demons are going to manage it. I bet it's all going wrong, sir, with Aggy bossing people around? I bet it is! I bet you really need me, right, sir?'

'Um, yes,' said Moist. 'Are they giving you medicine?'

'Hah, they *call* it medicine, sir. They gave me a lot of ol' mumbo-pocus about it being wonderful stuff, but it's got neither taste nor smell, if you want my opinion. They say it'll do me good but I told 'em it's hard work that does me good, sir, not sitting in soapy water with young wimmin lookin' at my rattle-and-flute. And they took my hair away! They called it unhygienic, sir! What a nerve! All right, it moves about a bit of its own accord, but that's only natural. I've had my hair a long time, sir. I'm used to its funny little ways!'

'Hwhat is going on here?' said a voice full of offended ownership.

Moist turned.

If one of the rules that should be passed on to a young man is 'don't get mixed up with crazy girls who smoke like a bellows', another one should be 'run away from any woman who pronounces "what" with two Hs'.

This woman might have been two women. She certainly had the cubic capacity and, since she was dressed entirely in white, looked rather like an iceberg. But chillier. And with sails. And with a head-dress starched to a cutting edge.

Two smaller women stood behind and on either side of her, in definite danger of being crushed if she stepped backwards.

'I've come to see Mr Groat,' said Moist weakly, while Groat gibbered and pulled the bedclothes over his head.

'*Quite* impossible! I am the matron here, young man, and I must insist that you leave at once! Mr Groat is in an extremely unstable condition.'

'He seems fine to me,' said Moist.

He had to admire the look the matron gave him. It suggested that Moist had just been found adhering to the sole of her shoe. He returned it with a chilly one of his own.

'Young man, his condition is *extremely* critical!' she snapped. 'I refuse to release him!'

'Madam, illness is not a crime!' said Moist. 'People are not released from hospital, they are discharged!'

The matron drew herself up and out, and gave Moist a smile of triumph. 'That, young man, is hwhat we are afraid of!'

* * *

Moist was sure doctors kept skeletons around to cow patients. *Nyer, nyer, we know what you look like underneath* . . . He quite approved, though. He had a certain fellow feeling. Places like the Lady Sybil were very rare these days, but Moist felt certain he could make a profitable career out of wearing a white robe, using long learned names for ailments like 'runny nose' and looking solemnly at things in bottles.

On the other side of the desk, a Dr Lawn – he had his name on a plate on his desk, because doctors are very busy and can't remember everything – looked up from his notes on Tolliver Groat.

'It was quite interesting, Mr Lipwig. It was the first time I've ever had to operate to remove the patient's clothing,' he said. 'You don't happen to know what the poultice was made of, do you? He wouldn't tell us.'

'I believe it's layers of flannel, goose grease and bread pudding,' said Moist, staring around at the office.

'Bread pudding? *Really* bread pudding?'

'Apparently so,' said Moist.

'Not something alive, then? It seemed leathery to us,' said the doctor, leafing through the notes. 'Ah, yes, here we are. Yes, his trousers were the subject of a controlled detonation after one of his socks exploded. We're not sure why.'

'He fills them with sulphur and charcoal to keep his feet fresh, and he soaks his trousers in saltpetre to prevent Gnats,' said Moist. 'He's a great believer in natural medicine, you see. He doesn't trust doctors.'

'Really?' said Dr Lawn. 'He retains some vestige of sanity, then. Incidentally, it's wisest not to argue with the nursing staff. I find the wisest course of action is to throw some chocolates in one direction and hurry off in the other while their attention is distracted. Mr Groat thinks that every man is his own physician, I gather?'

'He makes his own medicines,' Moist explained. 'He starts every day with a quarter of a pint of gin mixed with spirits of nitre, flour of sulphur, juniper and the juice of an onion. He says it clears the tubes.'

'Good heavens, I'm sure it does. Does he smoke at all?'

Moist considered this. 'No-o. It looks more like steam,' he said.

'And his background in basic alchemy is . . . ?'

'Non-existent, as far as I know,' said Moist. 'He makes some interesting cough sweets, though. After you've sucked them for two minutes you can feel the wax running out of your ears. He paints his knees with some sort of compound of iodine and—'

'Enough!' said the doctor. 'Mr Lipwig, there are times when we humble practitioners of the craft of medicine have to stand aside in astonishment. Quite a long way aside, in the case of Mr Groat, and preferably behind a tree. Take him away, please. I have to say that against all the odds I found him amazingly healthy. I can quite see why an attack by a banshee would be so easily shrugged off. In fact Mr Groat is probably unkillable by any normal means, although I advise you not to let him take up tap dancing. Oh, and do take his wig, will you? We tried putting it in a cupboard, but it got out. We'll send the bill to the Post Office, shall we?'

'I thought this said "Free Hospital" on the sign,' said Moist.

'Broadly, yes, broadly,' said Dr Lawn. 'But those on whom the gods have bestowed so many favours – one hundred and fifty thousand of them, I heard – probably have had all the charity they require, hmm?'

And it's all sitting in the Watch's cells, thought Moist. He reached into his jacket and produced a crumpled wad of green Ankh-Morpork one-dollar stamps.

'Will you take these?' he said.

The picture of Tiddles being carried out of the Post Office by Moist von Lipwig was, since it concerned an animal, considered to be full of human interest by the *Times* and was thus displayed prominently on the front page.

Reacher Gilt looked at it without displaying so much as a flicker of emotion. Then he reread the story next to it, under the headlines:

MAN SAVES CAT

'We'll Rebuild Bigger!' Vow as Post Office Blazes

$150,000 Gift From Gods

Wave of stuck drawers hits city

'It occurs to me that the editor of the *Times* must sometimes regret that he has only one front page,' he observed drily.

There was a sound from the men sitting round the big table in Gilt's office. It was the kind of sound you get when people are not really laughing.

'Do you think he *has* got gods on his side?' said Greenyham.

'I hardly imagine so,' said Gilt. 'He must have known where the money was.'

'You think so? If I knew where that much money was I wouldn't leave it in the ground.'

'No, you wouldn't,' said Gilt quietly, in such a way that Greenyham felt slightly uneasy.

'*Twelve and a half per cent! Twelve and a half per cent!*' screamed Alphonse, bouncing up and down on his perch.

'We're made to look fools, Reacher!' said Stowley. 'He *knew* the line would go down yesterday! He might as *well* have divine guidance! We're losing the local traffic already. Every time we have a shutdown you can bet he'll run a coach out of sheer devilment. There's nothing that damn man won't stoop to. He's turned the Post Office into a . . . a show!'

'Sooner or later all circuses leave town,' said Gilt.

'But he's laughing at us!' Stowley persisted. 'If the Trunk breaks down again I wouldn't put it past him to run a coach to Genua!'

'That would take weeks,' said Gilt.

'Yes, but it's cheaper and it gets there. That's what he'll say. And he'll say it loudly, too. We've got to do something, Reacher.'

'And what do you suggest?'

'Why don't we just spend some money and get some proper maintenance done?'

'You can't,' said a new voice. 'You don't have the men.'

All heads turned to the man at the far end of the table. He had a jacket on over his overalls and a very battered top hat on the table beside him. His name was Mr Pony, and he was the Trunk's chief engineer. He'd come with the company, and had hung on because at the age of fifty-eight, with twinges in your knuckles, a sick wife and a bad back, you think twice about grand gestures such as storming out. He hadn't seen a clacks until three years ago, when the first company was founded, but he was methodical and engineering was engineering.

Currently his greatest friend in the world was his collection of pink flimsies. He'd done his best, but he wasn't going to carry the can when this lot finally fell over and his pink flimsies would see to it that he didn't. White memo paper to the chairman, yellow flimsy to the file, pink flimsy you kept. No one could say he hadn't warned them.

A two-inch stack of the latest flimsies was attached to his clipboard. Now, feeling like an elder god leaning down through the clouds of some Armageddon and booming: 'Didn't I tell you? Didn't I warn you? Did you listen? Too late to listen now!', he put on a voice of strained patience.

'I've got six maint'nance teams. I had eight last week. I sent you a memo about that, got the flimsies right here. We ought to have eighteen teams. Half the lads are needin' to be taught as we go, and we ain't got time for teachin'. In the ol' days we'd set up walkin' towers to take the load an' we ain't got men even to do that now—'

'All right, it takes time, we *understand*,' said Greenyham. 'How long will it take if you . . . hire more men and get these walking towers working and—'

'You made me sack a lot of the craftsmen,' said Pony.

'We didn't sack them. We "let them go",' said Gilt.

'We . . . downsized,' said Greenyham.

'Looks like you succeeded, sir,' said Pony. He took a stub of pencil out of one pocket and a grubby notebook out of the other.

'D'you want it fast or cheap or good, gentlemen?' he said. 'The way things have gone, I can only give you one out of three . . .'

'How soon can we have the Grand Trunk running properly?' said Greenyham, while Gilt leaned back and shut his eyes.

Pony's lips moved as he ran his eyes over his figures. 'Nine months,' he said.

'I suppose if we're seen to be working hard nine months of erratic running won't seem too—' Mr Stowley began.

'Nine months shut down,' said Mr Pony.

'Don't be a fool, man!'

'I ain't a fool, sir, thank you,' said Pony sharply. 'I'll have to find and train new craftsmen, 'cos a lot of the old brigade won't come back whatever I offer. If we shut the towers down I can use the signallers; at least they know their way around a tower. We can get more work done if we don't have to drag walking towers and set them up. Make a clean start. The towers were never built that well to begin with. Dearheart never expected this sort of traffic. Nine months of dark towers, sirs.'

He wanted to say, oh, how he wanted to say: craftsmen. D'you know what that means? It means men with some pride, who get fed up and leave when they're told to do skimpy work in a rush, no matter what you pay them. So I'm employing people as 'craftsmen' now who're barely fit to sweep out a workshop. But you don't care, because if they don't polish a chair with their arse all day you think a man who's done a seven-year apprenticeship is the same as some twerp who can't be trusted to hold a hammer by the right end. He didn't say this aloud, because although an elderly man probably has a lot less future than a man of twenty, he's far more careful of it . . .

'You can't do better than that?' said Stowley.

'Mr Stowley, I'll be doin' well if it's only nine months,' said Pony, focusing again. 'If you don't want to shut down I can maybe get it done in a year and a half, if I can find enough men and you're ready to spend enough money. But you'll have shutdowns every day. It'll be crippled runnin', sir.'

'This man von Lipwig will walk all over us in nine months!' said Greenyham.

'Sorry about that, sir.'

'And how much will it cost?' asked Gilt dreamily, without opening his eyes.

'One way or the other, sir, I reckon maybe two hundred thousand,' said Pony.

'That's ridiculous! We paid less than that for the Trunk!' Greenyham burst out.

'Yes, sir. But, you see, you got to run maint'nance *all the time*, sir. The towers have been run ragged. There was that big gale back in Sektober and all that trouble in Uberwald. I haven't got the man-power. If you don't do maint'nance a little fault soon becomes a big one. I sent you gentlemen lots of reports, sir. And you cut my budget twice. I may say my lads did wonders with—'

'Mr Pony,' said Gilt quietly, 'I think what I can see here is a conflict of cultures. Would you mind strolling along to my study, please? Igor will make you a cup of tea. Thank you so much.'

When Pony had gone, Greenyham said: 'Do you know what worries me right now?'

'Do tell us,' said Gilt, folding his hands across his expensive waistcoat.

'Mr Slant is not here.'

'He has apologized. He says he has important business,' said Gilt.

'We're his biggest clients! What's more important than us? No, he's not here because he wants to be somewhere else! The damn old revenant senses trouble and he's never there when it all goes bad. Slant always comes out smelling of roses!'

'That is at least more fragrant than his usual formaldehyde,' said Gilt. 'Don't *panic*, gentlemen.'

'Somebody did,' said Stowley. 'Don't tell me that fire was accidental! Was it? And what happened to poor old Fatty Horsefry, eh?'

'Calm down, my friends, calm down,' said Gilt. They're just merchant bankers, he thought. They're not hunters, they're scavengers. They have no vision.

He waited until they had settled down and were regarding him with that strange and rather terrifying look that rich men wear when they think they may be in danger of becoming poor men.

'I expected something like this,' he said. 'Vetinari wants to harry us, that is all.'

'Reacher, you know we'll be in big trouble if the Trunk stops working,' said Nutmeg. 'Some of us have . . . debts to service. If the Trunk fails for good then people will . . . ask questions.'

Oh, those pauses, thought Gilt. Embezzlement is such a *difficult* word.

'Many of us had to work very hard to raise the cash,' said Stowley.

Yes, keeping a straight face in front of your clients must be tricky, Gilt thought. Aloud, he said, 'I think we have to pay, gentlemen. I think we do.'

'Two hundred thousand?' said Greenyham. 'Where do you think we can get that kind of money?'

'You got it before,' murmured Gilt.

'And what is *that* supposed to mean, pray?' said Greenyham, with just a little too much indignation.

'Poor Crispin came to see me the night before he died,' said Gilt, as calmly as six inches of snow. 'Babbled about, oh, all sorts of wild things. They hardly bear repeating. I think he believed people were after him. He did however insist on pressing a small ledger on me. Needless to say, it is safely locked away.'

The room fell silent, its silence made deeper and hotter by a number of desperate men thinking hard and fast. They were, by their own standards, honest men, in that they only did what they knew or suspected that everyone else did and there was never any visible blood, but just now they were men far out on a frozen sea who'd just heard the ice creak.

'I strongly suspect that it'll be a bit less than two hundred thousand,' said Gilt. 'Pony would be a fool if he didn't leave a margin.'

'You didn't warn us about this, Reacher,' said Stowley resentfully.

Gilt waved his hands. 'We must speculate to accumulate!' he said. 'The Post Office? Trickery and sleight of hand. Oh, von Lipwig is an ideas man, but that's *all* he is. He's made a splash, but he's not got the stamina for the long haul. Yet as it turns out he will do us a favour. Perhaps we have been . . . a little smug, a little lax, but we have learned our lesson! Spurred by the competition we are investing several hundred thousand dollars—'

'*Several* hundred?' said Greenyham.

Gilt waved him into silence, and continued: '—several hundred thousand dollars in a challenging, relevant and exciting systemic overhaul of our entire organization, focusing on our core competencies while maintaining full and listening co-operation with the communities we are proud to serve. We fully realize that our energetic attempts to mobilize the flawed infrastructure we inherited have been less than totally satisfactory, and hope and trust that our valued and loyal customers will bear with us in the coming months as we interact synergistically with change management in our striving for excellence. That is our mission.'

An awed silence followed.

'And thus we bounce back,' said Gilt.

'But you said several hundr—'

Gilt sighed. 'I *said* that,' he said. 'Trust me. It's a game, gentlemen, and a good player is one who can turn a bad situation to their advantage. I have brought you this far, haven't I? A little cash and the right attitude will take us the rest of the way. I'm sure you can find some more money,' he added, 'from somewhere it won't be missed.'

This wasn't silence. It went beyond silence.

'What are you suggesting?' said Nutmeg.

'Embezzlement, theft, breach of trust, misappropriation of funds . . . people can be so harsh,' said Gilt. He threw open his arms again and a big friendly smile emerged like the sun breaking through storm clouds. 'Gentlemen! I understand! Money was made to work, to move, to grow, not to be locked up in some vault. Poor Mr Horsefry, I believe, did not really understand that. So much on his mind, poor fellow. But we . . . we are businessmen. We understand these things, my friends.'

He surveyed the faces of men who now knew that they were riding a tiger. It had been a good ride up until a week or so ago. It wasn't a case of not being able to get off. They could get off. That was not the problem. The problem was that the tiger knew where they lived.

Poor Mr Horsefry . . . there had been rumours. In fact they were completely unsubstantiated rumours, because Mr Gryle had been excessively good at his job when pigeons weren't involved, had moved like a shadow with claws and, while he'd left a faint scent, it had been masked by the blood. In the nose of a werewolf, blood trumps everything. But rumour rose in the streets of Ankh-Morpork like mist from a midden.

And then it occurred to one or two of the board that the jovial 'my friends' in the mouth of Reacher Gilt, so generous with his invitations, his little tips, his advice and his champagne, was beginning, in its harmonics and overtones, to sound just like the word 'pal' in the mouth of a man in an alley who was offering cosmetic surgery with a broken bottle in exchange for not being given any money. On the other hand, they'd been safe so far; maybe it was worth following the tiger to the kill. Better to follow at the beast's heel than be its prey . . .

'And now I realize that I am inexcusably keeping you from your beds,' said Gilt. 'Good night to you, gentlemen. You may safely leave *everything* to me. Igor!'

'Yeth, marthter,' said Igor, behind him.

'Do see these gentlemen out, and ask Mr Pony to come in.'

Gilt watched them go with a smile of satisfaction, which became a bright and happy face when Pony was ushered in.

The interview with the engineer went like this:

'Mr Pony,' said Gilt, 'I am very pleased to tell you that the Board, impressed by your dedication and the hard work you have been putting in, have voted unanimously to increase your salary by five hundred dollars a year.'

Pony brightened up. 'Thank you very much, sir. That will certainly come in—'

'However, Mr Pony, as part of the management of the Grand Trunk Company – and we do think of you as part of the team – we must ask you to bear in mind our cash flow. We cannot authorize more than twenty-five thousand dollars for repairs this year.'

'That's only about seventy dollars a tower, sir!' the engineer protested.

'Tch, is it really? I told them you wouldn't accept that,' said Gilt. 'Mr Pony is an engineer of integrity, I said. He won't accept a penny less than fifty thousand, I told them!'

Pony looked hunted. 'Couldn't really do much of a job, sir, even for that. I could get some walking tower teams out there, yes, but most of the mountain towers are living on borrowed time as it is—'

'We're counting on you, George,' said Gilt.

'Well, I suppose . . . Could we have the Hour of the Dead back, Mr Gilt?'

'I really wish you wouldn't use that fanciful term,' said Gilt. 'It really does not present the right image.'

'Sorry, sir,' said Pony. 'But I still need it.'

Gilt drummed his fingers on the table. 'You're asking a lot, George, you really are. That's revenue flow we're talking about. The Board won't be very pleased with me if I—'

'I think I've got to insist, Mr Gilt,' said Pony, looking at his feet.

'And what could you deliver?' said Gilt. 'That's what the Board will want to know. They'll say to me: Reacher, we're giving good old George everything he asks for; what will we be getting in return?'

Forgetting for the moment that it was a quarter of what he'd asked for, good old George said: 'Well, we could patch up all round and get some of the really shaky towers back into some sort of order, especially 99 and 201 . . . Oh, there's just so much to do—'

'Would it, for example, give us a year of reasonable service?'

Mr Pony struggled manfully with the engineer's permanent dread of having to commit himself to anything, and managed, 'Well, if we don't lose too many staff, and the winter isn't too bad, but of course there's always—'

Gilt snapped his fingers. 'By damn, George, you've talked me into it! I'll tell the Board that I'm backing you and to hell with them!'

'Well, that's very kind of you, sir, of course,' said Pony, bewildered, 'but it's only papering over the cracks, really. If we don't have a major rebuild we're only laying up even more trouble for the future—'

'In a year or so, George, you can lay any plans you like in front of us!' said Gilt jovially. 'Your skill and ingenuity will be the saving of the company! Now I know you're a busy man and I mustn't keep you. Go and perform miracles of economy, Mr Pony!'

Mr Pony staggered out, proud and bemused and full of dread.

'Silly old fool,' said Gilt, and reached down and opened the bottom drawer of his desk. He pulled out a beartrap, which he set, with some effort, and then stood in the middle of the floor with his back to it.

'Igor!' he called.

'Yeth, thur,' said Igor, behind him. There was a snap. 'I think thith ith yourth, thur,' Igor added, handing Gilt the sprung trap. Gilt looked down. The man's legs appeared unscathed.

'How did you—' he began.

'Oh, we Igorth are no thtranger to marthterth of an enquiring mind, thur,' said Igor gloomily. 'One of my gentlemen uthed to thtand with hith back to a pit lined with thpiketh, thur. Oh how we chuckled, thur.'

'And what happened?'

'One day he forgot and thtepped into it. Talk about laugh, thur.'

Gilt laughed, too, and went back to his desk. He liked that kind of joke.

'Igor, would you say that I'm insane?' he said.

Igors are not supposed to lie to an employer. It's part of the Code of the Igors. Igor took refuge in strict linguistic honesty.

'I wouldn't find mythelf able to thay that, thur,' he said.

'I must be, Igor. Either that or everyone else is,' said Gilt. 'I mean, I *show* them what I do, I show them how the cards are marked, I tell them what I am . . . and they nudge one another and grin and each one of them thinks himself no end of a fine fellow to be doing business with me. They throw good money after bad. They believe themselves to be sharp operators, and yet they offer themselves like little lambs. How I love to see their expressions when they think they're being *astute*.'

'Indeed, thur,' said Igor. He was wondering if that job at the new hospital was still open. His cousin Igor was already working there and had told him it was wonderful. Sometimes you had to work all night! And you got a white coat, all the rubber gloves you could eat and, best of all, you got *rethpect*.

'It's so . . . basic,' said Gilt. 'You make money as it runs down, you make money building it up again, you might even make a little money running it, then you sell it to yourself when it collapses. The leases alone are worth a fortune. Give Alphonse his nuts, will you?'

'*Twelve and a half per cent! Twelve and a half per cent!*' said the cockatoo, sidling up and down the perch excitedly.

'Thertainly, thur,' said Igor, taking a bag out of his pocket and advancing cautiously. Alphonse had a beak like a pair of shears.

Or maybe try veterinary work like my other cousin Igor, Igor thought. That was a good traditional area, certainly. Pity about all that publicity when the hamster smashed its way out of its treadmill and ate that man's leg before flying away, but that was Progrethth for you. The important thing was to get out before the mob arrived. And when your boss started telling thin air how good he was, that was the time.

'Hope is the curse of humanity, Igor,' said Gilt, putting his hands behind his head.

'Could be, thur,' said Igor, trying to avoid the horrible curved beak.

'The tiger does not hope to catch its prey, nor does the gazelle hope to escape the claws. They *run*, Igor. Only the running matters. All they know is that they must run. And now I must run along to those nice people at the *Times*, to tell everyone about our bright new future. Get the coach out, will you?'

'Thertainly, thur. If you will excuthe me, I will go and fetch another finger.'

I think I'll head back to the mountains, he thought as he went down to the cellar. At least a monster there has the decency to look like one.

Flares around the ruins of the Post Office made the night brilliant. The golems didn't need them, but the surveyors did. Moist had got a good deal there. The gods had spoken, after all. It'd do a firm no harm at all to be associated with this phoenix of a building.

In the bit that was still standing, shored up and tarpaulined, the Post Office – that is, the people who were the Post Office – worked through the night. In truth there wasn't enough for everyone to do, but they turned up anyway, to do it. It was that kind of night. You had to be there, so that later you could say '. . . and I was there, that very night . . .'

Moist knew he ought to get some sleep, but he had to be there too, alive and sparkling. It was . . . amazing. They listened to him, they did things for him, they scuttled around as if he was a real leader and not some cheat and fraud.

And there were the letters. Oh, the letters hurt. More and more were coming in, and they were addressed to him. The news had got round the city. It had been in the paper! The gods *listened* to this man!

. . . we will deliver to the gods themselves . . .

He was the man with the gold suit and the hat with wings. They'd made a crook the messenger of the gods, and piled on his charred desk the sum of all their hopes and fears . . . badly punctuated, true, and in smudged pencil or free Post Office ink, which had spluttered across the paper in the urgency of writing.

'They think you're an angel,' said Miss Dearheart, who was sitting on the other side of his desk and helping him sort through the pathetic petitions. Every half-hour or so Mr Pump brought up some more.

'Well, I'm not,' snapped Moist.

'You speak to the gods and the gods listen,' said Miss Dearheart, grinning. 'They told you where the treasure was. Now that's what *I* call religion. Incidentally, how *did* you know the money was there?'

'You don't believe in any gods?'

'No, of course not. Not while people like Reacher Gilt walk under the sky. All there is, is us. The money . . . ?'

'I can't tell you,' said Moist.

'Have you *read* some of these letters?' said Miss Dearheart. 'Sick children, dying wives—'

'Some just want cash,' said Moist hurriedly, as if that made it better.

'Whose fault is that, Slick? You're the man who can tap the gods for a wad of wonga!'

'So what shall I do with all these . . . prayers?' said Moist.

'Deliver them, of course. You've got to. You are the messenger of the gods. And they've got stamps on. Some of them are *covered* in stamps! It's your *job*. Take them to the temples. You promised to do that!'

'I never promised to—'

'*You promised to when you sold them the stamps!*'

Moist almost fell off his chair. She'd wielded the sentence like a fist.

'And it'll give them hope,' she added, rather more quietly.

'False hope,' said Moist, struggling upright.

'Maybe not this time,' said Miss Dearheart. 'That's the point of hope.' She picked up the battered remains of Anghammarad's arm-band. '*He* was taking a message across the whole of Time. You think you've got it tough?'

'Mr Lipwig?'

The voice floated up from the hall, and at the same time the back-ground noise subsided like a bad soufflé.

Moist walked over to where a wall had once been. Now, with the scorched floorboards creaking underfoot, he looked right down into the hall. A small part of him thought: we'll have to put a big picture window here when we rebuild. This is just too impressive for words.

There was a buzz of whispering and a few gasps. There were a lot of customers, too, even in the early foggy hours. It's never too late for a prayer.

'Is everything all right, Mr Groat?' he called down.

Something white was waved in the air.

'Early copy of the *Times*, sir!' Groat shouted. 'Just in! Gilt's all over the front page, sir! Where you ought to be, sir! You won't like it, sir!'

If Moist von Lipwig had been raised to be a clown, he'd have visited shows and circuses and watched the kings of fooldom. He'd have marvelled at the elegant trajectory of the custard pie, memorized the new business with the ladder and the bucket of whitewash and watched with care every carelessly juggled egg. While the rest of the audience watched the display with the appropriate feelings of terror, anger and exasperation, he'd make notes.

Now, like an apprentice staring at the work of a master, he read Reacher Gilt's words on the still-damp newspaper.

It was garbage, but it had been cooked by an expert. Oh, yes. You had to admire the way perfectly innocent words were mugged, ravished, stripped of all true meaning and decency and then sent to walk the gutter for Reacher Gilt, although 'synergistically' had probably been a whore from the start. The Grand Trunk's problems were clearly the result of some mysterious spasm in the universe and had nothing to do with greed, arrogance and wilful stupidity. Oh, the Grand Trunk management had made mistakes – oops, 'well-intentioned judgements which, with the benefit of hindsight, might regrettably have been, in some respects, in error' – but these had mostly occurred, it appeared, while correcting 'fundamental systemic errors' committed by the previous management. No one was sorry for anything because no living creature had done anything wrong; bad things had happened by spontaneous generation in some weird, chilly, geometrical otherworld, and 'were to be regretted'.*

The *Times* reporter had made an effort but nothing short of a stampede could have stopped Reacher Gilt in his crazed assault on the meaning of meaning. The Grand Trunk was 'about people' and the reporter had completely failed to ask what that meant, *exactly*? And then there was this piece called 'Our Mission' . . .

Moist felt the acid rise in his throat until he could spit lacework in a sheet of steel. Meaningless stupid words, from people without wisdom or intelligence or any skill beyond the ability to water the currency of expression. Oh, the Grand Trunk was for *everything*, from life and liberty to Mum's home-made Distressed Pudding. It was for everything, except anything.

Through a pink mist his eye caught the line: 'safety is our foremost consideration'. Why hadn't the lead type melted, why hadn't the paper

---

* Another bastard phrase that'd sell itself to any weasel in a tight corner.

blazed rather than be part of this obscenity? The press should have buckled, the roller should have cleaved unto the platen . . .

That was bad. But then he saw Gilt's reply to a hasty question about the Post Office.

Reacher Gilt *loved* the Post Office and blessed its little cotton socks. He was very grateful for its assistance during this difficult period and looked forward to future co-operation, although of course the Post Office, in the real modern world, would never be able to compete on anything other than a very local level. Mind you, someone has to deliver the bills, ho ho . . .

It was masterly . . . the *bastard*.

'Er . . . are you okay? Could you stop shouting?' said Miss Dearheart.

'What?' The mists cleared.

Everyone in the hall was looking at him, their mouths open, their eyes wide. Watery ink dripped from Post Office pens, stamps began to dry on tongues.

'You were shouting,' said Miss Dearheart. 'Swearing, in fact.'

Miss Maccalariat pushed her way through the throng, with an expression of determination.

'Mr Lipwig, I hope never to hear such language in this building again!' she said.

'He was using it about the chairman of the Grand Trunk Company,' said Miss Dearheart, in what was, for her, a conciliatory tone of voice.

'Oh.' Miss Maccalariat hesitated, and then remembered herself. 'Er, in that case . . . perhaps a teensy bit quieter, then?'

'Certainly, Miss Maccalariat,' said Moist obediently.

'And perhaps not the K-word?'

'No, Miss Maccalariat.'

'And also not the L-word, the T-word, both of the S-words, the V-word and the Y-word.'

'Just as you say, Miss Maccalariat.'

'"Murdering conniving bastard of a weasel" was acceptable, however.'

'I shall remember that, Miss Maccalariat.'

'Very good, Postmaster.'

Miss Maccalariat turned on her heel and went back to haranguing someone for not using blotting paper.

Moist handed the paper to Miss Dearheart. 'He's going to walk away with it,' he said. 'He's just throwing words around. The Trunk's too big to fail. Too many investors. He'll get more money, keep the system going just this side of disaster, then let it collapse. Buy it up then via another company, maybe, at a knock-down price.'

'I'd suspect him of anything,' said Miss Dearheart. 'But you sound *very* certain.'

'That's what I'd do,' said Moist, 'er . . . if I was that kind of person. It's the oldest trick in the book. You get the punt— you get others so deeply involved that they don't dare fold. It's the dream, you see? They think if they stay in it'll all work out. They daren't think it's all a dream. You use big words to tell them it's going to be jam tomorrow and they *hope*. But they'll never win. Part of them knows that, but the rest of them never listens to it. The house always wins.'

'Why do people like Gilt get away with it?'

'I just told you. It's because people hope. They'll believe that someone will sell them a real diamond for a dollar. Sorry.'

'Do you know how I came to work for the Trust?' said Miss Dearheart.

Because clay people are easier to deal with? Moist thought. They don't cough when you talk to them? 'No,' he said.

'I used to work in a bank in Sto Lat. The Cabbage Growers' Co-operative—'

'Oh, the one on the town square? With the carved cabbage over the door?' said Moist, before he could stop himself.

'You know it?' she said.

'Well, yes. I went past it, once . . .' Oh no, he thought, as his mind ran ahead of the conversation, oh, please, *no* . . .

'It wasn't a bad job,' said Miss Dearheart. 'In our office we had to inspect drafts and cheques. Looking for forgeries, you know? And one day I let four through. Four fakes! It cost the bank two thousand dollars. They were cash drafts, and the signatures were perfect. I got sacked for that. They said they had to do something, otherwise the customers would lose confidence. It's not fun, having people think you might be a crook. And that's what happens to people like us. People like Gilt always get away with it. Are you all right?'

'Hmm?' said Moist.

'You look a bit . . . off colour.'

That *had* been a good day, Moist thought. At least, up until now it had been a good day. He'd been quite pleased with it at the time. You weren't supposed ever to meet the people afterwards. Gods damn Mr Pump and his actuarial concept of murder!

He sighed. Oh well, it had come to this. He'd known it would. Him and Gilt, arm-wrestling to see who was the biggest bastard.

'This is the country edition of the *Times*,' he said. 'They don't go to press with the city edition for another ninety minutes, in case of late-breaking news. I think I can wipe the smile off his face, at least.'

'What are you going to do?' said Miss Dearheart.

Moist adjusted the wingèd hat. 'Attempt the impossible,' he said.

CHAPTER TWELVE

The Woodpecker

The Challenge – Moving Mountains – The Many Uses of Cabbage – The Board Debates – Mr Lipwig on his Knees – The Smoking Gnu – The Way of the Woodpecker

IT WAS THE NEXT MORNING.

Something prodded Moist.

He opened his eyes, and stared along the length of a shiny black cane, past the hand holding the silver Death's head knob and into the face of Lord Vetinari. Behind him, the golem smouldered in the corner.

'Pray, don't get up,' said the Patrician. 'I expect you have had a busy night?'

'Sorry, sir,' said Moist, forcing himself upright. He'd fallen asleep at his desk again; his mouth tasted as though Tiddles had slept in it. Behind Vetinari's head he could see Mr Groat and Stanley, peering anxiously round the door.

Lord Vetinari sat down opposite him, after dusting some ash off a chair.

'You have read this morning's *Times*?' he said.

'I was there when it was printed, sir.' Moist's neck seemed to have developed extra bones. He tried to twist his head straight.

'Ah, yes. Ankh-Morpork to Genua is about two thousand miles, Mr Lipwig. And you say you can get a message there faster than the clacks. You have issued that as a challenge. Most *intriguing*.'

'Yes, sir.'

'Even the fastest coach takes almost two months, Mr Lipwig, and I'm given to understand that if you travelled non-stop your kidneys would be jolted out of your ears.'

'Yes, sir. I know that,' said Moist, yawning.

'It would be cheating, you know, to use magic.'

Moist yawned again. 'I know that too, sir.'

'Did you *ask* the Archchancellor of Unseen University before you suggested that he should devise the message for this curious race?' Lord Vetinari demanded, unfolding the newspaper. Moist caught sight of the headlines:

THE RACE IS ON!
'Flying Postman' vs. Grand Trunk

'No, my lord. I said the message should be prepared by a well-respected citizen of great probity, *such as* the Archchancellor, sir.'

'Well, he's hardly likely to say no now, is he?' said Vetinari.

'I'd like to think so, sir. Gilt won't be able to bribe him, at least.'

'Hmm.' Vetinari tapped the floor once or twice with his cane. 'Would it surprise you to know that the feeling in the city this morning is that you'll win? The Trunk has never been out of commission for longer than a week, a clacks message can get to Genua in a few hours and yet, Mr Lipwig, people think you can do this. Don't you find that amazing?'

'Er . . .'

'But, of course, you are the man of the moment, Mr Lipwig,' said Vetinari, suddenly jovial. 'You are the golden messenger!' His smile was reptilian. 'I do hope you know what you are doing. You *do* know what you are doing, don't you, Mr Lipwig?'

'Faith moves mountains, my lord,' said Moist.

'There are a lot of them between here and Genua, indeed,' said Lord Vetinari. 'You say in the paper that you'll leave tomorrow night?'

'That's right. The weekly coach. But on this run we won't take paying passengers, to save weight.' Moist looked into Vetinari's eyes.

'You wouldn't like to give me some little clue?' said the Patrician.

'Best all round if I don't, sir,' said Moist.

'I suppose the gods haven't left an extremely fast magical horse buried somewhere nearby, have they?'

'Not that I'm aware, sir,' said Moist earnestly. 'Of course, you never know until you pray.'

'No-o,' said Vetinari. He's trying the penetrating gaze, Moist thought. But we know how to deal with that, don't we? We let it pass right through.

'Gilt will have to accept the challenge, of course,' said Vetinari. 'But he is a man of . . . ingenious resource.'

That seemed to Moist to be a very careful way of saying 'murderous bastard'. Once away, he let it pass.

His lordship stood up. 'Until tomorrow night, then,' he said. 'No doubt there will be some little ceremony for the newspapers?'

'I haven't actually planned that, sir,' said Moist.

'No, of course you haven't,' said Lord Vetinari, and gave him what could only be called . . . a *look*.

Moist got very much the same look from Jim Upwright, before the man said: 'Well, we can put out the word and call in some favours and we'll get good horses at the post houses, Mr Lipwig, but we only go as far as Bonk, you know? Then you'll have to change. The Genua Express is pretty good, though. We know the lads.'

'You sure you want to hire the whole coach?' said Harry, as he rubbed down a horse. 'It'll be expensive, 'cos we'll have to put on another for the passengers. It's a popular run, that one.'

'Just the mail in that coach,' said Moist. 'And some guards.'

'Ah, you think you'll be attacked?' said Harry, squeezing the towel bone dry with barely an effort.

'What do *you* think?' said Moist.

The brothers looked at one another.

'I'll drive it, then,' said Jim. 'They don't call me Leadpipe for nothing.'

'Besides, I heard there were bandits up in the mountains,' said Moist.

'Used to be,' said Jim. 'Not as many now.'

'That's something less to worry about, then,' said Moist.

'Dunno,' said Jim. 'We never found out what wiped them out.'

Always remember that the crowd which applauds your coronation is the same crowd that will applaud your beheading. People like a show.

People like a show . . .

. . . and so mail was coming in for Genua, at a dollar a time. A lot of mail.

It was Stanley who explained. He explained several times, because Moist had a bit of a blind spot on this one.

'People are sending envelopes with stamps *inside* envelopes to the coach office in Genua so that the first envelope can be sent back in the second envelope,' was the shape of explanation that finally blew on some sparks in Moist's brain.

'They want the envelopes back?' he said. 'Why?'

'Because they've been used, sir.'

'That makes them valuable?'

'I'm not sure how, sir. It's like I told you, sir. I think some people think that they're not real stamps until they've done the job they were invented to do, sir. Remember the first printing of the one penny stamps that we had to cut out with scissors? An envelope with one of those on is worth two dollars to a collector.'

'Two hundred times more than the stamp?'

'That's how it's going sir,' said Stanley, his eyes sparkling. 'People post letters to themselves just to get the stamp, er, stamped, sir. So they've been used.'

'Er . . . I've got a couple of rather crusty handkerchiefs in my pocket,' said Moist, mystified. 'Do you think people might want to buy *them* at two hundred times what they cost?'

'No, sir!' said Stanley.

'Then why should—'

'There's a lot of interest, sir. I thought we could do a whole set of stamps for the big guilds, sir. All the collectors would want them. What do you think?'

'That's a very clever idea, Stanley,' said Moist. 'We'll do that. The one for the Seamstresses' Guild might have to go *inside* a plain brown envelope, eh? Haha!'

This time it was Stanley who looked perplexed. 'Sorry, sir?'

Moist coughed. 'Oh, nothing. Well, I can see you're learning fast, Stanley.' Some things, anyway.

'Er . . . yes, sir. Er . . . I don't want to push myself forward, sir—'

'Push away, Stanley, push away,' said Moist cheerfully.

Stanley pulled a small paper folder out of his pocket, opened it, and laid it reverentially in front of Moist.

'Mr Spools helped me with some of it,' he said. 'But I did a lot.'

It was a stamp. It was a yellowy-green colour. It showed – Moist peered – a field of cabbages, with some buildings on the horizon.

He sniffed. It smelled of cabbages. Oh, yes.

'Printed with cabbage ink and using gum made from broccoli, sir,' said Stanley, full of pride. 'A Salute to the Cabbage Industry of the Sto Plains, sir. I think it might do very well. Cabbages are so popular, sir. You can make so many things out of them!'

'Well, I can see that—'

'There's cabbage soup, cabbage beer, cabbage fudge, cabbage cake, cream of cabbage—'

'Yes, Stanley, I think you—'

'—pickled cabbage, cabbage jelly, cabbage salad, boiled cabbage, deep-fried cabbage—'

'Yes, but now can—'

'—fricassee of cabbage, cabbage chutney, Cabbage Surprise, sausages—'

'Sausages?'

'Filled with cabbage, sir. You can make practically anything with cabbage, sir. Then there's—'

'Cabbage stamps,' said Moist, terminally. 'At fifty pence, I note. You have hidden depths, Stanley.'

'I owe it all to you, Mr Lipwig!' Stanley burst out. 'I have put the childish playground of pins right behind me, sir! The world of stamps, which can teach a young man much about history and geography as well as being a healthy, enjoyable, engrossing and thoroughly worthwhile hobby that will give him an interest that will last a lifetime, has opened up before me and—'

'Yes, yes, thank you!' said Moist.

'—and I'm putting thirty dollars into the pot, sir. All my savings. Just to show we support you.'

Moist heard all the words, but had to wait for them to make sense.

'Pot?' he said at last. 'You mean like a bet?'

'Yes, sir. A *big* bet,' said Stanley happily. 'About you racing the clacks to Genua. People think that's funny. A lot of the bookmakers are offering odds, sir, so Mr Groat is organizing it, sir! He said the odds aren't good, though.'

'I shouldn't think they are,' said Moist weakly. 'No one in their right mind would—'

'He said we'd only win one dollar for every eight we bet, sir, but we reckoned—'

Moist shot upright. 'Eight to one *odds on*?' he shouted. 'The *bookies* think I'm going to *win*? How much are you all betting?'

'Er . . . about one thousand two hundred dollars at the last count, sir. Is that—'

Pigeons rose from the roof at the sound of Moist von Lipwig's scream. '*Fetch Mr Groat right now!*'

It was a terrible thing to see guile on the face of Mr Groat. The old man tapped the side of his nose.

'You're the man that got money out o' a bunch of gods, sir!' he said, grinning happily.

'Yes,' said Moist desperately. 'But supposing I – I just did that with a trick . . .'

'Damn good trick, sir,' the old man cackled. '*Damn* good. A man who could *trick* money out of the gods'd be capable of anything, I should think!'

'Mr Groat, there is no way a coach can get to Genua faster than a clacks message. It's two thousand miles!'

'Yes, I realize you've got to say that, sir. Walls have ears, sir. Mum's the word. But we all had a talk, and we reckoned you've been very good to us, sir, you really believe in the Post Office, sir, so we thought: it's time to put our money in our mouth, sir!' said Groat, and now there was a touch of defiance.

Moist gaped once or twice. 'You mean "where your mouth is"?'

'You're the man who knows a trick or three, sir! The way you just went into the newspaper office and said, we'll race you! Reacher Gilt walked right into your trap, sir!'

Glass into diamond, thought Moist. He sighed. 'All right, Mr Groat. Thank you. Eight to one on, eh?'

'We were lucky to get it, sir. They went up to ten to one on, then they closed the books. All they're accepting now is bets on *how* you'll win, sir.'

Moist perked up a little. 'Any good ideas?' he asked.

'I've got a one-dollar flutter on "by dropping fire from the sky", sir. Er . . . you wouldn't like to give me a hint, p'raps?'

'Please go and get on with your work, Mr Groat,' said Moist severely.

'Yessir, of course, sir, sorry I asked, sir,' said Groat, and crabbed off.

Moist put his head in his hands.

I wonder if it's like this for mountain climbers, he thought. You climb bigger and bigger mountains and you know that one day one of them is going to be just that bit too steep. But you go on doing it, because it's so-o good when you breathe the air up there. And you know you'll die falling.

How could people be so stupid? They seemed to cling to ignorance because it smelled familiar. Reacher Gilt sighed.

He had an office in the Tump Tower. He didn't like it much, because the whole place shook to the movement of the semaphore, but it was necessary for the look of the thing. It did have an unrivalled view of the city, though. And the site alone was worth what they'd paid for the Trunk.

'It takes the best part of two months to get to Genua by coach,' he said, staring across the rooftops to the Palace. 'He might be able to shave something off that, I suppose. The clacks takes a few hours. What is there about this that frightens you?'

'So what's his game?' said Greenyham. The rest of the board sat around the table, looking worried.

'I don't know,' said Gilt. 'I don't care.'

'But the gods are on his side, Reacher,' said Nutmeg.

'Let's talk about that, shall we?' said Gilt. 'Does that claim strike anyone else as odd? The gods are not generally known for no-frills gifts, are they? Especially not ones that you can bite. No, these days they restrict themselves to things like grace, patience, fortitude and inner strength. Things you can't see. Things that have no value. Gods tend to be interested in prophets, not profits, haha.'

There were some blank looks from his fellow directors.

'Didn't quite get that one, old chap,' said Stowley.

'Pro*phets*, I said, not pro*fits*,' said Gilt. He waved a hand. 'Don't worry yourselves, it will look better written down. In short, Mr Lipwig's gift from above was a big chest of coins, some of them in what look remarkably like bank sacks and all in modern denominations. You don't find this strange?'

'Yes, but even the high priests say he—'

'Lipwig is a *showman*,' snapped Gilt. 'Do you think the gods will carry his mail coach for him? Do you? This is a *stunt*, do you understand? It got him on page one again, that's all. This is not hard to follow. He has no plan, other than to fail heroically. No one expects him actually to win, do they?'

'I heard that people are betting heavily on him.'

'People enjoy the experience of being fooled, if it promises a certain amount of entertainment,' said Gilt. 'Do you know a good bookmaker? I shall have a little flutter. Five thousand dollars, perhaps?'

This got some nervous laughter, and he followed it up. 'Gentlemen, be sensible. No gods will come to the aid of our Postmaster. No wizard, either. They're not generous with magic and we'll soon find out if he uses any. No, he's looking for the publicity, that's all. Which is not to say,' he winked, 'that we shouldn't, how shall I put it, make certainty doubly sure.'

They perked up still more. This sounded like the kind of thing they wanted to hear.

'After all, accidents can happen in the mountains,' said Greenyham.

'I believe that is the case,' said Gilt. 'However, I was referring to the Grand Trunk. Therefore I have asked Mr Pony to outline our procedure. Mr Pony?'

The engineer shifted uneasily. He'd had a bad night. 'I want it recorded, sir, that I have urged a six-hour shutdown before the event,' he said.

'Indeed, and the minutes will show that I have said that is quite impossible,' said Gilt. 'Firstly because it would be an unpardonable loss of revenue, and secondly because sending no messages would send quite the wrong message.'

'We'll shut down for an hour before the event, then, and clear down,' said Mr Pony. 'Every tower will send a statement of readiness to the Tump and then lock all doors and wait. No one will be allowed in or out. We'll configure the towers to run duplex – that is,' he translated for management, 'we'll turn the down-line into a second up-line, so the message will get to Genua twice as fast. We won't have *any* other messages on the Trunk while the, er, race is on. No Overhead, nothing. And from now on, sir, from the moment I walk out of this room, we take no more messages from feeder towers. Not even from the one in the Palace, not even from the one in the University.' He sniffed, and added with some satisfaction: ''specially not them students. Someone's been having a go at us, sir.'

'That seems a bit drastic, Mr Pony?' said Greenyham.

'I hope it is, sir. I think someone's found a way of sending messages that can damage a tower, sir.'

'That's impossi—'

Mr Pony's hand slapped the table. 'How come you know so much, sir? Did you sit up half the night trying to get to the bottom of it?

Have you taken a differential drum apart with a tin opener? Did you spot how the swage armature can be made to jump off the elliptical bearing if you hit the letter K and then send it to a tower with an address higher than yours, but *only* if you hit the letter Q first and the drum spring is fully wound? Did you spot that the key levers wedge together and the spring forces the arm up and you're looking at a gearbox full of teeth? Well, I did!'

'Are you talking about sabotage here?' said Gilt.

'Call it what you like,' said Pony, drunk with nervousness. 'I went to the yard this morning and dug out the old drum we took out of Tower 14 last month. I'll swear the same thing happened there. But mostly the breakdowns are in the upper tower, in the shutter boxes. That's where—'

'So our Mr Lipwig has been behind a campaign to sabotage us . . .' Gilt mused.

'I never said that!' said Pony.

'No name need be mentioned,' said Gilt smoothly.

'It's just sloppy design,' said Pony. 'I dare say one of the lads found it by accident and tried it again to see what happened. They're like that, the tower boys. Show 'em a bit of cunning machinery and they'll spend all day trying to make it fail. The whole Trunk's a lash-up, it really is.'

'Why do we employ people like this?' said Stowley, looking bewildered.

'Because they're the only people mad enough to spend their life up a tower miles from anywhere pressing keys,' said Pony. 'They *like* it.'

'But somebody in a tower must press the keys that do all these . . . terrible things,' said Stowley.

Pony sighed. They never took an interest. It was just money. They didn't know how anything *worked*. And then suddenly they needed to know, and you had to use baby talk.

'The lads follow the signal, sir, as they say,' he said. 'They watch the next tower and repeat the message, as fast as they can. There's no time to think about it. Anything for their tower comes out on the differential drum. They just pound keys and kick pedals and pull levers, as fast as they can. They take pride in it. They even do all kinds of tricks to speed things up. I don't want any talk about sabotage, not right now. Let's just get the message sent, as fast as possible. The lads will enjoy that.'

'The image is attractive,' said Gilt. 'The dark of night, the waiting towers, and then, one by one, they come alive as a serpent of light speeds across the world, softly and silently carrying its . . . whatever. We must get some poet to write about it.' He nodded at Mr Pony. 'We're in your hands, Mr Pony. You're the man with the plan.'

'I don't have one,' said Moist.

'No plan?' said Miss Dearheart. 'Are you telling me you—'

'Keep it down, keep it down!' Moist hissed. 'I don't want everyone to know!'

They were in the little café near the Pin Exchange which, Moist had noticed, didn't seem to be doing much business today. He'd had to get out of the Post Office, in case his head exploded.

'You challenged the Grand Trunk! You mean you just talked big and hoped something would turn up?' said Miss Dearheart.

'It's always worked before! Where's the sense in promising to achieve the achievable? What kind of success would that be?' said Moist.

'Haven't you ever heard of learning to walk before you run?'

'It's a theory, yes.'

'I just want to be absolutely clear,' said Miss Dearheart. 'Tomorrow night – that's the day after today – you are going to send a coach – that's a thing on wheels, pulled by horses, which might reach fourteen miles an hour on a good road – to race against the Grand Trunk – that's all those semaphore towers, which can send messages at hundreds of miles an hour – all the way to Genua – that's the town which is a very long way away indeed?'

'Yes.'

'And you have no wonderful plan?'

'No.'

'And why are you telling me?'

'Because, in this city, right now, *you* are the only person who would possibly *believe* I don't have a plan!' said Moist. 'I told Mr Groat and he just tapped the side of his nose, which is something you wouldn't want to watch, by the way, and said, "Of course you haven't, sir. Not you! Hohoho!"'

'And you just hoped something would turn up? What made you think it would?'

'It always has. The only way to get something to turn up when you need it is to need it to turn up.'

'And I'm supposed to help you how?'

'Your father built the Trunk!'

'Yes, but I didn't,' said the woman. 'I've never been up in the towers. I don't know any big secrets, except that it's always on the point of breaking down. And everyone knows that.'

'People who can't afford to lose are betting money on me! And the more I tell them they shouldn't, the more they bet!'

'Don't you think that's a bit silly of them?' said Miss Dearheart sweetly.

Moist drummed his fingers on the edge of the table. 'All right,' he said, 'I can think of another good reason why you might help me. It's a little complicated, so I can only tell you if you promise to sit still and not make any sudden movements.'

'Why, do you believe I will?'

'Yes. I think that in a few seconds you'll try to kill me. I'd like you to promise not to.'

She shrugged. 'This should be interesting.'

'Promise?' said Moist.

'All right. I hope it's going to be exciting.' Miss Dearheart flicked some ash off her cigarette. 'Go on.'

Moist took a couple of calm breaths. This was it. The End. If you kept changing the way people saw the world, you ended up changing the way you saw yourself.

'I am the man who lost you that job at the bank. I forged those bills.'

Miss Dearheart's expression didn't change, apart from a certain narrowing of the eyes. Then she blew out a stream of smoke.

'I did promise, did I?' she said.

'Yes. Sorry.'

'Did I have my fingers crossed?'

'No. I was watching.'

'Hmm.' She stared reflectively at the glowing end of her cigarette. 'All right. You'd better tell me the rest of it.'

He told her the rest of it. All of it. She quite liked the bit where he was hanged, and made him repeat it. Around them, the city happened. Between them, the ashtray filled up with ash.

When he'd finished she stared at him for some time, through the smoke.

'I don't understand the bit where you give all your stolen money to the Post Office. Why did you do that?'

'I'm a bit hazy on that myself.'

'I mean, you're clearly a self-centred bastard, with the moral fibre of a, a—'

'—rat,' Moist suggested.

'—a rat, thank you . . . but suddenly you're the darling of the big religions, the saviour of the Post Office, official snook-cocker to the rich and powerful, heroic horseman, all-round wonderful human being and, of course, you rescued a cat from a burning building. Two humans, too, but everyone knows the cat's the most important bit. Who are you trying to fool, Mr Lipwig?'

'Me, I think. I've fallen into good ways. I keep thinking I can give it up any time I like, but I don't. But I know if I *couldn't* give it up any time I liked, I wouldn't go on doing it. Er . . . there is another reason, too.'

'And that is—?'

'I'm not Reacher Gilt. That's sort of important. Some people might say there's not a lot of difference, but I can see it from where I stand and it's there. It's like a golem not being a hammer. Please? How can I beat the Grand Trunk?'

Miss Dearheart stared through him until he felt very uncomfortable.

Then she said, in a faraway voice: 'How well do you know the Post Office, Mr Lipwig? The building, I mean.'

'I saw most of it before it burned down.'

'But you never went on to the roof?'

'No. I couldn't find a way up. The upper floors were stuffed with letters when . . . I . . . tried . . .' Moist's voice trailed off.

Miss Dearheart stubbed out her cigarette. 'Go up there tonight, Mr Lipwig. Get yourself a little bit closer to heaven. And then get down on your knees and pray. You know how to pray, don't you? You just put your hands together – and hope.'

Moist got through the rest of the day somehow. There were postmastery things to do – Mr Spools to speak to, builders to shout at, the everlasting clearing up to oversee and new staff to hire. In the case of the staff, though, it was more ratifying the decisions of Mr Groat and Miss Maccalariat, but they seemed to know what they were doing. He just had to be there to make the occasional judgement, like:

'Do we embrace divertingly?' said Miss Maccalariat, appearing in front of his desk.

There was a pregnant pause. It gave birth to a lot of little pauses, each one more deeply embarrassing than its parent.

'Not as far as I know,' was the best Moist could manage. 'Why do you ask?'

'A young lady wants to know. She said that's what they do at the Grand Trunk.'

'Ah. I suspect she means embrace diversity,' said Moist, recalling Gilt's speech to the *Times*. 'But we don't do that here because we don't know what it means. We'll employ anyone who can read and write and reach a letter box, Miss Maccalariat. I'll hire vampires if they're a member of the League of Temperance, trolls if they wipe their feet, and if there're any werewolves out there I'd *love* to hire postmen who can bite back. Anyone who can do the job, Miss Maccalariat. Our job is moving the mail. Morning, noon and night, we deliver. Was there anything else?'

Now there was a glint in her eye. 'I don't have any difficulties with anyone who speaks up about what they are, Mr Lipwig, but I must protest about dwarfs. Mr Groat is hiring them.'

'Fine workers, Miss Maccalariat. Keen on the written word. Hardworking, too,' said Moist briskly.

'But they do not tell you what their— what they— which— if they're ladies or gentlemen dwarfs, Mr Lipwig.'

'Ah. This is going to be about the privies again?' said Moist, his heart sinking.

'I feel I am responsible for the moral welfare of the young people in my charge,' said Miss Maccalariat sternly. 'You are smiling, Postmaster, but I will not be funned with.'

'Your concern does you credit, Miss Maccalariat,' said Moist. 'Special attention will be paid to this in the design of the new building, and I will tell the architect that you are to be consulted at every stage.' Miss Maccalariat's well-covered bosom inflated noticeably at this sudden acquisition of power. 'In the meantime, alas, we must make do with what the fire has left us. I do hope, as part of the *management* team, you will reassure people on this.'

The fires of dreadful pride gleamed off Miss Maccalariat's spectacles. Management!

'Of *course*, Postmaster,' she said.

But, mostly, Moist's job was just to . . . be. Half of the building was a blackened shell. People were squeezed into what was left; mail was even being sorted on the stairs. And things seemed to go better when he was around. He didn't have to do anything, he just had to be there.

He couldn't help thinking of the empty plinth, where the god had been taken away.

He was ready when dusk came. There were plenty of ladders around, and the golems had managed to shore up the floors even up here. Soot covered everything and some rooms opened on to blackness, but he climbed ever up.

He struggled through what remained of the attics, and clambered through a hatch and on to the roof.

There wasn't much of it. The descent of the rainwater tank had brought down a lot of burning roof with it, and barely a third remained over the great hall. But the fire had hardly touched one of the legs of the U, and the roof there looked sound.

There was one of the old postal pigeon lofts there, and someone had been living in it. That wasn't too surprising. Far more people wanted to live in Ankh-Morpork than there was Ankh-Morpork for them to live in. There was a whole sub-civilization at rooftop level, up here among the towers and ornamental domes and cupolas and chimneys and—

—clacks towers. That's right. He'd seen the clacks tower, and someone up here, just before his life had taken a turn for the strange. Why would a loft built for carrier pigeons have a semaphore tower? Surely the pigeons didn't use it?

Three gargoyles had colonized this one. They liked clacks towers anyway – being up high was what being a gargoyle was all about – and they'd fitted into the system easily. A creature that spent all its time watching and was bright enough to write down a message was a vital component. They didn't even want paying, and they never got bored. What could possibly bore a creature that was prepared to stare at the same thing for years at a time?

Around the city, the clacks towers were lighting up. Only the University, the Palace, the Guilds and the seriously rich or very nervous ran their towers at night, but the big terminal tower on the Tump blazed like a Hogswatch tree. Patterns of yellow squares ran up and down the main tower. Silent at this distance, winking their signals above the rising mists, outlining their constellations against the evening sky, the towers were more magical than magic, more bewitching than witchcraft.

Moist stared.

What was magic, after all, but something that happened at the snap of a finger? Where was the *magic* in that? It was mumbled words and weird drawings in old books and in the wrong hands it was dangerous as hell, but not one half as dangerous as it could be in the right hands. The universe was full of the stuff; it made the stars stay up and the feet stay down.

But what was happening now . . . this was *magical*. Ordinary men had dreamed it up and put it together, building towers on rafts in swamps and across the frozen spines of mountains. They'd cursed and, worse, used logarithms. They'd waded through rivers and dabbled in trigonometry. They hadn't dreamed, in the way people usually used the word, but they'd imagined a different world, and bent metal round it. And out of all the sweat and swearing and mathematics had come this . . . thing, dropping words across the world as softly as starlight.

The mist was filling the streets now, leaving the buildings like islands in surf.

Pray, she'd said. And, in a way, the gods owed him a favour. Well, didn't they? They'd got a handsome offering and a lot of celestial cred for not, in fact, doing anything at all.

Get down on your knees, she'd said. It hadn't been a joke.

He knelt, pressed his hands together, and said, 'I address this prayer to any god who—'

With a silence that was frightening, the clacks tower across the street lit up. The big squares glowed into life one after the other. For a moment, Moist saw the shape of the lamplighter in front of one of the shutters.

As he disappeared into the dark, the tower started to flicker. It was close enough to illuminate the roof of the Post Office.

There were three dark figures at the other end of the roof, watching Moist. Their shadows danced as the pattern of lights changed, twice every second. They revealed the figures were human, or at least humanoid. And they were walking towards him.

Gods, now, gods could be humanoid. And they didn't like to be messed about.

Moist cleared his throat. 'I'm certainly glad to see you—' he croaked.

'Are you Moist?' said one of the figures.

'Look, I—'

'She said you'd be kneeling down,' said another member of the celestial trio. 'Fancy a cup of tea?'

Moist got up slowly. This was not godly behaviour.

'Who *are* you?' he said. Emboldened by the lack of thunderbolts, he added: 'And what are you doing on my building?'

'We pay rent,' said a figure. 'To Mr Groat.'

'He never told me about you!'

'Can't help you there,' said the shadow in the centre. 'Anyway, we've only come back to get the rest of our stuff. Sorry about your fire. It wasn't us.'

'You being—' said Moist.

'I'm Mad Al, he's Sane Alex, and that's Adrian, who says he's not mad but can't prove it.'

'Why do you rent the roof?'

The trio looked at one another.

'Pigeons?' suggested Adrian.

'That's right, we're pigeon fanciers,' said the shadowy figure of Sane Alex.

'But it's dark,' said Moist. This information was considered.

'Bats,' said Mad Al. 'We're trying to breed homing bats.'

'I don't believe bats have that kind of homing instinct,' said Moist.

'Yes, it's tragic, isn't it?' said Alex.

'I come up here at nights and see those empty little perches and it's all I can do not to cry,' said Undecided Adrian.

Moist looked up at the little tower. It was about five times the height of a man, with the control levers on a polished panel near the bottom. It looked . . . professional, and well used. And portable.

'I don't think you breed any kind of birds up here,' he said.

'Bats are mammals,' said Sane Alex. Moist shook his head.

'Lurking on rooftops, your own clacks . . . you're the Smoking Gnu, aren't you?'

'Ah, with a mind like that I can see why you're Mr Groat's boss,' said Sane Alex. 'How about a cup of tea?'

Mad Al picked a pigeon feather out of his mug. The pigeon loft was full of the flat, choking smell of old guano.

'You have to like birds to like it up here,' he said, flicking the feather into Sane Alex's beard.

'Good job you do, eh?' said Moist.

'I didn't say I did, did I? And we don't live up here. It's just that you've got a good rooftop.'

It was cramped in the pigeon loft, from which pigeons had, in fact, been barred. But there's always one pigeon that can bite through wire netting. It watched them from the corner with mad little eyes, its genes remembering the time it had been a giant reptile that could have taken these sons of monkeys to the cleaners in one mouthful. Bits of dismantled mechanisms were everywhere.

'Miss Dearheart told you about me, did she?' said Moist.

'She said you weren't a complete arse,' said Undecided Adrian.

'Which is praise coming from her,' said Sane Alex.

'And she said you were so crooked you could walk through a corkscrew sideways,' said Undecided Adrian. 'She was smiling when she said it, though.'

'That's not necessarily a good thing,' said Moist. 'How do you know her?'

'We used to work with her brother,' said Mad Al. 'On the Mark 2 tower.'

Moist listened. It was a whole new world.

Sane Alex and Mad Al were old men in the clacks business; they'd been in it for almost four years. Then the consortium had taken over, and they'd been fired from the Grand Trunk on the same day that Undecided Adrian had been fired from the Alchemists' Guild chimney, in their case because they'd spoken their mind about the new management and in his case because he hadn't moved fast enough when the beaker started to bubble.

They'd all ended up working on the Second Trunk. They'd even put money into it. So had others. It had all kinds of improvements, it would be cheaper to run, it was the bee's knees, mutt's nuts and various wonderful bits of half a dozen other creatures. And then John Dearheart, who always used a safety lanyard, landed in the cabbage field and that was the end of the Second Trunk.

Since then, the trio had done the kinds of jobs available to new square pegs in a world of old round holes, but every night, high above, the clacks flashed its messages. It was so close, so inviting, so . . . *accessible*. Everyone knew, in some vague, half-understood way, that the Grand Trunk had been stolen in all but name. It belonged to the enemy.

So they'd started an informal little company of their own, which used the Grand Trunk without the Grand Trunk's knowing.

It was a little like stealing. It was exactly like stealing. It was, in fact, stealing. But there was no law against it because no one knew the crime existed, so is it really stealing if what's stolen isn't missed? And is it stealing if you're stealing from thieves? Anyway, all property is theft, except mine.

'So now you're, what was it again . . . crackers?' Moist said.

'That's right,' said Mad Al. 'Because we can crack the system.'

'That sounds a bit over-dramatic when you're just doing it with lamps, doesn't it?'

'Yes, but "flashers" was already taken,' said Sane Alex.

'All right, but why "Smoking Gnu"?' said Moist.

'That's cracker slang for a very fast message sent throughout the system,' said Sane Alex proudly.

Moist pondered this. 'That makes sense,' he said. 'If I was a team of three people, who all had a first name beginning with the same letter, that's just the kind of name I'd choose.'

They'd found a way into the semaphore system, and it was this: at night, all clacks towers were invisible. Only the lights showed. Unless you had a good sense of direction, the only way you could identify *who* the message was coming from was by its code. Engineers knew lots of codes. Ooh, lots.

'You can send messages *free*?' said Moist. 'And nobody notices?'

There were three smug smiles. 'It's easy,' said Mad Al, 'when you know how.'

'How did you know that tower was going to break down?'

'We broke it,' said Sane Alex. 'Broke the differential drum. They take hours to sort out because the operators have to—'

Moist missed the rest of the sentence. Innocent words swirled in it like debris caught in a flood, occasionally bobbing to the surface and waving desperately before being pulled under again. He caught 'the' several times before it drowned, and even 'disconnect' and 'gear chain', but the roaring, technical polysyllables rose and engulfed them all.

'—and that takes at least half a day,' Sane Alex finished.

Moist looked helplessly at the other two. 'And that means what, exactly?' he said.

'If you send the right kind of message you can bust the machinery,' said Mad Al.

'*The whole Trunk?*'

'In theory,' said Mad Al, 'because an execute and terminate code—'

Moist relaxed as the tide came back in. He wasn't interested in machinery; he thought of a spanner as something which had another person holding it. It was best just to smile and wait. That was the thing about artificers: they loved explaining. You just had to wait until they reached your level of understanding, even if it meant that they had to lie down.

'—can't do that any more in any case, because we've heard they're changing the—'

Moist stared at the pigeon for a while, until silence came back. Ah. Mad Al had finished, and by the looks of things it hadn't been on a high note.

'You can't do it, then,' said Moist, his heart sinking.

'Not now. Old Mr Pony might be a bit of an old woman but he sits and niggles at problems. He's been changing all the codes all day! We've heard from one of our mates that every signaller will have to have a personal code now. They're being very careful. I know Miss Adora Belle thought we could help you, but that bastard Gilt has locked things up tight. He's worried you're going to win.'

'Hah!' said Moist.

'We'll come up with some other way in a week or two,' said Undecided Adrian. 'Can't you put it off until then?'

'No, I don't think so.'

'Sorry,' said Undecided Adrian. He was playing idly with a small glass tube, full of red light. When he turned it over, it filled with yellow light.

'What's that?' Moist asked.

'A prototype,' said Undecided Adrian. 'It could have made the Trunk almost three times faster at night. It uses perpendicular molecules. But the Trunk's just not open to new ideas.'

'Probably because they explode when dropped?' said Sane Alex.

'Not *always*.'

'I think I could do with some fresh air,' said Moist.

They stepped out into the night. In the middle distance the terminal tower still winked, and towers were alight here and there in other parts of the city.

'What's that one?' he said, like a man pointing to a constellation.

'Thieves' Guild,' said Undecided Adrian. 'General signals for the members. I can't read 'em.'

'And that one? Isn't that the first tower on the way to Sto Lat?'

'No, it's the Watch station on the Hubwards Gate. General signals to Pseudopolis Yard.'

'It *looks* a long way off.'

'They use small shutter boxes, that's all. You can't see Tower 2 from here – the University's in the way.'

Moist stared, hypnotized, at the lights.

'I wondered why that old stone tower on the way to Sto Lat wasn't used when the Trunk was built? It's in the right place.'

'The old wizard tower? Robert Dearheart used it for his first experiments, but it's a bit too far and the walls aren't safe and if you stay in there for more than a day at a time you go mad. It's all the old spells that got into the stones.'

There was silence and then they heard Moist say, in a slightly strangled voice: 'If you *could* get on to the Grand Trunk tomorrow, is there anything you could do to slow it down?'

'Yes, but we can't,' said Undecided Adrian.

'Yes, but if you could?'

'Well, there's something we've been thinking about,' said Mad Al. 'It's very crude.'

'Will it knock out a tower?' said Moist.

'Should we be telling him about this?' said Sane Alex.

'Have you ever met *anyone* else that Killer had a good word for?' said Mad Al. 'In theory it could knock out *every* tower, Mr Lipwig.'

'Are you insane as well as mad?' said Sane Alex. 'He's *government*!'

'Every tower on the Trunk?' said Moist.

'Yep. In one go,' said Mad Al. 'It's pretty crude.'

'*Really every* tower?' said Moist again.

'Maybe not *every* tower, if they catch on,' Mad Al admitted, as if less than wholesale destruction was something to be mildly ashamed of. 'But plenty. Even if they cheat and carry it to the next tower on horse-back. We call it . . . *the Woodpecker*.'

'The woodpecker?'

'No, not like that. You need, sort of, more of a pause for effect, like . . . *the Woodpecker*.'

'. . . *the Woodpecker*,' said Moist, more slowly.

'You've got it. But we can't get it on to the Trunk. They're on to *us*.'

'Supposing *I* could get it on to the Trunk?' said Moist, staring at the lights. The towers themselves were quite invisible now.

'You? What do you know about clacks codes?' said Undecided Adrian.

'I treasure my ignorance,' said Moist. 'But I know about people. You think about being cunning with codes. I just think about what people see—'

They listened. They argued. They resorted to mathematics, while words sailed through the night above them.

And Sane Alex said: 'All right, all right. Technically it could work, but the Trunk people would have to be stupid to let it happen.'

'But they'll be thinking about codes,' said Moist. 'And I'm good at making people stupid. It's my job.'

'I thought your job was postmaster,' said Undecided Adrian.

'Oh, yes. Then it's my vocation.'

The Smoking Gnu looked at one another.

'It's a totally mad idea,' said Mad Al, grinning.

'I'm glad you like it,' said Moist.

*   *   *

There are times when you just have to miss a night's sleep. But Ankh-Morpork never slept; the city never did more than doze, and would wake up around 3 a.m. for a glass of water.

You could buy *anything* in the middle of the night. Timber? No problem. Moist wondered whether there were vampire carpenters, quietly making vampire chairs. Canvas? There was bound to be someone in the city who'd wake up in the wee small hours for a wee and think, 'What I could really do with right now is one thousand square yards of medium grade canvas!' and, down by the docks, there were chandlers open to deal with the rush.

There was a steady drizzle when they left for the tower. Moist drove the cart, with the others sitting on the load behind him and bickering over trigonometry. Moist tried not to listen; he got lost when maths started to get silly.

Killing the Grand Trunk . . . Oh, the towers would be left standing, but it would take months to repair them all. It'd bring the company down. No one would get hurt, the Gnu said. They meant the men in the towers.

The Trunk had become a monster, eating people. Bringing it down was a beguiling idea. The Gnu were full of ideas for what could replace it – faster, cheaper, easier, streamlined, using imps specially bred for the job . . .

But something irked Moist. Gilt had been right, damn him. If you wanted to get a message five hundred miles very, very fast, the Trunk was the way to do it. If you wanted to wrap it in a ribbon, you needed the Post Office.

He liked the Gnu. They thought in a refreshingly different way; whatever curse hung around the stones of the old tower surely couldn't affect minds like theirs, because they were inoculated against madness by being a little bit crazy all the time. The clacks signallers, all along the Trunk, were . . . a different kind of people. They didn't just *do* their job, they lived it.

But Moist kept thinking of all the *bad* things that could happen without the semaphore. Oh, they used to happen before the sema-phore, of course, but that wasn't the same thing at all.

He left them sawing and hammering in the stone tower, and headed back to the city, deep in thought.

CHAPTER THIRTEEN

The Edge of the Envelope

In which we learn the Theory of Baize-Space – Devious Collabone – The Grand Trunk Burns – So Sharp You'll Cut Yourself – Finding Miss Dearheart – A Theory of Disguise – Igor Moveth On – 'Let This Moment Never End' – A Brush with the Trunk – The big sail unfurls – The Message is Received

MUSTRUM RIDCULLY, ARCHCHANCELLOR of Unseen University, levelled his cue and took careful aim.

The white ball hit a red ball, which rolled gently into a pocket. This was harder than it looked because more than half of the snooker table served as the Archchancellor's filing system,* and indeed to get to the hole the ball had to pass *through* several piles of paperwork, a tankard, a skull with a dribbly candle on it and a lot of pipe ash. It did so.

'Well done, Mr Stibbons,' said Ridcully.

'I call it baize-space,' said Ponder Stibbons proudly.

Every organization needs at least one person who knows what's going on and why it's happening and who's doing it, and at UU this role was filled by Stibbons, who often wished it wasn't. Right now he was present in his position as Head of Inadvisably Applied Magic, and his long-term purpose was to see that his department's budget went through on the nod. To this end, therefore, a bundle of thick pipes led from under the heavy old billiard table, out through a hole in the wall and across the lawn into the High Energy Magic building, where – he sighed – this little trick was taking up 40 per cent of the rune-time of Hex, the University's thinking engine.

'Good name,' said Ridcully, lining up another shot.

'As in *phase*-space?' said Ponder, hopefully. 'When a ball is just

---

* Ridcully practised the First Available Surface method of filing.

about to encounter an obstacle that is not another ball, you see, Hex moves it into a theoretical parallel dimension where there is un-occupied flat surface and maintains speed and drag until it can be brought back to this one. It really is a most difficult and intricate piece of unreal-time spell casting—'

'Yes, yes, very good,' said Ridcully. 'Was there something else, Mr Stibbons?'

Ponder looked at his clipboard. 'There's a polite letter from Lord Vetinari asking on behalf of the city whether the University might consider including in its intake, oh, twenty-five per cent of less able students, sir?'

Ridcully potted the black, through a heap of university directives.

'Can't have a bunch of grocers and butchers telling a university how to run itself, Stibbons!' he said firmly, lining up on a red. 'Thank them for their interest and tell them we'll continue to take one hundred per cent of complete and utter dullards, as usual. Take 'em in dull, turn 'em out sparklin', that's always been the UU way! Anythin' else?'

'Just this message for the big race tonight, Archchancellor.'

'Oh, yes, that thing. What should I do, Mr Stibbons? I hear there's heavy betting on the Post Office.'

'Yes, Archchancellor. People say the gods are on the side of Mr Lipwig.'

'Are *they* betting?' said Ridcully, watching with satisfaction as the ball rematerialized on the other side of a neglected ham sandwich.

'I don't think so, sir. He can't possibly win.'

'Was he the fella who rescued the cat?'

'That was him, sir, yes,' said Ponder.

'Good chap. What do we think of the Grand Trunk? Bunch of bean-crushers, I heard. Been killin' people on those towers of theirs. Man in the pub told me he'd heard the ghosts of dead signallers haunt the Trunk. I'll try for the pink.'

'Yes, I've heard that, sir. I think it's an urban myth,' said Ponder.

'They travel from one end of the Trunk to the other,' he said. 'Not a bad way to spend eternity, mark you. There's some splendid scenery up in the mountains.' The Archchancellor paused, and his big face screwed up in thought. 'Haruspex's *Big Directory of Varying Dimensions*,' he said at last.

'Pardon, Archchancellor?'

'That's the message,' said Ridcully. 'No one said it had to be a letter, eh?' He waved a hand over the tip of the cue, which grew a powdering of fresh chalk. 'Give them a copy each of the new edition. Send 'em to our man in Genua . . . what's his name, thingummy, got a funny name . . . show him the old Alma Pater is thinkin' of him.'

'That's Devious Collabone, sir. He's out studying Oyster Communications in a Low Intensity Magical Field for his B.Thau.'

'Good gods, *can* they communicate?' said Ridcully.

'Apparently, Archchancellor, although thus far they're refusing to talk to him.'

'Why'd we send him all the way out there?'

'Devious H. Collabone, Archchancellor?' Ponder prompted. 'Remember? With the terrible halitosis?'

'Oh, you mean *Dragonbreath* Collabone?' said Ridcully, as realization dawned. 'The one who could blow a hole in a silver plate?'

'Yes, Archchancellor,' said Ponder patiently. Mustrum Ridcully always liked to triangulate in on new information from several positions. 'You said that out in the swamps no one would notice? If you remember, we allowed him to take a small omniscope.'

'Did we? Far-thinking of us. Call him up right now and tell him what's going on, will you?'

'Yes, Archchancellor. In fact I'll leave it a few hours because it's still night time in Genua.'

'That's only their opinion,' said Ridcully, sighting again. 'Do it now, man.'

Fire from the sky . . .

Everyone knew that the top half of the towers rocked as the messages flew along the Trunk. One day, someone was going to do something about it. And all old signallers knew that if the connecting rod operating the shutters on the down-line was pushed up to open them *on the same blink* as the connecting rod on the up-line was pulled down to close the shutters on the other side of the tower, the tower lurched. It was being pushed from one side and pulled from the other, which would have roughly the same effect as a column of marching soldiers could have on an old bridge. That wasn't too much of a problem, unless it occurred again and again so that the rocking built up to a dangerous level. But how often would that happen?

Every time the Woodpecker arrived at your tower, that was how often. And it was like an illness that could only attack the weak and sick. It wouldn't have attacked the old Trunk, because the old Trunk was too full of tower captains who'd shut down instantly and strip the offending message out of the drum, secure in the knowledge that their actions would be judged by superiors who knew how a tower worked and would have done the same thing themselves.

It *would* work against the new Trunk, because there weren't enough of those captains now. You did what you were told or you didn't get paid and if things went wrong it wasn't your problem. It was the fault of whatever idiot had accepted this message for sending in the first place. No one cared about you, and everyone at headquarters was an idiot. It wasn't your fault; no one listened to you. Headquarters had even started an Employee of the Month scheme to show how much they cared. *That* was how much they didn't care.

And today you'd been told to shift code as fast as possible, and *you* didn't want to be the one accused of slowing the system down, so you watched the next tower in line until your eyes watered and you hit keys like a man tapdancing on hot rocks.

One after another, the towers failed. Some burned when the shutter boxes broke free and smashed on the cabin roofs, spilling blazing oil. There was no hope of fighting fire in a wooden box sixty feet up in the air; you slid down the suicide line and legged it to a safe distance to watch the show.

Fourteen towers were burning before someone took their hands off the keys. And then what? You'd been given orders. There were to be no, repeat no other messages on the Trunk while this message was being sent. What did you do next?

Moist awoke, the Grand Trunk burning in his head.

The Smoking Gnu wanted to break it down and pick up the pieces, and he could see why. But it wouldn't work. Somewhere on the line there was going to be one inconvenient engineer who'd risk his job to send a message ahead saying: it's a killer, shift it slowly. And that would be that. Oh, it might take a day or two to get the thing to Genua, but they had weeks to work with. And someone else, too, would be smart enough to compare the message with what had been sent by the first tower. Gilt would wriggle out of it – no, he'd storm out of it. The message had been tampered with, he'd say, and he'd be right. There had to be another solution.

The Gnu were on to something, though. Changing the message was the answer, if only he could do it in the right way.

Moist opened his eyes. He was at his desk, and someone had put a pillow under his head.

When was the last time he'd slept in a decent bed? Oh, yes, the night Mr Pump had caught him. He'd spent a couple of hours in a rented bed that had a mattress which didn't actually move and wasn't full of rocks. Bliss.

His immediate past life scampered before his eyes. He groaned.

'Good Morning, Mr Lipvig,' said Mr Pump from the corner. 'Your Razor Is Sharp, The Kettle Is Hot And I Am Sure A Cup Of Tea Is On The Way.'

'What time is it?'

'Noon, Mr Lipvig. You Did Not Get In Until Dawn,' the golem added reproachfully.

Moist groaned again. Six hours to the race. And then so many pigeons would come home to roost it'd be like an eclipse.

'There Is Much Excitement,' said the golem, as Moist shaved. 'It Has Been Agreed That The Starting Line Will Be In Sator Square.'

Moist stared at his reflection, barely listening. He always raised the stakes, automatically. Never promise to do the possible. Anyone could do the possible. You should promise to do the impossible, because sometimes the impossible *was* possible, if you could find the right way, and at least you could often extend the limits of the possible. And if you failed, well, it *had* been impossible.

But he'd gone too far this time. Oh, it'd be no great shame to admit that a coach and horses couldn't travel at a thousand miles an hour, but Gilt would strut about it and the Post Office would remain just a little, old-fashioned thing, behind the times, small, unable to compete. Gilt would find some way to hold on to the Grand Trunk, cutting even more corners, killing people out of greed—

'Are You All Right, Mr Lipvig?' said the golem behind him.

Moist stared into his own eyes, and what flickered in the depths.

Oh, boy.

'You Have Cut Yourself, Mr Lipvig,' said Mr Pump. 'Mr Lipvig?'

Shame I missed my throat, Moist thought. But that was a secondary thought, edging past the big dark one now unfolding in the mirror.

Look into the abyss and you'll see something growing, reaching towards the light. It whispered: Do this. This will work. Trust me.

Oh, boy. It's a plan that *will* work, Moist thought. It's simple and deadly, like a razor. But it'd need an unprincipled man to even think about it.

No problem there, then.

I'll kill you, Mr Gilt. I'll kill you in our special way, the way of the weasel and cheat and liar. I'll take away everything *but* your life. I'll take away your money, your reputation and your friends. I'll spin words around you until you're cocooned in them. I'll leave you nothing, not even hope . . .

He carefully finished shaving, and wiped the remnant of the foam off his chin. There was not, in truth, that much blood.

'I think I could do with a hearty breakfast, Mr Pump,' he said. 'And then I have a few things to do. In the meantime, can you please find me a broomstick? A proper birch besom? And then paint some stars on the handle?'

The makeshift counters were crowded when Moist went down, but the bustle stopped when he entered the hall. Then a cheer went up. He nodded and waved cheerfully, and was immediately surrounded by people waving envelopes. He did his best to sign them all.

'A lot o' extra mail for Genua, sir!' Mr Groat exulted, pushing his way through the crowd. 'Never seen a day like it, never!'

'Jolly good, well done,' Moist murmured.

'And the mail for the gods has gone right up, too!' Groat continued.

'Pleased to hear it, Mr Groat,' said Moist.

'We've got the first Sto Lat stamps, sir!' said Stanley, waving a couple of sheets above his head. 'The early sheets are *covered* in flaws, sir!'

'I'm very happy for you,' said Moist. 'But I've got to go and prepare a few things.'

'Aha, yes!' said Mr Groat, winking. ' "A few things", eh? Just as you say, sir. Stand aside, please, Postmaster coming through!'

Groat more or less pushed customers out of the way as Moist, trying to avoid the people who wanted him to kiss babies or were trying to grab a scrap of his suit for luck, made it out into the fresh air.

Then he kept to the back streets, and found a place that did a very reasonable Double Soss, Egg, Bacon and Fried Slice, in the hope that food could replace sleep.

It was all getting out of hand. People were putting out bunting and setting up stalls in Sator Square. The huge floating crowd that was the street population of Ankh-Morpork ebbed and flowed around the city, and tonight it would contract to form a mob in the square, and could be sold things.

Finally he plucked up his courage and headed for the Golem Trust. It was closed. A bit more graffiti had been added to the strata that now covered the boarded-up window. It was just above knee-level and said, in crayon: 'Golms are Made of p0o.' It was good to see the fine old traditions of idiot bigotry being handed down, in a no-good-at-all kind of way.

Dolly Sisters, he thought wildly, staying with an aunt. Did she ever mention the aunt's name?

He ran in that direction.

Dolly Sisters had once been a village, before the sprawl had rolled over it; its residents still considered themselves *apart* from the rest of the city, with their own customs – Dog Turd Monday, Up Needles All – and almost their own language. Moist didn't know it at all. He pushed his way through the narrow lanes, looking around desperately for— what? A column of smoke?

Actually, that wasn't a bad idea . . .

He reached the house eight minutes later, and hammered on the door. To his relief, she opened it, and stared at him.

She said: 'How?'

He said: 'Tobacconists. Not many women around here have a hundred-a-day habit.'

'Well, what do you want, Mr Clever?'

'If you help me, I can take Gilt for everything he's got,' said Moist. 'Help me. Please? On my honour as a totally untrustworthy man?'

That at least got a brief smile, to be replaced almost immediately by the default expression of deep suspicion. Then some inner struggle resolved itself.

'You'd better come into the parlour,' she said, opening the door all the way.

That room was small, dark and crowded with respectability. Moist sat on the edge of a chair, trying not to disturb anything, while he strained to hear women's voices along the hallway. Then Miss Dearheart slipped in and shut the door behind her.

'I hope this is all right with your family,' said Moist. 'I—'

'I told them we were courting,' said Miss Dearheart. 'That's what parlours are for. The tears of joy and hope in my mother's eyes were a sight to see. Now, what do you want?'

'Tell me about your father,' said Moist. 'I've got to know how the Grand Trunk was taken over. Have you still got any paperwork?'

'It won't do any good. A lawyer looked at it and said it would be very hard to make a case—'

'I intend to appeal to a higher court,' said Moist.

'I mean, we can't *prove* a lot of things, not actually *prove*—' Miss Dearheart protested.

'I don't have to,' said Moist.

'The lawyer said it would take months and months of work to—'
she went on, determined to find a snag.

'I'll make someone else pay for it,' said Moist. 'Have you got books?
Ledgers? Anything like that?'

'What are you intending to do?' Miss Dearheart demanded.

'It's better if you don't know. It really is. I know what I'm doing,
Spike. But *you* shouldn't.'

'Well, there's a big box of papers,' said Miss Dearheart uncertainly.
'I suppose I could just sort of . . . leave it in here while I'm tidying
up . . .'

'Good.'

'But can I trust you?'

'On this? My gods, no! Your father trusted Gilt, and look what
happened! I wouldn't trust me if I was you. But I would if I was me.'

'The funny thing is, Mr Lipwig, that I find myself trusting you all
the more when you tell me how untrustworthy you are,' said Miss
Dearheart.

Moist sighed. 'Yes, I know, Spike. Wretched, isn't it? It's a people
thing. Could you fetch the box, please?'

She did so, with a puzzled frown.

It took all afternoon and even then Moist wasn't sure, but he'd filled
a small notebook with scribbles. It was like looking for piranhas in a
river choked with weeds. There were a lot of bones on the bottom.
But, although sometimes you thought you'd glimpsed a flash of silver,
you could never be sure you'd seen a fish. The only way to be certain
was to jump in.

By half past four Sator Square was packed.

The wonderful thing about the golden suit and the hat with wings
was that, if Moist took them off, he wasn't him any more. He was just
a nondescript person with unmemorable clothes and a face you
might vaguely think you'd seen before.

He wandered through the crowd, heading towards the Post Office.
No one gave him a second glance. Most didn't bother with a first

glance. In a way he'd never realized until now, he was alone. He'd always been alone. It was the only way to be safe.

The trouble was, he *missed* the golden suit. Everything was an act, really. But the Man in the Golden Suit was a good act. He didn't want to be a person you forgot, someone who was one step above a shadow. Underneath the wingèd hat, he could do miracles or, at least, make it appear that miracles had been done, which is nearly as good.

He'd have to do one in an hour or two, that was certain.

Oh well . . .

He went round the back of the Post Office, and was about to slip inside when a figure in the shadow said, 'Pissed!'

'I suspect you mean Psst?' said Moist. Sane Alex stepped out of the shadows; he was wearing his old Grand Trunk donkey jacket and a huge helmet with horns on.

'We're running slow with the canvas—' he began.

'Why the helmet?' said Moist.

'It's a disguise,' said Alex.

'A big horned helmet?'

'Yes. It makes me so noticeable that no one will suspect I'm trying not to be noticed, so they won't bother to notice me.'

'Only a very intelligent man would think of something like that,' said Moist carefully. 'What's happening?'

'We need more time,' said Alex.

'What? The race starts at six!'

'It won't be dark enough. We won't be able to get the sail up until half past at least. We'll be spotted if we poke our heads over the parapet before then.'

'Oh, come on! The other towers are far too far away!'

'People on the road aren't,' said Alex.

'Blast!' Moist had forgotten about the road. All it would take later was someone saying he'd seen people on the old wizarding tower . . .

'Listen, we've got it all ready to raise,' said Alex, watching his face. 'We can work fast when we're up there. We just need half an hour of darkness, maybe a few minutes more.'

Moist bit his lip. 'Okay. I can do that, I think. Now get back there and help them. But don't start until I get there, understand? Trust me!'

I'm saying that a lot, he thought after the man had hurried away. I just hope they will.

He went up to his office. The golden suit was on its hanger. He put it on. There was work to do. It was dull, but it had to be done. So he did it.

At half past five the floorboards creaked as Mr Pump walked into the room, dragging a broomstick behind him.

'Soon It Will Be Time For The Race, Mr Lipvig,' he said.

'I must finish a few things,' said Moist. 'There's letters here from builders and architects, oh, and someone wants me to cure their warts . . . I really have to deal with the paperwork, Mr Pump.'

In the privacy of Reacher Gilt's kitchen, Igor very carefully wrote a note. There were niceties to be observed, after all. You didn't just leg it like a thief in the night. You tidied up, made sure the larder was stocked, washed the dishes and took exactly what you were owed from the petty cash box.

Shame, really. It had been a pretty good job. Gilt hadn't expected him to do much, and Igor had enjoyed terrorizing the other servants. Most of them, anyway.

'It's so sad you're going, Mr Igor,' said Mrs Glowbury, the cook. She dabbed at her eyes with a handkerchief. 'You've been a real breath of fresh air.'

'Can't be helped, Mrthth Glowbury,' said Igor. 'I thall mith your thteak and kidney pie, and no mithtake. It doth my heart good to thee a woman who can really make thomething out of leftoverth.'

'I've knitted you this, Mr Igor,' said the cook, hesitantly proffering a small soft package. Igor opened it with care, and unfolded a red and white striped balaclava.

'I thought it would help keep your bolt warm,' said Mrs Glowbury, blushing.

Igor agonized for a moment. He liked and respected the cook. He'd never seen a woman handle sharp knives so skilfully. Sometimes, you had to forget the Code of the Igors.

'Mrthth Glowbury, you did thay you had a thithter in Quirm?' he said.

'That's right, Mr Igor.'

'Now would be a very good time for you to go and vithit her,' said Igor firmly. 'Do not athk me why. Goodbye, dear Mrthth Glowbury. I thall remember your liver with fondneth.'

Now it was ten minutes to six.

'If You Leave Now, Mr Lipvig, You Will Be Just In Time For The Race,' the golem rumbled, from the corner.

'This is work of civic importance, Mr Pump,' said Moist severely, reading another letter. 'I am showing rectitude and attention to duty.'

'Yes, Mr Lipvig.'

He let it go on until ten minutes past the hour, because it'd take five minutes to get to the square, at a nonchalant saunter. With the golem lumbering beside him, in something approaching the antithesis of both nonchalance and sauntering, he left the Post Office behind.

The crowd in the square parted at his approach, and there were cheers and some laughter when people saw the broomstick over his shoulder. It had stars painted on it, therefore it must be a magic broomstick. Of such beliefs are fortunes made.

Find The Lady, Find The Lady . . . there was a science to it, in a way. Of course, it helped if you found out how to hold three cards in a loose stack; that was really the key. Moist had learned to be good at that, but he had found mere mechanical tricks a bit dull, a bit beneath him. There were other ways, ways to mislead, to distract, to anger. Anger was always good. Angry people made mistakes.

There was a space in the centre of the square, round the stagecoach on which Leadpipe Jim sat proudly. The horses gleamed, the coachwork sparkled in the torchlight. But the group standing around the coach sparkled rather less.

There were a couple of people from the Trunk, several wizards and, of course, Otto Chriek the iconographer. They turned and welcomed Moist with expressions ranging from relief to deep suspicion.

'We were considering disqualification, Mr Lipwig,' said Ridcully, looking severe.

Moist handed the broom to Mr Pump. 'I do apologize, Archchancellor,' he said. 'I was checking some stamp designs and completely lost track of time. Oh, good evening, Professor Pelc.'

The Professor of Morbid Bibliomancy gave him a big grin and held up a jar. 'And Professor Goitre,' he said. 'The old chap thought he'd like to see what all the fuss is about.'

'And this is Mr Pony of the Grand Trunk,' said Ridcully.

Moist shook hands with the engineer. 'Mr Gilt not with you?' he said, winking.

'He's, er, watching from his coach,' said the engineer, looking nervously at Moist.

'Well, since you are both here, Mr Stibbons will hand you each a copy of the message,' said the Archchancellor. 'Mr Stibbons?'

Two packages were handed over. Moist undid his, and burst out laughing.

'But it's a book!' said Mr Pony. 'It'll take all night to code. And there's diagrams!'

Okay, let's begin, thought Moist, and moved like a cobra. He snatched the book from the startled Pony, thumbed through it quickly, grabbed a handful of pages and ripped them out, to a gasp from the crowd.

'There you are, sir,' he said, handing the pages back. 'There is your message! Pages 79 to 128. We'll deliver the rest of the book and the recipient can put your pages in later, if they arrive!' He was aware of Professor Pelc glaring at him, and added: 'And I'm sure it can be repaired *very neatly*!'

It was a stupid gesture but it was big and loud and funny and cruel and if Moist didn't know how to get the attention of a crowd he didn't know anything. Mr Pony backed away, clutching the stricken chapter.

'I didn't mean—' he tried, but Moist interrupted with: 'After all, we've got a big coach for such a small book.'

'It's just that pictures take time to code—' Mr Pony protested. He wasn't used to this sort of thing. Machinery didn't answer back.

Moist allowed a look of genuine concern to cross his face. 'Yes, that does seem unfair,' he said. He turned to Ponder Stibbons. 'Don't you think that's unfair, Mr Stibbons?'

The wizard looked puzzled. 'But once they've coded it it'll only take them a couple of hours to get it to Genua!' he said.

'Nevertheless, I must insist,' said Moist. 'We don't want an unfair advantage. Stand down, Jim,' he called up to the coachman. 'We're going to give the clacks a head start.' He turned to Ponder and Mr Pony with an expression of innocent helpfulness. 'Would an hour be all right, gentlemen?'

The crowd exploded. Gods, I'm good at this, Moist thought. I want this moment to go on for ever . . .

'Mr Lipwig!' a voice called out. Moist scanned the faces, and spotted the caller.

'Ah, Miss Sacharissa. Pencil at the ready?'

'Are you seriously telling us you'll *wait* while the Grand Trunk prepares their message?' she said. She was laughing.

'Indeed,' said Moist, grasping the lapels of his gleaming jacket. 'We in the Post Office are fair-minded people. May I take this opportunity to tell you about our new Green Cabbage stamp, by the way?'

'Surely you're going too far, Mr Lipwig?'

'All the way to Genua, dear lady! Did I mention the gum is cabbage-flavoured?'

Moist couldn't have stopped himself now for hard money. This was where his soul lived: dancing on an avalanche, making the world up as he went along, reaching into people's ears and changing their minds. For this he offered glass as diamonds, let the Find The Lady cards fly under his fingers, stood smiling in front of clerks examining fake bills. This was the feeling he craved, the raw naked excitement of pushing the envelope—

Reacher Gilt was moving through the crowd, like a shark among minnows. He gave Moist a carefully neutral look, and turned to Mr Pony.

'Is there some problem, gentlemen?' he said. 'It's getting late.'

In a silence punctuated by chuckles from the crowd, Pony tried to explain, in so far as he now had any grip of what was going on.

'I see,' said Gilt. 'You are pleased to make fun of us, Mr Lipwig? Then allow me to say that we of the Grand Trunk will not take it amiss if you should leave now. I think we can spare you a couple of hours, eh?'

'Oh, certainly,' said Moist. 'If it will make you feel any better.'

'Indeed it will,' said Gilt gravely. 'It would be best, Mr Lipwig, if you were a long way away from here.'

Moist heard the tone, because he was expecting it. Gilt was being reasonable and statesmanlike, but his eye was a dark metal ball and there was the harmonic of murder in his voice. And then Gilt said: 'Is Mr Groat well, Mr Lipwig? I was sorry to hear of the attack.'

'Attack, Mr Gilt? He was hit by falling timber,' said Moist. And that question entitles you to no mercy at all, no matter what.

'Ah? Then I was misinformed,' said Gilt. 'I shall know not to listen to rumours in future.'

'I shall pass on your good wishes to Mr Groat,' said Moist.

Gilt raised his hat. 'Goodbye, Mr Lipwig. I wish you the best of luck in your gallant attempt. There are some dangerous people on the road.'

Moist raised his own hat and said: 'I intend to leave them behind very soon, Mr Gilt.'

There, he thought. We've said it all, and the nice lady from the newspaper thinks we're good chums or, at least, just business rivals being stiffly polite to each other. Let's spoil the mood.

'Goodbye, ladies and gentlemen,' he said. 'Mr Pump, be so good as to put the broom on the coach, would you?'

'Broom?' said Gilt, looking up sharply. 'That broom? The one with stars on it? You're taking a *broomstick*?'

'Yes. It will come in handy if we break down,' said Moist.

'I protest, Archchancellor!' said Gilt, spinning round. 'This man intends to fly to Genua!'

'I have no such intention!' said Moist. 'I resent the allegation!'

'Is this why you appear so confident?' snarled Gilt. And it *was* a snarl, there and then, a little sign of a crack appearing.

A broomstick could travel fast enough to blow your ears off. It wouldn't need too many towers to break down, and heavens knew they broke down all the time, for a broomstick to beat the clacks to Genua, especially since it could fly direct and wouldn't have to follow the big dog-leg the coach road and the Grand Trunk took. The Trunk would have to be really unlucky, and the person flying the broom would be really frozen and probably really dead, but a broomstick could fly from Ankh-Morpork to Genua in a day. That might just do it.

Gilt's face was a mask of glee. *Now* he knew what Moist intended.

Round and round she goes, and where she stops, nobody knows . . .

It was the heart of any scam or fiddle. Keep the punter uncertain or, if he *is* certain, make him certain of the wrong thing.

'I demand that no broomstick is taken on the coach!' said Gilt to the Archchancellor, which was not a good move. You didn't demand anything from wizards. You *requested*. 'If Mr Lipwig is not confident in his equipment,' Gilt went on, 'I suggest he concedes right now!'

'We'll be travelling alone on some dangerous roads,' said Moist. 'A broomstick might be essential.'

'However, I am forced to agree with this ... gentleman,' said Ridcully, with some distaste. 'It would not look *right*, Mr Lipwig.'

Moist threw up his hands. 'As you wish, sir, of course. It is a blow. May I request even-handed treatment, though?'

'Your meaning?' said the wizard.

'There is a horse stationed at each tower to be used when the tower breaks down,' said Moist.

'That is normal practice!' snapped Gilt.

'Only in the mountains,' said Moist calmly. 'And even then only at the most isolated towers. But today, I suspect, there's one at every tower. It's a pony express, Archchancellor, with apologies to Mr Pony. They could easily beat our coach without sending a word of code.'

'You can't possibly be suggesting that we'd take the message all the way on horseback!' said Gilt.

'You were suggesting I'd fly,' said Moist. 'If Mr Gilt is not confident in his equipment, Archchancellor, I suggest he concedes now.'

And there it was, a shadow on Gilt's face. He was more than just irate now; he'd passed into the calm, limpid waters of utter, visceral fury.

'So let's agree that this isn't a test of horses against broomsticks,' said Moist. 'It's stagecoach against clacks tower. If the stage breaks down, we repair the stage. If a tower breaks down, you repair the tower.'

'That seems fair, I must say,' said Ridcully. 'And I so rule. However, I must take Mr Lipwig aside to issue a word of warning.'

The Archchancellor put his arm round Moist's shoulders and led him round the coach. Then he leaned down until their faces were a few inches apart.

'You are aware, are you, that painting a few stars on a perfectly ordinary broomstick doesn't mean it will get airborne?' he said.

Moist looked into a pair of milky blue eyes that were as innocent as a child's, particularly a child who is trying hard to look innocent.

'My goodness, doesn't it?' he said.

The wizard patted him on the shoulder. 'Best to leave things as they are, I feel,' he said happily.

Gilt smiled at Moist as they returned.

It was just too much to resist, so Moist didn't. Raise the stakes. Always push your luck, because no one else would push it for you.

'Would you care for a little *personal* wager, Mr Gilt?' he said. 'Just to make it . . . interesting?'

Gilt handled it well, if you couldn't read the tells, the little signs . . .

'Dear me, Mr Lipwig, do the gods approve of gambling?' he said, and gave a short laugh.

'What is life but a lottery, Mr Gilt?' said Moist. 'Shall we say . . . one hundred thousand dollars?'

That did it. That was the last straw. He saw something snap inside Reacher Gilt.

'One hundred thousand? Where would you lay your hands on that kind of money, Lipwig?'

'Oh, I just place them together, Mr Gilt. Doesn't everyone know that?' said Moist, to general amusement. He gave the chairman his most insolent smile. 'And where will *you* lay *your* hands on one hundred thousand dollars?'

'Hah. I accept the wager! We shall see who laughs tomorrow,' said Gilt bluntly.

'I'll look forward to it,' said Moist.

And now I have you in the hollow of my hand, he thought to himself. The hollow of my hand. You're enraged, now. You're making wrong decisions. You're walking the plank.

He climbed up on to the coach and turned to the crowd. 'Genua, ladies and gentlemen. Genua or bust!'

'Someone will!' yelled a wag in the crowd. Moist bowed, and, as he straightened up, looked into the face of Adora Belle Dearheart.

'Will you marry me, Miss Dearheart?' he shouted.

There was an 'Oooh' from the crowd, and Sacharissa turned her head like a cat seeking the next mouse. What a shame the paper had only one front page, eh?

Miss Dearheart blew a smoke ring. 'Not yet,' she said calmly. This got a mixture of cheers and boos.

Moist waved, jumped down beside the driver and said: 'Hit it, Jim.'

Jim cracked his whip for the sound of the thing, and the coach moved away amidst cheering. Moist looked back, and made out Mr Pony pushing determinedly through the crowd in the direction of the Tump Tower. Then he sat back and looked at the streets, in the light of the coach lamps.

Perhaps it was the gold working its way in from outside. He could feel something filling him, like a mist. When he moved his hand, he was sure that it left a trail of flecks in the air. He was still flying.

'Jim, do I look all right?' he said.

'Can't see much of you in this light, sir,' said the coachman. 'Can I ask a question?'

'Go ahead, please.'

'Why'd you give those bastards just those middle pages?'

'Two reasons, Jim. It makes us look good and makes them look like whiny kids. And the other is, it's the bit with all the colour illustrations. I hear it takes *ages* to code one of those.'

'You're so sharp you'll cut yourself, Mr Lipwig! Eh? Damn straight!'

'Drive like the blazes, Jim!'

'Oh, I know how to give them a show, sir, you can bank on it! Hyah!' The whip cracked again, and the sound of hooves bounced off the buildings.

'*Six* horses?' said Moist, as they rattled up Broadway.

'Aye, sir. Might as well make a name for myself, sir,' said the coachman.

'Slow down a bit when you get to the old wizard tower, will you? I'll get off there. Did you get some guards?'

'Four of them, Mr Lipwig,' Jim announced. 'Lying low inside. Men of repute and integrity. Known 'em since we were lads: Nosher Harry, Skullbreaker Tapp, Grievous Bodily Harmsworth and Joe "No Nose" Tozer. They're mates, sir, don't you worry, and they're looking forward to a little holiday in Genua.'

'Yeah, we've all got our buckets and spades,' growled a voice from inside.

'I'd rather have them than a dozen watchmen,' said Jim happily.

The coach rattled on, leaving the outlying suburbs behind. The road under the wheels became rougher, but the coach swung and danced along on its steel springs.

'When you've dropped me off you can rein them in a bit. No need to rush, Jim,' said Moist, after a while.

In the light of the coach lamps Moist saw Jim's red face glow with guile.

'It's your Plan, eh, sir?'

'It's a wonderful plan, Jim!' said Moist. And I shall have to make sure it doesn't work.

The lights of the coach disappeared, leaving Moist in chilly darkness. In the distance the faintly glowing smokes of Ankh-Morpork made a great trailing mushroom of cloud that blotted out the stars. Things rustled in the bushes, and a breeze wafted the scent of cabbages over the endless fields.

Moist waited until he got some night vision. The tower appeared, a column of night without stars. All he had to do was find his way through the dense, brambly, root-knotted woodland—

He made a noise like an owl. Since Moist was no ornithologist, he did this by saying 'woo woo'.

The woodland exploded with owl hoots, except that these were owls that roosted in the old wizarding tower, which drove you mad in a day. It had no obvious effect on them except that the noises they made resembled every possible sound that could be made by a living or even dying creature. There was definitely some elephant in there, and possibly some hyena, too, with a hint of bedspring.

When the din had died down a voice from a few feet away whispered: 'All right, Mr Lipwig. It's me, Adrian. Grab my hand and let's go before the others start fighting again.'

'Fighting? What about?'

'They drive each other up the wall! Feel this rope? Can you feel it? Right. You can move fast. We scouted out a trail and strung the rope—'

They hurried through the trees. You had to be really close to the tower to see the glow coming through the ruined doorway at the base. Undecided Adrian had fixed some of his little cold lights up the inner wall. Stones moved under Moist's feet as he scrambled to the summit. He paid them no attention, but ran up the spiral stair so fast that when he reached the top he spun.

Mad Al caught him by the shoulders. 'No rush,' he said cheerfully. 'We've got ten minutes to go.'

'We'd have been ready twenty minutes ago if *somebody* hadn't lost the hammer,' muttered Sane Alex, tightening a wire.

'What? I put it in the tool box, didn't I?' said Mad Al.

'In the spanner drawer!'

'So?'

'Who in their right mind would look for a hammer in the spanner drawer?'

Down below, the owls started up again.

'Look,' said Moist quickly, 'that's not important, is it? Right now?'

'This man,' said Sane Alex, pointing an accusing wrench, 'this man is mad!'

'Not as mad as someone who keeps his screws neatly by size in jam jars,' said Mad Al.

'That counts as sane!' said Alex hotly.

'But everyone knows rummaging is half the fun! Besides—'

'It's done,' said Undecided Adrian.

Moist looked up. The Gnu's clacks machine rose up into the night, just as it had done on the Post Office roof. Behind it, in the direction of the city, an H-shaped structure climbed even further. It looked a little like a ship's mast, an effect maybe caused by the wires that steadied it. They rattled in the faint breeze.

'You must have upset someone,' Adrian went on, while the other two settled down a bit. 'A message was sent through twenty minutes ago, from Gilt himself. He said the big one will go through duplex, great care must be taken not to change it in any way, there is to be no other traffic at all until there's a restart message from Gilt, and he'll personally sack the entire staff of any tower that does not strictly follow those instructions.'

'It just goes to show, the Grand Trunk *is* a people company,' said Moist.

Undecided Adrian and Mad Al walked over to the big frame and began to unwind some ropes from their cleats.

Oh well, thought Moist, now for it . . .

'There's just one alteration to the plan,' he said, and took a breath. 'We're not sending the Woodpecker.'

'What do you mean?' said Adrian, dropping his rope. 'That *was* the plan!'

'It'll destroy the Trunk,' said Moist.

'Yes, that was the plan, sure enough,' said Al. 'Gilt's as good as painted "kick me" on his pants! Look, it's falling down of its own accord anyway, okay? It was an experiment in the first place! We can rebuild it faster and better!'

'How?' said Moist. 'Where will the money come from? I know a way to destroy the company but leave the towers standing. They were stolen from the Dearhearts and their partners. I can give them back! But the only way to build a better line of towers is to leave the old ones intact. The Trunk's got to earn!'

'That's the sort of thing Gilt would say!' snapped Al.

'And it's true,' said Moist. 'Alex, you're sane, tell the man! Keep the Trunk operating, replace one tower at a time, never dropping any code!' He waved a hand towards the darkness. 'The people out on the towers, they want to be proud of what they do, yes? It's tough work and they don't get paid enough but they live to shift code, right? The company's running them into the ground but they still shift code!'

Adrian tugged at his rope. 'Hey, the canvas is stuck,' he announced to the tower in general. 'It must have been caught up when we furled it . . .'

'Oh, I'm sure the Woodpecker will work,' said Moist, plunging on. 'It might even damage enough towers for long enough. But Gilt will twist his way out of it. Do you understand? He'll shout about sabotage!'

'So what?' said Mad Al. 'We'll have this lot back on the cart in an hour and no one will know we were ever here!'

'I'll climb up and free it, shall I?' said Undecided Adrian, shaking the canvas.

'I said it won't *work*,' said Moist, waving him away. 'Look, Mr Al, this isn't going to be settled by fire. It's going to be settled with words. We'll tell the world what happened to the Trunk.'

'You've been talking to Killer about that?' said Alex.

'Yes,' said Moist.

'But you can't prove anything,' said Alex. 'We heard it was all legal.'

'I doubt it,' said Moist. 'But that doesn't matter. I don't have to prove anything. I said this is about words, and how you can twist them, and how you can spin them in people's heads so that they think the way you want them to. We'll send a message of our own, and do you know what? The boys in the towers will *want* to send it, and when people know what it says they'll *want* to believe it, because they'll want to live in a world where it's true. It's my words against Gilt's, and I'm better at them than he is. I can take him down with a sentence, Mr Mad, and leave every tower standing. And no one will ever know how it was done—'

There was a brief exclamation behind them, and the sound of canvas unrolling quite fast.

'Trust me,' said Moist.

'We'll never get another chance like this,' said Mad Al.

'Exactly!' said Moist.

'One man has died for every three towers standing,' said Mad Al. 'Did you know that?'

'You know they'll never really die while the Trunk is alive,' said Moist. It was a wild shot, but it hit something, he sensed it. He rushed on: 'It lives while the code is shifted, and they live with it, always Going Home. Will you stop that? You can't stop it! I won't stop it! But I *can* stop Gilt! *Trust* me!'

The canvas hung like a sail, if as someone intended to launch the tower. It was eighty feet high and thirty feet wide and moved a little in the wind.

'Where's Adrian?' said Moist.

They looked at the sail. They rushed to the edge of the tower. They looked down into darkness.

'Adrian?' said Mad Al uncertainly.

A voice from below said: 'Yes?'

'What are you doing?'

'Just, you know . . . hanging around? And an owl has just landed on my head.'

There was a small tearing noise beside Moist. Sane Alex had cut a hole in the canvas.

'Here it comes!' he reported.

'What?' said Moist.

'The message! They're sending from Tower 2! Take a look,' Alex said, backing away.

Moist peered through the slit, back towards the city. In the distance, a tower was sparkling.

Mad Al strode over to the half-sized clacks array and grabbed the handles.

'All right, Mr Lipwig, let's hear *your* plan,' he said. 'Alex, give me a hand! Adrian, just . . . hang on, all right?'

'It's trying to push a dead mouse in my ear,' said a reproachful voice from below.

Moist shut his eyes, lined up the thoughts that had been buzzing for hours, and began to speak.

Behind and above him, the huge expanse of canvas was just enough to block the line of sight between the two distant towers. In front of him, the Smoking Gnu's half-sized tower was just the *right* size to look, to the next tower in line, like a bigger tower a long way off. At night all you could see were the lights.

The clacks in front of him shook as the shutters rattled. And now a new message was dropping across the sky . . .

It was only a few hundred words. When Moist had finished, the clacks rattled out the last few letters and then fell silent.

After a while Moist said: 'Will they pass it along?'

'Oh, yes,' said Mad Al, in a flat voice. 'They'll send it. You're sitting up in a tower in the mountains and you get a signal like that? You'll get it away and out of your tower as fast as you can.'

'I don't know if we ought to shake your hand or throw you off the tower,' said Sane Alex sullenly. 'That was evil.'

'What sort of person could dream up something like that?' said Mad Al.

'Me. Now let's pull Adrian up, shall we?' said Moist quickly. 'And then I'd better get back to the city . . .'

An omniscope is one of the most powerful instruments known to magic, and therefore one of the most useless.

It can see everything, with ease. Getting it to see *anything* is where wonders have to be performed because there is so much Everything – which is to say, everything that can, will, has, should or might happen in all possible universes – that anything, any previously specified *thing*, is very hard to find. Before Hex had evolved the control thaumarhythms, completing in a day a task that would have taken five hundred wizards at least ten years, omniscopes were used purely as mirrors because of the wonderful blackness they showed. This, it turned out, is because 'nothing to see' is what most of the universe consists of, and many a wizard has peacefully trimmed his beard while gazing into the dark heart of the cosmos.

There were very few steerable omniscopes. They took a long time to make and cost a great deal. And the wizards were not at all keen on making any more. Omniscopes were for them to look at the universe, not for the universe to look back at them.

Besides, the wizards did not believe in making life too easy for people. At least, for people who weren't wizards. An omniscope was a rare, treasured and delicate thing.

But today was a special occasion, and they had thrown open the doors to the richer, cleaner and more hygienic sections of Ankh-Morpork society. A long table had been set for Second Tea. Nothing too excessive – a few dozen roast fowls, a couple of cold salmon, one hundred linear feet of salad bar, a pile of loaves, one or two kegs of beer and, of course, the chutney, pickle and relish train, one trolley not being considered big enough. People had filled their plates and were standing around chatting and, above all, Being There. Moist slipped in unnoticed, for now, because people were watching the University's biggest omniscope.

Archchancellor Ridcully thumped the side of the thing with his hand, causing it to rock.

'It's still not *working*, Mr Stibbons!' he bellowed. 'Here's that damn enormous fiery eye again!'

'I'm sure we have the right—' Ponder began, fiddling with the rear of the big disc.

'It's me, sir, Devious Collabone, sir,' said a voice from the omniscope. The fiery eye pulled back and was replaced by an enormous fiery nose. 'I'm here at the terminal tower in Genua, sir. Sorry about the redness, sir. I've picked up an allergy to seaweed, sir.'

'Hello, Mr Collabone!' yelled Ridcully. 'How are you? How's the—'

'—shellfish research—' murmured Ponder Stibbons.

'—shellfish research comin' along?'

'Not very well, actually, sir. I've developed a nasty—'

'Good, good! Lucky chap!' Ridcully yelled, cupping his hands to increase the volume. 'I wouldn't mind bein' in Genua myself at this time of year! Sun, sea, surf and sand, eh?'

'Actually it's the wet season, sir, and I'm a bit worried about this fungus that's growing on the omni—'

'Wonderful!' shouted Ridcully. 'Well, I can't stand here and chew your fat all day! Has anything arrived? We are agog!'

'Could you just stand back a little bit further, please, Mr Collabone?' said Ponder. 'And you don't really need to speak so . . . loudly, Archchancellor.'

'Chap's a long way away, man!' said Ridcully.

'Not as such, sir,' said Ponder, with well-honed patience. 'Very well, Mr Collabone, you may proceed.'

The crowd behind the Archchancellor pressed forward. Mr Collabone backed away. This was all a bit too much for a man who spent his days with no one to talk to but bivalves.

'Er, I've had a message by clacks, sir, but—' he began.

'Nothin' from the Post Office?' said Ridcully.

'No, sir. Nothing, sir.'

There were cheers and boos and general laughter from the crowd. From his shadowy corner, Moist saw Lord Vetinari, right by the Archchancellor. He scanned the rest of the crowd and spotted Reacher Gilt, standing off to one side and, surprisingly, not smiling. And Gilt saw him.

One look was enough. The man wasn't certain. Not *totally* certain.

Welcome to *fear*, said Moist to himself. It's hope, turned inside out. You know it can't go wrong, you're sure it can't go wrong . . .

But it might.

I've got you.

Devious Collabone coughed. 'Er, but I don't think this is the message Archchancellor Ridcully sent,' he said, his voice gone squeaky with nervousness.

'What makes you think that, man?'

'Because it says it isn't,' Collabone quavered. 'It says it's from dead people . . .'

'You mean it's an old message?' said Ridcully.

'Er, no, sir. Er . . . I'd better read it, shall I? Do you want me to read it?'

'That's the *point*, man!'

In the big disc of glass, Collabone cleared his throat.

' "*Who will listen to the dead? We who died so that words could fly demand justice now. These are the crimes of the Board of the Grand Trunk: theft, embezzlement, breach of trust, corporate murder—*" '

CHAPTER FOURTEEN

Deliverance

Lord Vetinari Requests Silence – Mr Lipwig Comes Down – Mr Pump
Moves On – Fooling No One But Yourself – The Bird – The Concludium
– Freedom of Choice

THE GREAT HALL WAS IN uproar. Most of the wizards took the opportunity to congregate at the buffet, which was now clear. If there's one thing a wizard hates, it's having to wait while the person in front of them is in two minds about coleslaw. It's a salad bar, they say, it's got the kind of stuff salad bars have, if it was surprising it wouldn't *be* a salad bar, you're not here to *look* at it. What do you expect to find? Rhino chunks? Pickled coelacanth?

The Lecturer in Recent Runes ladled more bacon bits into his salad bowl, having artfully constructed buttresses of celery and breastworks of cabbage to increase its depth five times.

'Any of you Fellows know what this is all about?' he said, raising his voice above the din. 'Seems to be upsetting a lot of people.'

'It's this clacks business,' said the Chair of Indefinite Studies. 'I've never trusted it. Poor Collabone. Decent young man in his way. A good man with a whelk. Seems to be in a spot of bother . . .'

It was quite a large spot. Devious Collabone was opening and shutting his mouth on the other side of the glass like a stranded fish.

In front of him, Mustrum Ridcully reddened with anger, his tried and tested approach to most problems.

'. . . sorry, sir, but this is what it says and you asked me to read it,' Collabone protested. 'It goes on and on, sir—'

'And that's what the clacks people gave you?' the Archchancellor demanded. 'Are you *sure*?'

'Yes, sir. They did look at me in a funny way, sir, but this is definitely it. Why should I make anything up, Archchancellor? I spend most of my time in a tank, sir. A boring, boring, lonely tank, sir.'

'Not one more word!' screamed Greenyham. 'I forbid it!' Beside him, Mr Nutmeg had sprayed his drink across several dripping guests.

'Excuse me? You *forbid*, sir?' said Ridcully, turning on Greenyham in sudden fury. 'Sir, I am the Master of this college! I will not, sir, be told what to do in my own university! If there is anything to be forbidden here, sir, *I* will do the forbidding! Thank you! Go ahead, Mr Collabone!'

'Er, er, er . . .' Collabone panted, longing for death.

'I said carry on, man!'

'Er, er . . . yes . . . "*There was no safety. There was no pride. All there was, was money. Everything became money, and money became everything. Money treated us as if we were things, and we died—*"'

'Is there no law in this place? That is outright slander!' shouted Stowley. 'It's a trick of some sort!'

'By whom, sir?' roared Ridcully. 'Do you mean to suggest that Mr Collabone, a young wizard of great integrity, who I may say is doing wonderful work with snakes—'

'—shellfish—' murmured Ponder Stibbons.

'—shellfish, is playing some kind of *joke*? How dare you, sir! Continue, Mr Collabone!'

'I, I, I—'

'That is an *order*, Dr Collabone!'*

'Er . . . "*Blood oils the machinery of the Grand Trunk as willing, loyal people pay with their lives for the Board's culpable stupidity—*"'

The hubbub rose again. Moist saw Lord Vetinari's gaze traverse the room. He didn't duck in time. The Patrician's stare passed right through him, carrying away who knew what. An eyebrow rose in interrogation. Moist looked away, and sought out Gilt.

He wasn't there.

In the omniscope Mr Collabone's nose now glowed like a beacon. He struggled, dropping pages, losing his place, but pressing on with

---

* Archchancellor Ridcully was a great believer in retaliation by promotion. You couldn't have civilians criticizing one of *his* wizards. That was *his* job.

the dogged, dull determination of a man who could spend all day watching one oyster.

'—nothing less than an attempt to blacken our good names in front of the whole city!' Stowley was protesting.

' "—*unaware of the toll that is being taken. What can we say of the men who caused this, who sat in comfort round their table and killed us by numbers? This*—" '

'I will sue the University! I will sue the University!' screamed Greenyham. He picked up a chair and hurled it at the omniscope. Halfway to the glass it turned into a small flock of doves, which panicked and soared up to the roof.

'Oh, *please* sue the University!' Ridcully bellowed. 'We've got a *pond* full of people who tried to sue the University—'

'Silence,' said Vetinari.

It wasn't a very loud word, but it had an effect rather like that of a drop of black ink in a glass of clear water. The word spread out in coils and tendrils, getting everywhere. It strangled the noise.

Of course, there is always someone not paying attention. 'And furthermore,' Stowley went on, oblivious of the hush unfolding in his own little world of righteous indignation, 'it's plain that—'

'I *will* have silence,' Vetinari stated.

Stowley stopped, looked around and deflated. Silence ruled.

'Very good,' said Vetinari quietly. He nodded at Commander Vimes of the Watch, who whispered to another watchman, who pushed his way though the crowd and towards the door.

Vetinari turned to Ridcully. 'Archchancellor, I would be grateful if you would instruct your student to continue, please?' he said in the same calm tone.

'Certainly! Off you go, Professor Collabone. In your own time.'

'Er, er, er, er . . . it says further on: "*The men obtained control of the Trunk via a ruse known as the Double Lever, in the main using money entrusted to them by clients who did not suspect that*—" '

'Stop reading that!' Greenyham shouted. 'This is ridiculous! It is just slander upon slander!'

'I'm certain I spoke, Mr Greenyham,' said Vetinari.

Greenyham faltered.

'Good. Thank you,' said Vetinari. 'These are very serious allegations, certainly. Embezzlement? Murder? I'm sure that Mr— sorry,
Professor Collabone is a trustworthy man' – in the omniscope Devious
Collabone, Unseen University's newest professor, nodded desperately
– 'who is only reading what has been delivered, so it would appear
that they have originated from within your own company. *Serious*
allegations, Mr Greenyham. Made in front of all these people. Are
you suggesting I should treat them as some sort of prank? The city is
watching, Mr Greenyham. Oh, Stowley appears to be ill.'

'This is not the place for—' Greenyham tried, aware once more of
the creaking of ice.

'It is the *ideal* place,' said Vetinari. 'It is *public*. In the circumstances,
given the nature of the allegations, I'm sure everyone would require
that I get to the bottom of them as soon as possible, if only to prove
them totally groundless.' He looked around. There was a chorus of
agreement. Even the upper crust loved a show.

'What do *you* say, Mr Greenyham?' said Vetinari.

Greenyham said nothing. The cracks were spreading, the ice was
breaking up on every side.

'Very well,' said Vetinari. He turned to the figure beside him.

'Commander Vimes, be so kind as to send men to the offices of the
Grand Trunk Company, Ankh-Sto Associates, Sto Plains Holdings,
Ankh Futures and particularly to the premises of the Ankh-Morpork
Mercantile Credit Bank. Inform the manager, Mr Cheeseborough,
that the bank is closed for audit and I wish to see him in my office at
his earliest convenience. Any person in any of those premises who so
much as moves a piece of paper before my clerks arrive will be
arrested and held complicit in any or all of such offences as may
be uncovered. While this is happening, moreover, no person
concerned with the Grand Trunk Company or any of its employees is
to leave this room.'

'You can't do that!' Greenyham protested weakly, but the fire had
drained out of him. Mr Stowley had collapsed on the floor, with his
head in his hands.

'Can I not?' said Vetinari. 'I am a tyrant. It's what we do.'

'What is happening? Who am I? Where is this place?' moaned Stowley, a man who believed in laying down some groundwork as soon as possible.

'But there's no evidence! That wizard's lying! Someone must have been bribed!' Greenyham pleaded. Not only had the ice broken up, but he was on the floe with the big hungry walrus.

'Mr Greenyham,' said Lord Vetinari, 'one more uninvited outburst from you and you will be imprisoned. I hope that is clear?'

'On what charge?' said Greenyham, still managing to find a last reserve of hauteur from somewhere.

'*There doesn't have to be one!*' Robe swirling like the edge of darkness, Vetinari swung round to the omniscope and Devious Collabone, for whom two thousand miles suddenly wasn't far enough. 'Continue, Professor. There will be no further interruptions.'

Moist watched the audience as Collabone stuttered and mispronounced his way through the rest of the message. It dealt with generalities rather than particulars, but there were dates, and names, and thundering denunciations. There was nothing new, not *really* new, but it was packaged in fine language and it was delivered by the dead.

We who died on the dark towers demand this of you . . .

He ought to be ashamed.

It was one thing to put words in the mouths of the gods; priests did it all the time. But this, this was a step too far. You had to be some kind of bastard to think of something like this.

He relaxed a bit. A fine upstanding citizen wouldn't have stooped so low, but he hadn't got this job because he was a fine upstanding citizen. Some tasks needed a good honest hammer. Others needed a twisty corkscrew.

With any luck, he could believe that, if he really tried.

There had been a late fall of snow, and the fir trees around Tower 181 were crusted with white under the hard, bright starlight.

Everyone was up there tonight – Grandad, Roger, Big Steve-oh,

Wheezy Halfsides, who was a dwarf and had to sit on a cushion to reach the keyboards, and Princess.

There had been a few muffled exclamations as the message came through. Now there was silence, except for the sighing of the wind. Princess could see people's breath in the air. Grandad was drumming his fingers on the woodwork.

Then Wheezy said: 'Was that all real?'

The breath clouds got denser. People were relaxing, coming back to the real world.

'You saw the instructions we got,' said Grandad, staring across the dark forests. 'Don't change anything. Send it on, they told us. We sent it on. We damn well did send it on!'

'Who was it from?' said Steve-oh.

'It doesn't matter,' said Grandad. 'Message comes in, message goes out, message moves on.'

'Yeah, but was it really from—' Steve-oh began.

'Bloody hell, Steve-oh, you really don't know when to *shut up*, do you?' said Roger.

'Only I heard about Tower 93, where the guys died and the tower sent a distress signal all by itself,' mumbled Steve-oh. He was fast on the keys, but not knowing when to shut up was only one of his social failings. In a tower, it could get you killed.

'Dead Man's Handle,' said Grandad. 'You should know that. If there's no activity for ten minutes when a signature key is slotted, the drum drops the jacquard into the slot and the counterweight falls and the tower sends the help sign.' He spoke the words as if reading them from a manual.

'Yeah, but I heard that in Tower 93 the jacquard was wedged and—'

'I can't stand this,' muttered Grandad. 'Roger, let's get this tower working again. We've got local signals to send, haven't we?'

'Sure. And stuff waiting on the drum,' said Roger. 'But Gilt said we weren't to restart until—'

'Gilt can kiss my—' Grandad began, then remembered the present company and finished: '—donkey. You read what went through just now! Do you think that bas— that man is still in charge?'

Princess looked out from the upstream window. '182's lit up,' she announced.

'Right! Let's light up and shift code,' Grandad growled. 'That's what we do! And who's going to stop us? All those without something to do, get out! We are *running*!'

Princess went out on to the little platform, to be out of the way. Underfoot the snow was like icing sugar, in her nostrils the air was like knives.

When she looked across the mountains, in the direction she'd learned to think of as downstream, she could see that Tower 180 was sending. At that moment, she heard the thump and click of 181's own shutters opening, dislodging snow. We shift code, she thought. It's what we do.

Up on the tower, watching the star-like twinkle of the Trunk in the clear, freezing air, it was like being part of the sky.

And she wondered what Grandad most feared: that dead clacksmen could send messages to the living, or that they couldn't.

Collabone finished. Then he produced a handkerchief and rubbed away at whatever the green stuff was that had begun to grow on the glass. This made a squeaking sound.

He peered nervously through the smear. 'Is that all right, sir? I'm not in some sort of trouble, am I?' he asked. 'Only at the moment I think I'm close to translating the mating call of the giant clam . . .'

'Thank you, Professor Collabone; a good job well done. That will be all,' said Archchancellor Ridcully coldly. 'Unhinge the mechanism, Mr Stibbons.' A look of fervid relief passed across Devious Collabone's face just before the omniscope went blank.

'Mr Pony, you are the chief engineer of the Grand Trunk, are you not?' said Vetinari, before the babble could rise again.

The engineer, suddenly the focus of attention, backed away waving his hands frantically. 'Please, your lordship! I'm just an engineer, I don't *know* anything—'

'Calm yourself, please. Have you heard that the souls of dead men travel on the Trunk?'

'Oh, yes, your lordship.'

'Is it true?

'Well, er . . .' Pony looked around, a hunted man. He'd got his pink flimsies, and they would show everyone that he was nothing more than a man who'd *tried* to make things work, but right now all he could find on his side was the truth. He took refuge in it. 'I can't see how, but, well . . . sometimes, when you're up a tower of a night, and the shutters are rattlin' and the wind's singing in the rigging, well, you might think it's true.'

'I believe there is a tradition called "Sending Home"?' said Lord Vetinari.

The engineer looked surprised. 'Why, yes, sir, but . . .' Pony felt he ought to wave a little flag for a rational world in which, at the moment, he didn't have a lot of faith, 'the Trunk was dark before we ran the message, so I don't see how the message could have got on—'

'Unless, of course, the dead put it there?' said Lord Vetinari. 'Mr Pony, for the good of your soul and, not least, your body, you will go now to the Tump Tower, escorted by one of Commander Vimes's men, and send a brief message to all the towers. You will obtain the paper tapes, which I believe are known as drum rolls, from all the towers on the Grand Trunk. I understand that they show a record of all messages originating at that tower, which cannot be readily altered?'

'That will take weeks to do, sir!' Pony protested.

'An early start in the morning would seem in order, then,' said Lord Vetinari.

Mr Pony, who had suddenly spotted that a spell a long way from Ankh-Morpork might be a very healthy option just now, nodded and said, 'Right you are, my lord.'

'The Grand Trunk will remain closed in the interim,' said Lord Vetinari.

'It's private property!' Greenyham burst out.

'Tyrant, remember,' said Vetinari, almost cheerfully. 'But I'm sure that the audit will serve to sort out at least some aspects of this mystery. One of them, of course, is that Mr Reacher Gilt does not seem to be in this room.'

Every head turned.

'Perhaps he remembered another engagement?' said Lord Vetinari. 'I think he slipped out some time ago.'

It dawned on the directors of the Grand Trunk that their chairman was absent and, which was worse, they weren't. They drew together.

'I wonder if, uh, at this point at least we could discuss the matter with you privately, your lordship?' said Greenyham. 'Reacher was not an easy man to deal with, I'm afraid.'

'Not a team player,' gasped Nutmeg.

'Who?' said Stowley. 'What is this place? Who are all these people?'

'Left us totally in the dark most of the time—' said Greenyham.

'I can't remember a thing—' said Stowley. 'I'm not fit to testify, any doctor will tell you . . .'

'I think I can say on behalf of all of us that we were suspicious of him all along—'

'Mind's a total blank. Not a blessed thing . . . what's this thing with fingers on . . . who am I . . .'

Lord Vetinari stared at the Board for five seconds longer than was comfortable, while tapping his chin gently with the knob of his cane. He smiled faintly.

'Quite,' he said. 'Commander Vimes, I think it would be iniquitous to detain these gentlemen here any longer.' As the faces in front of him relaxed into smiles full of hope, that greatest of all gifts, he added: 'To the cells with them, Commander. Separate cells, if you please. I shall see them in the morning. And if Mr Slant comes to see you on their behalf, do tell him I'd like a little chat, will you?'

That sounded . . . good. Moist strolled towards the door, while the hubbub rose, and had almost made it when Lord Vetinari's voice came out of the throng like a knife.

'Leaving so soon, Mr Lipwig? Do wait a moment. I shall give you a lift back to your famous Post Office.'

For a moment, just a slice of a second, Moist contemplated running. He did not do so. What would be the point?

The crowd parted hurriedly as Lord Vetinari headed towards the door; behind him, the Watch closed in.

Ultimately, there is the freedom to take the consequences.

The Patrician leaned back in the leather upholstery as the coach drew away. 'What a strange evening, Mr Lipwig,' he said. 'Yes, indeed.'

Moist, like the suddenly bewildered Mr Stowley, considered that his future happiness lay in saying as little as possible.

'Yes, sir,' he said.

'I wonder if that engineer *will* find any evidence that the strange message was put on the clacks by human hands?' he wondered aloud.

'I don't know, my lord.'

'You don't?'

'No, sir.'

'Ah,' said Vetinari. 'Well, the dead are known to speak, sometimes. Ouija boards and séances, and so on. Who can say they wouldn't use the medium of the clacks?'

'Not me, sir.'

'And you are clearly enjoying your new career, Mr Lipwig.'

'Yes, sir.'

'Good. On Monday your duties will include the administration of the Grand Trunk. It is being taken over by the city.'

Oh well, so much for future happiness . . .

'No, my lord,' said Moist.

Vetinari raised an eyebrow. 'There is an alternative, Mr Lipwig?'

'It really *is* private property, sir. It belongs to the Dearhearts and the other people who built it.'

'My, my, how the worm turns,' said Vetinari. 'But the trouble is, you see, they weren't good at business, only at mechanisms. Otherwise they would have seen through Gilt. The freedom to succeed goes hand in hand with the freedom to fail.'

'It was robbery by numbers,' said Moist. 'It was Find The

Lady done with ledgers. They didn't stand a chance.'

Vetinari sighed. 'You drive a hard bargain, Mr Lipwig.' Moist, who wasn't aware he had tried to drive a bargain at all, said nothing. 'Oh, very well. The question of ownership will remain in abeyance for now, until we have plumbed the sordid depths of this affair. But what I truly meant was that a great many people depend on the Trunk for their living. Out of sheer humanitarian considerations, we must do something. Sort things out, Postmaster.'

'But I'm going to have my hands more than full with the Post Office!' Moist protested.

'I hope you are. But in my experience, the best way to get something done is to give it to someone who is busy,' said Vetinari.

'In that case, I'm going to keep the Grand Trunk running,' said Moist.

'In honour of the dead, perhaps,' said Vetinari. 'Yes. As you wish. Ah, here is your stop.'

As the coachman opened the door Lord Vetinari leaned towards Moist. 'Oh, and before dawn I do suggest you go and check that everyone's left the old wizarding tower,' he said.

'What do you mean, sir?' said Moist. He knew *his* face betrayed nothing.

Vetinari sat back. 'Well done, Mr Lipwig.'

There was a crowd outside the Post Office, and a cheer went up as Moist made his way to the doors. It was raining now, a grey, sooty drizzle that was little more than fog with a slight weight problem.

Some of the staff were waiting inside. He realized the news hadn't got around. Even Ankh-Morpork's permanent rumour-mill hadn't been able to beat him back from the University.

'What's happened, Postmaster?' said Groat, his hands twisting together. 'Have they won?'

'No,' said Moist, but they picked up the edge in his voice.

'Have *we* won?'

'The Archchancellor will have to decide that,' said Moist. 'I suppose we won't know for weeks. The clacks has been shut down, though. I'm sorry, it's all complicated . . .'

He left them standing and staring as he trudged up to his office, where Mr Pump was standing in the corner.

'Good Evening, Mr Lipwig,' the golem boomed.

Moist sat down and put his head in his hands. This was victory, but it didn't feel like it. It felt like a mess.

The bets? Well, if Leadpipe got to Genua you could make a case under the rules that he'd won, but Moist had a feeling that all bets were off now. That meant people would get their money back, at least.

He'd have to keep the Trunk going, gods knew how. He'd sort of promised the Gnu, hadn't he? And it was amazing how people had come to rely on the clacks. He wouldn't know how Leadpipe had fared for *weeks*, and even Moist had got used to daily news from Genua. It was like having a finger cut off. But the clacks was a big, cumbersome monster of a thing, too many towers, too many people, too much effort. There had to be a way of making it better and sleeker and cheaper . . . or maybe it was something so big that no one could run it at a profit. Maybe it was like the Post Office, maybe the profit turned up spread around the whole of society.

Tomorrow he'd have to take it all seriously. Proper mail runs. *Many* more staff. Hundreds of things to do, and hundreds of other things to do before you could do *those* things. It wasn't going to be fun any more, cocking a snook, whatever a snook was, at the big slow giant. He'd won, so he'd have to pick up the pieces and make everything work. And come in here the next day and do it all again.

This wasn't how it was supposed to end. You won, and you pocketed the cash and walked away. That was how the game was supposed to go, wasn't it?

His eye fell on Anghammarad's message box, on its twisted, corroded strap, and he wished he was at the bottom of the sea.

'Mr Lipwig?'

He looked up. Drumknott the clerk was standing in the doorway, with another clerk behind him.

'Yes?'

'Sorry to disturb you, sir,' said the clerk. 'We're here to see Mr Pump. Just a minor adjustment, if you don't mind?'

'What? Oh. Fine. Whatever. Go ahead.' Moist waved a hand vaguely.

The two men walked over to the golem. There was some muted conversation, and then it knelt down and they unscrewed the top of its head.

Moist stared in horror. He knew it was done, of course, but it was shocking to see it happening. There was some rummaging around that he couldn't make out, and then the cranium was replaced, with a little pottery noise.

'Sorry to have disturbed you, sir,' said Drumknott, and the clerks left.

Mr Pump stayed on his knees for a moment, and then rose slowly. The red eyes focused on Moist, and the golem stuck out his hand.

'I Do Not Know What A Pleasure Is, But I Am Sure That If I Did, Then Working With You Would Have Been One,' he said. 'Now I Must Leave You. I Have Another Task.'

'You're not my, er, parole officer any more?' said Moist, taken aback.

'Correct.'

'Hold on,' said Moist, as light dawned, 'is Vetinari sending you after Gilt?'

'I Am Not At Liberty To Say.'

'He is, isn't he? You're not following me any more?'

'I Am Not Following You Any More.'

'So I'm free to go?'

'I Am Not At Liberty To Say. Good Night, Mr Lipvig.' Mr Pump paused at the door. 'I Am Not Certain What Happiness Is, Either, Mr Lipvig, But I Think – Yes, I Think I Am Happy To Have Met You.'

And, ducking to get through the doorway, the golem left.

That only leaves the werewolf, thought part of Moist's mind, faster than light. And they're not much good at boats and completely lost when it comes to oceans! It's the middle of the night, the Watch are running around like madmen, everyone's busy, I've got a bit of cash and I've still got the diamond ring and a deck of cards . . . who'd notice? Who'd care? Who'd worry?

He could go *anywhere*. But that wasn't really him thinking that, was it . . . it was just a few old brain cells, running on automatic. There wasn't anywhere to go, not any more.

He walked over to the big hole in the wall and looked down into the hall. Did *anyone* go home here? But now the news had got around, and if you wanted any hope of anything delivered anywhere tomorrow, you came to the Post Office. It was quite busy, even now.

'Cup of tea, Mr Lipwig?' said the voice of Stanley, behind him.

'Thank you, Stanley,' said Moist, without looking round. Down below, Miss Maccalariat was standing on a chair and nailing something to the wall.

'Everyone says we've won, sir, 'cos the clacks has been shut down 'cos the directors are in prison, sir. They say all Mr Upwright has to do is get there! But Mr Groat says the bookies probably won't pay up, sir. And the king of Lancre wants some stamps printed, but it'll come a bit pricey, sir, since they only write about ten letters a year up there. Still, we've showed them, eh, sir? The Post Office is back!'

'It's some kind of banner,' said Moist, aloud.

'Sorry, Mr Lipwig?' said Stanley.

'Er . . . nothing. Thank you, Stanley. Have fun with the stamps. Good to see you standing up so . . . straight . . .'

'It's like having a new life, sir,' said Stanley. 'I'd better go, sir, they need help with the sorting . . .'

The banner was crude. It read: 'Thank You Mr Lipwic!'

Gloom rolled around Moist. It was always bad after he'd won, but this time was the worst. For days his mind had been flying and he'd felt alive. Now he felt numb. They'd put up a banner like that, and he was a liar and a thief. He'd fooled them all, and there they were, thanking him for fooling them.

A quiet voice from the doorway behind him said: 'Mad Al and the boys told me what you did.'

'Oh,' said Moist, still not turning round. She'll be lighting a cigarette, he thought.

'It wasn't a nice thing to do,' Adora Belle Dearheart went on, in the same level tone.

'There wasn't a nice thing that would work,' said Moist.

'Are you going to tell me that the ghost of my brother put the idea in your head?' she said.

'No. I dreamed it up myself,' said Moist.

'Good. If you'd tried that, you'd be limping for the rest of your life, believe me.'

'Thank you,' said Moist leadenly. 'It was just a lie I knew people would want to believe. Just a lie. It was a way to keep the Post Office going and get the Grand Trunk out of Gilt's hands. You'll probably get it back, if you want it. You and all the other people Gilt swindled. I'll help, if I can. But I don't want thanking.'

He felt her draw nearer.

'It's not a lie,' she said. 'It's what ought to have been true. It pleased my mother.'

'Does *she* think it's true?'

'She doesn't want to think it isn't.'

No one does. I can't stand this, Moist thought. 'Look, I know what I'm like,' he said. 'I'm not the person everyone thinks I am. I just wanted to prove to myself I'm not like Gilt. More than a hammer, you understand? But I'm still a fraud by trade. I thought you knew that. I can fake sincerity so well that even I can't tell. I mess with people's heads—'

'You're fooling no one but yourself,' said Miss Dearheart, and reached for his hand.

Moist— *shook her off, and ran out of the building, out of the city and back to his old life, or lives, always moving on, selling glass as diamond, but somehow it just didn't seem to work any more, the flair wasn't there, the fun had dropped out of it, even the cards didn't seem to work for him, the money ran out, and one winter in some inn that was no more than a slum he turned his face to the wall—*

And an angel appeared.

'What just happened?' said Miss Dearheart.

Perhaps you do get two . . .

'Only a passing thought,' said Moist. He let the golden glow rise. He'd fooled them all, even here. But the good bit was that he could go on doing it; he didn't have to stop. All he had to do was remind himself, every few months, that he could quit any time. Provided he knew he could, he'd never have to. And there was Miss Dearheart, without a cigarette in her mouth, only a foot away. He leaned forward—

There was a loud cough behind them. It turned out to have come from Groat, who was holding a large parcel.

'Sorry to interrupt, sir, but this just arrived for you,' he said, and sniffed disapprovingly. 'Messenger, not one of ours. I thought I'd better bring it straight up 'cos there's something moving about inside it . . .'

There was. And airholes, Moist noted. He opened the lid with care, and pulled his fingers away just in time.

'*Twelve and a half per cent! Twelve and a half per cent!*' screamed the cockatoo, and landed on Groat's hat.

There was no note inside, and nothing on the box but the address.

'Why'd someone send you a parrot?' said Groat, not caring to raise a hand within reach of the curved beak.

'It's Gilt's, isn't it?' said Miss Dearheart. 'He's *given* you the bird?'

Moist smiled. 'It looks like it, yes. Pieces of eight!'

'*Twelve and a half per cent!*' yelled the cockatoo.

'Take it away, will you, Mr Groat?' said Moist. 'Teach it to say . . . to say . . .'

'Trust me?' said Miss Dearheart.

'Good one!' said Moist. 'Yes, do that, Mr Groat.'

When Groat had gone, with the cockatoo balancing happily on his shoulder, Moist turned back to the woman.

'And tomorrow,' he said, 'I'll *definitely* get the chandeliers back!'

'What? Most of this place doesn't have a ceiling,' said Miss Dearheart, laughing.

'First things first. Trust me! And then, who knows? I might even find the fine polished counter! There's no end to what's possible!'

And out in the bustling cavern white feathers began to fall from the roof. They may have been from an angel, but were more likely to be coming from the pigeon that a hawk was just disembowelling on a beam. Still, they *were* feathers. It's all about style.

*   *   *

Sometimes the truth is arrived at by adding all the little lies together and deducting them from the totality of what is known.

Lord Vetinari stood at the top of the stairs in the Great Hall of the Palace, and looked down on his clerks. They'd taken over the whole huge floor for this Concludium.

Chalked markings – circles, squares, triangles – were drawn here and there on the floor. Within them, papers and ledgers were piled in dangerously neat heaps. And there were clerks, some working inside the outlines and some moving noiselessly from one outline to another bearing pieces of paper as if they were a sacrament. Periodically clerks and watchmen arrived with more files and ledgers, which were solemnly received, assessed and added to the relevant pile.

Abacuses clicked everywhere. Clerks would pad back and forth and sometimes they would meet in a triangle and bend their heads in quiet discussion. This might result in their heading away in new directions or, increasingly as the night wore on, one clerk would go and chalk a new outline, which would begin to fill with paper. Sometimes an outline would be emptied and rubbed out and its contents distributed among nearby outlines.

No enchanter's circle, no mystic's mandala was ever drawn with such painfully meticulous care as the conclusions being played out on the floor. Hour after hour it went on, with a patience that at first terrified and then bored. It was the warfare of clerks, and it harried the enemy through many columns and files. Moist could read words that weren't there but the clerks found the numbers that weren't there, or were there twice, or were there but going the wrong way. They didn't hurry. Peel away the lies, and the truth would emerge, naked and ashamed and with nowhere else to hide.

At 3 a.m. Mr Cheeseborough arrived, in a hurry and bitter tears, to learn that his bank was a shell of paper. He brought his own clerks, with their nightshirts tucked into hastily donned trousers, who went down on their knees alongside the other men and spread out more papers, double-checking figures in the hope that if you stared at numbers long enough they'd add up differently.

And then the Watch turned up with a small red ledger, and it was given a circle of its own, and soon the whole pattern re-formed around it . . .

It wasn't until almost dawn that the sombre men arrived. They were older and fatter and better – but not showily, never showily – dressed, and moved with the gravity of serious money. They were financiers too, richer than kings (who are often quite poor), but hardly anyone in the city outside their circle knew them or would notice them in the street. They spoke quietly to Cheeseborough as to one who'd suffered a bereavement, and then talked among themselves, and used little gold propelling pencils in neat little notebooks to make figures dance and jump through hoops. Then quiet agreement was reached and hands were shaken, which in this circle carried infinitely more weight than any written contract. The first domino had been steadied. The pillars of the world ceased to tremble. The Credit Bank would open in the morning, and when it did so bills would be honoured, wages would be paid, the city would be fed.

They'd saved the city with gold more easily, at that point, than any hero could have managed with steel. But in truth it had not exactly been gold, or even the promise of gold, but more like the fantasy of gold, the fairy dream that the gold is there, at the end of the rainbow, and will continue to be there for ever provided, naturally, that you don't go and look.

This is known as Finance.

On the way back home to a simple breakfast, one of them dropped off at the Guild of Assassins to pay his respects to his old friend Lord Downey, during which current affairs were only lightly touched upon. And Reacher Gilt, wherever he had gone, was now certainly the worst insurance risk in the world. The people who guard the rainbow don't like those who get in the way of the sun.

Some Time After

THE FIGURE IN THE CHAIR did not have long hair, or an eyepatch. It didn't have a beard or, rather, it wasn't intending to have a beard. It hadn't shaved for several days.

It groaned.

'Ah, Mr Gilt,' said Lord Vetinari, looking up from his playing board. 'You are awake, I see. I'm sorry for the manner in which you were brought here, but some quite expensive people wish to see you dead and I thought it would be a good idea if we had this little meeting before they did.'

'I don't know who you're talking about,' said the figure. 'My name is Randolph Stippler, and I have papers to prove it—'

'And wonderful papers they are, Mr Gilt. But enough of that. No, it is about angels that I wish to talk to you now.'

Reacher Gilt, wincing occasionally as the aches from three days of being carried by a golem made themselves felt, listened in mounting puzzlement to the angelic theories of Lord Vetinari.

'. . . brings me on to my point, Mr Gilt. The Royal Mint needs an entirely new approach. Frankly, it's moribund and not at all what we need in the Century of the Anchovy. Yet there is a way forward. In recent months Mr Lipwig's celebrated stamps have become a second currency in this city. So light, so easy to carry, you can even send them through the post! Fascinating, Mr Gilt. At last people are loosening their grip on the idea that money should be shiny. Do you know that a typical one penny stamp may change hands up to twelve times before being affixed to an envelope and redeemed? What the Mint needs to see it through is a man who understands the *dream* of currency. There will be a salary and, I believe, a hat.'

'*You* are offering me a *job*?'

'Yes, Mr Stippler,' said Vetinari. 'And, to show the sincerity of my offer, let me point out the door behind you. If at any time in this interview you feel you wish to leave, you have only to step through it and you will never hear from me again . . .'

Some little time later the clerk Drumknott padded into the room. Lord Vetinari was reading a report on the previous night's secret meeting of the Thieves' Guild *inner* inner council.

He tidied up the trays quite noiselessly, and then came and stood by Vetinari.

'There are ten overnights off the clacks, my lord,' he said. 'It's good to have it back in operation.'

'Indeed yes,' said Vetinari, not looking up. 'Otherwise how in the world would people be able to find out what we want them to think? Any foreign mail?'

'The usual packets, my lord. The Uberwald one has been most deftly tampered with.'

'Ah, dear Lady Margolotta,' said Vetinari, smiling.

'I've taken the liberty of removing the stamps for my nephew, my lord,' Drumknott went on.

'Of course,' said Vetinari, waving a hand.

Drumknott looked around the office and focused on the slab where the little stone armies were endlessly in combat. 'Ah, I see you have won, my lord,' he said.

'Yes. I must make a note of the gambit.'

'But Mr Gilt, I notice, is not here . . .'

Vetinari sighed. 'You have to admire a man who *really* believes in freedom of choice,' he said, looking at the open doorway. 'Sadly, he did not believe in angels.'